Green Criminology

Over the past ten years, the study of environmental harm and 'crimes against nature' has become an increasingly popular area of research amongst criminologists. This book represents the first international, comprehensive and introductory text for green criminology, offering a concise exposition of theory and concepts and providing extensive geographical coverage, diversity and depth to the many issues pertaining to environmental harm and crime.

Divided into three sections, the book draws on a range of international case studies and examples, and looks at the conceptual and methodological foundations of green criminology, before examining in detail areas of environmental crime and harm, and how they are addressed, including:

- climate change and social conflict;
- abuse and harm to animals;
- threats to biodiversity;
- pollution and toxic waste;
- environmental victims;
- environmental regulation, law enforcement and courts;
- environmental forensic studies;
- environmental crime prevention.

Green Criminology is packed with pedagogical features, including dialogue boxes, case examples, discussion questions and lists of further reading and is perfect for students around the world engaged with green criminology and crime against the environment.

Rob White is Professor of Criminology at the University of Tasmania, Australia, and author of *Crimes Against Nature*, *Global Environmental Harm*, *Environmental Crime: A Reader* and *Transnational Environmental Crime*, all published by Routledge.

Diane Heckenberg is a Research Associate in the School of Social Sciences at the University of Tasmania, Australia, and recently completed a PhD on toxic toys and the transference of harm.

Green Criminology

An introduction to the study of environmental harm

Rob White and Diane Heckenberg

Routledge
Taylor & Francis Group
LONDON AND NEW YORK

First published 2014
by Routledge
2 Park Square, Milton Park, Abingdon, Oxon, OX14 4RN

and by Routledge
711 Third Avenue, New York, NY 10017

Routledge is an imprint of the Taylor & Francis Group, an informa business

© 2014 Rob White and Diane Heckenberg

The right of Rob White and Diane Heckenberg to be identified as authors of this work has been asserted by them in accordance with sections 77 and 78 of the Copyright, Designs and Patents Act 1988.

All rights reserved. No part of this book may be reprinted or reproduced or utilised in any form or by any electronic, mechanical, or other means, now known or hereafter invented, including photocopying and recording, or in any information storage or retrieval system, without permission in writing from the publishers.

Trademark notice: Product or corporate names may be trademarks or registered trademarks, and are used only for identification and explanation without intent to infringe.

British Library Cataloguing in Publication Data
A catalogue record for this book is available from the British Library

Library of Congress Cataloging-in-Publication Data
White, R. D. (Robert Douglas)
Green criminology: an introduction to the study of environmental harm/
Rob White, Diane Heckenberg. – 1st Edition.
pages cm
1. Offenses against the environment. 2. Criminology–Environmental aspects.
I. Heckenberg, Diane. II. Title.
HV6401.W454 2014
364.1'445–dc23
2013026312

ISBN: 978-0-415-63209-6 (hbk)
ISBN: 978-0-415-63210-2 (pbk)
ISBN: 978-0-203-09610-9 (ebk)

Typeset in Times New Roman
by Cenveo Publisher Services

Printed and bound by CPI Group (UK) Ltd, Croydon, CR0 4YY

Contents

List of figures	vii
List of tables	viii
List of boxes	ix
List of case vignettes	xi
Acknowledgements	xii
Introduction	1

PART I
Conceptual and methodological foundations   **5**

1	Green criminology and environmental crime	7
2	Eco-global criminology and transnational environmental crime	25
3	Eco-justice and ecocide	45
4	Dimensions of environmental crime	60
5	Researching environmental harm	79

PART II
Transgression and victimization   **99**

6	Climate change and social conflict	101
7	Abuse and harm to animals	117
8	Threats to biodiversity	137
9	Pollution and toxic waste	156
10	Environmental victims	175

PART III
Intervention and prevention 195

11	Environmental regulation	197
12	Environmental law enforcement	217
13	Environmental forensic studies	235
14	Environmental courts	256
15	Environmental crime prevention	276
	Conclusion	296
	Glossary	298
	References	304
	Index	332

Figures

5.1	Map of the world	87
7.1	Methods used in each stage of the illegal abalone market	132
11.1	Tiers and types of regulation: Australia	201
11.2	The regulatory pyramid	202
11.3	Understanding non-compliance in the Australian waste sector	206
11.4	The regulatory toolbox	208

Tables

2.1	Geographical scale and environmental harm	28
3.1	An eco-justice perspective – three approaches to justice, rights and harms	48
3.2	Dimensions and notions of justice	50
4.1	Key considerations of environmental harm	67
5.1	Steps to doing environmental horizon-scanning	83
5.2	Types of data sources	89
5.3	Issues, limitations and constraints in data collection and analysis	90
6.1	Crime and climate change	110
10.1	Types of engagement between activists, the state and corporations	188
11.1	The environmental regulation continuum	202
12.1	Environmental enforcement agencies at different tiers: Australia	219
13.1	Discourses and the languaging of environmental issues	245
13.2	Challenges to necessary and sufficient knowledge in assessing toxic towns	249
15.1	Approaches and techniques of situational prevention	279
15.2	Focus for market reduction approach to wildlife crime	285

Boxes

1.1	Perspectives within green criminology	18
2.1	Three approaches to conceptualizing environmental harm	30
2.2	Capitalism and the transformation of nature	34
2.3	The conceptual basis of environmental horizon-scanning	41
3.1	Four propositions about justice	53
4.1	Necessary factors for the successful construction of an environmental problem	63
4.2	Colouring environmental issues	70
4.3	Features of different types of spaces	73
5.1	The global commons, place and harm: student exercise	86
5.2	Alternative data sources	91
6.1	Climate change issues	105
6.2	Climate change and social conflict	107
7.1	Animal categories	120
7.2	Key issues relating to animal abuse	126
7.3	Wildlife poaching and theft	129
8.1	Appendixes to Convention on International Trade in Endangered Species	139
8.2	Encouraging better vegetation management	150
8.3	Survival status of species	153
9.1	E-waste facts and figures	160
9.2	Interfaces and hazardous waste	165
10.1	Mapping victim issues	181
10.2	Eco-justice and victims	182
11.1	Exploratory research on environmental compliance and enforcement	209
11.2	Differing views of Environmental Management Systems	212
12.1	The enforcement chain	225
12.2	NGOs compared with official environmental law enforcement	230
13.1	Community risk assessment in relation to chemical hazards	244
13.2	Elder knowledge about toxic legacy in Tasmania	250

14.1 Criteria to determine seriousness of environmental offences 262
15.1 Approaches and techniques of crime prevention dealing
     with illegal fishing 281
15.2 Crime prevention applied to different types of wildlife crime 283
15.3 Key issues relating to organized crime and the environment 288

Case vignettes

1.1	Green criminology in Slovenia, 1981	15
2.1	Horizon-scanning the impacts of climate change	42
3.1	The Niger delta	55
4.1	BP Horizon oil spill	74
8.1	Salvinia – a floating aquatic menace	151
9.1	The river runs black in Guiyu	163
9.2	Coal seam fire	170
10.1	A river gets 'rights'	184
14.1	Lessons from a defunct South African environment court	273
15.1	Mafia and wind farms	289

Acknowledgements

This book builds upon work undertaken by us, separately and together, over the past two decades. In addition to this we have incorporated ideas and materials from as wide a range of sources as possible with the intent of acknowledging and recognizing the many diverse influences on 'green criminology' as an emerging field. Chapter 5 on Researching environmental harm draws heavily from a chapter in the *Routledge International Handbook of Green Criminology*, edited by Nigel South and Avi Brisman. The Glossary is taken from *Environmental Crime: A Reader*, edited by Rob White. We are grateful to our many colleagues worldwide who, in many different ways, have supported and contributed to this textbook. It is to them that we dedicate the present work.

Introduction

For many thousands of years humans have done things to the environment that have fundamentally transformed local landscapes and regional biodiversities. From bringing plants and animals from one region to new parts of the world, to polluting rivers and seas with industrial outfall and filling land and soils with human refuse, to fire burning in particular local biospheres, ecological change has been part and parcel of how humans have worked with each other, and nature, for millennia. Not all such activities have been viewed as harmful, nor has the transformation of local environments always been seen as a negative.

In ecological terms, however, today there are several areas of acknowledged harm that are garnering ever greater attention and concern from the scientific community and from the population at large. Global warming, threats to biodiversity, and new and ever more toxic forms of pollution and waste are combining to destroy ecological balance and in the process put the well-being and health of humans, eco-systems, non-human animals and plants at risk. We are killing the world as we know it.

In response to growing discontent about the state of the environment a distinctive, critical 'green criminology' has emerged in recent years that takes its focus from issues relating to the environment (in the widest sense possible) and social harm (as defined in ecological as well as strictly legal terms). Much of this work has been directed at exposing different instances of substantive environmental injustice and ecological injustice. It has also involved critique of the actions of nation-states and transnational capitalism for fostering particular types of harm, and for failing to adequately address or regulate harmful activity. Given the pressing nature of many environmental issues, it is not surprising that criminologists around the world are now seeing environmental crime and environmental victimization as areas for concerted analytical and practical attention.

This book

The purpose of this book is to introduce readers to the landscape of green criminology, a field characterized by convention and complexity, conversation and confrontation. The text is divided into three main sections:

Part I: Conceptual and methodological foundations provides an account of the theoretical and research foundations of green criminology. It outlines different perspectives and approaches to the study of environmental harm, including definitions of and challenges to legal notions of harms against the environment. This section identifies the different types of environmental crime, the varied ways in which researchers and scholars define such crimes, and how such analysis links to considerations of environmental, ecological and species justice.

Part II: Transgression and victimization involves a closer look at particular areas of environmental crime and harm. Here the concern is to provide detailed examination of specific topics such as climate change, abuse and harm to animals, threats to biodiversity, the problem of pollution and waste, and the plight of environmental victims. This section explores the effects of environmental harm through the lens of specific processes and activities that are diminishing ecological and species well-being.

Part III: Intervention and prevention takes up the question of what is to be done about environmental crime. Knowing about the damage and about criminality is one thing. But in the end it is how groups, organizations, institutions and societies respond to environmental harm that ultimately counts. This section discusses the nature of environmental regulation, the dynamics of environmental law enforcement and crime prevention, the limits and possibilities of environmental forensics and the role of environmental courts in stemming the tide of environmentally destructive practices and conduct.

A key question is how to conceptualize the nature and causes of environmental harm arising from human actions. In responding to this, green criminology traverses a very broad intellectual territory and canvasses many different concrete issues. Each chapter of this book features a series of topics for discussion, designed to take up some of the key issues and viewpoints on particular topics.

The chapters in the book are designed to stimulate student curiosity, to encourage thinking about the wide-ranging nature of environmental harms and crimes that have been (past), that are (present) and that are likely to be (future) perpetrated. Some of the discussions will resonate as shared concerns (e.g. many people can relate to issues of pollution and waste; less so perhaps to food riots). Regardless of where these events occur and whether they are currently prohibited (by law) or condoned (by the global marketplace) they represent issues for study. We hope you will use the ideas and information in this book as a springboard for identifying and researching environmental crimes and harms that arouse your interest, with a view to building upon the existing knowledge repository in the growing research frontier of green criminology.

Looking to the future

From the point of view of international affairs we appear to be looking at a future of fortresses and scarcities, of social conflicts over resources that are increasingly culminating in expressions of public anger. These types of issues are cutting much closer to the bone than perhaps they used to – they are affecting real people in our time, and real people are making their voices heard (through street level protest and social media). This is all due to the pressures that we are collectively putting on the environment. As we modify, degrade and destroy the lifeblood of this planet, the tendency is to retreat into a fortress mentality that is protective of immediate perceived personal and community interests. Climate change will only exacerbate these tendencies as food, energy (i.e., oil) and water come into short supply, and climate-induced migration increases due to these and other pressures.

The scramble for what is left in terms of both renewable and non-renewable resources (i.e., minerals, fish, water, trees), in the context of climate-related scarcity and the accelerating limits to ecology, heighten the sense of foreboding and insecurity felt around the world. It also means that unscrupulous methods may be used in order to satisfy immediate (rather than long-term) self-interests – as in the case of illegal fishing and the substitution of horsemeat for beef. Environmental crimes such as these are, in effect, generated by global systemic pressures on the world's ecology.

The contribution of green criminology is to frame these kinds of general issues in terms of transgressions against humans, eco-systems and animals, and more broadly in the context of global economic and political pursuits. The concept of eco-justice embodies this, as it refers to the interrelated fields of environmental justice (humans and equity), ecological justice (intrinsic value of eco-systems) and species justice (rights and needs of animals). The tendency toward the 'fortress' society (again, at all levels) undermines the possibility and practice of eco-justice in its various manifestations.

Going against this fortress mentality requires a global vision, one that views universal human interests as achievable through a global ecological citizenship. If self-interest is only defined in terms of corporate profit and the 'national interest', then basically we are doomed to a life that is short, nasty and brutal. Sectional interests of this sort can only serve to divide the world into 'winners' and 'losers', an arrangement that has marked the advance of human history to date – but which cannot be sustained in the light of the catastrophic circumstances posed by climate change.

Our hope is that this book will inspire this and future generations of students to take up the issues, to research and critique environmental crimes (the unlawful) and environmental harms (the lawful but awful), and to demand a different future, one that embraces the study of environmental crimes and harms but also seeks out innovative approaches to negotiating this landscape in ways that lead to solutions. It is easy to raise and critique the issues, but it is much more difficult to be part of solutions that promote alternative ways of thinking about and solving the problems. The potential for change or action is all the more reason to get involved. If we remain silent about the destruction of the planet, the planet itself will go silent – because it no longer *is*. Green criminology as a field of study has great potential to make a contribution to altering the planet for the better, for all. This is its promise and its greatest challenge.

Part I

Conceptual and methodological foundations

Chapter 1

Green criminology and environmental crime

Introduction

This chapter will discuss the following topics:

- what green criminology is;
- studying environmental harm;
- environmental crime and environmental harm;
- perspectives within green criminology;
- the systemic causes of environmental harm.

The term 'green criminology' first emerged in the early 1990s to describe a critical and sustained approach to the study of environmental crime (Lynch, 1990; South, 1998a and b). This chapter introduces the reader to green criminology and the different ways in which researchers and scholars examine issues pertaining to environmental crimes and harms. It outlines the distinctive features of green criminology, the main concepts and foci of analysis and the ongoing debates that mark its further and continuing development as a *bona fide* perspective within criminology.

A series of intriguing questions arise about precisely what it is that we are talking about when we invoke the name 'green criminology'. The term can refer to a specific focus on environmental crimes or harms: that is, a particular topic for sustained criminological analysis (such as poaching of parrots). Alternatively, it may refer to a conceptual approach premised upon certain notions of justice and particular moral frameworks, such as environmental justice or species justice. It may involve 'old' (that is, conventional) theories and perspectives (general strain theory, for example) applied to new areas (such as climate change), as well as 'new' methods and approaches (such as horizon-scanning) applied to old areas (e.g. illegal waste disposal). For some, green criminology is defined by networks and collaborations between scholars and researchers; for others, it is the objective content of the research that defines this field of enquiry.

Our view is that the field of green criminology ought to be defined as widely as possible, thereby allowing for diverse conceptual and empirical insights into the nature and dynamics of environmental wrongdoing. For the purposes of this textbook, therefore, a wide spectrum of approaches, methods and perspectives are canvassed, accommodated and utilized under the broad canopy of green criminology.

What is green criminology?

Green criminology refers to the study by criminologists of environmental harms (that may incorporate wider definitions of crime than are provided by strictly legal definitions); environmental laws (including enforcement, prosecution and sentencing practices); and environmental regulation (systems of criminal, civil and administrative law designed to manage, protect and preserve specified environments and species, and to manage the negative consequences of particular industrial processes) (White 2008a, 2011a).

In general, green criminology takes as its focus issues relating to the environment (in the widest possible sense) and harm (as defined in ecological as well as strictly legal terms). Much of this work has been directed at exposing different instances of substantive social and ecological injustice. It has also involved critique of the actions of nation-states and transnational companies for fostering particular types of harm, and for failing to adequately address or regulate harmful activity.

The key focus of green criminology is environmental crime but green criminologists also study environmentally harmful activities not currently defined as crimes. Environmental crime is conceptualized in several different ways within the broad framework of green criminology. For some scholars, environmental crime is defined narrowly within strict legal definitions – it is what the law says it is. For others, environmental harm is itself deemed to be a social and ecological crime, regardless of legal status – if harm is done to environments or animals, then from the point of view of the critical green criminologist, it is argued that such harms ought to be considered a 'crime'.

The interface of criminology with environmental issues, as a discrete field of study, and in a manner that involves increased and concerted professional attention and hands-on intervention has been forcefully advocated by Lynch and Stretesky (2003: 231):

> In general, criminologists have often left the study of environmental harm, environmental laws and environmental regulations to researchers in other disciplines. This has allowed little room for critical examination of individuals or entities who/which kill, injure and assault other life forms (human, animal or plant) by poisoning the earth. In this light, a green criminology is needed to awaken criminologists to the types of major environmental harm and damage that can result from environmental harms; the conflicts that

arise from attempts at defining environmental crime and deviance; and the controversies still raging over possible solutions, given extensive environmental regulations already in place.

From a criminological perspective, taking up the challenge offered here will require rigorous and sophisticated analysis of the social dynamics that shape and allow certain types of activities harmful to the environment (including to human and non-human species) to take place over time. This approach demands that environmental issues be framed within the context of a sociological and socio-criminological imagination (see Wright Mills 1959, White 2003, Young 2011). That is, study must appreciate the importance of situating environmental harm within its social and historical context. It is context (the economic, social and political conditions in which environmental transgressions occur) that gives a study specificity. Interpretation and analysis need to take into account how current trends reflect the make-up of global and local societies, the overall direction in which those societies are heading, and the ways in which diverse groups of people are being affected by particular social, economic and political processes.

The kinds of harm and crime studied within green criminology include illegal trade in endangered species, such as the trade in exotic birds or the killing of elephants for their ivory tusks; illegal harvesting of 'natural resources', such as illegal fishing and logging; and illegal disposal of toxic substances and the resultant pollution of air, land and water. Wider definitions of environmental crime extend the scope of analysis to consider harms associated with legal activities (such as the clear felling of old-growth forests) and the negative ecological consequences of new technologies – such as use of genetically modified organisms in agriculture (e.g. reduction of biodiversity through extensive planting of GMO corn). More recent considerations include the criminological aspects of climate change, from the point of view of human contributions to global warming (e.g. carbon emissions from coal-fired power plants) and the criminality associated with the aftermath of natural disasters (e.g. incidents of theft and rape in the wake of Hurricane Katrina in New Orleans).

Environmental crime and environmental harm

The study of environmental crime is not new, although green criminology as a distinctive perspective within criminology is. Environmental crime frequently embodies a certain ambiguity. This is because it is not only located in models of risk (e.g. the precautionary principle) or evaluated in terms of actual harms (e.g. polluter pays), but is also judged in the context of cost-benefit analysis (e.g. license to trade or to pollute or to kill or capture). This goes to the heart of why environmental crime itself is consistently undervalued in law. The label of environmental crime tends to be applied to specific activities that are otherwise lawful or licensed (e.g. cutting down trees, pulling fish from the ocean), since these are viewed as not being intrinsically criminal or 'bad'. It is the context that makes something allowable or problematic. To take another example, harm to the environment is, in many situations, considered to be acceptable (for instance in certain circumstances we are prepared to allow pollution under licence or authorization) because it is an inherent consequence of many industrial activities which are seen to provide significant benefits.

The 'wrongdoing' studied within green criminology is initially informed by legal conceptions and constructions of harm. The nature and seriousness of harm – what makes something 'criminal' or not – is captured in the distinction between illegality (*malum prohibitum*) and serious harm (*malum in se*).

Illegality – malum prohibitum

This area of law refers to conduct that is prohibited by law but generally considered less serious than other types of social harms (homicide for example). In many situations harm to the environment is considered to be acceptable because it is an inherent consequence of industrial activities linked to significant economic benefits. Cutting down trees and pulling species out of the ocean are thus NOT intrinsically criminal or 'bad' activities from the point of view of the law. So the main issue here is 'managing the problem' (usually framed in terms of catch limits and allowable levels of pollution or toxicity); this is essentially a matter of regulation. Examples include the Convention on International Trade in Endangered Species of Wild Fauna and Flora (CITES) and the Basel Convention on the Control of Transboundary Movement of Hazardous Wastes and Their Disposal – the first, designed to regulate the international movement of species, and the second, to control the transfer of hazardous substances between countries. Within this framework, it is the illegal aspects of ordinary legitimate practices that are problematic. A key practical focus is developing the best tools and strategies possible to ensure compliance with licensing provisions and specific environmental regulations.

Serious harm – malum in se

This area of law refers to conduct inherently wrong by nature, and which is considered serious. The main issue here is 'eradicating the problem' (usually framed in terms of banning of specific substances and/or activities). The intent of the law is to prevent and abolish harmful practices, as seen for example in the application of public interest law in India to stop polluting industries from destroying sites of national significance (Mehta 2009). Another example of this approach is the Montreal Protocol, which effectively bans the use of ozone-depleting substances. An emergent demand, aligned to some extent with calls for recognition of Earth Rights (already manifest in some country's constitutions) is for a new international law on 'ecocide' (Higgins 2010). This would make extensive damage to, destruction of or loss of ecosystem(s) of a given territory an international crime (the fifth crime against peace).

Environmental crime is typically defined on a continuum ranging from strict legal definitions through to broader harm perspectives (see also Bricknell 2010). For example: 'an unauthorized act or omission that violates the law and is therefore subject to criminal prosecution and criminal sanction' (Situ and Emmons 2000: 3); 'an act committed with the intent to harm or with a potential to cause harm to ecological and/or biological systems and for the purpose of securing business or personal advantage' (Clifford and Edwards 1998: 26); 'criminal conduct that may have negative consequences for the environment' (UNODC 2011: 95); 'environmental harm is a crime' (White 2011a: 1).

The matter of legality does not prevent criminologists from critiquing certain types of ecologically harmful activities that happen to be legal, such as the clear felling of forests. From a criminal justice perspective, however, the issue of legality goes much deeper, to the heart of why *environmental crime itself is consistently under-valued in law*:

> Of note is the consistent use of the preface 'illegal' in the listed activities constituting environmental crime, a preface not regularly employed when describing other categories of crime. This reflects the fact that some component or level of these activities is still condoned and that it only becomes illegal once a set boundary has been passed. The tipping point of illegality contrasts environmental crimes with other established criminal offences
> (Bricknell 2010: 4)

Specific types of environmental harm as described in law include things such as illegal transport and dumping of toxic waste, the illegal transfer of hazardous materials (e.g. ozone-depleting substances), the illegal traffic in radioactive or nuclear substances, the illegal trade in flora and fauna, and illegal fishing and logging. However, within green criminology there is a more expansive definition of environmental crime or harm that includes (White 2011a):

- transgressions that are harmful to humans, environments and non-human animals, regardless of legality per se; and
- environmental-related harms facilitated by the state, as well as corporations and other powerful actors, insofar as these institutions have the capacity to shape official definitions of environmental crime in ways that allow or condone environmentally harmful practices.

Issues pertaining to state crime (the state as perpetrator of environmental harm) and transnational corporate crime (including the legitimacy granted to ecologically destructive acts and omissions on the part of large firms) demand attention in their own right.

So, too, do definitions of crime – such as *ecocide* – that embody challenges to the powerful. Ecocide has been defined as 'the extensive damage, destruction to or loss of ecosystems of a given territory, whether by human agency or by other causes, to such an extent that peaceful enjoyment by the inhabitants of that territory has been severely diminished' (Higgins 2012: 3). Where this occurs as a result of human agency, then it can be argued that such harm can be defined as a crime. The targets for action around ecocide include both nation-states and transnational corporations.

The label of environmental crime tends to be applied to specific activities that are otherwise lawful or licensed (e.g. illegal cutting down of trees) but rarely if ever to environmental harms involving wide-scale regional environmental destruction, such as war-related degradation (deforestation due to use of Agent Orange, for example) (see Al-Damkhi *et al.* 2009), or to harms generated at a systems level (e.g. ever-expanding production and consumption of commodities) (White 2013a).

Harm has been described as a 'normative concept that reflects underlying social judgements about the good and the bad', and environmental harm specifically has been defined as 'a setback to human interests that community norms have deemed to be significant' (Lin 2006: 901). The varied dimensions of harm are demonstrated in the contemporary proliferation of information about chains of causation that generate direct, indirect, immediate and cumulative harms (Lin 2006; Heckenberg 2010). Harm in this context is complex and transferable.

Harm can also be defined, negatively, in terms of loss or diminishment. A key concept here is that of sustainability, where this refers to notions of ongoing ecological and environmental balance over time (Merchant 2005; Al-Damkhi *et al.* 2009). A loss of environmental resources or biological diversity can thus be construed as harmful if 'sustainability' is the yardstick by which harm is measured. The deliberate destruction or depletion of resources that significantly impact a region's economic or ecological stability would therefore be considered an environmental crime (Al-Damkhi *et al.* 2009: 121), as would those harms associated with the concept of ecocide (Higgins 2012).

Green criminology's broader conceptualizations of environmentally adverse activities are essential in evaluating systemic, as well as particularistic, environmental harms (Beirne and South 2007). For example, the current environmental regulatory apparatus, informed by the ideology of 'sustainable development', is directed at bringing ecological sustainability to the present mode of producing and consuming – one based upon the logic of growth, expanded consumption of resources and the commodification of more and more aspects of nature. Harm, in this case, is built into the system (see Boyd 2003; White 2013a).

It is important therefore to distinguish (and make the connection between) specific instances of harm arising from imperfect operational practices (such as pollution spills), and systemic harm created by normatively sanctioned forms of activity (such as clear felling of Australian, Brazilian and Indonesian forests). The first is deemed to be 'criminal' or 'harmful' and thus subject to coercive social control. The second is not considered a criminal matter, although subject to regulation. The overall consequence is for global environmental problems to get worse, even in the midst of the proliferation of a greater range of regulatory mechanisms, agencies and laws.

Green criminology is premised upon the idea that we need to take environmental harm seriously. For some exponents this also means that we need conceptualizations of harm that go beyond conventional understandings of crime (Beirne and South 2007). Every green criminologist agrees that destructive and damaging human activities that harm environments warrant greater attention than has hitherto been the case within criminology. Yet, if ecological (and social and economic) welfare is to be maximized, then there is also a need to expand notions of what actually constitutes environmental crime. Harm, as conceived by critical green criminologists, for example, demands more encompassing definitions than that offered by mainstream law and criminology. This is because some of the most ecologically destructive activities, such as clear felling of old growth forests, is quite legal; while more benign practices, such as growing hemp for productive purposes, is criminalized.

Green criminology therefore provides an umbrella under which to theorize and critique both *illegal* environmental harms (that is, environmental harms currently defined as unlawful and therefore punishable) and *legal* environmental harms (that is, environmental harms currently condoned as lawful but which are, nevertheless, socially and ecologically harmful). How harm is conceptualized is thus partly shaped by how the legal–illegal divide is construed within specific research and analysis.

Studying environmental harm

There are a number of intersecting dimensions that need to be considered in any analysis of environmental harm (White 2008a). These include consideration of who the victim is (human or non-human); where the harm is manifest (global through to local levels); the main site in which the harm is apparent (built or natural environment); the scale of the harm (contained, dispersed, cumulative) and the time frame within which harm can be analysed (immediate and delayed consequences). Many of the main features pertaining to environmental harm are inherently international in scope and substance, although they can be acutely local in terms of their impact.

Indeed, the categorization of environmental harm is varied, in that there are different ways in which environmental crimes have been conceptualized and classified. From the point of view of environmental law, for example, environmental harm encapsulates a wide range of concerns, some of which are subject to criminal sanctions but many of which are not (Boyd 2003). The kinds of issues canvassed under environmental law relate to laws and policies intended to protect water (e.g. pollution), air (e.g. ozone depletion), land (e.g. pesticide regulation) and biodiversity (e.g. endangered species). From the point of view of harm, writers have also incorporated under the environmental harm umbrella concerns relating to employee health (e.g. exposure to radioactivity) and pathological indoor environments (e.g. the home, hospitals, workplaces) (Rosoff, Pontell and Tillman 1998; Curson and Clark 2004). Criminologists and others thus categorize environmental crimes in varying ways, and how they do so has implications for their study.

14 Conceptual and methodological foundations

For instance, Carrabine *et al.* (2004) discuss environmental crimes in terms of primary and secondary crimes. Green crimes are broadly defined simply as crimes against the environment. *Primary crimes* are those crimes that result directly from the destruction and degradation of the earth's resources, through human actions. *Secondary or symbiotic green crime* is that crime arising out of the flouting of rules that seek to regulate environmental disasters. The first set of crimes relates to the harm as being bad in itself; the second relate to breaches of law or regulation associated with environmental management and protection.

In recent years researchers have studied a wide range of environmental harms associated with both 'green' and 'brown' issues.

'Green' types of environmental crime

Studying these types of crimes has been motivated by either a concern with species justice or an interest in conventional environmental crimes, such as illegal fishing. For instance, work over the past decade has been carried out in respect to:

- deforestation and the devastation to plant, animal and human welfare and rights that has accompanied this process (Boekhout van Solinge 2008a and b, 2010a and b; Halsey 2005; Green, Ward and McConnachie 2007; Bisschop 2012a);
- the illegal theft and trade in reptiles in South Africa (Herbig 2010);
- fishing-related crimes, including the poaching of abalone and of lobster (Tailby and Gant 2002; McMullan and Perrier 2002; Petrossian 2012);
- animal abuse that involves both systemic uses of animals, such as factory farming, and one-on-one abuse of animals (Beirne 2009; Sollund 2008);
- crime prevention and the illicit trade in endangered species involving many different kinds of animals (Wellsmith 2010; Schneider 2008);
- the illegal wildlife market in Africa, in particular the trade in elephant ivory (Lemieux and Clarke 2009) and the illegal wildlife trade in Russia (South and Wyatt 2011).

'Brown' types of environmental crime

In regard to 'brown' issues, the production and disposal of waste is a matter of significant concern to academic researchers interested in questions of environmental harm. Relevant examples of such research include:

- the role of organized criminal syndicates in the dumping of waste, including toxic waste (Block 2002; Ruggiero 1996);
- inequalities associated with the location of disadvantaged and minority communities near toxic waste sites (Saha and Mohai 2005; Pellow 2007; Pinderhughes 1996);

- the use of medical and epidemiological evidence in demonstrating the nature and dynamics of toxic crimes (Lynch and Stretesky 2001);
- the global trade in electronic waste as a form of environmental crime, which is of particular concern at the present time (Gibbs, McGarrell and Axelrod 2010b; Interpol 2009; Bisschop 2012b; Bisschop and Vande Walle 2013);
- the social and cultural context within which local residents come to perceive what it is that pollutes their neighbourhoods and local rivers (Natali 2010);
- environmental racism linked to the social status of being poor, part of a minority group or indigenous community (Bullard 1994; Bullard 2005a and Brook 1998);
- specific incidents where toxic materials have been dumped into developing countries by unscrupulous companies (White 2009d).

The range of substantive topic areas presently being investigated by green criminologists is growing. For example, there are also a variety of 'white' types of environmental crime (that is, those based upon laboratory procedures) that are likewise garnering attention. This is particularly true of the analysis and critique of genetically modified organisms (GMOs). The abrogation of human rights and United Nations agreements in attempts to impose GMO crops on reluctant nation-states (Walters, R. 2004, 2005, 2011) has been studied, as have the implications of GMO technology for third-world food producers (Mgbeoji 2006).

Perspectives within green criminology

Scholars and researchers have been working on issues pertaining to environmental crime for many years, although without necessarily using the label 'green criminology' to describe their work. For instance, environmental harm and crime has been linked to the activities of corporations and also to organized criminal syndicates in regard to the control and manipulation of waste disposal processes and the production and distribution of toxic chemicals (Pearce and Tombs 1998; Ruggiero 1996; Massari and Monzini 2004).

Case vignette 1.1 Green criminology in Slovenia, 1981

Opinions about the origins of environmental or green criminology differ but for criminologists in the European country of Slovenia, environmental crime and its consequences were on the horizon as early as 1981, when Pečar warned about new forms of criminality relating to green and environmental issues. Pečar was far-sighted and anticipated a need to define and forewarn about the advent of environmental crimes – he even spoke about the crime of ecocide. In 1981 environmental crime according to Pečar (1981: 40) was defined as:

> every permanent or temporary act or process which has a negative influence on the environment, people's health or natural resources, including; building, changing, abandonment and destruction of buildings; waste processing and elimination of waste; emissions into water, air or soil; transport and handling of dangerous substances; damaging or destructing of natural resources; reduction of biological diversity or reduction of natural genetic resources; and other activities or interventions, which put the environment at risk.
>
> (Cited in Eman *et al*. 2009: 578)
>
> He characterized the pollution of nature and the environment as a devaluation of the environment, something he also called 'ecocide' – intentional destruction of the living environment. Under this term he classified examples of waste dumping and negative environmental interventions (Pečar 1981). Later, he identified the motivations for much environmental crime when he said: 'environmental crime results from selfishness, which is determined by the need for profit associated with the control of nature' (Pečar 1988: 116 (cited in Eman *et al*. 2009: 578)).

Others have looked specifically at environmental crime, but generally within conventional frameworks. Here the focus has been on traditional illegal activities associated with the environment (such as illegal fishing), analysed within traditional criminological theoretical approaches. The key concepts and concerns of this kind of conventional work have been based upon legal concepts of environmental crime, existing legislative and regulatory measures around environmental crime, and the nature of official environmental law enforcement (Situ and Emmons 2000; Fyfe and Reeves 2009; Shelley and Crow 2009). Related to this, a conventional legal approach to the study of environmental crime sees it as a violation of criminal law and civil statutes; essentially legal studies with environmental crime as the object of analysis (Brickey 2008; Bell and McGillivray 2008; Mehta 2009).

Questions pertaining specifically to environmental justice have also been of long-standing interest. The main thrust of this work has been to explore the empirical links between toxic environments and certain categories of people (inevitably the poor, the dispossessed and people of colour), and to actively struggle against the discrimination and racism which underpins such injustice. However, the key concepts and concerns of this work have emphasized issues relating to the distribution of environmental advantage and disadvantage, rather than crime *per se* (Bullard 2005a and b; Pellow 2007).

The early pioneers of a distinctive 'green criminology' sought to provide a particular and self-conscious branding of the kind of work they engaged in. This occurred in the 1990s and was characterized by writing about the need for criminology to take environmental crimes seriously, and to do so in ways that would force criminology to rethink how it does what it does, and how to conceptualize the issues. Key concepts and concerns included the notion of green criminology itself as a concept, the idea that green criminology is a perspective not a theory, and the social and ecological importance of studying environmental crime and harm (Lynch 1990; South 1998a and b; Clifford 1998).

Green criminology has emerged in the last 20 years as a distinctive area of research, scholarship and intervention. It is distinctive in the sense that it has directed much greater attention to environmental crime and harm than mainstream criminology, and has heightened awareness of emergent issues, such as the problems arising from disposal of electronic waste (e-waste) and the social and ecological injustices linked to the corporate colonization of nature (including bio-piracy and imposition of GMO crops in developing countries).

While the unifying link between and among green criminologists is the focus on environmental issues, important theoretical and political differences are nonetheless becoming more apparent over time. For example, some scholars argue that green criminology must necessarily be anti-capitalist and exhibit a broad radical orientation (Lynch and Stretesky 2003). Others construe the task as one of conservation and natural resource management within the definitional limits of existing laws (Herbig and Joubert 2006; Gibbs *et al.* 2010a). Still others promote the idea that the direction of research should be global and ecological, and that new concepts need to be developed that will better capture the nature and dynamics of environmental harms in the twenty-first century (White 2011a).

As green criminology has grown as a specific area of concentrated scholarship and research, so, too, it has developed distinct sub-areas or perspectives that express quite different conceptualizations of the problem and how best to respond to it. Some of these are briefly summarized in Box 1.1. Importantly, any one writer may be aligned with more than one of the perspectives listed here – the categorizations are not mutually exclusive.

The hallmark of green criminology, regardless of diversity of opinion and the plurality of views, is that proponents argue for more attention to be given to environmental and ecological issues. It is interesting in this respect that a number of prominent criminologists are now utilizing their expertise from mainstream areas of criminology (e.g. situational crime prevention, general strain theory) to study specifically environmental issues such as illegal trade in elephant tusks, industrial pollution and social problems arising from climate change (Agnew 2012; Meško, Dimitrijevic and Fields 2010; Lemieux and Clarke 2009). Green criminology is not only expanding in its own right, but simultaneously there is a greening of criminology more generally.

Systemic causes of environmental harm

For many green criminologists the biggest threat to environmental rights, ecological justice and non-human animal well-being are system-level structures and pressures

Box 1.1 Perspectives within green criminology

Radical green criminology

A generic term to describe a *broad radical orientation* towards issues pertaining to *environmental harm* and crimes against nature.

Key concepts and concerns:

- ecological, environmental and species justice;
- anti-capitalist, anti-anthropocentric (or human-centred);
- environmentalist, animal rights.

Exemplar: Lynch and Stretesky (2003), who provide a trenchant critique of corporations and argue that green criminology ought to be defined precisely by its radical critique of the status quo.

Eco-global criminology

Designates a specific concern with the *transnational nature of environmental harm* and the ways in which transgressions against humans, ecosystems and animals manifest at a global level.

Key concepts and concerns:

- climate change;
- transnational environmental crime;
- ecological justice.

Exemplar: White (2011a), who argues that ecological criteria should underpin analysis, and that such analysis should be highly cognizant of the importance of scale, that incorporates the intersections of the local, national, regional and international.

Conservation criminology

Designates a specific concern with *natural resource conservation* and management that draws upon criminological concerns, and with environmental law enforcement and *environmental crime as legally defined*.

Key concepts and concerns:

- conservation;
- natural resource management;
- risk assessment and analysis.

Exemplar: Gibbs *et al.* (2010a), who argue for an integration of criminology with natural resource disciplines and the risk and decision sciences, so that the study of environmental crimes and risks better incorporates interdisciplinary scholarship.

Environmental criminology

Designates a conventional criminological approach to dealing with environmental crime as legally defined, drawing mainly upon place-based criminology (also known as 'environmental criminology') that concentrates on *situational crime prevention.*

Key concepts and concerns:

- situational crime prevention;
- market reduction approach;
- illegal wildlife trade.

Exemplar: Wellsmith (2010), who argues that place-based criminology and situational crime prevention have much to offer in reducing environmental harm, especially in areas such as 'wildlife crime' and endangered species conservation.

Constructivist green criminology

Designates an approach to the study of environmental harm and crime from the point of view of constitutive or constructivist criminology that emphasizes how categories and labels are socially and politically constructed.

Key concepts and concerns:

- language of criminological analysis;
- subjective elements of crime constitution;
- media studies.

Exemplar: Brisman (2012a), who argues for the need to deconstruct categories such as 'crime', 'criminal' and 'victim' in analyses of environmental harm, so that underlying relations of power and the labelling processes can be exposed, as in the case of contrarianism and climate change (see also Brisman and South 2012).

Specieist criminology

Designates a focus on *specieism* as the main target for criminological research and *critique of anthropocentrism* in the construction of environmental issues,

> insofar as species and individual members of species are seen to have intrinsic value and rights.
>
> *Key concepts and concerns:*
>
> - specieism as a form of discrimination;
> - abuse of animals, including factory farms;
> - illegal wildlife trade.
>
> Exemplar: Beirne (2009), who argues that abuse and degradation of animals has to be analysed in its historical and social contexts, and that major questions need to be answered regarding how, why, where and when animal abuse occurs.
>
> Source: White 2013b

that commodify all aspects of social existence, that are based upon the exploitation of humans, non-human animals and natural resources, and that privilege the powerful over the interests of the vast majority. It is for this reason that assessment of environmental wrongdoing also requires critical scrutiny of how nation-states themselves intervene with regard to specific environmental harm issues.

Consideration of who is responsible for environmental harm can be approached by acknowledging that, in part, the answer depends upon the level of abstraction one applies. Even though they are intrinsically linked, there are major differences between explanations that focus on systemic answers and those that examine immediate situational causes of harm or risk. Here students might consider several of the more general explanations for ecological calamity that point to particular sorts of 'perpetrator' as the source of the problem (see White 2011a for more detailed exposition).

Humans are responsible

The argument here is that humans are responsible for much of the destruction of ecological systems and, as such, are the key agents of environmental harm/crime in the contemporary time period. The argument is that the problem lies in how humans as a whole transform their immediate environments for their own purposes. The net result is to the detriment of both human and non-human, but the causal force of environmental degradation is ultimately human. The idea of blaming the human species, however, can be subjected to counter-factual analysis. That is, if all humans are implicated in the harm, then all humans must by their own 'human' nature be destructive. Yet we know from accounts of indigenous relationships with nature, to take one example, that some humans have lived countless years in harmonious relationship with their local ecosystems (see Robyn 2002). We also know that some contemporary communities in places such as India are actively reconfiguring their relationship with nature in ways that are ecologically sustainable and that promote biodiversity (see Shiva 2008). It is only at a very high level of abstraction, then, that we can place blame on humans. The more grounded the analysis becomes – the more reflective of specific groups and communities – the more tenuous the sweep of the generalization.

Technology is responsible

Another perspective places the emphasis on technology as a perpetrator or facilitator of environmental harm. In this scenario, technology is seen as that which creates the risks and harms. It is the motor car, the factory, the tractor, the coal-fired power station, the dam, the fertilizer, that is the problem. In response, proposals to downshift to a low-tech future might be interpreted as a 'blame the technology' kind of argument. Against this is the acknowledgement that the technology question is inherently about the social character of collective practice. Davison (2004: 144) points out that 'Technologies of genetics, biology, energy, matter and information cannot be neatly sorted into good and bad, or sustainable and unsustainable, piles'. What counts is the specific social and ecological conditions under which technologies are utilized and applied. The social context of technological use and development is therefore crucial.

Population is responsible

Overpopulation is frequently touted as the most important factor or variable in ecological destruction. Put simply, there are too many people on the planet for the planet to be able to sustain them. In ecological terms, this is often expressed in the language of ecological footprint. The solution is to reduce the number of people if we are to survive. Again, while it is true that the many billions of humans on the planet are contributing to global warming, loss of biodiversity and increased waste and pollution, to blame population *per se* risks pitching the problem at too abstract a level of explanation. For instance, the bulk of consumption is generated by consumers in advanced industrialized nations – the metropoles rather than the periphery. Moreover, it is the displacement of the poor and the profound social inequalities between North and South (and within these) that make for desperate people doing what they can to survive. Population growth is substantively linked to economic, social and political circumstance insofar as the more affluent one is, the less the proclivity to reproduce to the same extent as those who have little. Again, the question of power (and inequality) is a factor here, since it is those who 'have' who are most likely to favour controlling population policies in regard to those who do not.

Capitalism is responsible

Even a cursory examination of dominant world political economic trends reveals the close link between capitalism as a system and environmental degradation and transformation generally (see Chapter 2). The key aspects of contemporary political economy include accumulation as the economic engine: one that is based upon the exploitation of natural resources, non-human animals and people. While a system can be seen to be to blame (in the sense of being instrumental) for environmental degradation, it is nevertheless perplexing when it comes to assigning specific responsibility. Systems are deemed to be blameworthy, but they are not *responsible*, insofar as there is no single 'controlling mind'. Systems may be subjected to social and moral condemnation, and they may invoke substantive movements towards reform and revolutionary change. But there is no perpetrator as such. A simplistic blaming of capitalism therefore, provides little more than rhetorical shorthand for 'something is wrong', rather than providing a guide to who, precisely, is doing what within the overarching parameters of global capitalism.

Corporations are responsible

As with blaming capitalism for everything, there is a temptation to likewise blame transnational corporations (TNCs) for everything. A sizeable literature exists that spells out the many ways in which TNCs escape or minimize negative media coverage for acts or omissions that cause harm (Lynch, Stretesky and Hammond 2000), proactively use green-washing techniques to make them seem environmentally responsible or good corporate citizens (Beder 2002), threaten critics and environmental activists with lawsuits (Beder 2002; White 2005b) and generally make life difficult for those trying to expose their wrongdoing (White 2008a). The powerful have many ways in which to protect their interests. However, there is great variability between and within TNCs in terms of core activities, nature of executive decisions, and relationship to workers, consumers and environments. Again, more precision is needed in analysing the actual role and behaviour of specific companies, rather than relying upon stereotype and over-generalization (contrast, for example, Braithwaite and Drahos 2000 and Bakan 2004).

According to Williams (1996) it is important to phrase a definition of crime or harm as 'consequence of' rather than 'caused by'. This is because of the technical difficulties in proving causation in many instances of environmental harm. In the light of this it is not surprising that there are frequently deliberate denials of causal links, and hence the avoidance of liability and responsibility by perpetrators. Williams (1996: 26) argues that these are particularly important issues in relation to the environment insofar as 'the *complexity* of establishing causation creates an easy escape for perpetrators, and the *scale* of remediation is usually immense and so the incentive to avoid liability is great'. One task of green criminology is to expose the consequences of actions and omissions on the part of individuals, groups, organized gangs, corporations and nation-states.

Conclusion

The study of environmental crime is not new, although green criminology as a distinctive perspective within criminology is. The expansion of green criminology as a discrete body of work involving particular academics and practitioner networks is, ironically, based upon the notion of exclusivity – that is, that there is something unique and distinctive about this activity called 'green criminology' that sets it apart from other types of social scientific investigation. Conversely, the embrace of climate change and illegal wildlife trade within mainstream criminological circles represents a move toward inclusivity – that is, the field of criminology is sufficiently elastic to allow the incorporation of the study of environmental harm and crime more deeply into its conceptual and methodological universe.

The benefit of labelling this type of scholarly activity as 'green criminology' is that it has provided a focal point for people around the world who share a passionate interest in analysis of, and action around, environmental crimes and harms. This has been important in terms of building networks of scholars and researchers, and has led to an increasing number and variety of public forums where environmental crime is discussed and debated from diverse perspectives. While not precluding individuals from working on their own or in isolation from others, the sense of collective mission has been important in consolidating this area of work, in raising its status and profile within mainstream academic bodies and governmental organizations, and in engendering new conceptualizations and methodologies. The enhanced circulation and cross-fertilization of ideas and knowledge has been largely beneficial to all concerned. What unifies the diverse approaches under the green criminology umbrella is a concern with the environment informed by the pursuit of justice, whether this is legal, social or ecological.

The present and future directions for green criminology feature two key drivers that are propelling interest in this area. The first is the nature of contemporary environmental problems and the increasing realization of impending crisis related to these. The degradation and destruction of specific environments and the extinction of species is having manifestly negative impacts across the globe. This can no longer be ignored. Likewise, climate change is rapidly and radically altering the social and ecological landscape, in ways that warrant immediate and urgent attention from criminologists. The natural world, of which humans are a part, is demanding intervention which criminology can and must contribute to. The second is increasing awareness of interesting overlaps and synergies between green criminology and other areas of criminology. The latter include mainstream or conventional areas, for example, situational crime prevention and general strain theory. It also includes novel and more recent areas of concern, such as cultural criminology. Heightened interaction across conceptual domains is generating increasing interest in a green criminology that draws upon past knowledge, critiques the present and looks to the future.

Discussion topics

- Green criminology is a perspective not a theory. What does this mean, and how does it relate to the conceptual foundations and historical origins of green criminology?
- The state defines what is criminal or not. Why is this important to the development of extra-legal definitions of environmental harm?
- Why is it called 'green criminology'?
- What are some of the key differences between laws designed to regulate and manage an environmental problem (e.g. CITES and illegal trade in wildlife) and laws intended to eradicate a problem (e.g. Montreal Protocol and banning of ozone-depleting substances)?
- Different causes create different problems. Discuss this in reference to specific examples of environmental harm.

Further reading

Beirne, P., and South, N. (eds) (2007). *Issues in Green Criminology: Confronting harms against environments, humanity and other animals*. Cullompton: Willan Publishing.

Brisman, A., Beirne, P. and South, N. (2013). 'A guide to a green criminology', in N. South and A. Brisman (eds), *The Routledge International Handbook of Green Criminology*. London: Routledge.

Ellefsen, R., Sollund, R., and Larsen, G. (eds) (2012). *Eco Global Crimes: Contemporary problems and future challenges*. Farnham: Ashgate.

Nurse, A. (2013). *Animal Harm: Perspectives on why people harm and kill animals*. Farnham: Ashgate.

Walters, R., Westerhuis, D., and Wyatt, T. (eds) (2013). *Emerging Issues in Green Criminology*. Basingstoke: Palgrave Macmillan.

Chapter 2

Eco-global criminology and transnational environmental crime

Introduction

This chapter will discuss the following topics:

- eco-global criminology;
- the contours of global capitalism;
- transnational environmental crime; and
- horizon-scanning.

Eco-global criminology, as noted in Chapter 1, is one of several perspectives that fall under the broader rubric of green criminology. This chapter outlines the core concerns of eco-global criminology as these relate to concepts of harm, the globalization of harm, global political economy and the increasingly transnational nature of environmental crimes and harms. It closes with a discussion of eco-global criminology's adoption of horizon-scanning as a useful tool for examining over-the-horizon issues and trends that are likely to generate environmental crimes and harms now and into the future.

A concern with environmental crime inevitably leads the analytical gaze to acknowledge the fusion of the local and the global, and to ponder the ways in which many such transgressions transcend the normal boundaries of legality, jurisdiction, geography and social divide. This observation is important because so much environmental harm is intrinsically transnational in nature. Contemporary discussions of environmental crime, for example, deal with issues such as the illegal transport and dumping of toxic waste, the proliferation of electronic waste, transborder pollution that is either systematic (via location of factories) or related to accidents (e.g. chemical plant spills), the illegal trade in flora and fauna, and illegal fishing and logging. Whether conceptualized in conventional legal terms or based upon more encompassing ecologically-based conceptions, harm is by nature mobile and easily subject to transference.

Moreover, the systemic causal chains that underpin much environmental harm are located at the level of the global political economy – within which the transnational corporation stands as the central social force – and this, too, is reflected in the pressing together of the local-global at a practical level. International systems of production, distribution and consumption generate, reinforce and reward diverse environmental harms and those who perpetrate them (White 2002, 2008a, 2013a). These range from unsafe products to reliance upon genetically modified grains, the destruction of out-of-date ships and planes through to the transportation and dumping of hazardous wastes. Engaging with green criminology requires a sense of scale, and of the essential interconnectedness of issues, events, people and places.

Eco-global criminology

Eco-global criminology refers to a framework of analysis where the emphasis is on the ecological, the transnational and questions of justice. The substantive focus of eco-global criminology is transgressions against ecosystems, humans and animals. It draws upon three intertwined conceptual categories: the ecological, the global and transnational, and the harmful (White 2011a). It is not a 'theory' as such, since it does not purport to offer overarching causal explanations for transnational environmental crime (for example, to blame it on 'capitalism' or 'overpopulation' or 'specieism'). Instead the focus is on how things are as they are, and how they can be different in the future. Answers to the 'why' question are devolved to lower levels of abstraction (e.g. concrete cases relating to prosecution of offenders) and are specific to the topic at hand (e.g. explanations for the low penalties assigned to environmental offenders). The objective is to get to the bottom of what happened, how it happened, why it happened, and who knew about it and when – as these pertain to specific cases and events.

As a perspective, eco-global criminology is about seeing and analysing the world around us in certain ways. What marks it out from other green criminological perspectives is the attention given to specifically ecological considerations of harm (the lawful but awful) rather than criminal definitions (the unlawful) as such, as well as a global perspective on issues and events. The major threats to planetary well-being posed by climate change, diminished biodiversity, and pollution, for example, are considered core issues. Global environmental issues like climate change are altering the way we see the world, so that activities once considered lawful may become unlawful in the future, because of their consequences for people in other parts of the world as well as for future generations of all species and their habitats. Climate change has also heightened awareness of the mobility of certain environmental harms (e.g. toxic substances released from melting glaciers or leaching from clusters of industrial businesses during weather-related storms and floods).

To fully appreciate the nature of global environmental crime and injustice it is important to consider the physical location and scale of harm within particular geographical contexts. For eco-global criminology this means plotting out myriad different types of harm, recognizing that some are common across the world whilst others are specific to particular locales, regions and countries. The links between geographical scale and environmental harm can be spelled out through a simple mapping of environmental harms in different places around the world. In this way, layer after layer of harm, present and potential, can be determined by on the one hand investigating harmful ecological trends that involve degradation and destruction of environments (such as clear felling of forests), and on the other hand considering existing documentation of specific types of environmental crime (such as illegal international trade in plants and animals). These crimes are interconnected and intertwined in various ways. What happens at the local level has consequences for those on the other side of the planet. What happens in any one place is thus intrinsically important to what happens worldwide.

The production of global environmental harm is partly determined through complex processes of transference (Heckenberg 2010) that frequently relocate certain types of harm and harmful activities, to regions of least resistance. Harm can also be externalized from producers and consumers in ways that make it disappear (out of sight and outside the reach of adequate oversight). Producers may be unaware of or indifferent to the harms they cause to workers and consumers by what they produce. Consumers may be unaware of or indifferent to how what they consume creates harm elsewhere for humans and environments far removed from their everyday experience. The global trade in toxic waste (often under the cover of recycling), the illegal dumping of radioactive waste, carbon emission trading and the shifting of dirty industries to developing countries constitute some of the worst aspects of the 'not in my backyard' syndrome. The end result is a massive movement of environmentally harmful products, activities, processes and wastes to the most vulnerable places and most exploited peoples around the world

For eco-global criminology, the greatest threat to environmental rights, ecological justice and non-human animal well-being are system-level structures and pressures. Those who determine and shape the law are very often those whose activities need to be scrutinized and sometimes criminalized for the sake of planetary well-being. Environmental harm is thus highly contestable both at the level of definition, and in terms of visions of what remedies are required for desired social and ecological change.

Analysis of broad trends indicates that it is systemic imperatives and historical transformations associated with global capitalism that, in today's world, ultimately shape what it is that individuals do in and with their lives and their environments. Eco-global criminology thus is informed by ecological considerations and by a critical analysis that is worldwide in its scale and perspective. It is based upon eco-justice conceptions of harm that include consideration of transgressions against environments, non-human species and humans (see Chapter 3). For this kind of criminology the first question to ask is 'what harm is there in a particular activity?', rather than whether the activity is legal or not. Eco-global criminology incorporates substantive concerns based upon considerations of ecology, geography and justice.

Ecology

Eco-global criminology is distinctive in its attention to specifically ecological considerations of harm, and a global perspective on issues and events. A major concern, therefore, is to highlight the importance of research into and action around threats to planetary well-being posed by climate change, diminished biodiversity and pollution. For example, in large measure the problem of climate change is directly related to how humans across the globe produce and consume, distribute and exchange the fruits of their labour. While, to date, the impact of climate change on humans has been felt disproportionately in the developing countries, recent estimates indicate that more affluent countries in the West are now beginning to experience climate-related disasters (see UNEP 2007a). Plants and animals are affected not only by global warming (e.g. through threats to habitat and weather changes), but also by human efforts to mitigate and adapt to climate change (e.g. deforestation linked to planting of GMO crops). Threats to biodiversity (see Chapter 8) and the problem of waste (see Chapter 9) likewise contribute to unhealthy and insecure environments and futures.

Geography

To fully appreciate the nature of global environmental crimes it is essential to consider the physical location of harms within particular geographical contexts. There are myriad different types of harm, some common across the globe, others, however, specific to particular locales, regions and countries. This is illustrated in Table 2.1.

Table 2.1 Geographical scale and environmental harm

Scale	Example
The Local	Lobster poaching in Nova Scotia, Canada
	Abalone theft in Tasmania, Australia
The National	Pollution related to pastoral industry in New Zealand
	Issues of drinking water in Palestine, Israel and Jordan
The Regional	Logging in the forests of the Amazon
	Killing of elephants for their tusks in Africa
The Global	Global warming and natural disasters
	Formation of huge plastic dumps in oceans
The Transnational	Global trade in toxic waste
	Shifting of dirty industries to developing countries

Source: White 2011a

The harms so described are interconnected and intertwined in various ways: what happens at the local level has consequences for those on the other side of the planet. What happens in any one place is intrinsically important to what happens worldwide.

Crime and justice

From the point of view of eco-global criminology, analysis of transnational environmental crime needs to incorporate different, albeit inter-related, notions of harm (White 2011a). These include:

1 *Legal conceptions* of harm informed by laws, rules and international conventions, pertaining to unlawful practices such as illegal fishing or the transportation and transference of banned substances (major concerns of conventional criminology).
2 *Ecological conceptions* of harm, informed by holistic understandings of the interrelationship between species and environments, situate the key issue of ecological sustainability in the context of global warming and species extinction (major concerns of ecology and environmental studies).
3 *Justice conceptions* of harm, informed by notions of human, ecological and animal rights, and egalitarian concerns such as preserving complex ecosystems for their own value and preventing animal abuse (major concerns of green criminology).

These three approaches (see Box 2.1) incorporate competing yet overlapping notions of harm (both within and between each approach) that one way or another have to be acknowledged in eco-global criminological research.

The argument underpinning Box 2.1 is that if ecological (and social and economic, and human and non-human) welfare is to be maximized, then there is a need to expand existing notions of what actually constitutes an environmental crime (see Chapter 1). When criminalization does occur, it often reflects very limited anthropocentric (human-centred) notions of what is best (e.g. protection of legal fisheries and legal timber coups) that values 'nature' and 'wildlife' simply and mainly in terms of their worth as resources for human exploitation. It is about private property and business interests and monopolies and sustainable development. The intrinsic value of specific ecological areas and non-human species tends to be downplayed or ignored. Furthermore, exploitation of environments, plants and animals is treated as if they are equivalent – based upon their use-value to humans – rather than in the light of individual suffering and the lived experience of harm.

Rather than being restricted by the limitations of the legal/illegal divide, eco-global criminology asserts the prior importance of and urgency associated with *ecological sustainability*. This approach assesses 'harm' in many different

Box 2.1 Three approaches to conceptualizing environmental harm

Legal conceptions of harm (conventional criminology)

- Illegal taking of flora and fauna: includes activities such as illegal, unregulated and unreported fishing, illegal logging and trade in timber, and illegal trade in wild plants and animals.
- Pollution offences: relates to issues such as fly tipping (illegal dumping) through to air, water and land pollution associated with industry.
- Transportation of banned substances: refers to the illegal transport of radioactive materials and the illegal transfer of hazardous waste.

Ecological conceptions of harm (ecology and environmental studies)

- Problem of climate change: the concern is with those activities that contribute to global warming, such as the replacement of forests with cropland.
- Problem of waste and pollution: the concern is with those activities that defile the environment, leading to things such as the diminishment of clean water.
- Problem of biodiversity: the concern is to stem the tide of species extinction and the overall reduction in species resulting from certain forms of human production, including use of genetically modified organisms.

Justice conceptions of harm (green criminology)

- Environment rights and environmental justice: in which environmental rights are seen as an extension of human or social rights so as to enhance the quality of human life, now and into the future.
- Ecological citizenship and ecological justice: in which ecological citizenship acknowledges that human beings are merely one component of complex ecosystems that should be preserved for their own sake, via the notion of the rights of the environment.
- Animal rights and species justice: in which environmental harm is conceptualized in terms of the place of non-human animals within environments and their intrinsic right to not suffer abuse, whether this be one-on-one harm, institutionalized harm or harm arising from human actions that affect climates and environments on a global scale.

contexts and guises, regardless of legal status and existing institutional rationalizations as to why harmful activities should be allowed to occur.

The close relationship between the legal and the illegal, especially when it comes to environmental harm (White 2008a), also means that eco-global criminology frequently has to confront issues of power and powerful social interests. This has several implications in regard to gaining access to data and information, and for carrying out research in various parts of the world. The link between vested private interests, state interests and environmental harm is also of concern.

The contours of global capitalism

There is a close link between capitalism as a system and environmental degradation and transformation (see Stretsky, Long and Lynch 2013). The sphere of production is dominated by the production of commodities, the advance of technology and bio-technologies, and the exploitation of labour (in both developed and developing countries) in the service of mass production of goods and services that, in turn, demand a high turn-over rate. Extensive and intensive forms of consumption are essential to the realization of surplus value – that is, profit depends upon a critical mass of buyers purchasing mass-produced commodities. The link between production and consumption is found in the form of specific kinds of distribution processes (e.g. transportation of goods and services, retail outlets, storage, roads, railways, bridges, and ships) and exchange mechanisms (e.g. finance capital, credit availability) that sustain and contribute to extensive use of natural and human resources. Economic efficiency is measured in how quickly and cheaply commodities can be produced, channelled to markets, and consumed, a process inherently exploitive of both humans and nature.

In essence, the competition and waste associated with the capitalist mode of production have a huge impact on the wider environment, on humans and on non-human animals (for example, in the form of pollution and toxicity levels in air, water and land). These same processes pose major threats to biodiversity and the shrinking of the number of plant and animal species generally. This is related to both the legal and illegal trade in species, as well as to mass industrial production and extensive use of genetically modified organism (GMO) technologies.

At the heart of these processes is a political culture which takes for granted, but rarely sees as problematic, the proposition that continued expansion of material consumption is not only possible but will not harm the biosphere in any fundamental way. Built into the logic and dynamics of capitalism is the imperative to expand (Foster 2002), a tendency that is reinforced and facilitated by neo-liberal ideologies and policies. Arising from this growth imperative, there are several intertwined elements that have contributed to the dominance and entrenchment of the capitalist mode of production on a world scale. These include (White 2010b):

- *Privatization* – transition from common property to private property, accompanied by a shift toward concentrated private ownership and management, and greater reliance on market mechanisms rather than government controls to distribute goods and services, and protect environments.
- *Commodification* – transformation of use-value into exchange-value, as more and more aspects of social life and environment are commercialized, and 'worth' is gauged by how much something (including basic necessities, such as water) sells for on the commodity markets.
- *Massification* – mass production of goods and services, including for niche markets, facilitated by technologies such as the internet, but nonetheless accompanied by the simplification of consumables including foods (e.g. fewer varieties of tomato or corn) and other goods and services, which are reduced to a narrow range of choices (e.g. difference between specific products is superficial rather than substantive).
- *Globalization* – monopolization of control over production by corporate conglomerates via takeovers and mergers worldwide, and the penetration of the transnational corporation into local markets and practices, thus transforming the nature of production and consumption in these sites.

Capitalism in essence means expansion, and these social processes are intended precisely to bolster growth and further extend capital accumulation.

Systemic imperatives to expand imply that 'natural resources' are themselves subject to varying processes of commodification: that is, the transformation of existing or potential use-values into exchange-values (for example, clean drinking water becomes something to be bought and sold among consumers, rather than being a right for citizens). One consequence of commodification is that the distribution of goods and services using market mechanisms is privileged, rather than, for instance, being based upon communal and ecological assessments of need. In this context – and somewhat perversely – scarcity of, for example, clean drinking water, makes the natural commodity even more valuable to the owner. Scarcity thus equates to high profit levels (White 2003; South 2012).

The four elements – water, air, earth (land), sun (energy) – are ever more subject to conversion into something that produces value for private interests. Capitalism is always searching for things that can be transformed from simple use-values (i.e., objects of need) into exchange-values (i.e., commodities produced for exchange). This extends to 'nature' as it does to other kinds of objects. For example, what may have been formerly 'free' (e.g. drinking water), is now sold back to the consumer for a price (e.g. bottled water or metered water). Effectively consumption has been put at the service of production in the sense that consumer decisions and practices are embedded in what is actually produced and how it is produced. Yet it is via consumption practices, and the cultural contexts for constantly growing and changing forms of consumption, that production realizes its value.

Commodity production and consumption, then, takes place within the context of a global political system that is hierarchical and uneven. That is, sovereignty is historically and socially constructed through the prism of colonialism and imperialism, with certain nation-states holding greater power and resources (including military might) than others. The relationship between local, national, regional and global interests is construed within diverse social and political formations (e.g. United States, European Union, Association of South-East Asian Nations, African Union), but these, in turn, reflect the continuing legacy of a world divided into the 'haves' and 'have-nots'. The contours of this division are dictated by the strength of ownership and control over the means of production exerted regionally and globally by particular nation-states in conjunction with and in the interests of particular corporations. At the top of the hierarchy of nation-states is the United States.

The consolidation of a global capitalist system is at one and the same time reflective of gross inequalities within and between nation-states. There are winners and losers on the world stage, and this, too, is part of a broader historical and material process involving unequal trading relations between countries.

The appropriation of nature does not merely involve the turning of natural resources into commodities, and entrenching inequality via the global market but also frequently involves capital actually remaking nature and its products biologically and physically. It has been observed, for instance, that 'A precapitalist nature is transformed into a specifically capitalist nature' (O'Connor 1994: 158) in the form of genetic changes in food crops, the destroying of biological diversity through extensive use of plantation forestry, and so on. Indeed, the industrialization of agriculture (incorporating the use of seed and other patents) is one of the greatest threats to biodiversity, since this is one of the leading causes of erosion of plant genetic and species diversity. The basic means of life of humans is being reconstituted and reorganized through global systems of production (Croall 2007), and in many cases we still do not know the longer-term effects of new developments in the food area.

One impact of unsustainable environmental practices is the pressure exerted on companies to seek out new resources (natural and human) to exploit, as existing reserves dwindle due to over-exploitation and contamination from already produced wastes. Nature itself becomes a dumping ground, particularly in the invisible spaces of the open seas, in underground spaces and in less-developed countries. Waste is both an outcome and a driver of the production process (see Chapter 9).

Simultaneously, the social consequence of no work, no income, and no subsistence livelihood for significant numbers of people worldwide means that waste-producing and toxic forms of production (including recycling) are more likely to be accepted by the vulnerable. The imposition of such injustice is embedded in the wider systemic pressures associated with global capitalism. Profitability very often means adopting the most unsustainable practices for short-term gain. Transforming nature is part and parcel of what capitalism as a system does. How it does so, is what is of ecological significance as well as crucial to the well-being

> **Box 2.2 Capitalism and the transformation of nature**
>
> - *Resource depletion* – extraction of non-renewable minerals and energy without development of proper alternatives, over-harvesting of renewable resources such as fish and forest timbers.
> - *Disposal problems* – waste generated in production, distribution and consumption processes, pollution associated with transformations of nature, burning of fossil fuels and using up of consumables.
> - *Corporate colonization of nature* – genetic changes in food crops, use of plantation forestry that diminishes biodiversity, preference for large-scale, technology-dependent and high-yield agricultural and aquaculture methods that degrade land and oceans and affect species' development and well-being.
> - *Species decline* – destruction of habitats, privileging of certain species of grains and vegetables over others for market purposes, super-exploitation of specific plants and animals, due to presumed consumer taste and mass markets.

of the majority of humans on the planet (see Box 2.2). These transformations not only capitalistically change nature, but they simultaneously transform human relationships and the habitats of human and non-human alike.

The contours of global capitalism are crucial to any discussion of environmental harm, in that how, or whether, certain human activity is regulated and facilitated is still primarily a matter of state intervention. The strategies that nation-states use to deal with environmental concerns are contingent upon the class interests associated with political power. In most cases today the power of transnational corporations (TNCs) find purchase in the interface between the interests and preferred activities of the corporation and the specific protections and supports proffered by the nation-state. The latter can be reliant upon or intimidated by particular industries and companies. Tax revenue and job creation, as well as media support and political donations, may hinge upon particular state-corporate synergies. This of course can undermine the basic tenets of democracy and collective deliberation over how best to interpret the public or national interest

The structure and allocation of societal resources via the nation-state also has an impact upon how environmental issues are socially constructed. Spending on welfare, health, transportation, education and other forms of social infrastructure makes a big difference in people's lives. Recent fiscal crises (especially noticeable in European countries such as Greece, Ireland and Spain) and the effects of the global economic crisis have had the global impact of making ordinary workers extremely vulnerable economically. Under such conditions, there is even greater scope to either reduce environmental protection, or to increase environmentally destructive activity for short-term economic gain. In such circumstances, state legislation and company practices that are seen to put fetters on the profit-making enterprise will be withdrawn or markedly reduced. This is so whether the activity is in the metropole countries or in the periphery.

Yet the period since World War Two has seen major growth in the internationalization of treaties, agreements, protocols and conventions in relation to environmental protection and with respect to the securing of environmental resources. Nation-states have in recent years been more interested in taking governmental action on environmental matters, since much of this pertains to national economic interests. Moreover, the transboundary nature of environmental harm is evident in a variety of international protocols and conventions that deal with such matters as the illegal trade in ozone-depleting substances, the dumping and illegal transport of hazardous waste, illegal trade in chemicals such as persistent organic pollutants, and illegal dumping of oil and other wastes in oceans (Hayman and Brack 2002). A major concern today is the proliferation of 'e'-waste generated by the disposal of tens of thousands of computers, mobile phones and other equipment. Transnational environmental crime is still on the international agenda, albeit subject to the systemic constraints noted above.

Transnational environmental crime

Transnational environmental crime, as defined in conventional legal terms, refers to:

- unauthorized acts or omissions that are *against the law* and therefore subject to criminal prosecution and criminal sanctions;
- crimes that involve some kind of *cross-border transference* and an international or *global dimension*; and
- crimes related to *pollution* (of air, water and land), *crimes against wildlife* (including illegal trade in ivory as well as live animals) and *illegal fishing* (abalone, whales, dolphins and lobster, as well as fish).

These are the key focus of national and international laws relating to environmental matters, and are the main task areas for agencies such as Interpol. Some of the major international initiatives that formally specify certain activities as offences include (Forni 2010):

- Convention for Prevention of Maritime Pollution by Dumping Wastes and Other Matters;
- Convention on International Trade in Endangered Species of Wild Fauna and Flora (CITES);

- International Tropical Timber Agreement;
- Vienna Convention for the Protection of the Ozone Layer;
- Montreal Protocol on Substances that Deplete the Ozone Layer;
- Basel Convention on the Control of Transboundary Movements of Hazardous Wastes and their Disposal;
- United Nations Framework Convention on Climate Change;
- Kyoto Protocol.

In technical legal terms, transnational environmental crime has been defined as follows:

> ... transnational environmental crime involves the trading and smuggling of plants, animals, resources and pollutants in violation of prohibition or regulation regimes established by multilateral environmental agreements and/or in contravention of domestic law.
>
> (Forni 2010: 34)

This definition embodies huge complexities of scale, scope and content. For example, the legal framework governing environmental matters in international law is defined by over 270 Multilateral Environmental Agreements and related instruments (Forni 2010: 34). The laws and rules guiding action on environmental crime vary greatly at the local, regional and national levels, and there are overarching conventions and laws that likewise have different legal purchase depending upon how they are translated into action in each specific local jurisdiction. In part, differences in law-in-practice and conceptions of what is an environmental crime stem from the shifting nature of what is deemed harmful or not.

The notion of 'transnational' is, like crime generally, contentious from the point of view of definition and analytical focus. Mainstream concerns of criminal justice, as reflected in police agencies such as Interpol and the new international academic criminology, tend to view transnational crime in fairly conventional legal definitional terms (Madsen 2009; Van Dijk 2008). Specifically, the concern is with those activities that have been officially criminalized and thus are against the law. Those writing within a critical criminology tradition tend to raise issues that challenge both the conventional notion of crime (preferring often to use terms such as 'harm' or 'human rights' or 'ecological citizenship' as the appropriate yardstick) and the scope of analysis (which tends to go beyond conventional criminal categories or the standard criminological literature as such) (see Aas 2007).

Horizon-scanning

Looking over the horizon has two meanings that we explore in this section. The first relates to geographical scope – as in looking beyond our own borders. The second refers to temporal considerations – as in looking to the future and beyond. We begin with geographical notions of going beyond our own borders.

Locality is important when it comes to studying transnational environmental crimes and harms. Around the world different countries tend to have different types of environmental problems and issues. In New Zealand, for example, big questions have arisen over the use of pesticides and over-use of land for agriculture and pastoral purposes. Land and water is being contaminated through existing systems of production. By contrast, pressing issues of concern in Canada relate to the ecological impact of the huge oil tar sands projects in Alberta, and to the impact of insect blights on the pine trees of British Columbia. National context is important both in the objective nature of the problems at hand (e.g. pollution, deforestation, lack of adequate water) and in regard to subjective processes relating to the politicization of issues (e.g. the role of social movements in shaping public consciousness and state action on specific issues).

Most countries of the world have borders with another country. Rivers flow, mountains soar, air currents weave their way through the atmosphere, and plants and animals cross artificial boundaries that, for them, do not exist. There are issues that are specific to particular regions of the world. Huge tropical forests are found in the Amazon, an area that encompasses several different countries such as Brazil and Columbia. Such forests also cover parts of South-East Asia, spanning Indonesia, Malaysia, Thailand and Burma, among other countries. Africa is home to elephants, reptiles, giraffes and other creatures unique to particular parts of that continent, and not the preserve of any one country. Desertification and drought are phenomena associated with the dry lands of northern Africa and the island continent of Australia. Meanwhile, cross-border pollution in Europe, and between China and Russia, are matters that demand a regional rather than simply national response. Acid rain traverses provincial and state demarcations and can affect environments, animals and humans many kilometres away. A nuclear accident in Ukraine makes its presence felt in Britain, as well as the immediate vicinity of Chernobyl. Radioactivity stemming from the nuclear meltdown in Japan moves around the globe via ocean and air currents.

The opportunities for certain types of crime are influenced by very specific local and regional factors. For example, the penetration and dominance of the Mafia in the waste-disposal industry in Italy provides a unique but devastating illustration of national difference (compared to countries where organized crime is not involved in this industry) that has an international impact (through dumping of toxic waste in international waters). In central and western Africa, the global bush meat trade is driven by several different factors, with dire consequences for apes, chimpanzees, gorillas and other primates especially, which are threatened with extinction. Local habitats for these animals are also being lost through logging and commercial developments. Not only are adult primates being killed for food and body parts, but orphaned primates are being sold on the exotic pet market, further contributing to the degradation of these species.

Specific places demand specific analysis, yet these are intrinsically linked into considerations that are universal in their relevance and application. For instance, transnational environmental harm is always located somewhere. That is, while risk and harm can be analysed in terms of movements and transference from one place to another, it is nonetheless imperative that threats to the environment be situated in specific regional and national contexts. This is important for several reasons. First, environmental threats originate in particular factories, farms, firms, industries and localities. Second, the political and policy context within which threats to the environment emerge is shaped by the nature of and interplay between local, national, regional and international laws and conventions. What happens at the local and regional level counts – whether we are referring to the Nordic countries, those of south-eastern Europe, Australasia or Latin America.

What happens at the local level is likewise implicated in decisions and processes that transcend the local, given the complex international ties and connections between businesses, governments, workers and activists. For example, Australian conservationists have linked up with their activist counterparts in Japan to influence the relationship between Japanese paper companies and a Tasmanian forestry company engaged in the clear felling of old-growth forest. Protests have effectively been internationalized, although the destruction occurs in a specific place (White 2005b). Business associations and cross-national environmental campaigns are illustrative of how closely connected we all are in an increasingly globalized world.

The notion of transnational crime evokes at least two different conceptual concerns (see Madsen 2009). First, the crime must involve the movement of people, objects or decisions *across borders*. Secondly, the harm must be *recognized internationally* as a crime. There are limitations with each of these considerations. For example, genocide is universally acknowledged as an evil (even if there are disputes in practice as to whether or not genocide is in fact occurring – witness the debates over Sudan and how to interpret the tremendous loss of life in its southern regions due to systematic military interventions by various parties), but it may occur within a particular country's borders. Secondly, transnational harms may happen (such as the disposal and congregation of plastic waste in the ocean, or the migration of toxic substances from producer countries to formerly pristine wilderness areas, thereby affecting humans and animals in the latter even though they have no connection whatsoever with the former), but these may not be considered 'crimes' in international law. In other words, the study of transnational harm or crime always involves contested definitions (restrictive or expansive, depending upon the place of formal legality in the definition) and complexities related to scale (since it may manifest in specific local or regional contexts, as well as across regions).

The study of transnational crime involves different approaches that have various names. These include:

- *comparative* criminology (the nature of the crime problem in countries around the world);
- *transnational* criminology (cross-border forms of crime such as drug trafficking, arms trafficking, human trafficking and money laundering);
- *international* criminology (crime that is specifically recognized widely across nations as crimes against humanity, such as genocide);
- *global* criminology (how globalization and its consequences cause harm, such as structural adjustment policies of the World Bank); and
- *supranational* criminology (an encompassing study of international crimes, which includes terrorism, war crimes, state crime, and violations of human rights) (see Friedrichs 2007).

What recent global study has demonstrated is that methodologically it is essential to have both a sense of history and a sense of place in the study of the phenomenon at hand. It is through global, comparative and historical analyses that not only the differences (and similarities and paradoxes) in environmental crimes, but also differences in state and civil society responses to environmental harm, are best understood.

Consideration of scale and focus are implicit in the framing of research into transnational environmental crime. There are at least three different ways in which transnational research can be approached (White 2009a):

- *Global* – refers to transnational crimes, processes and agencies (universal effects, processes, agencies across the globe).
- *Comparative* – refers to differences between nation-states, including 'failed states' (particular differences between nation-states and regions).
- *Historical* – refers to epochal differences in modes of production and global trends (systemic differences over time, within and between different types of social formation).

The first approach focuses on globalization as a far-reaching process in which crime can be traced in its movements across the world and its presence documented in many different locales (Smandych and Larsen 2008). For example, the idea of globalization incorporates consideration of transnational harms, processes and agencies that span the globe. It implies that there are universal effects (such as climate change) that require united responses worldwide.

The second approach has a comparative focus, with a concern to study particular countries and regions, including failed states, in relation to each other (Gros 2008). The nature of similarities and differences is fundamental to this kind of study. Thus, the differences between nation-states and regions must be acknowledged and explained in their own right. For example, some countries and regions are more liable to be polluted than others.

The third approach is based upon historical appreciation of social change and social differences (Wright Mills 1959; Cornforth 1976). It views trends and issues in terms of major epochs, such as the transition from feudalism to capitalism, or the shift from competitive capitalism to global monopoly capitalism. There are differences in modes of production and global trends (e.g. peasant-based feudal agriculture versus capitalist agribusiness), and it is important to track systemic changes over time, within and between different types of social formation.

The use and need for horizon-scanning as an intellectual exercise and planning tool is related to the idea that many threats and opportunities are presently poorly recognized. Accordingly, a more systematic approach to identification and solution to issues is required rather than reliance upon ad hoc or reactive approaches. For example, Sutherland and Woodroof (2009: 1) point out that 'the need for horizon-scanning of environmental issues is illustrated by the recent failure to foresee both the widespread adoption of the range of biofuels currently in use, and the environmental consequences of biofuels production' (see also Chapter 8). Horizon-scanning can provide insight into risks (potential problems) and harms (actual problems). It provides a mechanism to discern where emerging threats (and positive opportunities) may arise and potential ways to mitigate or adapt to these.

In analysis of horizon issues a variety of concepts might be deployed. Certainly matters of time, space and scale are relevant. For example, risks and harms may be direct or indirect, and their consequences may be felt immediately or in the long-term. Harm may be specific to local areas (e.g. threats to certain species, like coral in the Great Barrier Reef) yet manifest as part of a general global pattern (such as being an effect of wide-scale temperature changes affecting coral everywhere). Harm is central, but this may be non-intentional (in the sense of being a by-product of some other agenda) or premeditated (insofar as the negative outcome, for some, is foreseen). The demise of the polar bear due to the impact of global warming in the Arctic is an example of the former. The displacement of local inhabitants from their land due to carbon sequestration schemes is an example of the latter.

Several other concepts are particularly relevant to horizon-scanning. Three of these look to the future: intergenerational equity, the precautionary principle and transference over time. Three of these address matters of justice, past, present and future: environmental justice, ecological justice and species justice. Collectively these concepts provide a values framework for assessing risks and harms as part of the exercise of looking over the horizon (see also Leiss and Hrudey 2005; White 2008a). Box 2.3 provides a summary of these key ideas.

The challenge for eco-global criminology is to marshal ideas and evidence from many different sources and disciplines in order to identify where harms and risks are emerging as matters of possible social and political importance, and to develop pre-emptive strategies to begin to address potential problems before they create further harms and risks pertaining to humans, specific eco-systems and animals.

In practice, horizon-scanning is premised upon three interrelated tasks. These include attempts to theorize causal forces in regard to any specific issue; to

Box 2.3 The conceptual basis of environmental horizon-scanning

Substantive orientation

- *Risk* – a prediction or expectation that includes the perspectives of those affected about what is important to them and concerns a hazard or danger in which there is uncertainty over occurrence but which may involve adverse consequences as the possible outcome within a certain time period.
- *Harm* – an actual danger or adverse effect, stemming from direct and indirect social processes, that negatively impinges upon the health and well-being and ecological integrity of humans, specific biospheres and non-human animals.
- *Cause* – analysis of causal chains that may involve many interrelated variables but which ultimately are linked to specific practices and human responsibility for environmental harm.

Justice orientation

- *Environmental justice* – in which environmental rights are seen as an extension of human or social rights so as to enhance the quality of human life, now and into the future.
- *Ecological justice* – in which it is acknowledged that human beings are merely one component of complex ecosystems that should be preserved for their own sake via the notion of the rights of the environment.
- *Species justice* – in which harm is constructed in relation to the place of non-human animals within environments and their intrinsic right to not suffer abuse, whether this be one-on-one harm, institutionalized harm or harm arising from human actions that affect climates and environments on a global scale.

Futures orientation

- *Intergenerational equity* – refers to the principle of ensuring that the generations to follow have at least the same or preferably better environments in which to live than those of the present generation.
- *Precautionary principle* – when an activity raises threats of harm to human health, non-human animals or the environment, precautionary

> measures should be taken even if some cause and effect relationships are not fully established scientifically.
> - *Transference over time* – in this context refers to the transfer of harm involving both cumulative impacts and compounding effects.
>
> Source: White 2011a

employ multidisciplinary methods; and to deliberate on potential policy responses. Theory, in this instance, is based upon the notion of anthropogenic causes – that is, the interest is in human responsibility for harm and thus issues pertaining to identification of specific perpetrators and degrees of culpability. Methodologically, the concern is to use a wide variety of methods and insights in an eclectic fashion in order to expose broad patterns of action (and omission) and causal chains of harm. Policy basically refers to matters relating to regulation and enforcement

> **Case vignette 2.1 Horizon-scanning the impacts of climate change**
>
> Horizon-scanning can be deployed to explore environmental issues that lie over the horizon. An example of this is Robert Agnew's work on the impact of climate change.
>
> > My arguments are speculative; but these speculations are based on the extensive research on climate change, are guided by several well-established theories of crime, and draw on a small body of research examining the effect of environmental factors on crime. The central argument I make is that climate change may foster a range of crimes at individual, corporate and state levels. These crimes include individual acts of violence and theft of the type that are illegal in virtually all states; corporate crimes such as environmental pollution and bribery, which are illegal in many states; and acts of state aggression that violate international law (Maier-Katkin *et al.* 2009). I also briefly discuss the effect of climate change on a variety of harmful acts that are not presently defined as crimes
> >
> > (Agnew 2011: 26)
>
> This description of criminology and climate change from a horizon-scanning perspective is intended to expose issues and to alert readers to impending issues, trends and challenges. By its nature, such work will always be contentious, provocative and tentative.

strategies, as well as issues of remediation and compensation. Any analysis based upon horizon-scanning will most likely involve creative lateral thinking and plans of intervention that may occasionally sit uncomfortably with the existing institutional status quo.

Conclusion

This chapter has provided an introduction to eco-global criminology by exploring its varied dimensions as an important perspective for the study of transnational environmental crimes and harms. As a perspective, it focuses on the ecological, the global and the application of three justice-related approaches to environmental crimes and harms. Of crucial importance is the bringing together of certain key concepts – the notion of movement or transference across borders, the idea that harm is related specifically to environmental concerns (including, for example, wildlife, as well as pollution) and the recognition that such crimes occur within specific geographical and social contexts. However, as indicated throughout this chapter, there are nevertheless ambiguities and controversies associated with defining transnational environmental crime. These primarily stem from diverse views of what criteria ought to be drawn upon in determining what is deemed to be a criminal or non-criminal activity.

Discussion topics

- What is the 'eco' in eco-global criminology?
- Provide examples of some of the ways in which 'nature' is being transformed as a result of applications of new technologies (such as genetics research) or new approaches to resource use (such as mass production techniques).
- What are the key dimensions that help to define transnational environmental crime?
- NIMBY refers to 'Not In My Back Yard'. Is it possible to isolate what happens in your back yard from what else is happening in the world today?
- Select an environmental harm (e.g. climate change, coal-seam fracking) and explore the use of horizon-scanning as a tool to analyse its possible consequences.

Further reading

Aas, K. (2007). *Globalization and Crime*. Los Angeles: Sage.
Agnew, R. (2011). 'Dire Forecast: A theoretical model of the impact of climate change on crime', *Theoretical Criminology*, 16(1): 21–42.
Boekhout van Solinge, T. (2010). 'Deforestation Crimes and Conflicts in the Amazon', *Critical Criminology*, 18: 263–77.

White, R. (2011). *Transnational Environmental Crime: Toward an eco-global criminology*. London: Routledge.

White, R., and Heckenberg, D. (2011). 'Environmental Horizon Scanning and Criminological Theory and Practice', *European Journal of Criminal Policy and Research*, 17(2): 87–100.

Chapter 3

Eco-justice and ecocide

Introduction

This chapter will discuss the following topics:

- green criminology and eco-justice;
- environmental, ecological and species justice;
- applying notions of justice;
- ecocide.

An eco-justice perspective refers to the broad orientation of green criminology which is largely directed at exposing different instances of substantive social and environmental injustice. From an eco-justice perspective, environmental harm is best seen in terms of justice, which in turn is based upon notions of human, ecological and animal rights and of broad egalitarian principles. A key issue is the weighing up of different kinds of harm and violation of rights, that may involve stretching the boundaries of conventional criminology to include other kinds of harms than those already deemed to be illegal.

How we understand the relationships between humans, the environment and non-human species is crucial to defining and responding to environmental issues. Embedded within different interpretations of these (inter)relationships are particular notions of harm. These notions, in turn, are reflected in specific conceptions of victimization, including who or what is subjected to which kinds of harm.

This chapter elaborates on the three approaches that singly and collectively contribute to and underpin an eco-justice perspective: environmental justice, ecological justice and species justice. It provides a general introduction to concepts of eco-justice, their application within a criminal-justice context, and their extension into new notions of harm as encapsulated for instance in the concept of 'ecocide'. As will be seen, the idea of justice is intertwined with notions of crime, harm and victimization.

Green criminology and eco-justice

A key distinguishing point of green criminology in comparison with mainstream or conventional criminology is its concern with the *non-human* as well as the human. To approach and appreciate this demands a different kind of analytical framework than is commonly provided within the usual criminological literature.

Our present interest is with three separate but interconnected justice-based approaches to harm pertaining to humans, eco-systems and animals. These approaches are the main components or elements that together constitute a broader eco-justice perspective (for elaboration see White 2013c). Environmental injustice (or victimization) can be considered from the point of view of transgressions against humans, specific bio-spheres or environments, and non-human animals.

A major factor that influences the study of environmental harm relates to the specific interests that count the most when conceptualizing the nature and seriousness of the harm. For example, when criminalization does occur, it often reflects human-centred (or anthropocentric) notions of what is best (e.g. protection of legal fisheries, legal timber coups) in ways that treat 'nature' and 'wildlife' simply and mainly as resources for human exploitation. The intrinsic value of specific ecological areas and particular species tends to be downplayed or ignored.

Nevertheless, recent years have seen greater legislative and judicial attention given to the rights of the environment per se, and to the rights of certain species of non-human animals to live free from human abuse, torture and degradation. This reflects both the efforts of eco-rights activists (e.g. conservationists) and animal-rights activists (e.g. animal-liberation movements) in changing perceptions – and laws – concerning the natural environment and non-human species. Vital to these social processes has been the promulgation of specific conceptualizations of 'justice'.

As we have said, within green criminology there are three broad approaches to justice, each with their own specific conceptions of what is harmful (see White 2008a). These include:

- *Human rights and environmental justice* – environmental rights are seen as an extension of human or social rights so as to enhance the quality of human life, now and into the future.
- *Ecological citizenship and ecological justice* – humans are acknowledged as merely one component of complex ecosystems that should be preserved for their own sake via the notion of the rights of the environment.
- *Animal rights and species justice* – environmental harm is constructed in relation to the place of non-human animals within environments and their intrinsic right to not suffer abuse, whether this be one-on-one harm, institutionalized harm or harm arising from human actions that affect climates and environments on a global scale.

Language shapes how 'harm' and 'value' are constructed in regard to (specific groups of) humans, specific biospheres and specific non-human animals, so a word about terminology is warranted before proceeding. To take one example of the importance of language, we might consider how criminologists and others speak about 'animals'. From a conservation criminology perspective (see for example, Gibbs *et al.* 2010a; Herbig and Joubert 2006) the language used in referring to animals tends to be anthropocentric and instrumental; thus, animals are categorized in terms of 'wildlife' and 'fisheries'. Environmental laws and laws specifically about animals likewise tend to define animals in ways that describe their existence and 'value' through reference to human conceptions and human uses (Sankoff and White 2009). Accordingly, the language used to frame the issues is informed by human-centred considerations.

By contrast, those criminologists who write primarily about animal rights and animal welfare issues describe such anthropocentric descriptions as a form of 'specieism' (see Beirne 2007; Sollund 2008). From their perspective, it is the suffering of non-human animals – whether construed as wild, domestic or commercial – that is of central concern, not whether the suffering stems from illegal criminal acts or not (since much animal suffering is linked to legal activities such as abattoirs and factory farms that rely upon animals as food sources). Accordingly, the language used to frame the issues is informed by animal-centred rather than human-centred considerations.

To put it differently, some green criminologists view nature instrumentally, and harm is viewed through the lens of legality; others view the exploitation of nature, particularly in relation to animals, as intrinsically bad and harmful. How or if this 'moral fissure' can be overcome is of major interest to a number of green criminology commentators (Beirne 2011; White 2013c). From the point of view of eco-justice, the core concern is with the object of harm or victimization. In other words, the emphasis is on identifying issues pertaining to the *victims of harm*, including how to define who (or indeed what) is an environmental 'victim' (Williams 1996). Many green criminologists believe that the concept of harm ought to encapsulate those activities that may be legal and legitimate but which nevertheless negatively impact on eco-systems and non-human animals, as well as humans (Lynch and Stretesky 2003; Beirne and South 2007). The former are precisely the fulcrum upon which rest many of the major differences within the eco-justice perspective.

Environmental justice, ecological justice and species justice

Eco-justice conceptions of harm include consideration of transgressions against environments, non-human species and humans (White 2008a, 2013c). Environmental harm can be distinguished on the basis of *who or what precisely is being harmed or victimized*.

Table 3.1 An eco-justice perspective – three approaches to justice, rights and harms

---

Environmental justice and human rights

FOCUS:	Environmental rights as an extension of human or social rights so as to enhance the quality of human life.
CONCEPTS:	*Intergenerational responsibility*: the present generation is responsible for ensuring environmental equity for future generations.
	Environmental justice: everyone has the right to a healthy environment, and there ought to be environmental equity for present generations.
EMPHASIS:	Environmental harm is constructed in relation to human-centred notions of value and use.

Ecological justice and ecological citizenship

FOCUS:	Human beings are merely one component of complex ecosystems that should be preserved for their own sake via the notion of the rights of the environment.
CONCEPTS:	*Ecological citizenship*: humans are responsible for the preservation and conservation of nature.
	Ecological justice: concerned with the quality of the biosphere and the rights of non-human species.
EMPHASIS:	Environmental harm is constructed in relation to notions of ecological harm and destructive techniques of human intervention.

Species justice and animal rights

FOCUS:	Non-human animals have rights based upon utilitarian notions (maximizing pleasure and minimizing pain), inherent value (right to respectful treatment) and an ethic of responsible caring.
CONCEPTS:	*Anti-speciesism and animal rights*: addressing the discriminatory treatments of animals as Other.
	Animal welfare: dealing with issues of animal abuse and suffering, and the nurturing of respectful relationships.
EMPHASIS:	Environmental harm is constructed in relation to the place of nonhuman animals within environments, and their intrinsic right to not suffer abuse, whether this be one-on-one harm, institutionalized harm or harm arising from human actions that affect climates and environments on a global scale.

Source: modified from White 2008a; see also White 2013c

As indicated in Table 3.1, there are three broad theoretical approaches (within green criminology) that frame how specific writers view the nature of environmental issues, including harm and responses to harm. These approaches present different dimensions of *in*justice which are relevant to an overarching eco-justice perspective. Each approach is concerned with particular conceptions of rights and different types of harmful transgression.

The following synopsis of each justice-based approach provides initial insight into the broad concerns of each (see White 2013c).

Environmental justice

Environmental justice refers to the distribution of environments among peoples in terms of access to, and use of, specific natural resources in defined geographical areas, and the impacts of particular social practices and environmental hazards on specific populations (e.g. ethnic minorities). In other words, the concern is with humans, who are at the centre of analysis. The focus is on human health and well-being and how these are affected by particular types of production and consumption. Within the environmental justice framework, it is humans that matter.

Ecological justice

Ecological justice refers to the relationship of humans generally to the rest of the natural world, and includes concerns relating to the health of the biosphere and, more specifically, plants and animals that also inhabit the biosphere. The main concern is with the quality of the planetary environment (that is frequently seen to possess its own intrinsic value) and the rights of other species (particularly animals) to live free from torture, abuse and destruction of habitat. The focus is on constantly evaluating how humans interact with their environment, in relation to potential harms and risks to specific creatures and specific locales, as well as the biosphere generally. Within the ecological justice framework, it is environments and specific eco-systems that matter.

Species justice

Species justice includes the particular consideration that animal welfare and rights ought to be of relevance to eco-justice. In specific terms, concepts such as speciesism may be invoked. This refers to the practice of discriminating against non-human animals because they are perceived to be inferior to the human species in much the same way that sexism and racism involve prejudice and discrimination against women and people of different colour. Within the species justice framework, it is animals that matter.

These three broadly different but connected approaches to justice together constitute the eco-justice perspective. They overlap in varying ways, but ultimately have distinctive foci around which scholars and activists tend to mobilize their efforts (i.e., stopping toxic waste dumping, saving forests and/or protecting animals). Within the particular conceptual and action frameworks of each approach there are important differences, based upon how specific 'interests' are conceptualized (White 2013c).

Applying notions of justice

Justice within an eco-justice perspective is initially framed in terms of the subject or victim that is liable to be harmed. However, justice in practice is usually

Table 3.2 Dimensions and notions of justice

Distribution
Justice as fairness/equality (need, desert, entitlement)

Recognition
Justice as acknowledgement (subordination, non-recognition, disrespect)

Participation
Justice as engagement (decision-making procedures, protecting interests)

Capacities
Justice as functionings (opportunities to 'do' and to 'be')

Source: Schlosberg 2007

articulated and understood as a balance of numerous interlinked elements. Schlosberg (2007) identifies the key categories or dimensions of justice, including distribution, recognition, participation and capacities. Table 3.2 summarizes these elements.

These dimensions of justice (distribution, recognition, participation, capacities) are summarized below according to the notions of justice (as fairness/equality, acknowledgement, engagement and functioning) associated with them.

Justice as fairness

The notion of justice as fairness is associated with questions of *distribution*. Justice, according to this conception, defines how we distribute various rights, goods and liberties, and how we define and regulate social and economic equality and inequality. What matters are the rules of distributive justice and how these are constructed. The rules may be procedure-based – such as providing equal opportunities for everyone to attain valued goods – or they may be oriented toward consequentialist and substantive conceptions of justice that ensure equal outcomes. Arguments occur over what the principles governing those proposed distributions should be (e.g. need, desert, entitlement). Such principles are deemed to be relevant to both human and non-human, particularly in the context of extending the notion of rights to environments and particular animals.

Justice as acknowledgement

The notion of justice as acknowledgement is associated with questions of *recognition*. According to this conception, justice refers to the equal dignity accorded to all, as well as the politics of difference where everyone is recognized for their particular distinctiveness. It is observed that, 'A lack of recognition in the social and political realms demonstrated by various forms of insults, degradation and devaluation at both the individual and cultural level inflicts damage to oppressed individuals and communities in the political and cultural realms' (Schlosberg 2007: 14). Derogatory language used in relation to animals provides one illustration of subordinated and disrespected identity, as this applies to the non-human (see Beirne 2009). Here it is argued that contemporary practices of cultural domination are such that the rights, interests and needs of eco-systems and animals are rendered invisible in ordinary life, and accordingly fewer legal, social and economic resources are put into acknowledging, supporting and respecting the non-human.

Justice as engagement

The notion of justice as participation is associated with questions of *engagement*. Justice, according to this conception, refers to the need for *participation*, which is also defined as an important component of justice. Participation generally refers to a person's membership and engagement in the greater community, and is supported by the institutionalization of democratic and participatory decision-making procedures. As applied to the non-human world, participation basically involves human advocacy, where the voice of animals or trees or eco-systems is 'heard' via the human third party. Humans thus can speak 'on behalf of' that and those which cannot participate directly for themselves in human affairs that affect them.

Justice as functioning

The notion of justice as *capacities* is associated with questions of *capability and functionings*. Justice according to this conception refers to the ability to achieve valuable functionings within the context of one's essential character and setting. For humans, capabilities are about a person's opportunities to do and to be what they choose in the context of a given society. Well-being is about 'doings' (activities) and 'beings' (states of existence), and enhancing capability means concentrating on the opportunity to be able to have combinations of functionings and on people being free to make use of this opportunity or not (Schlosberg 2007). Translated into an eco-justice context, capability means that each thing should be able to flourish as the thing it is. It is argued, for example, that, 'Every component of the Earth Community has three rights: the right to be, the right to habitat, and the right to fulfil its role in the ever renewing processes of the Earth Community' (Thomas Berry, quoted in Cullinan 2003). What this actually means in practice is difficult to determine, however, since nature by definition is complex, uncertain, interconnected and ever-changing. Capabilities (as possibilities) are therefore changing, open-ended, dynamic, and subject to ongoing deliberation.

In the context of the doing of justice there is a need to pinpoint those principles of justice that will most likely lead to desired outcomes. The notion of maximizing dominion or positive liberty is a useful starting point in this regard (White 2013c).

Secondly, there is the matter of establishing an institutional basis for action. This refers to implementing strategies that embody the justice principles identified above. Here it is suggested that repairing harm and restoration are practical ways in which justice can be done at a concrete level.

Specifically, the practices of justice ought to be informed by a moral statement that encapsulates what it is that we want to achieve by the doing of justice (see White and Graham 2010). Here, the republican theory of justice (Braithwaite and Pettit 1990) is particularly insightful and useful. Basically this theory is premised on the idea that if every act of crime represents damage to liberty and well-being, then the system's task is to promote positive liberty, by rectifying or remedying the damage caused by the crime. The theory incorporates many of the notions of justice cited above, in that it is interested in addressing harm as evident at different levels, examining the institutional consequences of intervention, and supporting restorative practices that foster individual and overall health and well-being.

While the focus is on human liberty and human societies, the basic approach to justice outlined here seems to make sense and have some application to justice as applied to the non-human. For example, when republican theory is translated into practice it usually takes the form of restorative justice. This refers to a justice process in which action is informed by two main considerations: repairing the harm, and ensuring widespread participation in justice decision-making. The point of intervention is to seek to heal and put right the wrongs (Zehr 1990). The concept of harm, as in republican theory, is extended to include not only direct victims (which in the context of this discussion ought to include eco-systems and animals and plants) but affected communities. The obligation to repair the harm is likewise a communal as well as individual obligation. Furthermore, the process of justice ought to maximize the opportunities for exchange of information, participation, dialogue and mutual consent as much as possible, and thereby ought to belong to the community as a whole (not just to vested interests, specific advocates or particular activist voices). Such justice also needs to be mindful of the outcomes, intended and unintended, of responses to harm and victimization – on people, on eco-systems and on animals.

Eco-justice concerns combined with the practical dimensions of justice can be translated into a series of interrelated propositions. These are summarized in Box 3.1.

What needs to constantly be weighed up is not only the type and degree of harm as this pertains to humans, eco-systems and animals. There is also a need to assess the type and degree of harm, in particular places (including global spaces), and how these harms impact humans, eco-systems and animals over time. The four propositions about justice outlined above provide some indication of the principles by which this might be achieved.

The destruction of the environment in ways that affect humans, eco-systems and non-human animals as well as plants can also be conceptualized in legal terms as evidence of a specific sort of crime. Justice in this case is defined not so

Box 3.1 Four propositions about justice

Proposition 1: Justice ought to be an active process

- Emphasis on participation – of victims, of offenders, of advocates, of communities.
- Emphasis on doing something – repairing harm, addressing the wrong.

Proposition 2: Justice is about maximizing liberty

- Emphasis on maximizing functioning – the right of the biotic and the abiotic 'to do' and 'to be'.
- Emphasis on maximizing status, capacities and worth – by acknowledging the value and rights of humans and non-human entities.

Proposition 3: Justice deals with issues holistically

- Emphasis on the historical and geographical context – locating creatures and environments within their unique social and ecological niche.
- Emphasis on the dynamic relationship between 'culture' and 'nature' – the ways in which humans live in and with nature.

Proposition 4: Justice has temporal and spatial dimensions

- Emphasis on the past, present and future – learn from what has gone on, and recognize that what we do now has consequences.
- Emphasis on potentials and what might be – forward looking and possibilities, with new knowledge and skills opening up new pathways and alternative horizons.

Source: drawing upon White 2013c

much by how we respond to harm, but by how we broadly define it to begin with. Ecocide is an example of this.

Ecocide

Ecocide has been defined as, 'the extensive damage, destruction to or loss of ecosystems of a given territory, whether by human agency or by other causes, to such an extent that peaceful enjoyment by the inhabitants of that territory has been severely diminished' (Higgins 2012: 3). Where this occurs as a result of human agency, then it is purported that a crime has occurred.

Ecocide as a concept has been used to refer to 'natural' processes of ecosystem decline and transformation, as well as human-created destruction of ecosystems. The former includes instances where, for example, kangaroos denude a paddock of its grasses and shrubs to the extent that both specific environment and the kangaroo mob are negatively affected. The migration and/or transportation of 'invasive' species, such as the crown of thorns starfish off the east coast of Australia or the introduction of trout into the central highland lakes of Tasmania, can lead to diminishment or death of endemic species of fish and coral – again a form of ecocide.

The term has also been applied to extensive environmental damage during war, as in the case of the use of defoliants (e.g. Agent Orange) in the Vietnam War, and the blowing up of oil wells and subsequent pollution during the first Gulf War in Iraq and Kuwait. These actions involved intent to actually produce environmental destruction in pursuit of military and other goals.

The notion of ecocide has been actively canvassed at an international level for a number of years, from at least the 1960s (Higgins, Short and South 2013). For example, there were major efforts to include it among the crimes associated with the establishment of the International Criminal Court, although the final document refers only to war and damage to the natural environment.

Nonetheless, environmental activists and international lawyers have continued to call for the establishment of either a specific crime of 'ecocide' and/or the incorporation of ecocide into existing criminal laws and international instruments (Higgins 2012).

Recent efforts, for example, have been directed at making 'ecocide' the fifth International Crime Against Peace (Higgins 2010, 2012). The urgency and impetus for this has been heightened by the woefully inadequate responses by governments, individually and collectively, to global warming. Climate change is rapidly and radically altering the very basis of world ecology, yet very little action has been taken by states or corporations to rein in the worst contributors to the problem. Carbon emissions are not decreasing, and 'dirty industries', such as coal and oil, continue to flourish.

In responding to this circumstance, reformers argue that the law itself must be radically altered. Indeed, there is growing momentum behind the idea of embedding the crime of ecocide as a 'crime against humanity' as well as other initiatives directed at entrenching certain environmental rights. In recent times, the concept of ecocide has been embraced by the Green Party of England and Wales and by Oxford local council in the United Kingdom, and is of continuing interest in relevant United Nations and other regional forums.

Potential support for the establishment of ecocide as a crime should be assessed in the light of parallel developments in the legal field. For example, the recent *Manual on Human Rights and the Environment* produced by the Council of Europe (2012) provides a platform for the exercise of both procedural and substantive rights in regard to the environment. Worldwide, public-trust and public-interest law have been used to establish future generations as victims of environmental crime, with the victims including human as well as the environment and non-human biota, for which surrogate victims (such as parents or NGOs) have provided representation (Preston 2011b; Mehta 2009). These developments are adding to the complexity of the law, and challenging many long-standing assumptions about the Nature–Human relationship.

> ### Case vignette 3.1 The Niger delta
>
> In 2008, serious ruptures occurred in the Bodo-Bonny trans-Niger pipeline, and three years later, in August 2011, a London law company and the local community brought a class action lawsuit against Dutch oil giant, Shell (Holtom 2011). If the proposal to have ecocide recognized as the fifth crime against peace was accepted, then this would change the legal landscape with respect to incidents like this. For instance, as Holtom notes 'the "eradicating ecocide" campaign also suggests that ecocide be a crime of strict liability – this means that to convict someone of ecocide all that needs to be proven is that they caused it, regardless of whether they had intended to'. The law, however, must for the moment, be content with 'being used reactively ... however one thing this law case cannot accomplish is to undo the decades of social and environment injustice caused to the Niger Delta's communities and natural environment' (Holtom 2011). Moreover, it could simply mean that companies headquartered in the West can transfer all the blame to their subsidiaries in the developing world. In June 2013 the UK's *Guardian* newspaper reported that:
>
>> Oil company Shell will resume talks next week in London with lawyers representing 15,000 of the poorest people in the world who are claiming millions of pounds compensation for oil spills on the Niger Delta. ... The Shell Petroleum Development Company of Nigeria (SPDC) has admitted liability for two spills from a pipeline in the Niger delta in 2008, but the company disputes the quantity of oil that was spilled and the damage that was done to livelihoods and the environment near the coastal village of Bodo in Rivers State. Oil spill experts working for the communities estimate that nearly 500,000 barrels leaked from the company pipeline over several months, Shell claims it was far less.
>>
>> (Vidal 2013)

An Earth jurisprudence is rapidly gaining traction amongst many of those with an interest in ecological sustainability and environmental justice (Cullinan 2003). These concerns are also finding their way into institutionalized statements and protections. For example, in 2008 the people of Ecuador by a 63 per cent majority voted for a new Constitution, the first in the world to comprehensively recognize ecosystem rights and nature rights (Walters, B. 2011). Article 71 provides:

> Nature or Pachamama, where life is reproduced and exists, has the right to exist, persist, maintain and regenerate its vital cycles, structure, functions and its processes in evolution. Every person, people, community or nationality, will be able to demand the recognition of rights for nature before the public organisms.

Progressive developments such as these are premised on the idea of Earth stewardship. Paradigms of trusteeship, of stewardship, are very different to those based upon private property conceptions of ownership. As Walters, B. (2011: 266) points out, 'Ownership implies that you can use land but don't have responsibility to others to care for it'. The Earth is seen to be 'held in trust', and it is humans who have the responsibility to provide the requisite stewardship. Threats to Nature rights can be conceptualized as, in essence, a crime of ecocide, and thus punishable by law.

This is precisely the point of a series of recent mock trials, each based upon the concept of ecocide. One trial was held on 30 September 2011 in the United Kingdom Supreme Court on the Canadian Athabasca tar sands (among other issues). Another was organized by the Environmental Defenders Office in Melbourne on 18 February 2012 on climate change and the provision of eight new coal mines in Queensland's Galilee Basin. Each of these trials drew upon notions of ecocide, Earth rights and superior responsibility of corporate managers as part of the deliberations. In most cases, the managers were found guilty of extensive destruction, damage to or loss of ecosystem(s) well-being.

Institutional structures within which such crimes could be tried will be needed. For this, it may well be that an International Environment Court (or equivalent) with requisite United Nations support is required. This is especially so if environmental matters such as those pertaining to the international spaces of the oceans (e.g. pollution, concentrations of plastic, illegal fishing, transference of toxic materials) and climate change (e.g. carbon emissions, victim compensation) are to be dealt with adequately (see also Chapter 14).

The notion of ecocide invites comparison with other crimes that, at least superficially, bear similarity. For instance, we can observe that:

- Ecocide is NOT the same as **homicide** – even though foreknowledge of consequences combined with anthropocentric causation imply preventable death.
- Ecocide is NOT the same as **suicide** – even though the agents of harm are themselves included as victims of harm.
- Ecocide is NOT the same as **genocide** – even though there are clear similarities in terms of disregard by perpetrators of the magnitude of the harm and disrespect of specific collectivities/victims.

Ecocide describes an attempt to criminalize human activities that destroy and diminish the well-being and health of ecosystems and species within these, including humans. Climate change and the gross exploitation of natural resources are leading to our general demise – hence increasing the need for just such a crime. From an eco-justice perspective, ecocide involves transgressions that violate the principles and central constituent elements of environmental justice, ecological justice and species justice.

The concept of ecocide also implies a non-anthropocentric understanding of nature and environmental crime. For example, conventional criminological accounts of environmental crime tend to see value in terms of natural resources, with measurement calculated in terms of industries and the value of illegal income generated by various environmental black markets related to wildlife smuggling, illegal fishing, illegal logging and illegal garbage/hazardous waste trafficking (see Liddick 2011). While occasionally reference is made to intrinsic values, it is human benefit that is a key driver in environmental law enforcement and regulation.

> In addition to the inherent value of the natural world and its denizens, concern for the severe environmental damage caused by these illegal industries implicates human health and prosperity across a number of dimensions. Overharvesting, the decimation of species, improper disposal of hazardous wastes, and loss in biodiversity will negatively impact humans not only by making the planet less habitable, but also by eliminating or reducing natural resources that, when used prudently, advance the human condition – the development of medicines being one prominent example.
> (Liddick 2011: 5)

Ecological well-being is thus construed primarily in terms of what nature can do for us rather than what we (humans) can do for nature.

In the light of this it is interesting to note that some of the key indicators used by the United Nations (UNEP 2011) to evaluate the 'state of the world' include:

- consumption of ozone-depleting substances;
- carbon dioxide emissions;
- carbon dioxide emission per capita;
- concentration of particulate matter;
- mountain glacier mass balance;
- renewable energy supply index;
- annual marine fish catch;
- global tuna catches;
- proportion of land area covered by forest;
- ratio of round-wood production and growing stock in forests;
- forest area FSC-certified;

- threatened species index;
- ratio of area protected to maintain biological diversity to surface area;
- municipal waste collection;
- proportion of water withdrawn for human use from renewable resources;
- levels of dissolved oxygen in surface waters;
- proportion of population with sustainable access to improved water source and with access to improved sanitation;
- number of parties to multilateral environmental agreements;
- number of certifications of the ISO 14001 standard.

It is claimed that 'this type of 'global environmental snapshot' can serve to draw attention to the most pressing issues and monitor major trends in areas such as climate change, freshwater quality, use of natural resources, biodiversity loss and environmental governance' (UNEP 2011: 61). From the point of view of ecocide, such indicators are also useful in assigning both costs and responsibilities that are important to consider in their own right.

Conclusion

The complexities of eco-justice do not lie only in its constituent elements, but in how these might be translated into moral choices and institutional practices. The justice framework of green criminology incorporates diverse understandings of what is 'good' and 'bad' and for whom or what. This inevitably leads to tensions and conflicts within green criminology as to what ought to be prioritized, protected and saved when it comes to difficult decisions surrounding environmental harm.

By the second half of the twentieth century the threat of ecocide began to assume global dimensions and could no longer be ignored (Teclaf 1994: 936). An effective international regime is an essential prerequisite for a world free of the fear of ecocide, but, if and when it is installed, it may give no more than a breathing space unless it is built upon a reconciliation of the twin needs for economic development and environmental preservation (Teclaf 1994: 956).

Discussion topics

- What does 'justice for all' mean in relation to environmental harm?
- Should species justice include plants as well as animals? Why or why not?
- Justice is always fundamentally about human justice. Discuss.
- What is Earth jurisprudence?
- The components of eco-justice are sometimes in conflict with each other. The rights and needs of humans, of specific eco-systems and of animals frequently appear to be in opposition to each other (for example, culling badgers in England for the sake of cattle farmers). Provide examples of this in your own locality or country.

Further reading

Agnew, R. (2013). 'The Ordinary Acts that Contribute to Ecocide: A criminological analysis', in N. South and A. Brisman (eds), *The Routledge International Handbook of Green Criminology*. London: Routledge.

Higgins, P. (2012). *Earth is Our Business: Changing the rules of the game*. London: Shepheard-Walwyn Publishers.

South, N. (2010). 'The Ecocidal Tendencies of Late Modernity: Transnational crime, social exclusions, victims and rights', in R. White (ed.), *Global Environmental Harm: Criminological perspectives*. Cullompton: Willan Publishing, pp. 228–47.

Teclaf, L.A. (1994). 'Beyond Restoration: The case of ecocide', *Natural Resources Journal*, Fall 1994: 933–56.

White, R. (2013). *Environmental Harm: An eco-justice perspective*. Bristol: Policy Press.

Chapter 4

Dimensions of environmental crime

Introduction

This chapter will discuss the following topics:

- the social construction of environmental harm;
- eco-philosophy and environmental issues;
- categorizing environmental harm;
- transference of harm across space and time; and
- disasters and crime.

The purpose of this chapter is to provide an outline of possible ways in which environmental crime can be understood and analysed. Green criminology generally adopts a stance toward the definitions and complexities of environmental harm that is critical and interpretive. Not all things are as they seem, and part of the mandate of green criminology is to unpack the nature and dynamics of environmental crime by exploring the spatial and temporal dimensions of such crime. Above all, the concern is with who or what has been harmed, and how and why this takes place.

Social construction of environmental harm

The theme of this section is how environmental crime is socially constructed. Specifically, the concern is to identify those elements that together result in activity being deemed harmful, and thereby worthy of investigation and prosecution.

Determining what is environmentally harmful is shaped by what gets publicly acknowledged to be an issue or problem warranting social attention. Environmental issues do not simply exist 'out there' as if they have an existence separate from human society. Rather, specific environmental problems and harms are always constructed as such through complex social processes of selection and affirmation. Objective harms do exist, but which harms come to public attention depends upon the successful mobilization of information, opinion and consciousness. It takes moral entrepreneurs to make people sit up and take notice.

How environmental problems are socially constructed always incorporates subjective and objective elements. To put it differently, while there are tensions between a 'realist' position and a 'hard constructionist' position, most commentators now agree that social problems are constructed through a combination of material and cultural factors (Hannigan 2006; Macnaghten and Urry 1998; Higgins and Natalier 2004).

- *Realism* refers to an analytical stance that sees 'nature' as objectively existing in its own right. Environmental problems are seen to originate in what is actually happening in the natural world.
- *Constructionism* refers to an analytical stance that sees 'nature' as a social construct, as something that is always constructed through the lens of a human culture that sifts and selects, names and categorizes, the natural world. Environmental problems are seen to be bounded by what humans determine to be important or significant.

In part these positions represent differences in analytical emphasis rather than absolutes. Beck (1992), for example, has a tendency to see environmental problems as objectively given phenomena. Others argue that the relationship between 'nature' and 'culture' is such that there is no reality whatsoever outside the symbolic world-building activities of humans (see Lockie 2004). The middle ground simply says that, yes, there is an objective 'nature', and, yes, humans interpret this nature through cultural filters (Lockie 2004; Hannigan 2006). The study of environmental problems is the study of real, existing problems; but these *become* social problems as the products of a 'dynamic social process of definition, negotiation and legitimation' (Hannigan 2006: 31). The problems may be 'real', but the definition, magnitude, impact, risk and origins of phenomena such as pollution, climate change and toxic waste are open to interpretation and dispute.

There are some very dramatic problems facing the planet when it comes to environmental issues. The severity of any particular issue, however, does not necessarily translate into the prominence given to that particular issue. The key question, therefore, is not so much severity but why certain issues become 'known' more than others. State intervention and social movement action around specific issues, similarly, rest upon the fact that these specific issues have become important enough to generate widespread, concrete social responses. What becomes prominent as a social issue reflects a social process in which certain claims – about nature, about environmental harm, about social impacts – are brought into the public domain and gain ascendancy. In this regard Hannigan (2006: 69) observes that, 'In researching the origins of environmental claims, it is important for the researcher to ask where a claim comes from, who owns or manages it, what economic and political interests claims-makers represent, and what type of resources they bring to the claims-making process'. Hannigan (1995, 2006) provides a useful analytical model that describes just this process.

The task of *assembling* refers to the process of basically determining the claim and supporting it with requisite information and evidence. It involves discovering and naming the problem and constructing 'proof' through appeal to scientific evidence. The more systematic and streamlined the knowledge claims, the more likely they can overcome pitfalls associated with lack of clarity, ambiguity and conflicting scientific evidence. A typical proposition might be, for example, that 'super-sized fish trawlers are bad for the environment'. Protagonists on both sides of this proposition would then engage in assembling their case, using whatever scientific and other evidence they could marshal in support of their position.

The task of *presenting* refers to the process of commanding attention and legitimating the claim. The central forum for this is the mass media, and the message is usually portrayed as a moral claim. A typical proposition might be, for example, that super fishing trawlers are bad, and we should stop their use now (or conversely, they are 'good' and should be encouraged). This task requires a communicator, someone who can gain public attention. This attention can be gained by using dramatic verbal and visual imagery, such as pictures of huge boats with huge nets or local recreational fishers with nothing in their fish pails. The key is visibility and keeping things in the public sphere.

The task of *contesting* means being able to invoke action and mobilizing support for the claims being made. This takes the issue into the political realm, and brings with it consideration of legal matters such as burden of proof and potential legislative change.

A typical proposition might be, for example: super trawlers are vital to the future economy of this region and will feed the people of Africa. Getting scientists on board, networking with like-minded people and organizations, and initiating public rallies (for example, of fishers, of consumers, of commercial operators) is all part of this process. It can be undermined by co-optation (for instance, allowing super trawlers to operate, but only under certain restrictive rules), issue fatigue (people do not want to hear about it anymore) or countervailing claims (fish farms are the sensible answer to marine ecological protection and sustainability).

The success or otherwise of claims-making in regard to environmental problems involves several interlocked factors. These are presented in Box 4.1, which summarizes what are in practice quite complicated and fluid social processes.

The social construction of environmental problems is complicated by a number of variables including the ambiguities of definition, redefining or relabelling of the harm, and routinization of the issues. Definitional ambiguity refers to the idea that what is environmental harm to one person may not be seen as environmental harm at all by another. For example, some people would say that resource depletion itself is a bad thing; others would argue that the issue is really about how to manage it, not that the activity is in and of itself bad.

Another factor that influences how environmental problems are socially constructed relates to changes in the type and extent of media coverage, and in popular participation, over time. For instance, social research has pointed to the phenomenon of the routinization of environmental concerns (Pakulski, Tranter and

Box 4.1 Necessary factors for the successful construction of an environmental problem

- Scientific authority for and validation of claims.
- Existence of 'popularizers' who can bridge environmentalism and science.
- Media attention in which the problem is 'framed' as novel and important.
- Dramatization of the problem in symbolic and visual terms.
- Economic incentives for taking positive action.
- Recruitment of an institutional sponsor who can ensure both legitimacy and continuity.

Source: Hannigan 2006: 78

Crook 1998). It is argued that a decline in membership and participation in environmental groups over a ten-year period was due in large part to the increasing familiarity of the public with environmental issues (because of persistent media coverage).

A change in the level of public concern about environmental issues was also attributed to a greater reliance upon experts rather than environmental activists to define and shape conceptions of environmental problems. The notion of 'having heard it all before' is also matched by more issues being identified, greater diffusion of concerns, and the clustering of issues into distinct categories (such as urban pollution or forest conservation). For claims-makers, their very success in getting the environment into the public agenda may well undermine later attempts to resuscitate interest in the issues that they specifically wish to mobilize sentiment around.

For scientists, the social processes associated with legitimating or delegitimating a problem can put them into an invidious occupational and personal situation. Environmental problems generally are bound to put more demands on science to come up with the diagnostic and remediation answers. Simultaneously, this opens science up to public scrutiny and criticism. Great care has to be taken in putting findings into context, and to communicating clearly the strengths and limitations of specific investigations. There is more than this at stake however. The perceived centrality of science and the scientist in determining environmental harm has been linked to the active suppression of environmental scientists through threats to employment conditions and prospects, and through censorship or blocking of publications and presentations (Kuehn 2004). Generally it is those in positions of power and authority who are likely to challenge the reputation, findings and skill of scientists who produce work not to their liking. Protection against suppression is likely to continue to be an issue of pressing concern well into the future.

The media obviously play a major role in constructing certain environmental issues as issues of public concern. It is important, therefore, to examine some of the ways in which media reporting of environmental issues takes place. Space precludes extensive and detailed assessment of the media, but even a cursory examination reveals significant trends and features that shape public views, attitudes and perceptions (see for example, Beder 2002; Cottle and Lester 2012; Pearse 2012; Brisman 2012b; Fitzgerald and Baralt 2010).

The gaining of a collective definition of social problems via the media involves issue selection. This is partly determined by the nature of the medium itself. It is also related to notions of what is newsworthy. Disasters, for example, are eminently newsworthy. They command attention and offer much in the way of televisuality. They tend not to be politically threatening. More complex and diffuse issues, such as global warming, are harder to present in simplistic form and in interesting formats. The content of the media coverage tends to be event-centred, to focus on milestones, catastrophes and court actions, rather than to be exploratory and explanatory of trends. The activist who risks life and limb against the Japanese whaler makes a good and sensational story. After all, the media are big business and the bottom line is sales and profit. For environmental claims-makers, this puts pressure to be dramatic rather than prosaic in their approach to conveying information about issues.

Analysis of the processes whereby environmental issues become translated into issues of public concern once again reaffirms the contingent nature of harm. Environmental harm is objective or material, in that certain trends and events can be discerned, and environmental and social impacts documented. But it is also subjective or cultural, in that the types of social phenomenon that are selected and categorized as environmentally harmful is a social process involving diverse actors. Study of the interplay between 'nature' and 'culture', especially around criminological topical concerns, should reveal further insight into the nature of environmental harm generally.

Specific matters that could also be looked at in greater depth include things such as the displacement of issues. For example, how do media and claims-makers construct environmental issues around different geographical orientations? Local and regional environmental issues may be more volatile politically than those pitched at the level of the global. Acknowledgement of global problems such as climate change is, in one sense, easier than dealing with more localized issues, since the scope of the problem also 'excuses' action on the part of authorities. Similarly, dealing with illegal logging or illegal fishing may appear to be more straightforward than trying to grapple with the complexities of biogenetics. Both geography and complexity can be used to displace attention from some issues in favour of others.

Environmental problems are socially constructed via public campaigns that legitimate claims and build support for reform and change. Rationality is crucial to this process, insofar as science is enlisted to provide evidence for this or that harm. However, it is often the emotions that go with environmental issues that can win the day for specific campaigns. Thus, affective elements (for example, images of a polar bear scrambling to stay afloat on a rapidly shrinking iceberg) are essential components in how issues are socially constructed.

Eco-philosophy and environmental issues

The development of green criminology as a field of sustained research and scholarship will by its very nature incorporate many different perspectives and strategic emphases. After all, it deals with concerns across a wide range of environments (e.g. land, air, water) and issues (e.g. fishing, pollution, toxic waste). It involves conceptual analysis as well as practical intervention on many fronts, and includes multi-disciplinary strategic assessment (e.g. economic, legal, social and ecological evaluations). It involves the undertaking of organizational analysis, as well as investigation of 'best practice' methods of monitoring, assessment, enforcement and education regarding environmental protection and regulation. Analysis needs to be conscious of local, regional, national and global domains and how activities in each of these overlap. It likewise requires cognizance of the direct and indirect, and immediate and long-term, impacts and consequences of environmentally sensitive social practices.

There are, then, significant issues surrounding scale, activities and legalities as these pertain to environmental harm. To define what constitutes environmental harm implies a particular philosophical stance on the relationship between human beings and nature. What is 'wrong' or 'right' environmental practice very much depends upon the criteria used to conceptualize the values and interests represented in this relationship, as reflected for instance in anthropocentric, biocentric and ecocentric perspectives.

Eco-philosophy has a major impact on how criminologists define crime and the varying ways in which they understand the victimization of humans, specific environments and non-human animals. Although the philosophies employed to explicate the nature of the relation between the 'social' and the 'natural' worlds are numerous (see for example, Lane 1998; Plumwood 2005; Halsey 2004), a useful analytical distinction can be made between anthropocentric (human-centred), biocentric (species-centred) and ecocentric (socio-ecological centred) perspectives (see Halsey and White 1998). Eco-philosophy, as manifested in regulatory practice, also leads to very different outcomes. Hence, the importance of acknowledging that how one views the relationship between humans and nature has material consequences in the real world of environmental politics.

The anthropocentric perspective emphasizes the biological, mental and moral superiority of *humans* over other living and non-living entities. Biocentrism views human beings as simply 'another species' to be attributed the *same* moral worth as such organisms as, for example, whales, wolves and birds. Ecocentrism refuses to place humanity either above or below the rest of nature. However, the unique capacity for human beings to develop and deploy methods of production which have global consequences, means that humans also have an explicit responsibility to ensure that such production methods do not exceed the ecospheric limits of the planet (White 2007). Moreover, this responsibility is a responsibility that extends to human *and* non-human life.

Each of these perspectives (anthropocentric, biocentric and ecocentric) conceives of the relationship between human beings and the environment in a different way, which in turn has major implications when it comes to defining and responding to instances of environmental harm. Consider, for example, how each philosophy might approach the practice of clear felling old-growth forest (see Halsey and White 1998).

Anthropocentric

An anthropocentric perspective views old-growth forests instrumentally, as a means to satisfy the demands of human beings. Economically, the philosophy requires that forests be exploited for their commercial potential and that the production methods used be those which incur the least cost to producers – such as clear felling. The aim of legislation is to facilitate the extraction and processing of particular resources (e.g. laws relating to the conditions whereby companies are guaranteed long-term access to particular geographical sites for the purposes of commercial activity such as mining, forestry or farming). Legislation is also directed at conserving particular natural resources through prohibiting over-use or over-extraction of particular resources (e.g. imposition of quotas on logging or fishing), or dealing with conflicts between certain industries (e.g. farming and mining), or between certain industries and specific population groups (e.g. mining companies and indigenous people).

Biocentric

A biocentric perspective views old-growth forests (and the organisms which dwell within them) as having intrinsic worth, whereby such forests have a significance independent of any value placed on them by human beings. Biocentrists consider old-growth forests to be significant because they are suitably diverse in structure and age as to provide the only habitat for certain forest-dependent species. In terms of conservation, biocentrism demands that there be no human impact on old-growth forest, since such ecosystems are considered too fragile to tamper with. Regulatory legislation should be directed first and foremost to preserving the natural environment, particularly those sites identified as being 'wilderness', in order to protect biodiversity and species integrity.

Ecocentric

An ecocentric perspective views old-growth forests as crucial to the long-term survival of humans and non-humans. Ecocentrism attempts to strike a balance between the need to utilize resources for human survival, and the need to develop rules which facilitate the benign use of the ecosphere. From an ecocentric position, ensuring the preservation of biocentric values (such as providing for the widest possible spectrum of species within a forested area), becomes integral to maintaining long-term human needs (such as the continued existence of clean air, unpolluted rivers and fertile soils). Ecocentrism advocates methods of production (such as selective logging techniques) which privilege the long-term requirements of ecosystem well-being over short-term economic demands. Legislation is ideally framed by the limits of ecology (of which humans are an integral part), instead of instrumental goals relating to economic growth and wealth accumulation.

We have seen that eco-philosophy, as manifested in regulatory practice, leads to very different outcomes. Hence, the importance of acknowledging that how one views the relationship between humans and nature has material consequences in the real world of environmental politics.

Categorizing environmental harm

The range of substantive topic areas that green criminology is presently investigating is growing. So, too, the complexities involved in studying environmental harm are likewise being acknowledged. For example, environmental harms can be analytically studied in regard to four types of perspective: focal considerations, geographical considerations, locational considerations and temporal considerations. Table 4.1 provides a summary of these.

Exploration of themes and issues within each of these areas can be used to explore the diversity of perspectives, approaches and concepts that are utilized in contemporary environmental criminology (see White 2005a). Each of these 'considerations' is explained in more detail below.

Table 4.1 Key considerations of environmental harm

Focal considerations

Identify issues pertaining to victims of harm:
| Environmental justice (humans) | Ecological justice (eco-systems) | Species justice (non-human animals) |

Geographical considerations

Identify issues pertaining to each geographical level:
| International | National | Regional/State | Local |

Locational considerations

Identify issues pertaining to specific kinds of sites:
| 'Built' environment (e.g. urban, rural, suburban) | 'Natural' environment (e.g. ocean, wilderness, desert) |

Temporal considerations

Identify issues pertaining to changes over time:
| Environmental effects (short-term/long-term) | Environmental impact (manifest/latent) | Social impact (immediate/lasting) |

Source: drawing on White 2005a, 2008a

Focal considerations

Focal considerations refer to concerns that centre on the key actors or players at the centre of investigation into environmental harm. In other words, the emphasis is on identifying issues pertaining to the victims of harm, including how to define who, or indeed what, is an environmental 'victim' (Williams 1996, 2009; Hall 2011, 2013a and b; Cardwell French and Hall 2011). Most green criminologists consider that the concept of 'harm' ought to encapsulate those activities that may be legal and 'legitimate' but which nevertheless negatively impact on people, environments and non-human animals (Lynch and Stretesky 2003; Beirne and South 2007). The emphasis placed upon either the human and/or the non-human, however, influences what to study and how to interpret the nature of environmental harm (see Chapter 3).

Geographical considerations

Varying types of environmental harm pertain to different geographical levels (see Chapter 2; see also Elliott 2007). Some issues are of a planetary scale (e.g. global warming), others regional (e.g. oceans and fisheries), some are national in geographical location (e.g. droughts in particular African countries), while others are local (e.g. specific oil spills). Similarly, laws tend to be formulated in particular geographically defined jurisdictions. The priority issues at any point in time will depend in part upon local contexts, and local environmental and criminogenic factors (e.g. rare species living in particular kinds of habitat). At the country level, different kinds of crimes and harms are linked to specific national contexts and particular geographical regions. For example, threats to biodiversity have been associated with illegal logging and deforestation in the Atlantic Forest of Brazil; illegal wildlife hunting and trade in Chiapas, Mexico; the commercial-scale illegal logging and shipment of illegal logs in Papua Province, Indonesia; and illegal fishing with dynamite and cyanide in Palawan, the Philippines (Akella and Cannon 2004).

Locational considerations

A distinction can be made between geographical area and 'place'. The latter refers to specific kinds of sites as described in the language of 'natural' and 'built' environment. The 'built' environment basically refers to significant sites of human habitation and residency. It includes urban and rural areas, and areas of cross-over between the two consisting of major regional concentrations of people, commuter suburbs and zones, and so on. The 'natural' environment consists of wilderness, oceans, rivers and deserts. These are sites in which human beings may be present, or through which they may traverse, but which are often seen as distinctive and 'separate' from human settlement per se (however, this needs to be qualified by acknowledging different ways in which humans interact with their environments, reflecting different cultural and material relationships to the land – see Langton 1998). Perceptions and consciousness of harm are in part linked to proximity of human habitation to the sources of harm themselves. A toxic spill in the middle of a major city, or contamination of its main harbour, is much more likely to capture public attention, and prompt government action, than something that happens in a remote wilderness area or on the high seas.

Temporal considerations

Another key issue for consideration relates to issues pertaining to changes over time. To some extent, such considerations are ingrained in contemporary environmental impact assessment in the guise of the 'precautionary principle' (Harvey 1998; Deville and Harding 1997). That is, what we do with and in the environment has consequences, some of which we cannot foresee. The short-term effects of environmental degradation include such things as the release of chlorofluorocarbons into the atmosphere, the long-term effect being the accumulation of greenhouse gases and ultimately climate warming. Environmental impacts begin with global warming as a manifest consequence of planetary change, and results in the latent consequences of changes in sea levels and changes in regional temperatures and precipitation (among other things). The social impact of environmental change is both immediate, as in the case of respiratory problems or increased probability of disease outbreak, and long-term (e.g. lower quality of life, alteration of physiological functioning).

In terms of public perceptions and public participation, environmental issues can also be categorized according to three different types of harm (Crook and Pakulski 1995; Tranter 2004; see also Curson and Clark 2004). As pointed out in Chapter 1, *brown* issues tend to be defined in terms of urban life and pollution (e.g. air quality); *green* issues mainly relate to wilderness areas and conservation matters (e.g. logging practices); and *white* issues refer to science laboratories and the impact of new technologies (e.g. genetically modified organisms). These are set out in Box 4.2.

The significance of conceptualizing environmental issues in this way is that it demonstrates the link between environmental action (usually involving distinct types of community and environmental groups), and particular sites (such as urban centres, wilderness areas or sea coast regions). Some issues tend to resonate more with members of the public than others; other issues generally only emerge if an accident or disaster brings them to the fore.

As discussed at the beginning of this chapter, the mobilization of opinion is crucial to determination of what is or is not considered a 'crime' (or 'harm') and how the state will in the end respond to the phenomenon in question. The complex relationship between human and non-human 'rights' is thus played out in practice through the importance of 'place' in the lives of diverse communities. This inevitably leads to conflicts over purposes, as each place or site is subject to competing demands – jobs (via logging), recreation (via tourism), sustenance (via settlement), aesthetics (via photography), and so on. Disputes over value and use are settled using the full range of political, ideological, legal, coercive and persuasive means available to stake-holder parties.

Box 4.2 Colouring environmental issues

'Brown' issues

- air pollution;
- pollution of urban stormwater;
- pollution of beaches;
- pesticides;
- oil spills;
- pollution of water catchments;
- disposal of toxic/hazardous waste.

'Green' issues

- acid rain;
- habitat destruction;
- loss of wildlife;
- logging of forests;
- depletion of ozone layer;
- toxic algae;
- invasive species via human transport;
- water pollution.

'White' issues

- genetically modified organisms;
- food irradiation;
- in vitro processes;
- cloning of human tissue;
- genetic discrimination;
- environmentally-related communicable diseases;
- pathological indoor environments;
- animal testing and experimentation;
- nano-technologies.

Source: drawing from White 2005a

Transference of harm across space and time

To fully appreciate the nature of environmental harm it is essential to consider the physical location and scale of the harm within particular geographical contexts. The production of global environmental harm is partly determined through complex processes of transference (Heckenberg 2010). Harm can move from one place to another. A toxic incident in Hungary provided a tragic illustration of this when a thick red torrent of sludge burst from a reservoir at an aluminium plant 100 kilometres south of Budapest in early October 2010. At least nine people died as a result of the sludge surge, some went missing, and over 100 people were physically injured as the toxic substance flowed into nearby villages and towns, subsequently threatening the Danube and the countries that border it.

The transformation of environments and the interplay between water, air and land, provides interesting challenges for interpretation and analysis of environmental risk. For example, it is essential to think of risk in dynamic rather than fixed terms. Environmental harm may originate in a specific location, but, due to natural processes of water and air movement and flow, it can spread to other parts of a city, region, country or continent. A localized problem thus contains the seeds of a global dilemma. Environmental harm such as dioxins in water is both temporal and spatial in nature. That is, the harm itself actually moves across time and space, covering wide areas and with long-lasting effects. Moreover, toxins accumulate over time. In other words, there is a cumulative impact on waterways and aquatic life, and small amounts of poison may eventually lead to great concentrations of toxicity in fish and other living creatures of the water, with major social consequences for fishers and human consumers of fish.

It is likewise important to appreciate the interrelationship between built and natural environments. On the one hand, it has long been recognized that the lungs of the planet are its forests, and therefore wilderness areas need to be protected not only for intrinsic but instrumental reasons. What happens to the global forests affects how humans, among other creatures, live in the built environments of the city. On the other hand, even where 'natural' areas are subject to conservation orders and state protection, as in the case of national parks, problems may flow from the cities to these areas. For example, some national parks in the United States are more polluted than cities; they have ozone levels that are higher than some major metropolitan areas. The source of the problem tends to be located elsewhere, taking the form of power-plant emissions, among other causes (Cooper 2002).

The transference of risk also manifests in other ways. For example, we can refer to the monetarization of risk – structural inequalities exploited by risk-producers (e.g. pressures placed on communities to accept toxic landfills on their land in return for financial compensation). At issue here is what to do about LULUs (Locally Unwanted Land Uses), and how the poor and disadvantaged are especially vulnerable to waste transfers relating to these. The traffic in risk also occurs at the global level where developing countries play the same role as poorer communities within developed nations (e.g. 'business-friendly' countries that accept hazardous industries and toxic wastes) (see Pellow 2007).

Also at issue is how to respond to NIMBY (not in my backyard) opposition within developed countries (Julian 2004). This is important because the direct result of the NIMBY effect is to transfer the problem somewhere else. Globalization means that we are connected in many different ways. It also means that producers and consumers are linked up through complex commodity chains.

In many cases, making one's own home safe contributes to making someone else's a hazard (see Adeola 2000). Harm is a consequence of intended actions as well as general negligence. In either case, there may be little consideration for the actual people who are victimized by acts or omissions, nor any sense of a duty of care. Who is exploited is partly a function of what is to be exploited, and where it is located.

> Multinational mining, oil and logging corporations are now using advanced exploration technology, including remote sensing and satellite photography, to identify resources in the most isolated and previously inaccessible parts of the world's tropical rain forests, mountains, deserts and frozen tundras. What the satellites don't reveal is the fact that native peoples occupy much of the land containing these resources.
>
> (Gedicks 2005: 168)

In a shrinking world, the search for new development green fields and for additional natural resources is intensifying and brings into play new technologies that allow ever greater extraction and processing of the Earth, as well as exploitation and victimization of its people (Klare 2012; Le Billon 2012; Tsing 2005).

Who is affected by activities carried out by powerful industries is also partly a matter of where and when. For example, the Arctic region is inhabited by some 4 million people including more than 30 indigenous peoples. Eight states – Canada, Denmark/Greenland, Finland, Iceland, Norway, the Russian Federation, Sweden and the United States – have territories in the Arctic region. While ostensibly a pristine environment where local peoples rely upon traditional food sources, for decades numerous pollutants have been impacting the Arctic and the people and animals that live there (UNEP 2007a; European Environment Agency 2010). This pollution originated elsewhere, especially in industrial heartlands such as the US, but the effect of transference has been devastating. In some parts of the Arctic, for example, breast-feeding mothers have been advised to supplement breast milk with powdered milk in order to reduce exposure to noxious chemicals.

The 'natural' and the 'social' are conjoined in very specific ways in particular geographical contexts. The study of environmental justice can be enhanced by appreciation of different types of spaces. These are summarized in Box 4.3, which outlines features pertaining to geographical, political-economic and globalizing spaces. How and why particular groups suffer from environmental victimization is framed by matters of location.

Geographical spaces are defined here by reference to key features of the natural environment. These determine the kinds of environmental harms that possibly and usually take place. For example, the nature of local air currents will bring in and prevent the flow of acid rain into a particular valley. Political economic spaces refer to features of the social environment, within which a range of stake-holders go about their business and live their lives. This includes such factors as transportation, technological devices and regulatory apparatus in a particular locale.

Globalizing spaces refers to the vertical integration of many different relationships and processes across the local-global continuum. People and places are interconnected in different ways, by social and business networks and through various human interactions. Spaces are unique and specific, but simultaneously conjoined and universal.

Specific incidents, trends and issues can be analysed in terms of local conditions and international influences. We might consider, for example, issues

---

Box 4.3 Features of different types of spaces

Geographical spaces: features of the 'natural environment'

- local and regional ecologies (e.g. biotic and abiotic characteristics);
- type of species (e.g. specific plant and animal species);
- topography and land form (e.g. mountains, valleys);
- flows and connections within and between areas (e.g. ocean currents, air currents, rivers and streams);
- climatic conditions (e.g. monsoonal rains, hours of sunlight).

Political economic spaces: features of the 'social and cultural environment'

- local and regional industries (e.g. agriculture, fishing, mining, tourism);
- role of local and transnational companies (e.g. business interests);
- role of local and national state in relation to regulation and governance (e.g. neoliberal policy, fiscal constraints);
- instrumental and intrinsic valuing of land, air, water, energy (e.g. commodification and profit, communal access and use);
- mechanisms of transference (e.g. technology, free-trade zones, shipping).

Globalizing spaces: key stake-holders dealing with localized issues

- integration of local, regional, national, international, transnational levels;
- transnational drivers (e.g. systemic imperatives of global capitalism);
- transnational actors (e.g. corporations, World Trade Organization);
- transnational activists (e.g. NGOs, governments in alliance);
- global networks (e.g. social networking, environmental law-enforcement agencies).

Source: White 2013c

pertaining to the ownership and control over heavily polluting factories in Mexico, the transfer of toxic waste to the Ivory Coast due to lax regulation and state corruption, the impact of forest sequestration schemes on local communities in Africa, the involvement of eco-Mafia in waste and pollution control in Naples, and the BP oil spill off the coasts of Louisiana and Florida in the Gulf of Mexico. Each case deserves close attention to specific factors arising from the particular 'spaces' in which they have emerged.

Case vignette 4.1 BP Horizon oil spill

In the Gulf of Mexico, the evidence of a massive oil spill has sunk beneath the surface of the ocean and disappeared off the pages of the global media. But it has left behind a trail of human and environmental devastation that 'has changed the lives of both the people and the ecosystem of the Gulf' (Snyder 2013). In April 2010 an exploratory well developed and operated by British Petroleum exploded, killing 11 people and causing 170 million gallons of oil (4 million barrels) to spill into the Gulf of Mexico over a period of approximately three months, polluting and destroying animals and plants along more than 100 miles of the Louisiana coastline. 'Declared as the worst ecological disaster in U.S. history, the damage was compounded by the chemical dispersants used to neutralize the slick' (Ruggiero and South 2010: 245). During the clean-up process an oil-dispersant (a toxic chemical called Corexit) was used in unprecedented quantities to attempt to disperse the oil, adding a further layer of toxicity to the Gulf's ecosystem, affecting fish, deep-water corals and marshes (Snyder 2013). In criminological terms this disaster brings to the fore several challenges that are summarized well by Ruggiero and South (2010: 246):

(a) the ambiguous nature of environmental harm, which is difficult to capture in a criminological framework as definitions of harm and definitions of crime do not always overlap;
(b) the high status of those causing the most harm who (like other powerful offenders) frequently reject the proposition that criminal definitions should apply to them while constantly striving to persuade legislators that a law imposing limits on the harm they cause would implicitly endanger the core values underpinning economic development and therefore be damaging to the collective well-being; and
(c) the barriers that impede the promotion of environmental justice and the production of relevant legislative tools for the defence of the earth.

The transference of environmental harm, and responses to it, is also contingent upon time. For example, the detection and origins of some types of environmentally related harm may be unclear due to significant time-lags in manifestation of the harm. Here it is important to acknowledge the notion of cumulative effects. For example, this could refer to the way in which dioxins accumulate in fish flesh over time. It could also refer to the cumulative impact of multiple sources of pollution as in cases where there are a high number of factories in one area (such as places along the US–Mexican border). Diseases linked to asbestos poisoning may surface many years after first exposure, and this, too, provides another example of long-term effects of environmental harm. Persistent use of pesticides in particular geographical areas may also have unforeseen consequences for local wildlife, including the development of new diseases among endemic animal species (as has been suggested has occurred in the case of facial tumour disease now rampant among the Tasmanian devil population in Australia).

From the point of view of eco-philosophy, the tendency has been for anthropocentric perspectives to dominate when it comes to answering the questions, *what to do*, over what period of time? And yet, protection of the environment very often requires criteria that go beyond a human-centred approach. To put it differently, the appropriate time scale for understanding resource and population stability is generally much longer than we are used to:

> Different systems move along different time scales. Geology works in the millions of years; economics in the tens of years; biology from a few minutes to a few centuries; evolutionary biology from a few years to millions of years. Appropriate time scales depend on how long it takes for things to happen in the subject area.
>
> (Page 1991: 64)

The importance of temporal concerns is reflected in cultures that view the relationship between people and the environment in holistic, reciprocal terms. The concept of 'balance' in some indigenous communities, for example, remains of vital significance (Robyn 2002). Here we see a value system and code of ethics that embodies living within one's means and living within and as part of nature (see also Langton 1998). It is an ecocentric approach to life.

The philosophy of living in and with nature is empirically reflected in two phenomena: one relating to 'place', the other to 'time'.

> The diversity of Native cultures and kinds of social organizations which developed through time represent a high degree of social/political complexity and are varied according to the demands and necessities of the environment. For example, American Indian nations organized at the band level of social/political development have used effective strategies to take advantage of

marginal habitats such as the Arctic and deserts of the Americas, where resources are limited

(Robyn 2002: 198–9)

Importantly, such systems are usually decentralized, communal and self-reliant: 'These societies live closely with and depend on the life contained in that particular ecosystem. This way of living enabled Indigenous communities to live for thousands of years in continuous sustainability' (Robyn 2002: 199). The point is that evaluation of environmental issues needs to consider the element of time: negatively, from the perspective of short- and long-term consequences of environmental harm; positively, from the perspective of 'what works' in protecting and preserving environments.

Disasters and crime

Since 2000, the world has witnessed some 2,500 disasters (UNEP 2010). When disasters occur, whether caused by humans or naturally occurring, anticipated or unanticipated, they involve destruction, loss, distress, injury, death and/or the disruption of norms (Volpe 2007: 611). What we also now know is that 'climate change is intensifying the hazards that affect human livelihoods, settlements and infrastructure. It is also weakening the resilience of livelihood systems in the face of increasing uncertainty and frequent disasters' (Masika 2002 cited in O'Brien *et al.* 2006: 68). While, to date, the impact of climate change has been felt disproportionately in developing countries, recent estimates indicate that the more affluent countries of the West are now beginning to experience climate-related disasters (see UNISDR 2007). The global financial crisis, earthquakes in Chile, Haiti and New Zealand, Hurricane Katrina and the recent corporate-related toxic spill in the Gulf of Mexico remind us that as global citizens we all share in the tragedy of disaster, whether as victims or bystanders.

Events during the past quarter-century have shown that natural disasters and the technological hazards that may accompany them (e.g. the co-occurring natural and technological disasters in Japan's Fukushima Nuclear Power Plant) are not problems that can be solved in isolation. Rather, they are symptoms of broader and more basic problems. Losses from hazards – and the fact that the nation cannot seem to reduce them – result from short-sighted and narrow conceptions of the human relationship to the natural environment (Mileti 1999: 2). Many disaster losses – rather than stemming from unexpected events – are the predictable result of interactions among three major systems – the physical environment which includes hazardous events; the social and demographic characteristics of the communities that experience them; and the buildings, roads, bridges and other components of the constructed environment (Mileti 1999: 3). As an example, 'about half of Japan's population and three-quarters of its economic assets are concentrated in flood-prone areas, and almost 5.5 million people live in areas below sea level' (OECD 2009: 7).

Natural disasters can be classified as 'slow-onset (e.g. droughts, El Niño and La Niña events, famines) and rapid-onset (e.g. floods, hurricanes, earthquakes, landslides, tsunamis, forest fires' (Delaney and Shrader 2000: 11). Hazards can be broadly grouped into three areas: natural, technological and complex emergencies (O'Brien et al. 2006: 65). The conventional approach to disasters is to see them as 'natural' (and to include such things as earthquakes, volcanoes and floods) or human-caused (relating to fires, explosions and oil spills). In the context of social inequality and global warming, this distinction needs to be interrogated and critiqued on the basis of social distributions of harm and causality arguments (Shiva 2008; White 2011a). For example, global warming is due to human activity, and a warmer world will generate more natural disasters and therefore more humanitarian crises (Purvis and Busby 2004).

For green criminology, the study of disasters is relevant from the point of view of both environmental crimes and conventional crimes, and in regard to issues surrounding victimization, crime prevention and law enforcement. It has been observed, for example, that:

> In New Orleans, the State failed to protect its citizens by giving them adequate assistance before and after the arrival of Hurricane Katrina, in the same way the national and local governments failed completely to prevent the daily crimes committed in that country. This shows that politics and law are closely bound up in the making of a catastrophe, and that from this point of view the same concept of foreseeability must be necessarily connected with the actions of institutions and governments.
>
> (Izzo 2009: 122)

In other words, what happens before, during and after a particular event can all be analysed from a criminological perspective. As Katrina demonstrated, there were major problems with law enforcement in the aftermath of the hurricane (Thornton and Voigt 2007; Nobo and Pfeffer 2012). But the problems did not begin or end there.

Indeed, the study of disasters (both human-created and natural) reveals substantial instances of criminality related to both the lead-up (e.g. shoddy building practices) and post-event (e.g. sex trade for aid) (see, for example, Green 2005; Bell 2010; Brezina and Kaufman 2008). Conventional street crimes such as looting, rape, assault and theft are matched in many instances by white-collar and corporate crimes such as contractor fraud, misappropriation of aid funds, price gouging (e.g. raising the price of emergency supplies to profit from increased demand) and illegal dumping of hazardous waste materials as part of the clean-up. Environmental harm may be evident in and arise from building collapses, breach of levees, major oil spills, chemical explosions and radioactive leaks. Macro-level changes to the environment, such as global warming, make study of disasters yet another key dimension of environmental crime that must be taken into account by green criminology.

Conclusion

The dimensions of environmental harm are diverse and complex. What gets defined as a 'problem' – its severity, its nature, its identification – is contingent upon the capacity of sectional interests to secure its definition. In other words, there is a differential ability of people to mobilize resources around their claims. In the end, environmental problems are always contingent in nature. This extends not only to what we normally conceive of as environmental issues, but to the study of disasters and hazards as well.

As knowledge of the interrelationship between the human and natural world increases, along with appreciation of the spatial and temporal nature of environmental harm, green criminology will need to further develop new and more extensive typologies of crime. In particular, this will necessarily involve a systematic process of documentation and classification – a 'naming' of harms.

Discussion topics

- What does 'time' have to do with environmental crime?
- What does 'space' have to do with environmental crime?
- Eco-philosophy describes the relationship between humans and nature. Why is this important in determining what is or is not harmful?
- What are some examples of 'brown', 'green' and 'white' environmental harms where you live?
- Disasters bring with them hazards that are not entirely insurmountable. It all depends upon foresight and planning. Discuss.

Further reading

Adeola, F. (2000). 'Cross-National Environmental Injustice and Human Rights Issues', *American Behavioral Scientist*, 43(4): 686–706.

Halsey, M., and White, R. (1998). 'Crime, Ecophilosophy and Environmental Harm', *Theoretical Criminology*, 2(3): 345–71.

Hannigan, J. (2006). *Environmental Sociology*, 2nd ed. London: Routledge.

Heckenberg, D., and Johnston, I. (2012). 'Climate Change, Gender and Natural Disasters: Social differences and environment-related victimisation', in R. White (ed.), *Climate Change from a Criminological Perspective*. New York: Springer.

Meško, G., Dimitrijevic, D., and Fields, C. (eds) (2010). *Understanding and Managing Threats to the Environment in South Eastern Europe*. Dordrecht: Springer.

Chapter 5

Researching environmental harm

Introduction

This chapter will discuss the following topics:

- the doing of research;
- global and local data collection;
- data collection sources;
- the subjects of research; and
- measuring environmental crime.

This chapter is not designed to provide a comprehensive overview of research methodologies and methods (readers can refer to general social-science texts for this purpose). Rather our intention is to concentrate on several key areas that are important for green criminologists to consider as they undertake research on environmentally related topics of their choice. As such, this chapter considers the different ways in which green criminology has been – or might be – conducted. It asks critical questions about current approaches, including when and where study should take place, how research might be undertaken, with whose participation, and in whose interests. Answering such questions requires an examination of existing conceptual and theoretical approaches to the practice of green criminology, with a view to identifying the complexities of researching transnational environmental harms and crimes. By understanding the challenges of working in this area, we also hope to identify directions for future methodological development.

Methodology here refers to the overall approach to the research process including the theoretical approach that influences the way the research is designed and conducted, and the lens through which the researcher views the social world. *Method* refers to the technique used to gather and analyse the research data (Walter 2013: 390). We argue that studying environmental crimes and harms demands new ways of looking at the world. It involves considering our location in the world, recognizing competing interests from the local to the global, shaping new knowledge alongside others, acknowledging the problems of difference and culture, understanding the impact of colonialism, crossing disciplinary and conceptual borders, coping with the pace of change (particularly new technologies), mapping sites of harm and transference, and discovering lost voices, to name a few. There is much to be done in this area.

At a practical level, methodology involves a series of decisions about which research questions to ask, which theories to use, what information and data to gather, how to manage, analyse and synthesize those data, and what interpretation to give to such information in the final analysis. These decisions are complicated by the subject matter at hand. For instance, the dimensions of environmental harm also pose particular challenges for researchers, insofar as different types of knowledge are required for dealing with specific kinds of environmental harm. Moreover, analysis needs to take into account considerable diversity in terms of:

- who the victim is (human or non-human);
- where the harm is manifest (local through to global);
- main site where the harm is apparent (built or natural environment);
- time frame within which the consequences of harm can be analysed (immediate, delayed, intergenerational).

Concepts that inform why we think it is important to conduct research in this area include the precautionary principle (forestalling future harms), questions of justice (issues of fairness and rights), intergenerational equity (the well-being of future generations), and compensation and rectification of harms (fixing the harm). We also want to get to the bottom of what happened, how it happened, why it happened, and who knew about it and when.

While the complexities of green criminological research need to be acknowledged, they should not deter researchers from engaging in such study. The point of discussing methodology and method is to orient researchers to important substantive and ethical issues, in order to critique and improve what we do now and into the future. Critical reflection on the practice of green criminology is a natural part of building knowledge and technique as we grapple with the challenges of studying environmental harm.

The doing of research

Temporal issues also need to be taken into account in approaching the study of environmental harms and crimes. We live in a constantly changing global society; consequently the forms of environmental crime are changing too, and we need to engage with more advanced and more flexible methodological approaches to aid our understanding of environmental crime (see Eman, Meško and Fields 2009: 574). One of the first questions to ask is at what point do we engage in such research – before something happens, as an event evolves, or after the event? The 'when' of research is important methodologically to the extent that where we focus our research gaze implies the tools we will use to undertake that research. Consider, for example, the following observations:

- If we choose to analyse harm, risk or crime *before* it occurs (e.g. climate change and the potential for natural disasters), then a method such as 'horizon-scanning' may be appropriate, since it is based upon extrapolating from what is currently known to forecast future environmental harms and crimes.
- If we choose to study harms and crimes *as they are presently evolving* (e.g. oil-rig explosions in ocean settings), then a case-study approach that brings together descriptive information and contemporary facts and figures may be the best method.
- If we choose to study a harmful event *after the fact* (e.g. land pollution from mining operations), then analysis of documents and use of interviews may be appropriate to reconstruct the factors which combined to create the problem.
- If we choose to examine an event that is *a number of years in the past* (e.g. poisoning of waterways over many years), then the historical method can be utilized, drawing upon documents, maps and photographs, and site records that facilitate a retrospective analysis of the phenomenon in question.

If we choose to re-examine significant events or trends (e.g. release of poisonous gases into the atmosphere due to a factory explosion), we may find it useful to adopt a 'cold case' type of approach, one that re-examines old evidence as well as utilizing new types of evidence-gathering (such as environmental DNA techniques) and new sources of evidence (such as narratives of retired factory workers) to provide fresh insights into older cases, and narratives of surviving victims of toxic harm.

If human, biosphere and non-human interests are to be protected in the future, environmental crime prevention must be forward-looking. This means implementing interventions now to guarantee environmental well-being later. It also means learning from the past in order to prevent harmful events from recurring. For example, a study of lobster poaching in Canada found a complex underground economy, with alliances between outlaw poachers, hotels, restaurants, community groups and private citizens. This occurred in a social environment in which the taking of lobster was seen as the natural right (and yearly ritual) of locals (McMullan and Perrier 2002). A futures orientation means grappling with such entrenched practices through innovative thinking at both a policy and grounded intervention level. An innovative temporal analysis might 'spotlight and compare categories of environmental crime that are presently tightly regulated, yet predicted to experience a resurgence in commission (e.g. illegal waste disposal); continue to be problematic in enforcing (e.g. native vegetation clearance); or that have been the recent target of substantial publicity and strengthening of penalties (e.g. water theft)' (Bricknell 2010: 115). In other words, not only can we approach research itself from the point of view of 'before the fact' and 'after the fact', but we can analyse how various activities are socially defined and re-defined over time, and why.

One example of a forward-looking methodological approach is the study of environmental crimes and harms that lie over the horizon, by integrating the core concerns of eco-global criminology (a framework of analysis concerned with ecological, transnational and justice matters) with the futures orientation of horizon-scanning (a systematic form of critical thinking about future risks, harms and precautions). As part of this approach, a conceptual framework has been developed as a tool for assessing and analysing environmental risks and harms (see Chapter 2). As already discussed, the three orientations in the framework – *substantive* (risk, harm and cause), *justice* (environmental, ecological and species) and *futures* (intergenerational equity, the precautionary principle and transference over time) – provide the conceptual building blocks for more detailed analysis of specific issues and trends. As a whole, these three orientations constitute the basis for the particular questions that are relevant to an environmental horizon-scanning exercise, as informed by eco-global criminology (White and Heckenberg 2011: 89–90).

In terms of practical research considerations, the conceptual framework for environmental horizon-scanning (see White 2011a) translates into a stepped approach, as illustrated in Table 5.1.

This table describes a research process that is more or less generic to any social research project. That is, the study of environmental harm – whether retrospective or prospective – demands a systematic approach to data collection and analysis. In addition to matters of timing, consideration of the spatial dimensions of research is also important. Delimiting green criminological research in terms of spatial dimensions may be informed by the geographical scale of the harm or crime itself, or by a decision to deliberately focus the research at a specific geographical level (from local through to global).

Global and local data collection

Sometimes it is best to concentrate on local-area matters, and to undertake research that delves into the complicated dynamics of the relatively small-scale, although the small-scale too can have global implications. For example, environmental harm is frequently associated with activities that occur in specific places that exhibit certain local cultural or historical traditions (e.g. cray potting, duck hunting, bird harvesting, four-wheel driving on beaches). In such situations, these activities may simply be considered 'folk crime' (i.e., everyone does it, everyone enjoys the benefits) and perceived as 'harmless fun' in the context of sporting and leisure pursuits.

Other forms of environmental harm are notable for their propensity to cross borders. This may involve all states on the planet, as in the case of ozone depletion or global warming. Or it may involve the international transference of toxic waste from developed countries of the North to less-developed countries of the South. Air and water pollution cross national borders and their effects extend beyond the local. Particular regions of the world are subject to certain types of crimes (e.g. killing elephants in Africa for their tusks, deforestation in the Amazon) that are specific to those regions.

Table 5.1 Steps to doing environmental horizon-scanning

Process	Example 1	Example 2
Step 1 Identify broad ecological issue	Land use	Climate change
Step 2 Ask what harm is related to this now and in the future?	Types of land use that threaten ecological well-being and social justice	Differential effects of climate change on specific population groups, particular ecosystems and particular species
Step 3 Draw upon a wide variety of sources (e.g. cross-disciplinary, multi-jurisdictional, cross-cultural), to investigate a broad ecological issue	Different types of land use, including, for example, replacement of forests by biofuel crops, use of subterranean spaces for radioactive waste	Conflict over resources, climate-induced migration, radical shifts in weather patterns
Step 4 Refine analysis by drilling down to a specific topic	Analysis of specific forms of land use, such as those that diminish biodiversity	Analysis of natural disasters associated with changing weather patterns
Step 5 Read widely on specific topic	Literature on genetically modified organisms and the role of transnational corporations, including, for example, United Nations reports on global biodiversity, and literature on deforestation	Disaster studies literature that links climate change to specific types of disaster (e.g. floods, cyclones) and that expounds issues surrounding cause and effect
Step 6 Collect information and data relevant to specific topic	Information about GMO crop substitution in countries such as Brazil, Argentina and Indonesia	Information about specific natural disasters, such as floods in Pakistan, or hurricane Katrina and associated storms in the United States
Step 7 Systematically investigate the phenomenon in question using the conceptual framework of environmental horizon-scanning (e.g. substantive, justice and futures orientations)	Identify which species are threatened, the reasons why, and the key variables that together have generated the harm in question (e.g. global agriculture markets)	Identify which places and populations are most at risk, the reasons why, and the key variables that together have generated the harm in question (e.g. lack of infrastructure)

(Continued)

Table 5.1 Steps to doing environmental horizon-scanning (Continued)

Process		Example 1	Example 2
Step 8	Analyse and interpret the information and data in the light of eco-global criminological considerations (e.g. transgressions against humans, ecosystems and animals)	Displacement of endemic species from habitat (including humans), and replacement of multiple species (plant and animal) with monoculture	Analysis of environmental victimization involving particularly vulnerable groups (e.g. women, children, poor, ethnic minorities), and effects of disasters on local ecosystems and species composition
Step 9	Extrapolate the key emerging patterns associated with the information and data on the particular topic	Forced removal of people from traditional lands, substitution of existing species with single species and further diminishment of biodiversity	Breakdown in law and order; prevalence of chaotic living conditions and massive changes to local ecosystems and species composition
Step 10	Analyse the information in the light of the varied discourses surrounding cause, harm and victimization from the point of view of relationships of power	Examine statements by governments, corporations, communities, experts and others about land-use issues	Examine statements by media outlets, governments, Non-Government Organizations and global agencies about a particular disaster
Step 11	Theorize the findings in relation to anthropogenic causes (e.g. human responsibility for harm, specific perpetrators and degrees of culpability)	Transnational corporations and governments that privilege sectional interests over those of local communities and particular species	Government officials and local building contractors who have a duty of care vis-à-vis requisite construction standards and provision of adequate preventive measures
Step 12	Reflect on possible avenues for action or strategic intervention that will best forestall or mitigate the impact and consequences of the future trend (e.g. application of the precautionary principle)	Community engagement in local and regional planning processes, including environmental impact assessments, United Nations involvement in protecting traditional ownership and land uses	Regulation of building codes and instigation of community policing models based around local participation and neighbourhood security
Step 13	Communicate the findings, bearing in mind the varied audiences for the particular research topic	Local communities, local councils, regional governments	Planning and municipal decision-makers, construction companies, law enforcement officials, non-government aid organizations

Source: White and Heckenberg 2011: 98–9

Expanding the scope and vision of research to include worldwide institutions, social processes and conduits of power (including resistance), is essential to contemporary green criminology. The important thing is that research needs to take place at different levels of scale from local through to global. The international nature of issues, trends, comparisons, and networks is vital and ought to complement work done at local, country and regional levels.

When we talk about scale, it is not only geography that matters. The notion of scale also applies to the size, nature and social organization of specific criminal activities. Illegal fishing, for example may involve huge factory ships that operate on the high seas and process thousands of tons of fish at any one time. Alternatively, it may be organized around dozens of smaller vessels, each of which is contracted to provide a catch that ultimately brings reward to the originating contractor. In other words, illegal production can be organized according to economies of scale (e.g. factory ships) or economies of scope (e.g. small independent fishers). In each case, however, there has to be a link to legitimate markets (e.g. for abalone, for lobsters) for the value of the commodity to be realized in dollar terms. In each case, as well, the damage is manifest in phenomena such as over-fishing and destruction of habitat that, in turn, affect subsequent market prices for the commodity in question. Scarcity is a major motivator for illegal as well as legal forays into particular kinds of harvesting and production activity (White 2008a, 2009a).

In practical terms, we suggest that the question concerning 'what level to study something' be informed by prior knowledge of scale more generally. To study transnational environmental crimes and harms, therefore, requires a knowledge of geography (where countries are), and an awareness of the way in which the world is divided up (politically, regionally, ecologically), as well as the geographies of power inherent in these divisions. We suggest, quite literally, that researchers post a map of the world on their wall to familiarize themselves with:

- continents (Africa, South America);
- countries (United States, Cambodia, Argentina);
- blocs (European Union, Latin America);
- regions (Amazon, South East Asia);
- countries with shared borders and waterways (transference of harm);
- global zones (subterranean, outer space, ocean gyres, Arctic);
- direction of ocean and air currents (transference of harm).

Examine the variety of maps that divide the world up in different ways:

- geographically (lowlands, mountains, rivers);
- politically (nation-states);
- militarily (top ten countries with armies);
- wealth (richest/poorest countries);

- crime rates (top ten countries with highest reported crime rates);
- religion;
- vegetation;
- language;
- literacy;
- climate;
- food consumption;
- wind and pressure;
- Gross Domestic Product;
- exports/imports;
- electricity consumption;
- seaports [See http://www.mapsofworld.com].

Part of this awareness involves locating ourselves as researchers in a global context, both geographically and in relation to the other features listed above. Studying environmental harms and crimes demands that we learn more about the world generally, how harm is circulated within this world, and where we fit into the overall global picture. An exercise related to this is provided in Box 5.1.

Box 5.1 The global commons, place and harm: student exercise

Exercise:

Examine the map of the world.

1 Pick a country that you know about or that you have a connection with, but which is not your home country (or the country that you normally live in).
2 Identify one or two key environmental issues that pertain to that country, and that could be investigated from the point of view of crime/harm.

Questions to consider:

- What is the importance of place? Describe the key features of the 'built' environment and the 'natural' environment.
- What is the cross-over harm from urban and built environments, to rural and wilderness areas?
- What is the cross-over harm from rural and wilderness areas, to urban and built environments?
- What are the harms distinctly associated with the 'built' environment? Are these also transnational in nature, and if so, in what ways?

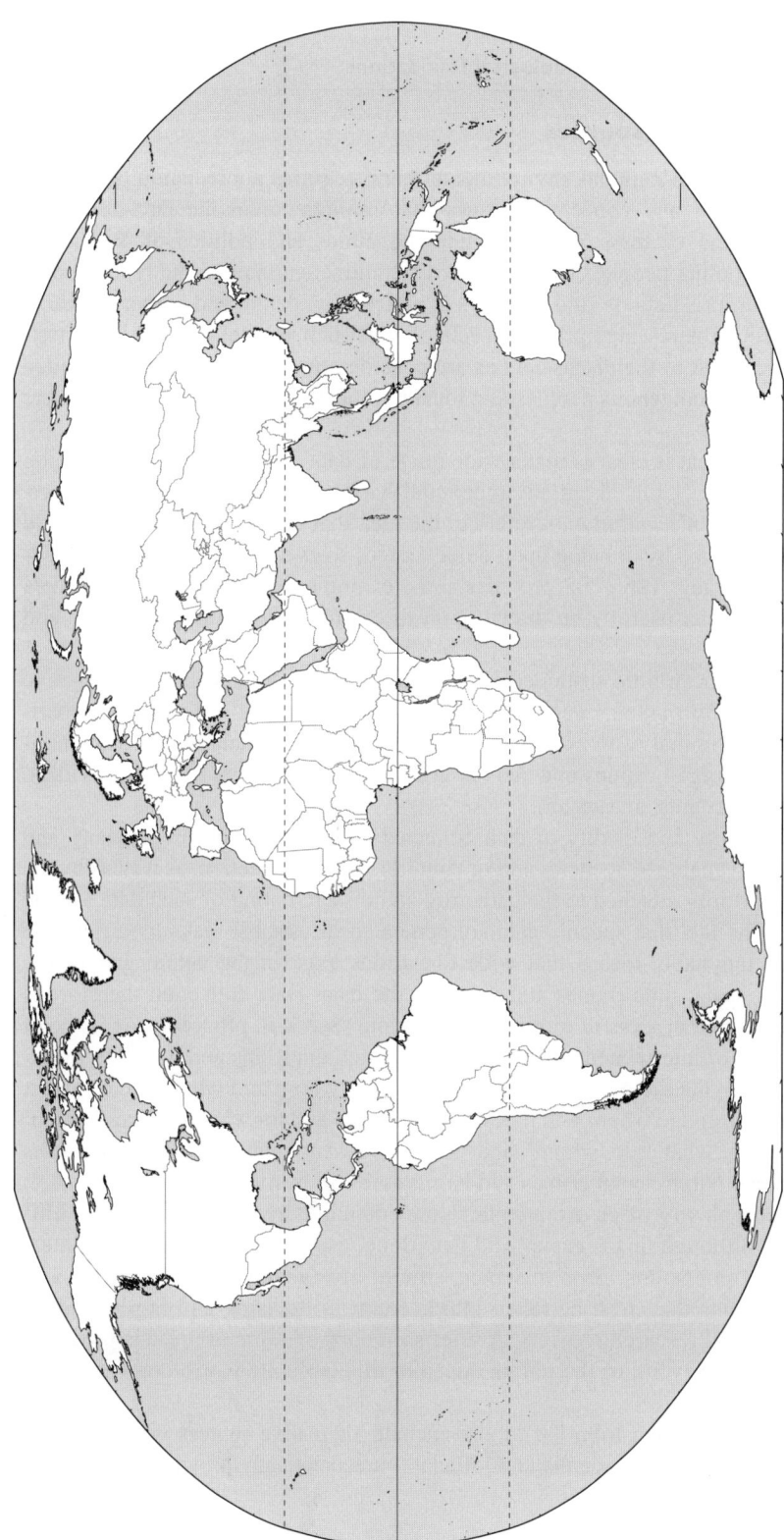

Figure 5.1 Map of the world. Source: http://johomaps.com/world/worldblank_bw.html.

Data collection sources

The study of transnational environmental harm requires appreciation of specific methodological and conceptual issues that impinge upon the data-collection process. Some of these issues include the ethics and politics of 'outsiders' researching other people's territory, the differential availability and types of data in different jurisdictions, and the ways in which state denial and corporate resistance impede the research process. Technologies such as satellites and DNA testing are relevant to the discussion, as are consideration of the expertise provided by scientists, indigenous peoples and local producers such as fishers and farmers (White 2009c).

One thing that is clear is that a wide range of data sources can be drawn upon to substantiate claims about environmental harms and crimes and their causes. The principle of *triangulation* refers to the idea that any one data source should be cross-checked by drawing upon other sources so as to ensure reliability, validity and accuracy. Table 5.2 provides some examples of different types of data sources that can usefully be drawn upon to examine environmental harms and crimes.

There has been little sustained effort to bring together official and alternative sources of information, much less data between different government departments and criminal justice agencies (such as police files, data collected by non-government organizations and activist groups, animal welfare service providers, journalist accounts, and so on).

The quantity and quality of data collected is influenced by the capacity and resources available to agencies and/or countries for its collection, as well as by the political priority attached to the gathering and disseminating of such data (White 2009c). The fact that specific data are generated in variable ways by a range of agencies inevitably means that wide disparities exist in the detail, geographic coverage, scale, time frames and scope of the data. Data collection therefore is always a social process in motion, a continuous 'work in progress'. At its heart are a series of interrelated matters: namely, which questions and which information will provide the most meaningful data, from whom and what sources will it be collected, and to whom will it be made available and for what purposes? 'Who' is collecting 'what', for 'whom', and 'why' are essential questions when it comes to data on environmental crimes and harms (see for example Whyte 2012).

The complexity of environmental issues demands responses that are multi-pronged, although this is easier said than done, especially if research has international dimensions. For instance, there are a number of issues and considerations that must be taken into account in devising and implementing cross-national research projects. A brief summary of some of these is provided in Table 5.3. Several of the points raised in this table are worth considering in greater depth.

What we can learn from has to also include alternative sources which go well beyond conventional academic and 'official' bureaucratically provided material, as

Table 5.2 Types of data sources

Data source	Example
Documents	Annual reports; correspondence such as emails, letters, memos; speeches; minutes of meetings; flow charts, decision trees
Media reports	Cartoons, newspaper editorials, articles, opinion pieces, letters to the editor, special documentaries
Official statistics	Census, Bureau of Statistics, Crime Commission, occupational health and safety statistics, consumer product safety incident reports
Court records	Environmental Law Courts – court opinions, prosecutions, sentences, sentencing rationales
Official enquiries	Panels, coronial inquests, state enquiries, commissions
Web-based records	Internet sites, home pages, video clips, blogs, corporate press releases
Paper based records	Diaries, journals, tracking records
Literature reviews	Journals, government reports, community research
Surveys	Questionnaires, telephone surveys, suggestion boxes
Group discussions	Invited respondents, public meetings, teleconferences
Focus groups	Specific sample group, briefing and debriefing sessions
Life histories	Selective in-depth discussions, story-telling, autobiographical narratives
Field observations	Field visits, participant observation
Peer research	Friendship, family and kinship networks
Social networking sites	Facebook, Twitter
Maps	Geographical, topographical, networks, systems and flows
Victim statements	Victim impact statements, narratives of families and carers
Health information	Disease clusters, toxicology reports, mortality statistics
Self-reports	Emissions by industry to air, water and land
Images	Photographs of environmental disasters, videos, images from closed-circuit cameras
Cinema and documentaries	Films about environmental issues, e.g. *Gomorrah*, *An Inconvenient Truth*
Unobtrusive measures	Remote cameras, satellite pictures, tracking devices
Legislation and enactment debates	Congressional and Parliamentary records (e.g. Hansard) to determine legislative intent
Television	Discovery Channel, National Geographic

illustrated in Box 5.2. It can include information from media stories, Non-Government Organizations, the internet, company records, medical information, traditions and legends, literature, and scientific studies of varying kinds.

Specific issues demand different approaches and the development of responses relevant to the nature of the problem. A case-study approach may be appropriate for some types of investigation; others will require statistical comparisons and analysis. Whatever methodology is selected, researchers need to be conscious of the diversity of social situations and situated knowledge – related to class, race, ethnicity, gender and age – that will have a bearing on their knowledge about the environment. A socially inclusive research programme is one that acknowledges this, as well as the intersections of class exploitation, colonial oppression, racial

Table 5.3 Issues, limitations and constraints in data collection and analysis

Practical issues	• Language differences (and subtleties of culture);
	• Access to countries and regions;
	• Expense of research;
	• Expertise required for the research (e.g. 'local' or outsider).
Scientific limitations	• Availability of data;
	• Diverse definitions of crime and harm;
	• Criteria used for comparisons;
	• Technical equipment and expertise in data collection;
	• Issues relating to the generalization of findings.
Political constraints	• Resistance to data collection;
	• Denial of harm on part of the powerful;
	• State denial and corporate resistance to research process;
	• Corruption of officials;
	• Misinformation.
Ethical issues	• Ethics and politics of 'outsiders' researching other people's territory;
	• Issues of parochialism and paternalism;
	• Whose knowledge is valued;
	• Whose voices are heard.

Source: drawing from White 2009c

injustice, gender inequality, age-based discrimination and environmental degradation (White 2009c: 245).

A typical case study (e.g. heavy metal pollution of soil in a mining town) involves interacting with key stake-holders (e.g. local doctors, local activists), being 'in the field' or conducting 'site' visits (e.g. to the town or affected community), 'participant observation' (observing first-hand in the research setting), conducting in-depth face-to-face interviews, and producing, sorting, transcribing and analysing 'interview data'. A case study may also rely upon secondary data gained and distilled off the web, including media statements, corporate press releases and video clips, transcripts of government inquiries, academic literature, company profiles on corporate websites, consumer and environmental activist voices, and statistics from wide-ranging sources. One approach to the perennial issue of generalization (i.e., how applicable is this one case to other instances of environmental harm?) is to consider the idea of 'naturalistic generalization' – this refers to context-specific knowledge gained by the *reader* of the case study. Melrose (2009) describes naturalistic generalization as the process by which the reader of the case study gains insight (or self-generated knowledge) by reflecting on the specifics of the case study and how the case resonates with their own experience. Thus, the reader reflects on how the details of a particular case study can be generalized to their own experience or research (Heckenberg 2011).

A specific case study, like the one suggested above for instance, may resonate with a reader examining a different form of harm, a different mode of transference

Box 5.2 Alternative data sources

NGOs and data collection

Non-Government Organizations (NGOs) are often engaged in data collection based upon their own research and through devising innovative systems and methods of counting and recording environmental harms across national boundaries. Greenpeace, for example, has a physical presence in 40 countries, and the International Fund for Animal Welfare has staff in 15 countries and projects in more than 40 countries. NGOs such as these, along with well-known agencies such as TRAFFIC and the Environmental Investigation Agency, provide extensive monitoring – and data collection – around issues such as illegal fishing, illegal trade in wildlife, deforestation and illegal trade in natural resources in special regions as well as globally.

Medical data to expose criminal harm

Lynch and Stretesky (2001) argue that harm exists where evidence can be presented that the products/processes in question are reasonably expected to harm human health (e.g. medical data); that toxic harms can be placed into context by comparing them with other harms that society considers serious (e.g. assault rifle homicide versus pesticide exposure deaths); and, that criminal responsibility exists where there is evidence that corporations have had knowledge of the risks they create or are indifferent to those risks (e.g. silence or rejection of alternatives). Importantly, any claims along these lines are not reliant upon traditional criminological evidence (the usual crime data sets and criminal justice statistics) to be empirically substantiated. Medical records and epidemiological data can be drawn upon to establish the reality of the harm and to raise the possibility of criminal action against the perpetrators.

Internet sources as data

The internet provides a rich source of information and data that includes everything from corporate profiles to video clips, media stories and individual blogs. There are, however, issues pertaining to reliability, copyright and currency that need to be considered, such as when webpages disappear overnight. A basic question is, how do researchers store links to internet data so that they retain currency for the length of a two- or three-year study? And what happens when corporations and others engage in 'sock puppeting' – the distortion of information for self-interested purposes (such as modifying entries in Wikipedia to show the company in the best possible light)?

or a different industry domain (e.g. with particular issues pertaining to power, evidence and control). Each case study undertaken may simultaneously add to an existing repository of similar stories and similar processes (e.g. thereby raising issues of time/space commonalities and differences). The findings from multidisciplinary research can contribute to a 'research frontier' (Mjoset 2009), in this case green criminology, while at the same time adding to a repository of work that examines specific environmental harms and crimes.

The subjects of research

All forms of knowledge are valuable. The knack is to validate the various forms of knowledge in ways that are respectful to their contributors, and to integrate them into our work while giving due acknowledgement to their strengths and limitations.

At the heart of investigations of transnational environmental harm is the question of whose knowledge of 'wrong' is right? In other words, whose voices are going to be heard, and which kinds of evidence are to be given credibility? It is rare that scientific evidence is uncontested and proof of environmental harm is simply a matter of 'let the facts decide'. For example, what counts as 'science', what counts as 'evidence', who counts as being a 'scientific expert' and what counts as 'sensible' public policy are all influenced by factors such as economic situations, the scientific tradition within a particular national context, the scientific standards used in relation to specific issues, and the style and mode of government (White 2008a). There are several different types of knowledge, including scientific, common-sense, experiential and technical. There are many different sources of knowledge in addition to scientific disciplines, including the knowledge of the lay person, the knowledge of workers such as farmers, fishers and loggers, the knowledge of indigenous peoples in diverse settings, and the knowledge of technicians who use particular instruments to measure and appraise aspects of the world around them.

Moving beyond one's own national borders to work with people in other locales and from other cultures is complicated by a range of factors. Gaining access to countries, regions and specific sites may be an issue, as is the expense associated with transnational study. University researchers may have to negotiate with relevant institutional review boards and human research ethics committees for permission to undertake research abroad. Language differences and the subtleties of culture may intrude into the research process by causing delays, leading to misunderstandings about substantive issues. The expertise required to undertake research is a perennial issue: outside 'experts' are the bane of many a developing country's existence insofar as local knowledge and capacity-building is ignored in favour of relying on 'trained' personnel from the metropole (see Stanley 2008). On the other hand, the political realities within some nation-states suggest that it may be best that an 'outsider' carry out the research if issues of safety, security and independent knowledge production are at stake. Insider/outsider relationships are contingent, therefore, upon local resources, staff availability and political contexts, and thus require 'sensitivity to situation' on the part of 'outside' researchers (White 2009c: 236).

Such sensitivity in turn points to the importance of working alongside others and respecting their knowledge as guiding concepts in transnational research. How is it possible to be sensitive to situation and context if you are not actually talking and engaging with local people (including local intellectuals, broadly defined)? The notion of outsider/insider is a real and meaningful distinction that is forged in the crucible of local experiences, long-standing cultural traditions, relationship to imperial power and positioning in the wider global political economy. Bridging the gap requires dialogue (not monologue), listening (not lecturing) and give-and-take interchange (not just giving, or just taking) (White 2009c : 236). Informed expertise is built upon processes that expand the horizons of knowledge and that, as part of this, incorporate the insights of people from many different backgrounds (see Connell 2007). This requires openness to the interplay between class, race, ethnicity, gender and other social variables in differentially positioning people (individually and collectively) in regard to social location and situated knowledge. It also demands adoption of multiple methods of study and a wide variety of ways in which to engage in dialogic social relationships (see for example, Banerjee and Bell 2007).

There are ways to ensure that researchers are not simply 'taking', that they are not exploiting the vulnerable, and that they are not misleading in their representations of situated knowledge. For instance, Dodson, Piatelli and Schmalzbauer (2007) describe the dilemmas and opportunities associated with research about the lives and perspectives of marginalized people living in a variety of social settings. Interestingly, and usefully, they speak of a methodological practice called 'interpretive focus groups'. On the one hand, research is oriented toward involving a wide range of participants in the research practice (i.e., hearing the voices from below, including the voices of those groups which historically have been disregarded or excluded from such research conversations). On the other hand, people from the same localities and social backgrounds are asked to participate in panels to discuss and interpret the findings (i.e., assessing the meaning of what has been said in the first phase of the research). This acknowledges that marginalized populations will, on occasion, be silent or hide certain things due to fears or suspicions related to what might be revealed about themselves and their lives that could make them vulnerable in relation to authority figures and mainstream institutions. The experience and expertise of local residents helps us understand why and how respondents speak as they do, and is thus considered alongside that of the 'academic' per se. Without this interpretive lens there may be misinterpretation of what people are actually saying. The process of utilizing interpretive focus groups enables researchers to collaboratively approach data analysis, and thus to capture more accurately and ethically, the 'truths' of those with whom they are interacting (White 2009c: 237–8).

Ascertaining 'truth', however, works in more than one direction. It is not only 'hearing' what is really being said, it also involves interpreting and contextualizing what is being conveyed. For example, specific groups who experience environmental problems may not always describe or see the issues in strictly environmental terms. This may be related to lack of awareness of the environmental harm, alternative explanations for the calamity (e.g. an act of God) and socio-economic pressures to 'accept' environmental risk in return for economic reward (see Julian 2004). Waldman (2007), for instance, describes a local community in South Africa that saw the contamination effects of asbestos as 'natural'. This was due to a combination of religious beliefs (that stressed a passive stance to the world around them) and the fact that often harms that are imperceptible to the senses only exist as a problem if they are constituted as such in public discourse (and in particular, the public discourse of the village community). Otherwise, what is, simply is as it is. Something that is seen to be 'naturally' caused or created tends to not generate the same anger, angst and conflict as that which is perceived to be due to human error and/or conscious intervention. In these circumstances appeal to scientific knowledge and a collaborative approach to making sense of what is happening is required. Otherwise, the 'common sense' knowledge belies the actual nature of the harm, and what is needed to address it. This is necessarily a highly political and sensitive process.

The imposition of outside frames of reference can also constitute a form of exploitation. This has both material, and socio-cultural consequences. This is seen, for example, in the acquisition of large areas of arable land in developing countries by foreign governments and private companies (Sutherland *et al.* 2009: 5). These land acquisitions are having major negative impacts on local people who are losing access and control over the resources on which they depend, and which are the rightful inheritance of future generations. Importantly, these problems are compounded in some cases by the ways in which 'conservation' is being foisted upon these same communities. As Duffy (2010: 11) points out:

> When wildlife reserves are established, local communities can suddenly find that their everyday subsistence activities have been outlawed and they have been redefined as criminals. ... Some of the world's best-known pristine wilderness areas are, in fact, engineered environments. Creating a national park means drawing up new conservation rules which outlaw the everyday subsistence activities of local communities, such as hunting for food and collecting wood.

From an historical perspective, the imposition of colonial power was intrinsically a matter of resource colonization, a phenomenon that affected many different indigenous peoples in places such as South America, North America and Australasia, as well as the native inhabitants of Africa, Asia and beyond. In places such as Australia, indigenous territories were considered frontier lands that were unowned, under-utilized and therefore open to exploitation. The prior ownership rights, interests and knowledges of indigenous inhabitants were treated as irrelevant by the European invaders. Environmental victimization has been central to dispossession and maltreatment of indigenous peoples over many continents and over a period of several centuries. Whose knowledge is privileged in interpreting 'the best interest' has been vital to dispossession and disregard in relation to indigenous and traditional cultures.

Issues of understanding and exploitation must be borne in mind even as green criminologists assert a more active role for themselves. 'As the twenty-first century unfolds and we witness continuing debate and contestation about "limits to growth", "peak oil", climate change and the urgency of limiting harm to the environment, there will be space for critical criminologists to take up the idea of the defence of the earth alongside advocacy of human rights as a global call for the future' (Ruggiero and South 2010). How we do this depends upon various concrete factors, including who, precisely, is to be included in this advocacy work and how we approach it.

Indeed, to talk about whose voices are heard means that we must also critically reflect on the dominant voices within our own field of green criminology itself. Key questions here include:

- Whose voices are heard?
- How and when are voices heard?
- Where are those voices located?
- What is the gender (class, race, etc.) bias in those voices?
- Which topics are studied and which issues are given priority?
- What do we know about scholars in regions of the world other than our own?
- Do we silence dissenting voices by not quoting them?
- Do we discount certain voices because of a failure to grasp what it is they are saying?
- In what ways can we collaborate, in practice, with those living, working and researching elsewhere?
- What languages are not privileged in the global dialogue about environmental harm, and is universal translation possible?

Funding is one issue that can affect whose voice(s) are heard in the academic landscape. Larger universities in developed countries are more likely to attract substantial funding than smaller universities in the developed world, and some universities in the developing world may attract little or no funding at all. Innovative approaches to research might also consider more cost-effective ways of moving beyond the parochial. One way of accomplishing this is to engage in well-designed research projects and programmes of study.

Measuring environmental crime

How environmental harm is conceived very much depends upon the yardstick by which worth is determined. To assess the severity of harm requires criteria linked to value, scale and measure (White 2013c). A clear divide exists between extrinsic and intrinsic value. The notion of 'intrinsic' value only makes sense relative to some idea of 'extrinsic' value. The common denominator in each case is who does the valuing: namely, humans. Here value is measured through quantitative assessments (the extent and type of harm) and moral or qualitative assessments (whether to include some types of activities as harm).

Value

Extrinsic
e.g. harm is measured in terms of human interests, mediated by what happens to the environment, animals and plants
Intrinsic
e.g. harm is measured according to criteria that presume certain things done to the environment and to animals and plants are inherently bad

This assessment of 'worth' is partly dependent upon the scale at which evaluation occurs. Is the focus on individual species or entire eco-systems? Should value also be applied to individual organisms, and if so, should this apply to all plants and animals? Eco-systems incorporate the biotic (plants, animals) and the abiotic (water, soil) that, arguably, have value in their own right as self-maintaining and self-perpetuating systems. How does one determine the relative value of individual organisms, particular species and overarching biotic communities relative to each other?

Scale

Individuals	*Particular species*	*Biotic community and abiotic context*
e.g. person	e.g. homo sapiens	e.g. Arctic eco-systems
e.g. plant	e.g. hemp	e.g. grasslands eco-systems
e.g. animal	e.g. apes	e.g. mountain eco-systems

At the same time, harms to specific eco-systems threaten all within them, human and non-human alike. Melting glaciers have implications for future flows of fresh water, and thus affect many different biotic communities in diverse territories and climates. Interconnection and overlapping interests are as important to consider as discrete needs, rights and concepts of justice.

Measuring harm

Form of harm
e.g. immediate and direct impact, indirect and diffuse
Seriousness of harm

e.g. injury, fatality
Wider effects of harm
e.g. spatial (local or transboundary), temporal (short- or long-term)
Characteristics of harm
e.g. cumulative effects, specific incidents

The value of human, eco-system and non-human species is reflected in how and why we measure harm. The 'why' of measuring harm may be informed by both intrinsic and instrumental criteria – a farmer's crops being contaminated by GMO products may combine elements of both considerations. The 'how' of measurement refers to efforts to put a value – monetary, ecological, aesthetic, cultural – on the harm. This involves attempts to make the harm visible and assess the magnitude of the harm (e.g. as minor, major or catastrophic, and in relation to what or whom). This can take the form of 'harm audits' (see Pantazis and Pemberton 2009). Key questions here are who is doing the valuing and what tools are utilized to assign value.

Environmental crime is socially constructed, both through definitional processes and by the ways in which environmental law enforcement is carried out in practice. As noted elsewhere, 'The ways in which we "measure crime" are thus intertwined with both "how crime is defined" (and what is deemed to be serious and harmful) and "how it is responded to by institutions of criminal justice" (through specific campaigns, programs, and interventions)' (White and Habibis 2005: 10). What is of concern to green criminologists is how best to measure the dark figure of environmental crime – those harms presently unreported or undocumented or unacknowledged as environmental crimes. Also of concern is how best to gauge institutional biases in what is deemed to be worthy of official attention and what is not. It is important, as well, to consider the question of victims and to establish some kind of baseline criteria that can be used to measure who or what suffers which kinds of environmental victimization.

Conclusion

The international nature of issues, trends, comparisons, and networks is vital and ought to complement work done at the local, regional and country levels. Expanding the scope and vision of green criminology to include worldwide institutions, social processes and conduits of power (including resistance), is essential. The important thing is that research ought to take place at different levels of scale (local through to global). To be truly global, we must not only foster the development of cross-disciplinary knowledge, but also capture the voices of researchers, scholars and activists from different parts of the world by considering their views and building them into our research and activities.

Specific issues such as illegal logging or trade in endangered species demand specific types of research and the development of responses that are specific to the nature of the problem. A case-study approach may be appropriate for some types of investigation; others will require statistical comparisons and analyses.

Whatever the specific methodology, it is essential to be conscious of the diversity of social situations and situated knowledge – related to class, race, ethnicity, gender and age – that will have a bearing on our knowledge about the environment. A socially inclusive research programme is one that acknowledges this, as well as the intersections of class exploitation, colonial oppression, racial injustice, gender inequality, age-based discrimination and environmental degradation.

Grounding research in the academic literature of different countries and cultures, incorporating the knowledge of diverse scholars, and engaging with the particular environmental crimes and harms that impact the lived realities of people in diverse places can bring a new energy and vitality to green criminological research. In other words, research on environmental harm is carried out for a purpose – namely, to help address issues of pressing concern that are destroying environments, non-human species and human lives in the here and now as well as those that threaten our planetary future.

Discussion topics

- What is 'data'?
- What kind of data collection do Non-Government Organizations such as Greenpeace, TRAFFIC and the Environmental Investigations Agency collect?
- Why is it important to corroborate information taken from internet searches in order to ensure its accuracy?
- What kind of statistics and facts and figures are available on environmental crime in your town/city, province/state, region/country?
- Why is 'do-it-yourself' research at the community level important to green criminology?

Further reading

Bisschop, L. (2011). 'Transnational Environmental Crime: Exploring (un)chartered territory', in M. Cools, Ruyver, B., Easton, M., Pauwels, L., Ponsaers, P., Vander Becken, T., Vander Laenen, F., Gande Walle, G., Verhage, A., and Vermeulen, G. (eds), *EU Criminal Justice, Financial & Economic Crime: New perspectives*. Antwerp: Maklu.

Eman, K., Meško, G., Dobovšek, B. and Sotlar, A. (2013). 'Environmental Crime and Green Criminology in South Eastern Europe – Practice and research', *Crime, Law, and Social Change*, 59(3): 341–58.

Gibbs, C., Gore, M., McGarrell, E., and Rivers, L. (2010). 'Introducing Conservation Criminology: Towards interdisciplinary scholarship on environmental crimes and risks', *British Journal of Criminology*, 50(1): 124–44.

Heckenberg, D., and White, R. (2013). 'Innovative Approaches to Researching Environmental Crime', in N. South and A. Brisman (eds), *Routledge International Handbook of Green Criminology*. London: Routledge.

Lynch, M., and Stretesky, P. (2006). 'Toxic Crimes: Examining corporate victimization of the general public employing medical and epidemiological evidence', in N. South and P. Beirne (eds), *Green Criminology*. Aldershot: Ashgate.

Part II

Transgression and victimization

Chapter 6

Climate change and social conflict

Introduction

This chapter will discuss the following topics:

- global warming and climate change;
- climate change, resources and social conflict;
- climate change and crime; and
- climate change, ecocide and state-corporate crime.

Climate change is the most important international issue facing humanity today, yet until recently criminology has devoted very little attention to this particular issue. This is changing (see Lynch and Stretesky 2010; Agnew 2011, 2012, 2013; White 2009b; 2011a, 2012a, b and c; Halsey 2013; South 2012; Fussey and South 2012). It is notable for example that a leading US criminologist recently observed that climate change will become one of the major, if not *the* major, forces driving crime as the twenty-first century progresses (Agnew 2011).

This chapter examines the nature and dynamics of climate change, and the implications and consequences of climate change for social order and criminal behaviour. It begins by describing global warming and climate change and then explores the social conflicts and crimes most likely associated with climate change, now and into the future. It concludes by considering the ways in which powerful social interests deny harm, to the detriment of all.

Global warming and climate change

Global warming describes the rising of the earth's temperature over a relatively short time span. *Climate change* describes the inter-related effects of this rise in temperature: from changing sea levels and changing ocean currents, through to the impacts of temperature change on local environments that affect the endemic flora and fauna in varying ways (for instance, the death of coral due to temperature rises in sea water, or the changed migration patterns of birds). *Weather* is the name we give to the direct local experience of things such as sunshine, wind, rain, snow and the general disposition of the elements. It is about the short-term and personal, not the long-term patterns associated with climate in general. As the planet warms up, the climate will change in ways that disrupt previous weather patterns – and will in some places even bring colder weather even though overall temperatures are on the rise (Lever-Tracy, 2011).

Concern about global warming had been expressed for many years, by many scientists in different disciplines. Even though it had been systematically denied and downplayed by contrarians, many of whom have friends in high places (Brisman 2012a; Kramer 2013), climate change is accepted by a majority of people today as a serious and urgent issue. Part of the reason for this is that climate and weather events seem to now touch or affect every person living on the planet. They do this directly and indirectly, in ways that are understandable and threatening to ordinary people. Unseasonal weather (such as droughts), extreme weather events (such as cyclones/hurricanes) and natural disasters (such as tsunamis) bring home the immediate effects of global warming to many millions of people. The longer-term effects, such as rising ocean levels, are also not so long-term for many people living in low-lying countries of the Pacific and Indian oceans.

The phenomenon of thermal-related deaths in France in August 2003 (Curson and Clark 2004) and the devastation wrought by Hurricane Katrina in New Orleans in 2005 (Hartman and Squires 2006) has also highlighted the lack of adequate preparation for such events and trends. It has also demonstrated that environmental injustice not only pertains to the siting of toxic facilities and the dumping of waste, but is entrenched in the priorities assigned to those whose safety, health and well-being matter the most. For the elderly, the poor and people of colour such differences are, literally, a matter of life and death.

The global media, including the internet, have been central to bringing awareness of climate change into more and more homes, at least in the more affluent nations where computers open many different portals to the world at large. For others, direct experience and changes in traditional social patterns are unmistakeable indicators of profound shifts in global climate (e.g. as with Inuit in northern Canada, who find the ice and snow arriving later and melting sooner, which affects their hunting and food-gathering activities). The world is smaller, and the issues more transparent. But the causes and solutions still generate considerable disagreement and, it seems, even less substantive action.

The lack of concerted global action on climate change is due in large measure to the actions of large transnational corporations, especially those in the 'old energy' sectors such as coal mining. Given that the top private corporations are economically more powerful than many nation-states, and given that they own and control great expanses of the world's land, water and food resources, these transnational corporations are individually and collectively a formidable force. On occasion, as well, business competitors may combine to use their collective muscle to influence world opinion or global efforts to curtail their activities.

For example, analysis of how big business has responded to global warming reveals a multi-pronged strategy to slow things down (Bulkeley and Newell 2010). Some of its elements were:

- challenging the science behind climate change;
- creating business-funded environmental NGOs;
- emphasizing the economic costs of tackling climate change;
- using double-edged diplomacy to create stalemates in international negotiations;
- using domestic politics (particularly in the United States) to stall international progress;
- directly influencing the climate-change negotiations through direct lobbying.

It is only through continuous pressure from below (grassroots groups and global activists), and the occasional exercise of political will from enlightened politicians from above (evident in some Latin American countries, such as Bolivia), that moderates the exercise of this kind of corporate power.

Nonetheless, today most governments acknowledge that there is a problem and that it must in some way be addressed. The divides between North and South, geographically and metaphorically, are already deepening as crises related to food production and distribution, energy sources and pollution, and changing climates re-arrange the old world order. Social inequality and environmental injustice will undoubtedly be the drivers of continuous conflict for many years to come, as the most dispossessed and marginalized of the world's population suffer the brunt of food shortages, undrinkable water, climate-induced migration and general hardship in their day-to-day lives. Women will suffer more than men, people of colour more than the non-indigenous and the non-migrant, the young and the elderly more than the adult, and the infirm and disabled of all ages.

The urgency and reality of climate-change issues were eloquently conveyed in a May 2010 letter signed by 284 members of the US National Academy of Sciences published in *Science* claiming that:

> There is compelling, comprehensive and consistent objective evidence that humans are changing the climate in ways that threaten our societies and the ecosystems on which we depend. Many recent assaults on climate science and, more disturbingly, on climate scientists by climate change deniers are typically driven by special interests or dogma, not by an honest effort to provide an alternative theory that credibly satisfies the evidence.
> (Quoted in Lever-Tracy 2011: 10–11)

If anything, most disagreement surrounding climate change today is over how quickly global warming is proceeding rather than over whether it is happening. By October 2012, for instance, it was reported (Boyer 2012) that:

- The Arctic is warming twice as quickly as was projected in the 'worst-case' scenarios for the last major international climate science report in 2007.
- In 2012, the rate of ice loss from the Greenland land ice was an all-time record.
- The global food crisis, with climate change as a major driver, is now in its fifth year, and is set to intensify as the effects of recent drought and flooding in key exporting countries are felt down the food chain.
- Half the corals of the Great Barrier Reef in Australia have disappeared since 1980.
- The water of the world's oceans now carries about double the heat energy it held in 1990.
- Current global emissions trajectory will see surface warming pass 2°C by 2040 and pass the catastrophic level of 5°C around 2100.

Even if human emissions were stopped right now, this moment, the atmosphere would continue warming for another 25 years. Moreover, 'the ocean will continue to store heat from the atmosphere for yet more years, preventing or inhibiting the cooling of the planet until long after we're dead and buried. The only question is, how far will the warming go? The more carbon dioxide we put into the atmosphere, the hotter it will get' (Boyer 2012: 14–15).

Part of the reason why responses to climate change have been so little and so late has to do with the nature of 'slow crisis' (White 2012a). Floods in Brazil, Australia and Sri Lanka in early 2011 have generally been interpreted publicly as once-in-a-hundred year phenomena. Much the same was said about 'Super Storm Sandy' along the East coast of the United States in 2012. Cyclones and hurricanes are 'normal' to certain regions of the world, even though the frequency and intensity might be changing. There is no one single earth-shattering event that demarcates the 'crisis' of climate change. Transformation is progressive and longitudinal. It is not abrupt, completed or singularly global in impact.

The damage caused by global warming will be felt in the form of extreme weather events, increased competition for dwindling natural resources, outbreaks of disease and viral infections, further extinctions of species, continued pressure to trade off food for fuel – the list goes on. As Box 6.1 indicates, there are a number of issues associated with climate change that demand attention.

There is no doubt that global warming, affecting the world's climate systems, will have massive and ongoing consequences for humanity, eco-systems and non-human animals for many years to come.

Climate change, resources and social conflict

Human subsistence is based upon the use of a combination of renewable resources (e.g. fresh water, forests, fertile soils) and non-renewable resources (e.g. oil and minerals), and the ability of the planet to provide a range of naturally provided goods and services. 'Ocean fisheries supply fish that are a *good*, while

Box 6.1 Climate change issues

- *Climate change and social conflicts over natural resources* – struggles over food, water, energy, and questions of national and international security.
- *Climate change and the body* – issues surrounding nutrition, the rights of the unborn, effects of reliance upon genetically modified crops, feminization of nature (e.g. fish) due to pollutants and climate-related processes.
- *Climate change and natural disasters* – crime and criminality related to events such as floods, earthquakes, volcanic activity, cyclones/hurricanes that will intensify in the coming years due to climate change.
- *Climate change and paradoxical harms* – issues pertaining to present solutions to climate change that, in turn, generate new forms of harm (e.g. mercury content of new energy-efficient light bulbs).
- *Climate change and carbon emission trading* – how the trading of carbon credits is linked to various kinds of crimes, including for example, fraud and the displacement of local people off their lands (e.g. as has occurred in Africa).
- *Climate change and victimization* – the ways in which climate change, and climate change policies, have implications for victimization both at a universal level (i.e., everyone in the world is affected) and differentially (i.e., the poor and marginalized are especially vulnerable to the worst impacts of environmental change).
- *Climate change and injustice* – this relates to who the key perpetrators of global warming are, and to patterns of production and consumption that illustrate the unequal relations upon which climate change has been built.
- *Climate change, the law and the precautionary principle* – issues relating to uncertainty and potential hazards, and the ways in which risk of harm and criminal activity might be anticipated in law through the application of the precautionary principle.

the stratosphere ozone layer renders a *service* by protecting life from high levels of ultraviolet radiation. Some renewables provide both goods and services: forests supply timber (a good) while also maintaining regional hydrological cycles (a service)' (Homer-Dixon 1999: 47). Climate change affects natural resources as goods and services, especially in conjunction with other ecologically unsustainable practices.

Exploitation of natural resources is a major cause of armed conflict within and between communities and nation-states (Klare 2001, 2012; Le Billon 2012;

Homer-Dixon 1999). This is largely due to scarcity of resources, which can arise from depletion or degradation of the resource (supply), increased demand for it (demand), and unequal distribution and/or resource capture (structural scarcity) (Homer-Dixon 1999). What humans do to the environment is directly implicated in the production of scarcity, and hence conflict. For instance, 'Deforestation increases the scarcity of forest resources, water pollution increases the scarcity of clean water, and climate change increases the scarcity of the regular patterns of rainfall and temperature on which farmers rely' (Homer-Dixon 1999: 9). Greenhouse gas emissions, a major cause of global warming, are generated by existing industries and result in even further pressures on already vulnerable ecosystems. Arable land and drinking water are at a premium under such circumstances. As mentioned, the race to exploit increasingly scarce environmental resources has been recognized as a key source of violence, crime and conflict (Homer-Dixon 1999; Klare 2012; Le Billon 2012). These will be exacerbated under conditions of wide-scale climate change.

Unsurprisingly, then, there is a wide range of existing and potential social conflicts surrounding global warming. Four trends have been identified where climate change is giving rise to significant social conflict (White 2009; see also Smith and Vivekananda 2007; Solano and Ferrero-Waldner 2008). These include: conflicts over environmental resources (e.g. access to water, preservation of forests); conflicts linked to global warming (e.g. climate-induced migration); conflicts over the differential exploitation of resources (e.g. foreign patents and imposition of genetically modified crops versus traditional knowledge and use of plants); and conflicts over the transference of harm (e.g. cross-border and global concentrations of pollutants that contribute to global warming) (see Box 6.2).

Climate change affects us all, regardless of where we live, regardless of social characteristics. However, the effects of climate change, while felt by everyone, are not the same for everyone. Claims to a universal victimization in fact belie crucial differences in how different groups and classes of people are placed quite differently in relation to key risk and protective factors. Social conflict linked to climate change is as much as anything a reflection of social inequality, and not simply determined by changes in environmental conditions. For example, it has been observed that those most vulnerable to the 'consequences of consequences' of climate change are people living in poverty, in underdeveloped and unstable states, under poor governance (Smith and Vivekananda 2007). The consequences of global warming will thus bear most heavily on those least able to cope with climate-related changes.

Climate change and crime

Climate change continues to generate ecological conditions that will engender considerable anxiety and conflict. Higher temperatures and drought will affect food production, well-being and safety, and water-reliant economic sectors, such as power-generation. For example, in a single year in 2003, melting reduced the

Box 6.2 Climate change and social conflict

Conflicts over environmental resources:

e.g. water – anti-privatization protests and diminished clean drinking water resources (Bolivia, South Africa, Israel, Palestine);

e.g. food – food riots, particularly in relation to grain prices, associated with tension between crops for food and crops for bio-fuel (Mexico, Haiti, Indonesia, Cameroon);

e.g. fish – competition between local fishers and commercial and industrial fishers, leading to 'war' over specific fisheries (Canada, Spain).

Conflicts linked to global warming:

e.g. climate-induced migration of peoples – 'environmental refugees' (South Pacific Islands);

e.g. demographics – population size and profile (such as structural ageing) linked to distribution, availability and carrying capacity of land (China);

e.g. loss of territory and border disputes – receding coastlines and desertification (Egypt, Greenland, Canada, Russia, USA).

Conflicts over differential exploitation of resources:

e.g. indigenous people and bio-piracy – theft of plants and indigenous knowledge and techniques under guise of legal patent processes (Brazil, Peru);

e.g. subsistence versus industrial production – uses of bio-technology such as GMOs and other forms of technology to increase yields beyond the norm and beyond precaution, for profit purposes (Zambia);

e.g. conflicts over energy supply – related to the concentration of world's hydrocarbon reserves in specific regions (Iraq, Iran, Venezuela).

Conflicts over transference of harm:

e.g. cross-border pollution – movement of pollutants through fluid medium, such as water, or via air currents (China, Russia, Germany, Hungary);

e.g. transborder movement of toxic waste – corruption of companies and organized crime in re-distributing waste to countries of least resistance, or the oceans and deserts of the world (Somalia, Ivory Coast, Nigeria);

e.g. circulation of pollution and waste – such as concentration of plastics in specific geographical locations, and planetary sinks (ocean gyres, Antarctic ozone hole).

Source: White 2009b

mass of Alpine glaciers in Europe by one-tenth, and tens of thousands of people died due to the severe heat wave (European Environment Agency 2010). Collective security will increasingly be tied up with notions of ecological sustainability within a particular social context. Pressures relating to food and water supply, and loss of habitat, will manifest in various class-related processes including certain types of criminality.

Various crimes tied to climate-related events, such as food riots and climate-induced migration, will become more prevalent. Some of these, for example, include looting and black-marketeering in relation to foodstuffs, illegal fishing and killing of birds and land animals, trafficking in humans and in valued commodities such as water and food, and carbon-emission trading fraud. A bifurcation of crime will occur. The rich and powerful will use their resources to dump toxic and radioactive waste on the lands of the less powerful, and to build up their carbon credits by exploiting the financial hardships of others. Crimes of the less powerful will be crimes of desperation generated by falls in rainfall, failure of crops and subsistence concerns. Child soldiers and armed gangs will flourish in conditions of welfare collapse or non-existent government support. People will flee and be criminalized for seeking asylum; others will stay, to fight for dwindling resources in their part of the world. Communities will be pitted against each other, and industries against communities. Law and order will be increasingly more difficult to maintain, much less enforce in other than repressive ways.

Criminologists are now looking at climate-related crime and criminality in more systematic fashion from a range of perspectives. For example, the situational nature of climate change and crime has been explored from the point of view of the relationship between *temperature changes and human behaviour* (see for example, Boyanowsky 1999; Rotton and Cohn 2003; Peng et al. 2011; Mares 2013). Typically, the relevant literature has focused on one of three levels of analysis:

- *Individuals* – aggression and crimes of violence. Discussion here centres on whether extreme weather conditions, especially heat waves, are related to increases in aggression and thereby criminal assaults and the like.
- *Place-based activities* – local weather and indoor/outdoor routines and opportunities and links to specific types of crimes. Discussion here focuses on the places where people spend their time, and with whom, and how this affects their propensity to engage in certain types of criminal activities.
- *Communities and change* – systemic crop failure, and survival and migration strategies. Changes in local weather conditions are seen to affect how people behave psychologically and socially, including participation in activities that may involve illegal poaching or harvesting for the purposes of subsistence.

Another approach is to describe climate-change-related crime from the point of view of *perpetrators*. Such analysis might include reference to:

- *Crimes by the less powerful* – basic survival (e.g. loss of land, lack of rain, change in temperatures), through illegal migration, foraging for food in reserves, water theft, street riots.
- *Crimes by the powerful* – protection of privilege and defence of profit-motive, through enclosures of land, hoarding of food and other basics, establishment of private armies/security.
- *Crimes by organized criminals* – new criminal opportunities, such as carbon-emission fraud, illegal trafficking of people and substances, dumping of waste, illegal trade in food and water.
- *Crimes by the state* – collusion with powerful interests, denial of human/ecological rights, failure to intervene or regulate, radioactive waste on indigenous land, buying of land for food production/consumption somewhere else; granting of logging concessions regardless of (indigenous) land ownership.

Another type of classification relates to the *criminal offences* associated with climate change (White 2012a). Specific criminal and environmental offences linked to the phenomenon of climate change are categorized according to offences that contribute to climate change, those arising from its consequences, civil unrest and organized criminal activities, and offences pertaining to regulation and law enforcement associated with mitigation and adaptation strategies (see Table 6.1). In this scenario it is anticipated that there will be changes in the type, rate and frequency of offences as the climate alters (Bergin and Allen 2008; Wallets and Martin 2013).

A useful attempt to combine observations about *different levels of analysis* and substantive areas of criminality is provided by Agnew (2011). This work explicates the impact of climate change on crime in terms of:

- *Factors associated with climate change* – rising temperature, rising sea level, extreme weather events, changing patterns of precipitation, habitat change, negative health effects, food/water shortages, loss of livelihood, migration, social conflict.
- *These factors are, in turn, linked to criminogenic mechanisms* – increased strain, reduced control, reduced social support, beliefs/values favourable to crime traits, conducive to crime, opportunities for crime, social conflict.
- *And these lead to higher levels of individual, group, corporate, and state crime.*

A large and growing body of work is also looking at those crimes associated with *natural disasters* (White and Heckenberg 2011; Rodriquez, Quarantelli and Dynes 2007; Heckenberg and Johnson 2012; Takemura 2012; Fussey and South 2012). Climate change has been associated with the advent of varying types of 'natural disaster' which are projected to increase in intensity and frequency in the foreseeable future. These include such phenomenon as floods, cyclones, earthquakes, volcanic activity, extreme heat spells, and so on. Study of

Table 6.1 Crime and climate change

Subject of offence	Nature of offence
Environmental offences (contributing to climate change):	
Forestry	illegal felling of trees
Air pollution	emissions of dark smoke
Industrial pollution	unlicensed pollution
Illegal land clearance	destruction of habitat and forests
Clearing native vegetation	reducing biotic mass
Environmental offences (consequences of climate change):	
Water theft	stealing water
Wildlife poaching	illegal killing of animals
Illegal fishing	diminishment of fish stocks
Associated offences (civil unrest and criminal activities):	
Public order offences	food riots
Eco-terrorism	arson, tree spiking
Trafficking	migration and people smuggling
Violent offences	homicide, gang warfare
Regulatory offences (arising from policy responses to climate change):	
Carbon trading	fraud
Carbon offsets	misreporting
Illegal planting	unauthorized use of genetically modified organisms
Collusion	regulatory corruption

Source: White 2012a

disasters (both human-created and natural) has revealed substantial instances of criminality (see for example, Green 2005; Thornton and Voigt 2007). These include crimes pre-disaster (e.g. poor construction standards, such as omission of steel reinforcement in concrete), during the disaster (e.g. looting, rape) and post-disaster (e.g. insurance fraud, misappropriation of aid funds). The kinds of crimes associated with disasters include crimes against the person as well as corporate, white-collar and state crimes. Moreover, the scale of recent disasters, such as the 2011 floods in Pakistan, indicate other forms of criminality are associated with these events, including the collapse of public order, enforced climate-induced migration and the prevalence of local gang cultures. Global warming is a powerful driver of natural disasters as climate change fundamentally generates greater propensity toward extreme weather events such as cyclones and heat waves.

Fundamentally, criminology needs to critically examine the consequences of global warming for national security, societal peace and social and ecological well-being. As Agnew (2011: 36) also points out, 'A complete model of climate change and crime will therefore require that criminologists move beyond their traditional focus on single nations', a role to which he feels eco-global criminology is well suited. He also states that 'future research should examine the impact of climate change on particular types of crime and harmful activity in more detail' (Agnew 2011: 27). Developing an integrated and detailed picture of crime and criminality is a major project of green criminology, and climate change is one area deserving highest priority.

Everyone is affected by global warming. As a form of 'universal victimization', climate change means that we all lose out, regardless of class, gender, ethnicity, race, tribe or caste – and regardless of whose fault it is. Superstorm Sandy is NOT a 'once in a generation' phenomenon. It was simply part of the beginning of the predicted consequences flowing from human-caused global warming.

However, climate change also takes the character of 'particular victimization'. For instance, the context of global warming, declining oil resources and food crises puts even more of the world's ecological and economic burdens on the backs of the poor. As Shiva (2008: 5–6) observes:

> First, they are displaced from work; then they bear a disproportionate burden of the costs of climate chaos through extreme droughts, floods, and cyclones; and then they lose once more when pseudo-solutions like industrial biofuels divert their land and their food. Whether it is industrial agriculture or industrial biofuels, car factories or superhighways, displacement and forced evictions of indigenous peoples and peasants from the land are an inevitable consequence of an economic model that creates growth by extinguishing people's rights.

Peasants, indigenous peoples and artisans who live outside the industrialized globalized economy, who have caused no harm to the earth or other people, are among the worst victims of climate change consequences. Over 96 per cent of disaster-related deaths in recent years have taken place in developing countries. In 2001 there were 170 million people affected by disasters around the world, of which 97 per cent were climate-related (Shiva 2008: 3).

These vulnerabilities to victimization are not only due to geographical location as such but also to other inequalities. For example, many countries have coastal areas that are vulnerable to sea-level rise. But the Netherlands has the technological and financial capacity to protect itself to a greater extent than Bangladesh. Thus, not only are poorer countries less responsible for the problem, they are simultaneously least able to adapt to the climate impacts they will suffer, because they lack the resources and capacity to do so. This raises three key questions surrounding matters of justice: the question of responsibility (e.g. the North owes the South an 'ecological debt'); the question of who pays for action on mitigation and adaptation; and the question of who bears the costs of actions and inactions (see Bulkeley and Newell 2010).

Climate change, ecocide and state-corporate crime

The question of justice in relation to climate change inevitably leads one to consider the nature and dynamics of state-corporate crime. This is because the perpetrators and the responders to global warming tend to be one and the same: namely, nation-states and transnational corporations.

State-corporate crime has been defined as 'illegal or socially injurious actions that result from a mutually reinforcing interaction between (1) policies and/or practices in pursuit of the goals of one or more institutions of political governance and (2) policies and/or practices in pursuit of the goals of one or more institutions of economic production and distribution' (Michalowski and Kramer 2006: 15). When it comes to climate change, it has been argued that this provides a classic example of state-corporate crime. Specifically, corporate and state actors in interaction with each other create harms in four ways (Kramer and Michalowski 2012):

1. by denying that global warming is caused by human activity;
2. by blocking efforts to mitigate greenhouse gas emissions;
3. by excluding progressive, ecologically just adaptations to climate change from the political arena; and
4. by responding to the social conflicts that arise from climate change by transforming themselves into fortress societies that exclude the rest of the world.

State-corporate crime relates to both *acts* (e.g. Alberta tar sands) and *omissions* (e.g. failure to regulate carbon emissions, reliance upon dirty energy sources). Failure to act, now, to prevent global warming is criminal. Yet things continue much as they have, the status quo is maintained, and the harms mount up. This is the essence of 'ecocide' (see Chapter 3).

The global status quo is protected under the guise of arguments about the 'national interest' and the importance of 'free trade', which usually reflect specific sectoral business interests. Humanity has certain common interests – universal human interests – such as the survival of the human race in the face of things like global warming and climate change. These common human interests need to take priority over any other kind of interests if humans, as a species, are to survive. Yet this is clearly not happening. In part this is due to resistance and contrarianism perpetrated by powerful lobby groups and particular industries. This is most evident in state support in countries like the United States, Canada and Australia for risky businesses:

- oil and coal industries and other 'dirty' industries;
- coal-seam fracking and other threats to prime agricultural land;
- deep-drill oil exploration and exploitation;
- mega-mines and open-cut mining.

Accompanying support for these industries, there is resistance to global agreements on carbon emissions and use of carbon taxes.

Simultaneously, there is agreement to changes in land use, such as deforestation in favour of cash crops, bio-fuels, mining and intensive pastoral industries. Besides being problematic for those immediately affected by it, like humans and animals living in and off those forests, tropical deforestation is now becoming an international political issue because it is responsible for 20 per cent of global greenhouse emissions (Boekhout van Solinge 2010a). Indonesia and Brazil have now become respectively the third and fourth CO_2 emitting countries of the world, mainly as a result of clearing rainforest. States have given permission and financial backing to those companies engaged in precisely what will radically alter the world's climate the most in the coming years – greenhouse gas emissions

The exploitation of Canada's Alberta tar sands provides another case in point. This massive industrial project involves the active collusion of provincial and federal governments with big oil companies. The project is based upon efforts to extract and refine naturally created tar-bearing sand into exportable and consumable oil. One result of the project is a wide range of different types of harm to the ecosystem, animals and humans. For example, it has been pointed out that the tar sands oil production is the single largest contributor to the increase of global warming pollution in Canada. It will lead to the destruction of vast swathes of boreal forest, it contributes greatly to air pollution, and it is having negative health impacts on aquatic life and animals, and for humans who live nearby (see Smandych and Kueneman 2010; Klare 2012).

For those who study this type of environmental degradation, one that is associated with considerable social and ecological harm, the concept of state-corporate environmental crime is considered entirely appropriate as a descriptor (Smandych and Kueneman 2010). Placed within the larger global context of climate change, the scale and impact of this project also fits neatly with the concept of ecocide (see Chapter 3). The role of the federal and provincial governments is crucial to the project, and to propelling it forward regardless of manifest negative environmental consequences.

The politics of denial (at both the level of ideology and policy) is propped up by various techniques of neutralization (see Sykes and Matza 1957; Cohen 1993, 2001; Lynch, Burns and Stretesky 2010). This refers to the ways in which business and state leaders attempt to prevent action being taken around climate change while actively supporting specific sectoral interests. Typically, such techniques involve the following kinds of denials:

- *Denial of responsibility* (against anthropocentric or human causes as source of problem);
- *Denial of injury* ('natural' disasters are 'normal');
- *Denial of the victim* (failure to acknowledge differential victimization especially amongst poor and Third World);
- *Condemnation of the condemners* (attacks on climate scientists);
- *Appeal to higher loyalties* (American economic interests ought to predominate).

The net result is inaction on addressing the key factors contributing to climate change, such as carbon emissions.

There is a close intersection, therefore, of global warming, government action or inaction and corporate behaviour (Lynch and Stretesky 2010) and how these contribute to the overall problem of climate change. In this instance the state is itself implicated as a perpetrator of harm. Government subsidies for coal-fired power stations and government approval of dams that destroy large swathes of rainforest constitute substantial crimes against nature. In the light of the existing scientific evidence on global warming, continued encouragement of such activities represents intentional harm that is immoral and destructive of collective public interest in the same moment that particular industries and companies benefit.

Given the stakes involved, we might well ask: Should the impending destruction of ecosystems, and the human collateral damage associated with this, be thought of as a form of environmental genocide – ecocide? If so, then it is state leaders and government bureaucrats, as well as corporate heads and key shareholders, who should ultimately be held responsible for this crime.

The political economic relations of global capitalism are crucial in any discussion of environmental harm, in that how, or whether, certain human activity is regulated and facilitated is still primarily a matter of state intervention. The ways in which nation-states (and varying other levels of government) attempt to deal with environmental concerns is contingent upon the class interests associated with political power. In most cases today the power of transnational corporations find purchase in the interface between the interests and preferred activities of the transnational corporation and the specific protections and supports offered by the nation-state. The latter can be reliant upon or intimidated by particular industries and companies. Tax revenue and job creation, as well as media support and political donations, may depend upon particular state-corporate synergies. This of course can undermine the basic tenets of democracy and collective deliberation over how best to interpret the public or national interest.

The structure and allocation of societal resources via the nation-state also has an impact upon how environmental issues are socially constructed. Spending on welfare, health, transportation, education and other forms of social infrastructure makes a big difference in people's lives. Recent fiscal crises (especially noticeable in European countries such as Greece, Ireland and Spain) and the impact of the global economic crisis have had the global impact of making ordinary workers extremely vulnerable economically. Under such conditions, there is even greater scope to either reduce environmental protection, or to increase environmentally destructive activity, to the extent that existing state legislation and company practices are seen to put fetters on the profit-making enterprise. This is so whether the activity is in the metropole countries or in the periphery.

Conclusion

Global warming is rapidly changing the ecological and economic landscape of the planet. Problems of scarcity will exacerbate social conflict in many parts of the world, and crimes of many different types will flourish. From a criminological perspective, several questions warrant close consideration.

With regard to mitigation, the issue is: What can be done to reduce the contributing causes of climate change? The obvious and science-based answer is to diminish greenhouse gas emissions. This could involve the *criminalization* of carbon emissions and the forced shut-down of dirty industries.

With regard to adaptation, the issue is: What can be done to enable communities and species to adapt and survive climate change? One answer here is to ensure that harm is explicitly acknowledged in public policy. This could involve recognition of *victimization* and some type of compensation and reparation.

More generally, actions for change on climate-change issues will require that concepts such as human rights, ecological citizenship and the global commons be developed in ways that assert the primacy of 'climate justice' over narrow sectional interests. For this to occur there is a need for strong action within civil society to progress a more radical social change agenda. As part of this, criminologists (among others) must insist upon the protection of democratic spaces within which popular struggles can occur, given the powerful social interests opposed to needed climate change solutions.

Finally, the role of criminology itself will come into question around these issues. In conventional terms, it could well be simply the handmaiden of a repressive state, if criminology uncritically accepts a 'National Security' agenda. This would translate into defence of dirty industries, resource protection internally and externally, and collusion of criminologists against climate-change activists (perhaps under the rubric of fighting against 'eco-terrorism').

Alternatively, a progressive and green criminology will be defined in terms of its role as defender of social and ecological justice. The task is to conduct research that explores different types of environmental harms and crimes, the modus operandi of the key perpetrators and the consequences of such transgressions, including their contribution to global warming and climate change. It could also be to draft instruments such as an Environmental Victims Charter that speaks of repairing the harm and ensuring compensation for human and non-human victims of climate change.

Discussion topics

- What is the difference between climate change and global warming?
- Climate change is a matter of science not belief. Discuss.
- What are some of the ways in which climate change is altering social and ecological landscapes around the world?
- The consequences of climate change are not socially neutral. Discuss.

- How are different governments around the world responding to the threat and impacts of climate change?

Further reading

Brisman, A. (2012). 'The Cultural Silence of Climate Change Contrarianism', in R. White (ed.), *Climate Change from a Criminological Perspective*. New York: Springer.

Farrall, S., Ahmed, T., and French, D. (eds) (2012). *Criminological and Legal Consequences of Climate Change*. Oxford: Hart Publishing.

Haines, F., and Reichman, N. (2008). 'The Problem that is Global Warming: An introduction', *Law & Policy*, 30(4): 385–93.

Kramer, R., and Michalowski, R. (2012). 'Is Global Warming a State-Corporate Crime?', in R. White (ed), *Climate Change from a Criminological Perspective*. New York: Springer.

Smith, D., and Vivekananda, J. (2007). *A Climate of Conflict: The links between climate change, peace and war*. London: International Alert.

Chapter 7

Abuse and harm to animals

Introduction

This chapter will discuss the following topics:

- animals and criminology;
- the human categorization of animals;
- animal abuse and cruelty;
- wildlife crime and the illegal trade in wildlife; and
- animal rights and animal protection.

An important strand of green criminology is that which focuses primarily on non-human animals. This chapter explores the criminological research and scholarship in this area, and the types of crimes and harms associated with animals. As with other areas of green criminology, there are complexities and ambiguities that permeate knowledge and action around animal-rights and welfare issues.

Animals and criminology

Within criminology, there are two main strands of concerted research on animals. The first strand deals with matters of illegal trade, and issues such as illegal fishing, abalone poaching, the trade in endangered species, elephant poaching and threats to the tiger population (see, for example, White 2008a, 2009a; Beirne and South 2007; Lemieux and Clark 2009; Pires and Moreto 2011; Pires 2012; Wyatt 2012, 2013). The second strand makes the link between animal abuse and interpersonal violence, including the co-occurrence of child abuse, family violence and cruelty to animals (see for example, Beirne 2009, 2011; Ascione 2010; Flynn 2011; Hackett and Uprichard 2007). This literature argues that what individuals do to animals is also reflected in what they do to each other. Within mainstream criminology, the so-called 'progressive thesis', for example, inquires into how young people who abuse animals progress to other types of criminal acts, including harm against humans (Dadds, Turner and McAloon 2002; Ascione 2001, 2010). Animal cruelty is linked to anti-social behaviour generally, the hypothesis being that one feeds the other. Issues pertaining to both these strands are discussed in more depth below.

Other research has argued that systematic abuse of animals via factory farms ought to be considered at the same time as specific instances of harm to particular animals (Cazaux 1999; Beirne 2004). Indeed, recent criminological commentary on the social impact of working in abattoirs suggests that those whose job it is to kill animals are probably disproportionately more likely to be less empathetic towards their fellow humans (see Beirne 2004; MacNair 2002). In other words, where cruelty is in a sense built into a job (such as working in a slaughterhouse), the ramifications are that the job itself desensitizes and perverts the ordinary sensibilities of workers and takes them psychologically and socially in an unhealthy and negative direction (see Fitzgerald, Kalof and Dietz 2009).

More broadly, writers have also identified a series of potential topics that deserve further attention, such as the prosecution and execution of animals, and bestiality as a form of sexual assault (Beirne 2011). These kinds of inquiry suggest that further work is needed in relation to the idea of animals as victims of crime in their own right. They also examine instances in which individual animals are periodically prosecuted as 'offenders'. At a group (or species) level, the latter is also reflected in the phenomenon of banned dogs. In this instance dog attacks and dog bites, particularly in relation to children in the 1–4 age group, are considered major potential risks in relation to companion animals (Gullone and Clarke 2010), and high profile cases in Australia and the UK in recent years have seen legislative efforts to ban certain dog breeds altogether (see Hallsworth 2011). In the media the 'blame' has been put squarely on the backs of the 'beasts', although poor human handling has also been cited. Nonetheless, the implication is that there are innately 'bad' kinds of dog that require extra special care and control. Inevitably this is accompanied by regular calls to destroy 'dangerous' breeds and to limit traffic of such animals worldwide. Interestingly, the branding of some dogs as 'bad' has, in turn, generated interest among street gang members, criminal groups and groups of friends to own precisely such breeds of dog (Hallsworth 2011; Maher and Pierpoint 2011). Dog and dog-owner thus can share and reinforce the same 'bad pedigree' through their close association. For some people, the point is to enhance social status by having a 'status' dog; but companionship and for socializing in the group can be important reasons too (Maher and Pierpoint 2011).

Another area of criminological interest relates to how the police and courts are responding to the activities of animal-rights activists. In recent years the language of counter-terrorism has been liberally used in relation to animal-rights activists by those wishing to discredit animal-rights movements. In some places the language of 'terrorism' has been translated into anti-terrorism laws and the setting up of specialist units within police services with the express purpose of monitoring and intervention in relation to activist groups (Corporate Watch 2009; Yates 2011). Counter-movements to animal rights, comprised of industry front groups and those with a vested interest in certain types of animal exploitation, have been accused of fostering negative and distorted images of animal protectionism (Regan 2004). As part of this, these counter-movements have 'profitably tuned into the current "war on terrorism" and seem to have been fairly successful in framing any concern for non-human animals beyond the confines of conventional animal welfarism as illegitimate, beyond the pale, unnecessary, and terroristic in nature' (Yates 2007: 154). The criminalization of certain types and styles of protest, many of which were formerly seen as peaceful and entirely conventional, under the rubric of counter-terrorism is seen to have major implications for the nature and dynamics of animal advocacy (see Yates 2011).

The use of animals positively within the criminal justice system has also attracted criminological attention. The topics have ranged from the use of animals such as dogs in police enforcement tactics, to the use of animals in prisoner rehabilitation schemes (see Cazaux 1999; Beirne 2011; White and Graham 2010). From a prevention perspective, benefit has been achieved from the use of animal-assisted therapy when working with at-risk youth, while 'dogs in prison' programmes have benefited participating inmates as well as community groups sponsoring the training of guide dogs. Animals have thus been perceived and used as agents of healing in regard to particular offenders, young and old.

The human categorization of animals

The ontological standing of non-human animals is largely a status conferred by humans. Unsurprisingly, such conferred status is generally based upon a calculus of human needs and wants, combined with statistical data on the prevalence or number of non-human animals. The calculus changes over time and varies according to social and cultural context. Nonetheless, it establishes the ground rules which guide how specific animals and specific species are valued and acknowledged by particular societies of humans at any point in time.

Attempts to categorize animals according to environment and/or human service are difficult to do well, due to the complexities involved. Different criteria inevitably provide different ways in which to categorize different types of species (see O'Sullivan 2009; Herbig and Joubert 2006). While not unproblematic, Box 7.1 provides an attempt to distinguish animals according to two main criteria (wildlife/domesticated), and within each of these categories according to how the animal is perceived relative to human needs (service to/service for). These are inherently anthropomorphic categorizations, in the sense that the ways in which animals are classified reflect human interventions over time, and human notions of usefulness. Yet, regardless of their human-centred origins and character, such descriptions are essential in assessing matters of animal rights and animal welfare as these are presently constituted in law and social practices.

Box 7.1 Animal categories

Wildlife

Introduced wild

- invasive/pests (e.g. cane toad in Australia);
- valued (e.g. trout in Tasmania);
- ambiguous (e.g. camels and wild donkeys in central Australia).

Native species with a value of their own

- avian (e.g. kookaburras, cockatoos);
- marine (e.g. whales, sharks);
- aquatic (e.g. Murray river cod, marron);
- terrestrial (e.g. koala, kangaroo).

Economic wild animals

- recreation (e.g. fish);
- food (e.g. mutton birds);
- eco-tourism (e.g. birdlife, crocodiles);
- collectables (e.g. lizards, exotic fish).

Wild animals as threat/pest

- to agriculture (e.g. kangaroos);
- to pastoral industry (e.g. dingos);
- to surfing/recreation (e.g. sharks);
- to angling (e.g. galaxia fish).

Domestic animals

Economic animals (humans doing something to them)

- farm animals (e.g. pigs, cows, chickens);
- aquaculture animals (e.g. fish, prawns, oysters);
- research animals (e.g. rats, mice);
- exhibited animals (e.g. lions, tigers, bears).

Economic animals (doing something for humans)

- law enforcement (e.g. dogs);
- industrial/transportation animals (e.g. oxen, horses);

- recreation/racing/rodeos (e.g. horses, dogs);
- performing animals/circuses (e.g. lions, monkeys).

Non-economic animals (other human purposes)
- companion animals (e.g. cats, dogs, exotic fish, rabbits);
- hunting/sport companions (e.g. horses, dogs).

Service animals
- disability assistance dogs;
- guide dogs for the blind.

Source: drawing from and adding to White 2011a

Domestic animals are a separate category to those considered wild. This categorization is based upon historical relationships between certain species and humans, which, over time have transformed the basic nature of the animals in question. 'Domestication is an evolutionary process that results in animals such as our companion dogs and cats undergoing substantial behavioural, anatomical, physiological, and genetic changes during the process' (Bekoff 2010: xxxi). Any movement to introduce wild animals into a domestic environment (such as adopting chimpanzees as household pets) or domesticated animals into the wild (for example, release of cats) inevitably carries with it certain risks and problems, from unexpected episodes of violence against humans through to the creation of feral predators that threaten endemic species of birds and other animals.

Animals are valued by humans in a highly stratified way. Put simply, we like some, we hate some, and some we don't really care or think about. Beirne (2009), for example, outlines the many different legal definitions given to the term 'animal' across different jurisdictions in the United States. What is defined, and what is valued, when it comes to animals is highly variable and subject to ongoing contestation at the level of philosophy as well as at the level of legislative practice (see Benton 1998, 2007; Beirne 2009; Sankoff and White 2009). This has important consequences for criminal justice and other types of human intervention.

For example, the idea of 'pest' reduces the life, energy, activity and well-being of creatures to that of threat, worthlessness and nuisance relative to human objectives. It tends to portray targeted species in ways that foster eradication and fear of species, rather than understanding or appreciation of broader ecological and zoological processes and imperatives. Similarly the use of 'invasive species' is highly charged, as it relies upon emotive language to again convey the sense of unwanted intrusion. The language of this threat reinforces human categorizations of species that present them as somehow inherently evil, rather than as *bona fide* sentient creatures in their own right. This, in turn, can lead to diminishment of 'normal' standards of treatment in the rush to get rid of them. It can thus lead to and/or reinforce the inhumane treatment of animals.

Many millions of animals, particularly rats, mice, birds and guinea pigs, are used for scientific research. But the biggest category of animals, numerically, is that of animals used by humans for food. Animal suffering is ingrained in the mass production of animals for food and is evident in poor living conditions, terrible transportation situations (as seen in the live export trade), cruel slaughterhouse techniques and conditions, and overall disregard and disrespect of so called food animals.

The lack of intrinsic value of farmed food animals is indicated as well in the fact that, for instance, some six million farmed animals, mostly chickens, lost their lives in Hurricane Katrina's path. While the media latched on to hearttugging stories about companion animals and struggling children, the plight of the less-valued creatures was largely ignored.

> It was difficult to get the attention of state agricultural authorities or corporate managers for the chickens' plight. The birds' value to the industry is very low, and our society in general doesn't value them much higher. In any case, the chickens in the hurricane zone were property and, like some of the homes and possessions lost to Katrina, they were insured. This meant the corporate owners could collect on their damaged or destroyed 'goods'.
>
> (Baur 2008: 169)

Contrast that story with the following:

> In September 2005, people watching news reports on the progress of the evacuation of New Orleans were horrified to see images of a small white dog scratching at the side of a bus. The dog had just been dragged from the arms of the boy who had been holding him so the boy could be placed on the bus to leave the city. The boy reportedly screamed, 'Snowball! Snowball!' before he became so distraught he vomited. The police officer who pulled the dog from the boy's arms was reported to have said that he 'didn't know what would happen to the dog'.
>
> (Baum 2011: 105)

In the aftermath of Katrina, little was publicly discussed about the fate of food animals such as chickens. On the other hand, the US Congress enacted the Pets Evacuation and Transportation Act of 2006 (PETS Act) in symbolic recognition of the value and status of companion animals and service animals (such as guide dogs). This provides for the evacuation and transportation of such animals, albeit only when human life would not be endangered as a consequence (Baum 2011).

The status of animals is not only reflected in how they are labelled and treated in domestic circumstances pertaining to human needs and wants. Status is also conferred on the basis of prevalence or number of animals. For example, the notions of endangered and threatened species essentially speak to the survival status of particular species. Some are extinct (as with the thylacine, the dodo and the passenger pigeon), while others hover on the brink of extinction (orangutan, polar bear). Human intervention in the form of zoos or conservationist policies reflect varying conceptions of animal rights and welfare, including differing perspectives on which animals ought to be saved, the urgency of the action needed and which species are prioritized over others when it comes to activist campaigns. Saving the tiger is publicly popular, for example; stopping the killing of sharks less so.

Ironically, it is the laws that humans design to protect certain species that may, in effect, put them most at jeopardy. For example, measures put in place to prevent the illegal trade in endangered species can make that species even more attractive to criminal syndicates or private collectors, since it confirms their scarcity (and thus increases the commercial and collectible 'value') of the species in question. The damage that is manifest in phenomena such as over-fishing and destruction of habitat (both of which may be legally undertaken) also affects the subsequent market prices for the commodity in question. Scarcity is a major motivator for illegal as well as legal forays into particular kinds of harvesting and production activity. The losers are animals and their environments.

Animal-rights supporters argue that there are two kinds of animals – human and non-human – and that both have rights and interests as sentient beings; they believe, however, that the dominant ideology of speciesism enables humans to exploit non-human animals as commodities to be eaten, displayed, hunted and dissected for human benefit. *Speciesism* was first coined in the 1970s as part of animal-rights and animal-liberation campaign work in the UK. It refers to the discrimination against or exploitation of certain animal species by humans, based upon an assumption of human superiority (Ryder 2010). The concept has been equated with racism and sexism, insofar as these likewise refer to forms of arbitrary discrimination. However, debate continues regarding the precise relationship – and differences – between humans and animals, and under what conditions, if any, it is right to privilege human interests over that of animals. For some, there is no dividing line; for others, ultimately it is the health and welfare of specific humans that ought to take precedence over that of specific non-human animals.

It has been observed that non-human animals are frequently considered in primarily instrumental terms (as 'pets', as food, as resources) in mainstream and conservation criminology, and are categorized in mainly anthropomorphic terms (such as 'wildlife', 'fisheries') that belie the ways in which humans create and classify animals as Other (Beirne 2007, 2009).

Animal abuse and cruelty

The focus of the welfarist approach to animals is the humane treatment of animals (Ibrahim 2006). This model advocates the protection of animals through increased welfare-based interventions, but not the prohibition of animal exploitation. The model is focused on improvements to the treatment of animals but does not challenge the embedded exploitation of animals that is a consequence of their social and legal status (Ibrahim 2006). Implicit in this is that animals may still be exploited for their flesh, fur and skin, provided their suffering is not 'unnecessary' or (as it is often put) the animals are treated humanely.

At the other end of the spectrum is the rights-based approach. At the extreme end this approach contends that animals have rights to live free from human interference. This approach argues for the abolition of animal exploitation through both legal and non-legal change and for the legal recognition of rights for animals. Central to this approach is changing the legal character of animals from property to legal, rights-bearing entities (see Wise 2001, 2004; Francione 2010).

Animal cruelty is variously defined depending upon the jurisdiction. It can also vary depending upon the 'use' context within which the animal is located, as certain types of cruel activity may be accepted in some situations (e.g. killing of farmed animals for food). In many cases animal cruelty is described through a list of acts of omission or commission rather than through a specific legal definition of cruelty. In the state of South Australia, for example, cruelty is defined in these terms (Gullone and Clarke 2010: 306):

- deliberately or unreasonably causes the animal unnecessary pain;
- fails to provide it appropriate and adequate, food, water, shelter or exercise;
- fails to take reasonable steps to alleviate any pain suffered by the animal;
- abandons the animal;
- neglects the animal so as to cause it pain;
- releases the animal from captivity for the purpose of it then being hunted or killed by another animal;
- organizes, participates in, or is present at an event at which the animal is encouraged to fight with another animal;
- having injured the animal, fails to take reasonable steps to alleviate any pain suffered by the animal;
- kills the animal in a manner that causes the animal unnecessary pain;
- unless the animal is unconscious, kills the animal by a method that does not cause death to occur as rapidly as possible.

Animal welfare laws aim to provide legal protection for animals in two ways. General animal welfare laws – those relating to animal cruelty for example – provide broad prohibitions against animal abuse and require the humane treatment of animals. Specific animal welfare laws may also be in place that require the protection of animal interests in specific 'use' contexts, such as the use of animals in experiments or the slaughter of animals for food (Francione 2010).

A key part of animal welfare is the prevention of animal suffering. Animals are not simply construed as property (with which the owner can do as they wish), but are deemed to be sentient creatures that, as such, demand a certain 'duty of care' on the part of humans. Human use thus should not reduce the status of animal to solely that of commodity. Rather, there are obligations that flow from a conception of animals that view them as having feelings that matter (Webster 2010). Put simply, the aim should be to give animals under human protection a sense of well-being in life and a humane death, as part of positive welfare.

Animal welfare can be conceptualized as having three distinctive dimensions (see Fraser 2010):

- the affective state of animals: how animals feel, as reflected in their experiences of comfort and being free from prolonged or intense pain or hunger;
- the biological condition of animals: how animals function, as reflected in their growth and reproduction, and being reasonably free from disease and malnutrition;
- the nature of animals: how animals live, as reflected in natural environments that provide for fresh air, sunshine and natural vegetation, and that allow them to express their natural behaviour.

While often agreeing in practice, the distinctions do represent views of welfare that may not necessarily coincide.

> A pig farmer using criteria based on biological functioning might conclude that the welfare of a group of confined sows is high because the animals are well-fed, reproducing efficiently, and free from disease and injury. Critics using other criteria might conclude that the welfare of the same animals is poor because they are unable to lead natural lives, or because they show signs of frustration and discomfort.
>
> (Fraser 2010: 48)

Arguments about animal welfare often hinge upon these distinctions. Debate thus occurs within the welfare sector, as well as between welfare and rights campaigners. This debate is also reflected in attempts to reform animal welfare legislation, particularly in regards to mass farmed animals.

Phenomena such as arranging dog fights for entertainment and betting sport have in recent years drawn much public condemnation in places such as the United States. The rise of both anti-cruelty movements (such as the Royal Society for the Prevention of Cruelty to Animals) and animal-rights movements (such as People for the Ethical Treatment of Animals) has been instrumental in raising awareness of animal-abuse issues, and promoting alternative ways of thinking about such abuse. For green criminology, there are a series of key questions that are particularly pertinent to consider when it comes to animal abuse and cruelty. These are set out in Box 7.2.

Regulations and laws pertaining to animals tend to approach the issues from the point of view of protecting the integrity of specific animals from abuse (i.e., individual animal welfare), protecting the integrity of markets involving animal products (e.g. by fixing access and limits to fish catches), protecting human health and well-being from inappropriate animal products (e.g. slaughterhouse production rules), and protecting endangered species (i.e., collective existence of certain animals).

Box 7.2 Key issues relating to animal abuse

- *Who harms which animals and why?* Different sorts of actors engage in illegally harming animals. Likewise there is variation in the actors engaged in, and motivations behind, different types of species theft, transportation and exchange.
- *Who is criminalized in relation to animal abuse, and in what ways?* This question also pertains to the criminalization of animal activists, and the diverse ways in which different countries penalize those who fight on behalf of abused animals (e.g. charges of eco-terrorism through to mainstreaming of 'hidden camera' exposures in the mass media).
- *What are the key debates within the animal abuse domain?* The tension between 'rights' and 'welfare' approaches fundamentally shapes how people respond to specific issues, such as for example how to deal with feral animals and so called 'dangerous dogs'.
- *What are the public debates emerging in relation to animal abuse and other simultaneous environmental and ecological issues?* Here there are important considerations to be given to tensions arising over species protection (which animal is to be protected over and against other animals) and also animal rights versus environmental protection (e.g. the growing size of the kangaroo population relative to the carrying capacity of the local eco-system).
- *What is to be done about animal abuse?* This incorporates discussion of how criminal justice systems respond to specific crimes and by whom (e.g. RSPCA versus other protection agencies and the police), through to the use of animals (instrumentally) within the criminal justice system to 'humanize' offenders and juvenile offenders by teaching them empathy and an ethic of care.

Considerable research has recently been carried out on the social processes associated with offending and the characteristics of offenders in regards to specific types of animal-related crimes. For instance, in a landmark study that explores why people harm and kill animals, Nurse (2011, 2013a and b) has developed a new typology of offender motivations. The classification of offenders is based upon systematic research undertaken in the United Kingdom (and the United States) that examined offender justifications for what they do. Nurse (2013a) identified five discrete, although not mutually exclusive, categories of offenders:

- *Traditional criminals* – personal benefit from crimes (e.g. wildlife trafficking);
- *Economic criminals* – employment-related crime (e.g. killing protected birds to ensure safety of local game and habitats);
- *Masculinities criminals* – exercise of stereotypical masculine nature (e.g. linked to sport and gambling);
- *Hobby criminals* – collection and acquisition (e.g. egg collectors);
- *Stress offenders* – involved in animal harm as a result of their own stress or abuse (e.g. children who suffer abuse).

The importance of this typology is not only that it provides more detailed knowledge about offenders. Nurse (2013a) also observes that understanding different motivations has major implications for how we might respond to these kinds of animal harms. Specifically, he argues that calls for harsher penalties for animal cruelty, often spearheaded by NGOs such as the RSPCA, are too simplistic and generally ineffective if and when translated into policy and practice. This is because such demands generally fail to account for the lack of success of the traditional criminal justice system already in dealing with serious crime (much less animal harms). Moreover, they miss the point that a 'one-size-fits-all' response is neither appropriate nor effective in the face of diverse motivations for and circumstances of animal harm crimes (see Chapter 15).

An emerging area of research deals with animal abuse directly, as a core topic. The concern is with both systematic uses of animals, such as factory farming, and one-on-one abuses of animals (Beirne 2009; Sollund 2008). However, what counts as animal 'abuse' varies enormously within and between cultures and societies. Is locking up chickens in small coops a form of abuse? What counts as 'animal' abuse likewise varies depending upon the type and status of the animal one is referring to. Is fishing a form of abuse? There are many questions that can be asked regarding which animals 'deserve' protection and freedom from abuse, and how abuse itself is to be defined in legal and social terms (see for example, Sunstein and Nussbaum 2006). To answer these questions, we need to appreciate why it is that human societies simultaneously respect and protect certain creatures (especially animal companions such as dogs and cats) while allowing, and even condoning, the utterly dreadful treatment of others (as in the case of factory farming of battery hens to produce eggs) (see Beirne 2004).

Legislation can cover a broad range of acts, such as protection from cruelty, from abandonment and from poisoning, and ensuring that animals are provided with necessary sustenance and shelter. There are nevertheless major ambiguities in terms of how laws are framed, and how they are translated into practice. For instance, the use of animals in laboratory testing may involve systematic mutilation; yet, this type of action is legally allowed as long as the animals are provided 'humane care and treatment' generally (see Beirne 2009; Sankoff and White 2009).

In addressing the issue of animal abuse, Beirne (2009) argues that if the violation of animals' rights is to be taken seriously, then we need to examine why some harms to animals are defined as criminal, others as abusive but not criminal, and still others as neither criminal nor abusive. In pointing this out, Beirne (2009) emphasizes that exploring these questions necessarily leads to a more inclusive concept of harm. It also means that much more empirical work needs to be done to examine how laws are actually put into practice, where specific human interests fit into the picture, and how the social control of animal abuse ought to be carried out at an institutional level. That basic argument is that animals should count.

> The animal protection cause simply asks that animals not be treated like things but respected as creatures with inherent rights. It also maintains that we have an ethical responsibility not to abuse them. Asserting the rights of animals to be protected from human cruelty is just the affirmative version of the timeless principle that it is wrong to treat them cruelly.
> (Baur 2008: 190)

How animals currently count and how they should count, though, is part of the conundrum raised by Beirne (2009). It is also part and parcel of wider debates within the animal-rights and welfare literature on how best to conceptualize the relationship between humans and non-human animals generally (see White 2013c).

Wildlife crime and illegal trade in wildlife

Wildlife crime, on the other hand, cannot be reduced to matters of cruelty and animal rights. As Nurse (2013a: 35–6) observes, wildlife crime 'does not always involve cruelty and can involve humane methods of trapping and utilizing wildlife, which, while being harmful to animals in one sense (the 'harm' of being forcibly removed from the wild, sometimes in a manner that causes temporary injury, and then being reduced into captivity), would not constitute cruelty by most legal definitions'. Nonetheless, from a species justice perspective, the taking of animals from their habitats is intrinsically problematic.

Wildlife crime is broader than simply illegal trade in wildlife (although much contemporary green criminology does in fact concentrate on that). It can include, for example, a wide range of types of criminal activity, from unlawful gambling through to illegal poisoning. In broader terms, wildlife offences generally tend to fall into the following categories (Nurse 2013a: 52):

- killing, taking or possession of a wild bird;
- killing, taking or possessing a wild animal or mammal;
- trade in wildlife (alive or dead);
- trade in endangered species;
- taking or possession of wild birds' eggs.

Notably, what defines the crime is the legislation that defines it. Shooting ducks in a legal duck hunt, for instance, is not a criminal offence, even though harm is being done to the animal.

The scale and the international nature of the problem of illegal trade in wildlife is indicated in Box 7.3. This illustrates the extent of the trafficking, the harmful consequences of such activity and the lucrative nature of the illegal wildlife market.

Box 7.3 Wildlife poaching and theft

- Trafficking in birds and other animals (alive or dead) constitutes one of the world's largest illegal trades, with an estimated value of 18 to 26 billion euros per year (Zimmerman 2003; Warchol, Zupan and Clarke 2003; Ayling 2013; Europol 2011).
- Birds and other animals are traded for medicine, gourmet foods, clothing, ornamentation, exotic pets, sport and trophies (CEC 2005; Lemieux and Clarke 2009; Herbig 2010; Sollund 2008, 2011).
- The number of rhinoceros poached in South Africa has increased every year from 2007 until 2012, with the total in 2012 almost a 50 per cent increase on the 2011 figure; given the current rates of decline the probable date for total extinction of wild rhinos in Africa is estimated to be 2025 (Ayling 2013).
- Many of the species involved in the international illegal trade are endangered, both by the trade itself and by other threats to their habitat (Boekhout van Solinge 2008b, 2010a and b).
- The biggest forum for the illegal trade in animals is the internet, with the United States the biggest marketplace, followed by the United Kingdom and China (International Fund for Animal Welfare 2009).

Specific countries and specific regions will be characterized by different types of wildlife crime. For example, in Australia the commonly smuggled species include reptiles, birds, insects and spiders, as well as sugar gliders. Of cases prosecuted, reptiles (such as snakes and lizards) were targeted most, followed by birds (such as parrots) (Alacs and Georges 2008). Regular illegal imports into Australia include avian and reptilian species, as well as exotic fish (for the aquarium trade) and body parts from endangered species (for traditional Chinese or complementary medicines) (Bricknell 2010). Species taken in southern Africa, India, Russia and Indonesia will vary according to local conditions and animal prevalence. Similarly, the parrot trade is highly linked to South American locations such as Bolivia, Colombia and Peru, while wildlife poaching in the United States and Canada includes deer, moose, bears, turkeys and lobsters.

An animal-welfare approach is probably the perspective most reflected in criminological work surrounding animals, although green criminologists concerned with speciesism have asserted the animal-rights perspective as well. Closely associated with animal welfarism is the notion of protection of endangered species, and efforts to maintain the sustainability of animals in certain industries. For example, the poaching of abalone or lobster is prohibited insofar as it impinges upon the property rights of licensed fishers and taxation powers of the state, while simultaneously depleting species numbers (Tailby and Gant 2002; McMullan and Perrier 2002). Legislation that prohibits the illegal trade of wildlife, particularly endangered wildlife, is meant to protect species from criminal exploitation, although why and how species become endangered is less frequently addressed (e.g. degradation of habitats generally and destruction of local ecology through, for instance, clear-fell forestry). Intervention is mainly pitched at the species level, with efforts being put into conserving and maintaining viable numbers of particular species.

In recent years much of the criminological scholarship in regard to animals has been motivated by an interest in conventional environmental crimes, such as illegal fishing, rather than species justice as such. For instance, work over the past decade has been carried out in respect to the illegal theft and trade in reptiles in South Africa (Herbig 2010), fishing-related crimes, including the poaching of abalone and of lobster (Tailby and Gant 2002; McMullan and Perrier 2002), and the illegal wildlife market in Africa (Warchol, Zupan and Clarke 2003), in particular the trade in elephant ivory (Lemieux and Clarke 2009). For much of this burgeoning literature the key or central category of analysis is that of legality rather than harm. This is reflected in the principle legal instruments that guide much work in this area.

For example, the *Convention on International Trade in Endangered Species of Wild Fauna and Flora (CITES)* aims to ensure that international trade in specimens of wild animals and plants does not threaten their survival. CITES works by subjecting international trade in specimens of listed species to certain controls, based upon where the roughly 5,000 species of animals and 28,000 species of plants are situated in the three Appendices to the Convention that reflect the extent of the threat to it, and the controls that apply to the trade. From an animal-rights perspective, CITES merely legitimates anthropocentric interests. This is because the intent of CITES is to regulate the trade in species, not to prevent the trade itself. Moreover, the mechanisms of the Convention – the Appendices that assign survival and scarcity values – create and help to sustain the illegal market for endangered and threatened species. Illegality raises prices, so banning the trade in certain animals creates a lucrative black market for such expensive 'commodities'. Yet, regulating such trade perpetuates the instrumental use of animals for human consumption (metaphorically as well as literally).

Beirne (2009) observes that rarely have animals been understood in criminology other than in terms of their legal status as the property of human masters. That is, laws against poaching – of deer, pheasants, rabbits and partridges – in England were designed not to protect animals, but the rights of the rich and powerful to do with these creatures as they willed at their exclusive command. The point was to protect one's property, not to protect the animal as such.

Much the same logic applies to law pertaining to animals and primary industry. The illegal trade in wildlife involves not only the threat to endangered species directly but, also that to the economic viability of industries such as agriculture, forestry and fisheries.

> Illegal exports of wildlife and wildlife products from Australia pose a threat to the protection of endangered species. Illegal imports are accompanied by the potential for the introduction of pests and diseases which could have a dramatic impact on agriculture, conservation of the environment, and specialist industries, such as aviculture.
> (Halstead 1992: 1)

Thus, the smuggling of wildlife across national borders has the potential to threaten the viability of endangered species, whether flora or fauna, as well as to provide a potential vehicle for the introduction of pests and diseases into formerly unaffected areas (Herbig 2010; Ferrier 2010; Rosen and Smith 2010).

Law and criminology have not only been oriented toward illegal animal trade issues and matters of protecting property. Historically, as well, laws have been enacted to forbid cruel and improper treatment of certain animals, although criminologists have seldom considered animal suffering as the explicit focus of study. Moreover, in practice, law enforcement has been at best haphazard, and the 'crime' has not rated highly in public consciousness or as a serious concern.

Similar observations and conclusions are evident in recent studies of poaching (see McMullan and Perrier 2002; Forsyth, Gramling and Wooddell 1998; Bell, Hampshire and Topalidou 2007; Zhang, Hua and Sun 2008; Green 2011; Pires and Clarke 2011; Kahler and Gore 2012). These studies establish that people are engaged in poaching for a variety of reasons, and these reasons are partly related to immediate social context (e.g. exotic consumer products for the new middle classes in China; traditional hunting practices in Greece; community and commercial collusion in the taking of lobster in the Canadian Maritime provinces; income supplementation in Bolivia). In some instances, poaching is perceived as a sort of 'folk crime' – something that everyone knows about and that everyone allows to happen, since it is not perceived to be 'really' wrong in most respects (unless certain informal protocols and boundaries are violated, such as being seen to be 'greedy', too 'commercially-oriented' or 'not leaving enough for other people'). Poaching therefore exists with considerable community support in some locales and under some conditions.

What criminological research demonstrates is that, like the abuse of animals (as discussed earlier), there is a variety of motivations and offenders who engage in poaching and the illegal animal trade. Consider for a moment the specific example of abalone poaching. Australian research on this has demonstrated that different actors are involved, using different methods, with diverse outcomes for the illegally taken abalone. This is shown in Figure 7.1.

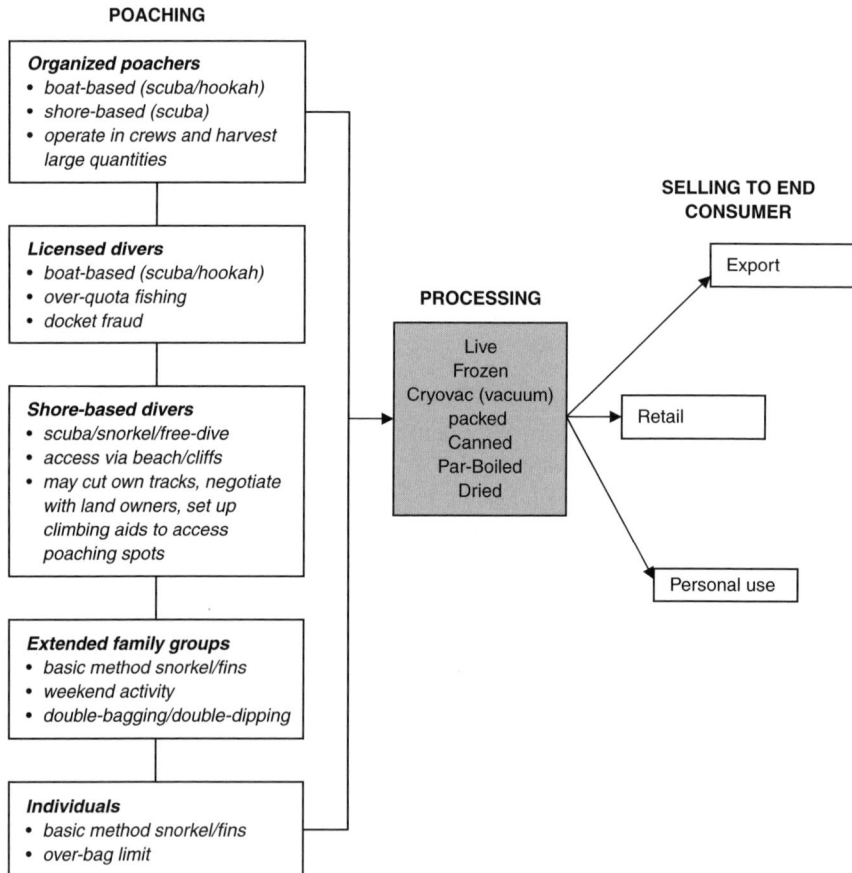

Figure 7.1 Methods used in each stage of the illegal abalone market. Source: Adapted from Tailby and Gant 2002.

Poaching is frequently embedded within local communities in ways that belie the possibility of imposing harsher sanctions without considerable resistance and pushback from local people (see Forsyth *et al.* 1998; Kahler and Gore 2012; White 2013b). The 'attractions' of poaching need to be counter-balanced in some way, and this will usually involve adoption of social, cultural, educational and economic measures that make sense to the local people themselves. This is particularly important given the wide range of actors and motivations to engage in poaching.

Animal rights and animal protection

The question of how best to protect the rights, needs and futures of animals is subject to considerable debate. It all depends on the starting premises from which one proceeds. For example, extensive work has been undertaken on how best to prevent the illegal trade in wildlife. This literature is growing rapidly, so much so that we deal with these issues separately again in the chapter on crime prevention (Chapter 15).

Most of this literature, however, is based entirely upon legal notions of harm and criminality. The underlying concern is with illegality, rather than the health and well-being of individual animals as such. The threat to elephants and rhinoceros from poachers, and illicit trade in parrots and reptiles, are problematic because they involve the breaking of laws. The laws themselves are based upon overarching judgements regarding the *number* of creatures living in the wild. When numbers are perceived to be low, then animal protection laws and international agreements such as the Convention on International Trade in Endangered Species of Wild Fauna and Flora (CITES) are put into play.

The logic behind this is not simply to protect endangered species because they are endangered; it is to manage these 'natural resources' for human use in the most equitable and least damaging manner. CITES does not prevent trade in species, it regulates it. Similar arguments can be made in regard to illegal fishing. It is not fishing itself which is viewed as the problem but over-fishing. The answer is natural resource management – that includes sanctions against trading or poaching particular species, use of enclosures and restricted access to other species, and breeding and assisted-migration schemes for others. Few of these measures stem from a concern with species justice per se. Rather they reflect human-centred or anthropocentric views of animals that value them through the lens of instrumental use.

Such views are not only restrictive when it comes to the narrow parameters within which to view animal interests (and needs and rights) in relation to illegal trade. They also have implications for how animal abuse and cruelty is framed. Protecting animals occurs within very particular social contexts. This is encapsulated in the following observation.

> Individual instances of animal abuse mostly refer to animals considered as individuals (companion animals, pets) with a visible and acknowledged personality and biography. On the other hand, the subjectivity of the millions of animals being exploited in animal husbandry, laboratories and other large-scale processes of animal abuse, is invisible and is concealed behind the anonymous production quotas and mortality rates.
>
> (Cazaux 1999: 120–1)

However, the emphasis on the individual within institutionalized animal-welfare regimes is turned on its head when considering animal protection, as this pertains to species as a whole. For the latter it is the population that matters, not the individual.

As has been observed by some writers (Cazaux 1999), consideration of human practices that are detrimental to the well-being of animals, such as loss and fragmentation of habitat, tend to focus on the effects regarding *animal populations* of a certain species (matters pertaining to the threat of extinction). Less attention is paid to the consequences of broad trends to the well-being of animals as *individual subjects*. The logic of species protection, over and above respect for the individual animal, means that in some instances animals are killed for no apparent reason or justification. In Norway, for example, efforts to protect the endangered species of polar fox, has nonetheless been accompanied by the killing of individual creatures which were guilty of the 'crime' of not fitting into the existing breeding programme (see Sollund 2012b). Their deaths served no apparent purpose, but their value (or lack thereof) was reflected in the actions taken to put them down. Respect and acknowledgement of the right of these individual creatures to live is confounded by the human emphasis on collective survival.

The question of legal versus illegal trade in animals also can be considered from the point of view of demand. In other words, there is a ready human consumer market for certain species of animal, regardless of how that animal is procured and transported to the consumer. Again, from the perspective of the transported animals, it matters little whether their displacement from habitat is criminal or not. What matters is that they are taken out of their natural habitats, and forced into living in human-defined modes of existence, and subject to human whim regarding activity, procreation and developmental capacity (see Sollund 2011). It is not only exotic animals which are subject to this form of treatment.

Companion animals refer to those animals primarily kept for companionship. It differs from the broader term of 'pet' which includes animals used for ornamental purposes and those kept for competitive or sporting activities (Serpell 2010: 133). The prevalence of companion animal ownership in the Western world is high, particularly in relation to cats and dogs. Birds are also kept as companion animals, as are fish and horses. In places like Latin America parrots are found in a high proportion of households (Sollund 2011).

The economic value of companion animals is reflected in the huge industries that have developed in relation to the feeding, grooming, health, training, provision of day care and longer-term temporary lodging, availability of specialist beaches and play areas, designer products including clothes and hats, and the list goes on. In the US alone, pet care is currently a $50 billion industry. The supply-chain emissions related to this industry make for a huge carbon footprint – so much so that the American Pet Products Association says that the number one trend is 'Reducing Your Pet's Carbon PAW print'. There are earth-friendly pet products being developed, but these are being sold in conjunction with designer shampoos and fashion, electric toothbrushes and self-flushing litterboxes, automatic doors and touch-activated toys, toy gyms, self-warming pet mats – and the list goes on (see Pearse 2012).

The enormous expansion of the pet and companion animal industries has left many animals vulnerable to abuse and exploitation in their human homes. It has also contributed to the endangerment of many species, such as parrots, which are abducted, trafficked and traded through both legal and illegal means (Sollund 2011). As the population of some species reduces in size, scarcity itself will generate lucrative markets for what is left in the wild. Accordingly, some writers argue that, rather than endorsing this kind of trade through legal mechanisms that legitimate it (such as CITES), there ought to be efforts to stop it altogether (Sollund 2011). Whether this would simply escalate the price of animals sold on the underground market is the flipside of the moral question of whether the trade itself is intrinsically defensible.

Law reform on behalf of animals is intended to address some of the issues pertaining to the status and valuing of animals. For example, in the United States the Animal Legal Defense Fund argues that animals are sentient beings and entitled to basic legal rights (Animal Legal Defense Fund 2007). In petitioning the US Congress, the ALDF states that Congress should pass legislation in support of the following basic rights for animals:

- The right of animals to be free from exploitation, cruelty, neglect and abuse.
- The right of laboratory animals not to be used in cruel or unnecessary experiments.
- The right of farm animals to an environment that satisfies their basic physical and psychological needs.
- The right of companion animals to a healthy diet, protective shelter and adequate medical care.
- The right of wildlife to a natural habitat, ecologically sufficient to a normal existence and self-sustaining species population.
- The right of animals to have their interests represented in court and safeguarded by the law of the land.

Translated into a practical model of advocacy, this construction of animal rights implies human guardianship (Pollard 2008). There is thus the presumption that human intervention – on the side of animals and as embedded in law – is necessary in order to protect them against exploitation and abuse. As with most areas of life, the law is a two-edged sword that can be wielded to defend interests as well as to undermine them. Protecting animals via the law is no exception to this rule, since the law embodies continued exploitation of animals in the same moment that it purports to protect them.

Conclusion

The number of green criminologists writing in the area of abuse and harm to animals has increased. Tensions can exist between both animal-rights and environmental-justice views, and animal-rights and ecological-justice approaches. Yet, very often conceptualization of environmental harm encapsulates the concerns of all three strands: protection of biodiversity within our forests is not incompatible with sustaining localized environments, protecting endangered species and ensuring human happiness. There are many concrete links between the health of natural environments, diverse human activity and the exploitation of animals. And, increasingly, the language of rights is being used to frame responses to harm and abuse that are evident across the three areas of concern (see Beirne and South 2007). This can sometimes lead to conflicts over which rights ought to take precedence in any given situation – human rights, rights of the environment, or animal rights (White 2013c).

Discussion topics

- What is an 'animal'?
- Should different types of animals (e.g. dogs) be granted more rights than other animals (fish)? Why or why not?
- Who harms animals and why?
- Is having a 'pet' wrong?
- What are the reasons why the illegal trade in animals is a criminal offence?

Further reading

Beirne, P. (2009). *Confronting Animal Abuse: Law, criminology, and human–animal relationships*. New York: Rowman & Littlefield.

Fitzgerald, A.J., Kalof, L., and Dietz, T. (2009). 'Slaughterhouses and Increased Crime Rates: An empirical analysis of the spillover from "the jungle" into the surrounding community', *Organisation and Environment*, 22(2): 158–84.

Nurse, A. (2013). *Animal Harm: Perspectives on why people harm and kill animals*. Farnham: Ashgate.

Sollund, R. (2011). 'Expressions of Specieism: The effects of keeping companion animals on animal abuse, animal trafficking and species decline', *Crime, Law and Social Change*, 55: 437–51.

Wyatt, T. (2012). *Green Criminology and Wildlife Trafficking: The illegal fur and falcon trades in Russia Far East*. Saarbrücken: Lambert Academic Publishing.

Chapter 8

Threats to biodiversity

Introduction

This chapter will discuss the following topics:

- the nature and importance of biodiversity;
- bio-insecurity and the exploitation of nature;
- reductions in biodiversity;
- biodiversity, flex crops and genetically modified organisms; and
- protecting biodiversity.

Biodiversity is generally defined as the variety of all species on earth. It refers to the different plants, animals and micro-organisms, and their genes, that together make up life on the planet. It also includes reference to the terrestrial (land), marine (ocean) and freshwater (inland water systems) ecosystems of which they are a part. It is also important to remember that ecosystems vary in size; for instance, a pond is a small ecosystem, while an ocean or a forest are considered large ecosystems, but they are all equally vulnerable. The loss of biodiversity in all three of its main components – genes, species and ecosystems – continues at a rapid pace. The five principal drivers of biodiversity loss (habitat change, over-exploitation, pollution, invasive alien species and climate change) are either constant or increasing in intensity (Secretariat of the Convention on Biological Diversity 2010).

In recent years criminologists have devoted concerted and detailed attention to questions relating to animal and plant life. Their work has been motivated by either a concern with species justice or an interest in conventional environmental crimes such as illegal fishing (see for example, Walters, B. 2005; Boekhout van Solinge 2008a and b; Herbig 2010; Beirne 2009; Sollund 2008). This scholarship has engaged with activities and circumstances spanning different parts of the globe. In part this arises from a growing recognition of the importance of studying the interconnectedness between producers and consumers, global markets and the institutions of world trade (both legal and illegal) and how these are linked in complex chains of transference and can involve quite sophisticated networks of relationships. The transnational nature of environmental crime is well established in and through such studies. For much of this burgeoning literature the focus of analysis is on legality rather than harm. If the latter is addressed, though, then 'harm' is generally constructed in the context of specific species or the human community affected.

In addition to definitions of environmental crime provided by conventional criminology, green criminology interprets transnational environmental issues through the lens of ecological concepts (see Chapters 2 and 3). From this perspective, *biodiversity* is the main frame of reference, rather than, for example, the offence of wildlife theft. This chapter explores the links between threats to biodiversity and the perpetration of a variety of environmental crimes and harms.

The nature and importance of biodiversity

With biodiversity, the key ecological message appears to be 'the more the merrier' – the greater the number of species the greater the resilience of the system as a whole to potential catastrophe, whether this is fire, drought or climate change. Any particular ecosystem is made up of both abiotic components (air, water, soil, atoms and molecules) and biotic components (plants, animals, bacteria and fungi). Changes to an ecosystem through human intervention occur through manipulation, contamination or destruction of these components (for example, through mining, land clearance and pesticide use). It is not only human intervention that can lead to change; the spread of invasive species can also transform local ecologies. It was recently reported that 'over 22 per cent of the world's plants are at risk of extinction, in large part due to loss of habitats through conversion of natural areas for agricultural use, including food and biofuel production' (UNEP 2011: 12).

A number of international instruments speak to matters pertaining to the protection of biodiversity. As previously noted a key international instrument of particular relevance to criminology is the *Convention on International Trade in Endangered Species of Wild Fauna and Flora (CITES)*, designed to ensure that international trade in specimens of wild animals and plants does not threaten their survival. CITES works by subjecting international trade in specimens of listed species to certain controls, based upon where the roughly 5,000 species of animals and 28,000 species of plants are situated in the three Appendices to the Convention, which reflect the extent of the threat to and the controls that apply to trade in a particular species. The appendixes are summarized in Box 8.1.

Box 8.1 Appendixes to Convention on International Trade in Endangered Species

Appendix I

Contains species threatened with extinction

Contains about 800 species deemed to be threatened with extinction and which are or may be affected by trade. Trade in wild-caught specimens of these species is illegal, permitted only in exceptional licensed circumstances (e.g. the red panda, gorilla, tigers, Asian elephant).

Appendix II

Contains species that, although not threatened with extinction now, might become so unless trade in them is strictly regulated

Contains about 32,500 species deemed to be not necessarily threatened with extinction, but that may become so unless trade in specimens of such species is subject to strict regulation, to avoid utilization incompatible with their survival. International trade in these specimens may be authorized by the granting of an export permit or re-export certificate (e.g. American black bear, African grey parrot, big-leaf mahogany tree).

Appendix III

Contains species that are protected in at least one country that has asked other CITES parties for help in controlling trade

Contains about 170 species, listed after at least one member country has asked other CITES parties for assistance in controlling trade in a species. Trade in these species is only permitted with an appropriate export permit and certificate of origin (e.g. two-toed sloth, African civet, alligator snapping turtle).

The legal and ecological importance of intervention around threatened and endangered species is illustrated by the sheer scale of this environmental crime. For example, in the early 1990s 'the value of legally traded wildlife products was estimated at US$160 billion per annum, legal wood exports at US$132 billion, and legal seafood exports at US$50 billion. The value of the illegal trade in wildlife products is harder to estimate, but is likely to be worth between US$10 and US$20 billion per year, second only to the international drugs trade in the ranks of illegal exchange' (Duffy 2010: 9–10).

Others likewise estimate that the illegal harvest, shipment and sale of protected animals and plants is second only to the illicit drug and arms trades in overall commercial value. In the area of illegal wildlife trade it has been noted that the extent of exploitation is driving many species to the brink of extinction (Schaedla 2007). There is lots of money to be made, but the consequences are devastating for biodiversity and overall ecological resilience on a world scale.

A green criminological approach to biodiversity is not solely concerned with legality, since many of the most damaging environmental activities are legal, or have yet to be criminalized, or are criminalized in one country but not another. Nor is it concerned with conservation as such, since the quality of life for species-level and individual animals is expressed within this approach in the notion of species justice (White 2013c). It is the wider conception of harm that marks off eco-global criminology from both mainstream criminology that deals with environmental issues (see Wellsmith 2010) and 'conservation criminology' as variously conceptualized (Herbig and Joubert 2006; Gibbs *et al.* 20010b).

Moreover, given the emphasis on global ecological constructions of well-being and harm, a further feature of eco-global criminology is the importance attached to big-picture construction of the issues – for instance, consideration of illegal trade in endangered species within the context of (and as only one contributing factor toward) loss of biodiversity. Accordingly the concern extends beyond a traditional criminological focus on illegal activity, or with nature as an exploitable resource, to those harms arising from both legal and illegal human interventions.

Bio-insecurity and the exploitation of nature

This section provides a discussion of indigenous and traditional people from the point of view of bio-insecurity. Bio-insecurity (for the many), state action (on behalf of the few) and the corporate colonization of nature (for the sake of profit) are interconnected. This was already evident, for example, in the early days of European global dominance, which saw specific trading companies (e.g. Hudson's Bay Company) being given exclusive monopolies to plunder the New World of animal and mineral products. Similar disrespect and exploitation continues today.

In Canada governments are eager to allow extraction industries to enter into and fully work lands occupied by indigenous peoples, regardless of the wishes of the local people (Rush 2002). Mining and logging operations create major environmental damage that directly affects the health and well-being of indigenous peoples. Meanwhile, in the United States, a history of repression of indigenous people is such that they were forcibly relocated to then unwanted lands that later proved to contain some of the richest mineral deposits and other natural resources in the US (such as uranium and low-sulphur coal). One consequence of their forced removal to lands that are now commercially desirable is that 'The quest for natural resources, then, imposes specific environmental risks on peoples such as Native Americans who reside near, and are dependent on, natural resources' (Field 1998: 80).

It is worth briefly reflecting here on how indigenous people around the world have traditionally lived in and with nature. For a start, the scale of human habitation tended to be tuned into local ecological conditions. People adapted to specific habitats (including marginal habitats such as deserts and Arctic regions), and specific systems were usually decentralized, communal and self-reliant: 'These societies live closely with and depend on the life contained in that particular ecosystem. This way of living enabled Indigenous communities to live for thousands of years in continuous sustainability' (Robyn 2002: 199). Over many years indigenous peoples developed unique, traditional local ecological knowledge supported by particular practices. In Australia, for instance, where the traditional indigenous people have been custodians of the land for 50,000 years, indigenous ecological knowledge (IEK) is deployed through 'traditional fire management practices that stimulate new growth for preferred animal species and increase the abundance of favoured bush medicine and bush tucker plants' (Central Land Council n.d.).

By contrast, the ethos of the colonizers saw the environment primarily as something to be exploited. This ran counter to an indigenous concept that understood the environment in terms of a balanced relationship between humans and the ecosystem.

Contemporary exploitation perpetuates this ethos through direct appropriation of lands that frequently reflect racist re-constructions and justification for this exploitation. This is made explicit in the case of bio-piracy. Bio-piracy relates to exploitation of third-world resources, indigenous and traditional peoples and their knowledge. Under the banner of free trade and the global (competitive) commons, the race to patent, for example, is a priority for many transnational companies. Bio-piracy can be understood in relation to 'traditional knowledge of the uses of plants' [TKUP] and the usurpation of indigenous ownership and control over plants using Western legal and political institutional mechanisms and forums.

> ... biopiracy may be defined as the unauthorized commercial use of biological resources and/or associated traditional knowledge, or the patenting of spurious inventions based on such knowledge, without compensation. Biopiracy also refers to the asymmetrical and unrequited movement of plants and TKUP from the South to the North through the processes of international institutions and the patent system.
>
> (Mgbeoji 2006: 13)

As Mgbeoji (2006) explains, corporate interests have used two methods to take what they want: institutional and juridical mechanisms (such as patents) and gendered and racist constructions of non-Western contributions to plant development and use (such as 'traditional' methods versus 'scientific').

> Most important, the legal and policy factors that facilitate the appropriation of indigenous peoples' knowledge operate within a cultural context that subtly but persistently denigrates the intellectual worth of traditional and indigenous peoples, especially local women farmers. Cultural biases in the construction of knowledge provide the epistemological framework within which plant genetic resources developed by indigenous peoples are continually construed as 'free-for-all' commodities – commodities that are just waiting to be appropriated by those with the cunning and resources to do so.
> (Mgbeoji 2006: 6)

Again, the assumption is that resource colonization is simply a natural part of doing business, and companies will do whatever it takes to gain and maintain competitive advantage.

A further example of the construction of bio-insecurity out of historical conditions of long-term stable food security is linked to the imposition of particular methods and types of production, especially agricultural production. The industrialization of agriculture (incorporating the use of seed and other patents) is one of the greatest threats to bio-security, causing significant erosion of plant genetic and species diversity. The imposition of genetically modified organisms (GMO) in crop planting and selection is highly contested worldwide. It has become a major social, economic and political issue – especially in countries with traditional techniques integrated into cultural systems that have sustained food production over many thousands of years (Walters, R. 2011; White 2011a).

Related to the issue of patented bio-technologies is the phenomenon of 'terminator technology'. This technology is precisely about market exploitation. It simultaneously threatens bio-security for local producers. The technology prohibits farmers from growing second-generation crops from the same seed. Also known as 'genetic use restriction technology', terminator technology also involves the use of chemicals that after one season block genetically altered seeds from germinating.

> Considering that at least 1.4 billion people rely on farm-saved seed for their annual crop and farming activities, the implications of terminator technology are devastating and irreversible. For example, unsuspecting farmers whose farms are near farms planted with terminator technology plants may have their crops ruined by escaped genes from the patented seeds. In other words, the impact may not be limited to farmers who purchase artificially sterilized seeds.
> (Mgbeoji 2006: 183)

Patent protection ensures that the big agribusiness conglomerates are able to control markets and production processes. This monopoly is facilitated by patents of existing organic materials (that is, through bio-piracy) and technological developments (that is, through genetic modification of organisms). The objective is to make direct producers – farmers – reliant upon commercially-bought seeds and related products such as fertilizers and pesticides.

The net result of these commercial activities, often facilitated and defended by particular nation-states, is global environmental destruction and degradation. This is occurring across a broad range of areas, from global warming through to diminishment of biodiversity. Waste and pollution (of air, water and land) continues to be a major problem. Simultaneously, 'natural resources' are being depleted at alarming rates with significant implications for both biotic (e.g. plants, animals) and abiotic (e.g. soils, water) constituents of the planet.

Reductions in biodiversity

According to the United Nations there are five principal threats to biodiversity (UNEP 2013). These are:

- the unsustainable harvesting of natural resources, including plants, animals and marine species;
- the loss, degradation or fragmentation of ecosystems through land conversion for agriculture, forest clearing, etc.;
- invasive non-native or 'alien' species being introduced to ecosystems to which they are not adapted (i.e., where they have no, or not enough, predators, to maintain an ecological balance);
- pollution; and
- climate change.

There are complex reasons why these threats appear as they do today, and the threats are interlinked in a variety of ways. The example of the intersections of biodiversity, deforestation and climate change will illustrate this point.

Climate change as manifest in changed weather patterns, combined with monoculture planting, has an impact on forest health and well-being. For example, the mountain pine beetle outbreak in North America has killed over 14 million hectares of mature pines in Canada alone since 2000 (UNEP 2011). This is due to the presence of an abundance of mature lodgepole pine (as a result of forestry management practices), the preferred host tree of the mountain pine beetle, and unusually high beetle survival during a series of mild winters. Previously, harsher winters and greater diversity of tree species had ensured that the pine beetle was unable to spread across the landscape to the same extent. Changes in weather patterns and climatic conditions will continue to alter ecosystems in unpredictable and unusual ways.

One consequence of the pine beetle outbreak has been to change the net carbon balance of Canada's forests, from that of carbon sink to carbon source. In other words, forest-based climate-mitigation strategies are based upon sequestration of carbon within 'living' forests – the direct impact of the pine-beetle outbreak was therefore to contribute to, rather than reduce, overall carbon emissions, via the decay of the dead trees (UNEP 2011). The threat to biodiversity is thus also simultaneously feeding into the risks and harms posed by climate change. Indeed, it has been predicted that world crop yields could fall as much as 20–40 per cent by mid-century because of climate change alone. We are also breaching the biophysical limits of the soil: world agricultural land productivity between 1990 and 2007 was 1.2 per cent a year, nearly half compared with 1950–90 levels of 2.1 per cent (Ahmed 2013).

Reduction in species includes both animals and plants. In regard specifically to trees and species that inhabit forests, 13 per cent of the world's total forest area is under formal protection, and almost 75 per cent of forests are covered by a national forest programme. Yet, despite progress in the regulatory sphere, and net gains in forest areas in Europe and Asia, total loss of forest cover during the last decade still averaged around 13 million hectares per year. Most deforestation is occurring in tropical forests, with substantial biodiversity impacts: 'Although the global rate of net forest cover loss has slowed, partly due to the expansion of plantations and to natural forest restoration, forest biodiversity loss continues to occur disproportionately since the highest levels of deforestation and of forest degradation are reported for biodiversity-rich natural forests in developing countries' (UNEP 2011: 48). Net losses are especially significant in South America and Africa.

Factors affecting deforestation, and reduction in forest biodiversity, include unsustainable harvesting of forest products for industrial use and livelihood needs, deforestation for agriculture, and severe drought and forest fires. Every year some 10 million hectares of forest are destroyed; industrial timber exports total around US$150 billion per year, and estimates of illegal logging account for about 25 per cent of removals worldwide (Setiono 2007: 27). Much of this illegal logging occurs with the involvement of corrupt government officials, including law enforcement officers, financial institutions and backers, and business people who import timber or wood-based products. Bribery and 'goodwill' payments, smuggling, illicit trafficking, money laundering and forging of documents are all part of the illegal logging industry (Setiono 2007).

Deforestation and species reduction are not the outcome solely of logging. Land clearance is also due to agricultural exploitation, cattle farming, mining, oil and gas installations, and hydroelectric dams (see Boekhout van Solinge 2008a and b, 2010; Khagram 2004; Boekhout van Solinge and Kuijpers 2013). There is also the phenomenon of 'conflict timber', associated with west Africa, for example, in which deforestation is linked to the funding of civil wars and armed conflicts (Boekhout van Solinge 2008a; see also Brisman and South 2013).

In these contexts, the ecological impact of logging and land clearance transcends the legal–illegal divide insofar as vast amounts of forest are destroyed in many different locations – from Peru and Brazil, Liberia and Sierra Leone, to Indonesia and Australia. The motivations, objectives and practices may vary depending upon the social context and specific industry interests, but the result is further depletion of many different kinds of trees and variety of forests.

Another reason for deforestation and biodiversity reduction is the increasing reliance on energy from organic sources. For example, maize for biofuels accounted for 25 per cent of US production in the 2007/08 crop year, and global vegetable oil supplies used for biodiesel production is on the increase: 'The largest biodiesel producers were the European Union, the United States, Brazil and Indonesia, with a combined use of vegetable oils for biodiesel of about 9 million tons in 2007 compared to global vegetable oils production of 132 million tons. ... The estimated increase in vegetable oils use for biodiesel was 6.6 million tons from 2004 to 2007, which would attribute 34 per cent of the increase in global consumption to biodiesel' (Mitchell 2008: 5). This translates into massive shifts in land use.

Indeed, the profitability of biofuel production is leading to large-scale plantations in places such as Indonesia, Brazil and Colombia. This has resulted in the clearing of rainforests and in some instances forcing indigenous people off their lands. Mol (2013: 254) critically observes that in Colombia:

> The gift of palm oil to the world leaves the people and the environment of the tropics with contaminated soils, groundwater, and rivers; habitat destruction; ecosystem disturbances; the loss of flora and aquatic and animal species; and processes of displacement and emplacement that inflict a whole range of physical, psychological, social, and cultural consequences upon local communities.

Cutting down trees also has a direct bearing on global warming. For instance, it has been estimated that by 2022 biofuel plantations could destroy 98 per cent of Indonesia's rainforests and that 'Every ton of palm oil used as biofuel releases 30 tons of CO_2 into the atmosphere, ten times as much as petroleum does' (Shiva 2008: 79).

Between 2006 and 2011, farmers in the US corn belt converted 1.3 million acres of temperate grassland and wetland into soybean and corn crops for biofuel (Bryce 2013). As a consequence, waterfowl habitats are infringed upon, and visiting pollinators will also decline as monocultural crops boom. A generous agricultural insurance is seen to encourage the exploitation of delicate grasslands and wetlands where the ground is too hilly or wet for crops. The result is that wetlands get 'tile-drained', and as farmers remove natural vegetation and till the earth, they release sequestered carbon. Threats to biodiversity are yet again linked back to forces that increase global warming.

Moreover, given the focus of the UN mechanism for Reducing Emissions from Deforestation and Forest Degradation (REDD) on minimizing carbon emissions caused by the destruction of living forest biomass, there will be greater pressures to convert or modify other ecosystems, especially savannahs and wetlands, for food or biofuel (Sutherland et al. 2009).

Powerful interests, including car manufacturers and grain farmers, have benefited from the search for organic energy alternatives to fossil fuels. The shift to biofuel is seen as a key source of green fuel supply for the world's car manufacturers. Greater demand for biofuel crops – such as corn, palm oil or soya – also means that farmers are finding the growing of such crops very lucrative economically. The industrialization of agriculture behind such ventures is not, however, without its ecological costs.

Biodiversity, flex crops and GMOs

The corporatization of agriculture has been accompanied by significant changes in land use. For example, there has been a major expansion in cropland worldwide. 'Viewed in a wider historical context, more land was converted to cropland in the 30 years after 1950, than in the 150 years between 1700 and 1850' (UNEP 2007a: 86). The environmental impact is loss of habitat and biodiversity; soil water-retention and regulation; disturbance of biological cycle; increases in soil erosion; nutrient depletion; salinity and eutrophication (that is, the depletion of oxygen in water). For humans, there is greater exposure to agrochemicals in air, soil and water.

Many of the contemporary environmental harms are related to how the basic means of life of humans is being reconstituted and reorganized through global systems of production. For example, the 'globalization of food production and manufacture and the use of new technologies and chemicals in farming and food processing have created a variety of risks to humans, non-human animals, the environment and health' (Croall 2007: 206), and in many cases we still do not know the longer-term effects of new developments in the food area. What is happening to food generally is symptomatic of how commodification is taking place in regard to all aspects of human life and in all parts of the globe.

One of the greatest threats to biodiversity is the industrialization of agriculture (incorporating the use of seed and other patents) since this is one of the leading causes of erosion of plant genetic and species diversity. This is reflected in the following observation.

> Today, a mere four crops account for two-thirds of the calories humans eat. When you consider that humankind has historically consumed some 80,000 edible species, and that 3,000 of these have been in widespread use, this represents a radical simplification of the food web.
>
> (Pollan 2007: 47)

The tendency toward fewer types of crops has been accelerated in recent decades with the rise of 'flex crops and commodities' (Borras, Franco and Wang 2013). These refer to a single crop/commodity that is highly valuable precisely because of its multiple characteristics and uses. These are not simply 'food' crops as such.

Typically, a flex crop straddles multiple:

- commodity sectors (food, feed, fuel, other industrial commodities);
- geographical spaces (e.g. North–South); and
- international political economy categories (e.g. OECD countries, non-OECD countries).

This makes flex crops very attractive to growers and buyers around the world insofar as everyone, it seems, can find a place in the market. The four key flex crops today are maize, palm oil, soya beans and sugar cane. Important producers and exporters of flex crops and commodities include, for example, Argentina for soya, Malaysia and Indonesia for palm oil, and Vietnam for fast-growing trees (Borras, Franco and Wang 2013). One type of crop, such as fast-growing trees, can be sold as a commodity in respect to diverse markets, including in this case timber products, biofuel and carbon offsets.

Multi-purpose crops exacerbate the push toward fewer varieties. Species reduction is also associated with ease of production, distribution and marketing. For instance, there is also a trend toward monoculture since uniformity means ease of cultivation and harvest, translating into higher profits. New agricultural and pastoral technologies reinforce this broad tendency toward simplification. The global political economy of genetically modified organisms (GMOs) provides a case in point.

According to New Zealand's Royal Commission on Genetic Modification, genetic modification can be defined as the use of genetic engineering techniques in a laboratory that involves:

- the deletion, multiplication, modification, or moving of genes within a living organism; or
- the transfer of genes from one organism to another; or
- the modification of existing genes or the construction of novel genes and their incorporation in any organism; or
- the utilization of subsequent generations or offspring of organisms modified by any of the activities described above.

The application of GM technologies to food production is perhaps one of the most publicly recognized, and fear-inspiring, uses of such technology. Countries that have been reluctant to adopt GM crops have been subjected to intense pressures to do so (Walters, R. 2004, 2011).

Ironically, given political claims that GM crops are vital in order to feed the world, GMO invasion of endemic species and crops is nonetheless seen to be capable of destroying unique genotypes, thereby creating the potential to threaten food security (i.e., diminishing diverse genetic material) (see Engdahl 2007). Such fears are not unfounded. Scientific studies report two issues of concern: first, that genetic contamination is occurring; and, secondly, that transgenes are unstable, meaning that once the GMO cross-pollinates with another plant, the transgene splits up and is inserted in an uncontrolled way – the displaced DNA could be creating utterly unpredictable effects (Robin 2010: 247).

The potential size of the problem is considerable, as the use of GMO crops has rapidly increased over the past decade.

> In 2007, transgenic crops (90 per cent of which, it should be recalled, have genetic traits patented by Monsanto) covered about 250 million acres: more than half were located in the United States (136.5 million acres), followed by Argentina (45 million), Brazil (28.8 million), Canada (15.3 million), India (9.5 million), China (8.8 million), Paraguay (5 million), and South Africa (3.5 million).
>
> (Robin 2010: 4)

Almost all of these crops were 'legally' planted, but the genetic and species consequences of transfer are potentially of a huge scale especially in terms of negative ecological impact.

Also of concern are those crops which have not been distributed through legitimate and legal means. For instance, in Mexico traditional corn has been found to be contaminated by GMO corn, despite the fact that in 1998 Mexico declared a moratorium on transgenic corn crops in order to preserve the extraordinary biodiversity of the plant. Meanwhile, in Paraguay, where (as of 2007) no law authorized the cultivation of GMOs, 'From 1996 to 2006, surfaces devoted to soybean cultivation went from less than 2.5 million acres to 5 million acres, an increase of 10 per cent a year' (Robin 2010: 275). To avoid losing markets and to ensure proper labelling of crops for markets such as the European Union, the Paraguayan government ended up simply legalizing the illegal crops. Much the same thing happened in Brazil and Poland (Engdahl 2007), and for much the same reasons (namely EU rules on traceability and labelling of GM foods intended for human and animal consumption) (Robin 2010).

Patent protection ensures that the big agribusiness companies are able to control markets and production processes. This is based upon patents of existing organic materials (that is, through bio-piracy) and technological developments (that is, through genetic modification of organisms). The point is to make direct producers – the farmers – reliant upon commercially-bought seeds (and related products such as fertilizer and pesticides).

The concentration of power and ownership of production in a handful of large corporations leads to simplification. The answer to wider health and environmental problems lies in rekindling, cherishing and protecting diversity. But this, in turn, would force a challenge to such monopolies.

> Biodiversity in diet means less monoculture in the fields. What does this have to do with your health? Everything. The vast monocultures that now feed us require tremendous amounts of chemical fertilizers and pesticides to keep from collapsing. Diversifying those fields will mean fewer chemicals, healthier soils, healthier plants and animals and, in turn, healthier people. It's all connected, which is another way of saying that your health isn't bordered by your body, and that what's good for the soil is probably good for you, too.
> (Pollan 2007: 70)

The economic forces that underpin bio-piracy, bio-security and bio-insecurity alike are precisely the forces that work most assiduously against biodiversity. As such, they operate against the interests of humans, environments and non-human animals. Profits come before people, profits come before ecological sustainability, and the outcome is a perpetual cycle of transnational environmental harm.

This simplification of production generates paradoxical harm from the point of view of biodiversity and potential threats to future food production. That is, to feed the world (at least in this scenario) means depleting the genetic plant pool and prioritizing certain species over others, and this, in turn, creates further problems.

> One consequence of the erosion of plant genetic diversity is that the capacity of the economically preferred plants to resist pests and diseases is compromised. The marketability of plant produce is not necessarily coterminous with the inherent superior quality of the plants to be marketed or selected for mono-cropping. Given the potential utility of plants that market forces may erroneously dismiss as economically useless, the short-sighted depletion of the plant genetic pool can be both costly and dramatic.
> (Mgbeoji 2006: 181)

Put simply, 'over the ages farmers have relied upon diverse crop varieties as protection from pests, blights and other forms of crop failure' (French 2000: 61). Reducing this diversity affects the inbuilt mechanisms that help to protect the soil and the vitality of the overall agricultural process. Moreover, intensive use of land and soils that rely upon chemical additives to ensure productivity – rather than, for example, traditional methods of crop rotation – further diminishes longer-term agricultural viability. Contemporary farming practices that feature biodiverse fields (based upon up to 12 different types of seed crops) have not only been found to be more resilient to frost, drought and variations in rainfall, but to produce more food and cash earnings than that of corn monoculture (Shiva 2008). Diversity is strength.

However, reducing capability to resist potential calamity – as is evident for example with the Canadian pine trees mentioned earlier – can also serve to increase general anxieties among farmers and heighten their sensitivity to potential threats. For example, at a political level, concerns about bio-security incorporate this sense of unease at being vulnerable to pests and disease (invasive species). For instance, in Australia there is great resistance to the entry of New Zealand apples (due to the perceived threat of fire blight disease) and Canadian wild salmon (due to the perceived threat of specific salmon-related diseases to the salmon aquaculture industry in Australia). Reliance upon a shrinking pool of genetic resources will do little to forestall the potential risks and harms from external as well as internal threats.

Protecting biodiversity

Responding to the threats to biodiversity takes many different forms. On the one hand it can involve the criminalization of acts and omissions that involve endangered species, as with CITES, or the illegal cutting down of trees (as an individual land owner or as part of an industry syndicate). On the other hand, it can consist of incentives for individuals and groups to change existing ways of doing things that have the effect of allowing greater species protection. Given that a major reason for biodiversity loss relates to land use, attempts to control and regulate land clearance are important. A positive approach to dealing with land clearance issues is provided in Box 8.2.

Box 8.2 Encouraging better vegetation management

In the Australian state of Victoria several initiatives are in place to offer landowners an incentive to encourage better vegetation management, and thereby protection of endemic species of plants and animals.

Bush tender – where the land owner receives periodic payments for land management practices above and beyond those required by legislation;

Carbon tender – which involves carbon offset contracts with land-holders who revegetate their properties;

Bush broker – which involves a native vegetation credit and trading scheme, whereby clearance on one landholding (by developers) can be offset on another through the purchase of native vegetation credits.

Source: Bricknell 2010: 88

Another response to biodiversity loss has been official and unofficial establishment of seed banks. These are a form of 'gene bank', the purposes of which are to preserve seed varieties for their own sake, because the plant may be a rare species, and just in case of catastrophic events (such as fires, hurricanes, volcanos, war). Seeds may be stored in special facilities such as nuclear-bomb-proof multi-story underground vaults and underground tunnels. They may also be preserved through *in situ* conservation of seed-producing plant species in places such as national parks and national wildlife refuges.

Such initiatives, however, do little to address the reasons for biodiversity loss in the first place. They are last-ditch attempts to preserve and hold on to species that otherwise would be extinguished. Other initiatives are also being adopted in order to protect biodiversity, in some cases forcing hard decisions on what to save and how to save it.

Due to climate change and massive shifts in land use worldwide, a large-scale shift in plant and animal species that is invasive to the endemic or native population of particular geographical areas is taking place (Secretariat of the Convention on Biological Diversity 2010). Simultaneously, local species may be placed under threat, due to changes in temperature, moisture, wind and carbon dioxide that may diminish their ability to withstand hitherto familiar pathogens, much less competing species invading their spaces. The problem of salvinia – a floating fern from South America – provides a case in point. This plant has destroyed local economies in Africa and South-east Asia by preventing fishing and essential river transport systems (Rowe 2007: 26). The weed has had and continues to have devastating impacts, as seen in Case vignette 8.1.

Case vignette 8.1 Salvinia – a floating aquatic menace

In Australia, Salvinia, a native of south-eastern Brazil, is regarded as one of the worst weeds in the nation, because of its invasiveness, potential for spread and economic and environmental impacts. It was first recorded as a weed near Sydney in 1952, and a year later near Brisbane. Since then it has infested most coastal streams from Cairns in northern Queensland to Moruya on the south coast of New South Wales. It has spread from backyards in all capital cities, and remote infestations affect the top end of the Northern Territory and regions of Western Australia. There is a belief that many infestations have been deliberately spread in order to harvest the plants for sale in the aquarium and horticulture industries (National Heritage Trust 2003). The weed is also a threat in other parts of the world including Africa, India, Sri Lanka, South East Asia, the Philippines, Papua New Guinea, New Zealand, Fiji, Hawaii and mainland United States. In March 2013, after severe flooding across the mid-north coast of Australia,

> salvinia moved throughout the wetlands and into the Maria River near Kempsey. The floating aquatic plant threatened to completely choke the freshwater wetlands and streams with major consequences for the natural ecosystem including severe impacts on the native fish throughout the Maria River port system (*MacLeay Argus* 2013).

What to do to preserve and protect species is not without its moral and ethical dilemmas. For example, life-and-death situations extend to instances where individual animals of one species may be sacrificed for the sake of the preservation of an entire other species, which can be either plant or animal. In a 1996 case the US Fish and Wildlife Service acted to poison 6,000 gulls at Monomoy National Wildlife Refuge off Cape Cod, in order to save 35 piping plovers, an endangered species. In another case, San Clemente Island, off the coast of California, has both endemic plant species and a population of feral goats. In order to protect plants numbering in the few hundreds, the Fish and Wildlife Service and the US Navy have shot tens of thousands of feral goats (Rolston 2010: 605–6).

Endemic species are not always the species that are most valued and most likely to gain support from human backers when it comes to situations of species competition. Such is the fate of the galaxias fish in Tasmania relative to the introduced trout (see Chapter 7). When it comes to animals, human intervention has major ramifications for species survival and biodiversity. The phenomenon of 'assisted colonization' involves the moving of species to sites where they do not currently occur or have not been known to occur in recent history. The introduction of 'alien' species was not uncommon during the course of European settlement outside Europe, as the example of trout in Tasmania exemplifies (see Franklin 2006). Today, however, this is happening in response to climate change, and usually is directed at species in the wild. 'In the UK, two native species of butterfly were recently translocated approximately 65 km northward into areas identified by modelling as climatically suitable for occupancy by the butterflies' (Sutherland *et al.* 2009).

The problem is that non-native species moving into new ecosystems are already recognized as a major conservation problem (Secretariat of the Convention on Biological Diversity 2010). This is evidenced, for example, by the rapid expansion in the numbers of Indo-Pacific lionfish along the east coast of the United States and in the Caribbean to the detriment of native coral reef fish (Sutherland *et al.* 2009). Assisted colonists could be viewed as invasive and as constituting a potential danger to existing ecosystems and their inhabitants. Classic cases where considerable damage has resulted include the introduction of the cane toad into Australia. Its subsequent spread has had colossal impacts on native species; with no or few natural predators, it has proliferated and continues to take over more and more territories previously held by other endemic species.

> **Box 8.3 Survival status of species**
>
> *Extinct*: the last remaining member of the species has died, or is presumed beyond reasonable doubt to have died (e.g. thylacine, dodo, passenger pigeon).
> *Extinct in the wild*: captive individuals survive, but there is no free-living, natural population (e.g. alagoas curassow, dromedary).
> *Critically endangered*: faces an extremely high risk of extinction in the immediate future (e.g. mountain gorilla, Javan rhino).
> *Endangered*: faces a very high risk of extinction in the near future (e.g. blue whale, orangutan).
> *Vulnerable*: faces a high risk of extinction in the medium-term (e.g. polar bear, cheetah, Komodo dragon).
> *Conservation dependent*: not severely threatened but must depend on conservation programmes (e.g. spotted hyena, leopard shark).
> *Near threatened*: may be considered threatened in the near future (e.g. tiger shark, blue-billed duck).
> *Least concern*: no immediate threat to the survival of the species (e.g. wood pigeon, house mouse).
> *Data deficient*: inadequate information to make a direct or indirect assessment of risk of extinction.
> *Not evaluated*: not evaluated against the Red list criteria.

Certainly a major area of governmental concern and criminological examination relates to issues pertaining to endangered species. The International Union for the Conservation of Nature's (2011) categorization of the status of species is provided in Box 8.3.

The illegal trade in plants and wildlife involves not only transnational environmental crime but also threatens biodiversity more generally. The threat here is not only to endangered species directly but, as well, to the economic viability of industries such as agriculture, forestry and fisheries.

> Illegal exports of wildlife and wildlife products from Australia pose a threat to the protection of endangered species. Illegal imports are accompanied by the potential for the introduction of pests and diseases which could have a dramatic impact on agriculture, conservation of the environment, and specialist industries, such as aviculture.
>
> (Halstead 1992: 1)

Thus, the smuggling of wildlife across national borders has the potential to threaten the viability of endangered species, whether flora or fauna, as well as to provide a potential vehicle for the introduction of pests and diseases into formerly unaffected areas (Herbig 2010).

The point has been made that: 'Illegal logging, fishing, and wildlife trade are almost invariably carried out at unsustainable levels, running down the natural capital from which poor people derive their livelihoods' (Duncan Brack, quoted in Schmidt 2004: A97). From a socio-legal point of view, it is the perceived value of a species – plant or animal – that determines the regulation of human behaviour in relation to that species. This extends to law-enforcement and crime-prevention measures, as well as incorporating how 'crime' is institutionalized in relation to specific kinds of plants and animals. What activities (and omissions) get criminalized depends upon how value is construed at any point in time. This will also vary depending upon the species in question.

From a broader systems perspective, however, the diminishment of biodiversity is due to the normal operating practices of the dominant mode of production. The methods and techniques of industry, from mining to agribusiness, set in train a long line of offences and infringements that, in turn, reinforce the basic problem – namely, the rapid deterioration of biodiversity across the plant and animal kingdoms. In the context of climate change, such developments are life-threatening to all species, insofar as resilience and adaptation demand versatility and difference.

Conclusion

This chapter illustrates that the threats to biodiversity are many and profound, with major ramifications for the number and well-being of plant and animal species now and into the future. Particular threats to biodiversity differ for different regions but include, for example: population growth; pollution (industrial emissions that cause acid rain); global climate change (the greenhouse effect and destruction of the ozone layer); habitat destruction (burning or felling of old-growth forests); over-exploitation of natural resources (illegal trade of fauna and flora); and invasion of introduced species (CapeNature 2007).

It is likely that the risk of extinction for many species may have been underestimated (McGrath 2008), a situation likely to be made worse by the consequences of climate change (Secretariat of the Convention on Biological Diversity 2010). Moreover, as local climates and temperatures change, greater pressure will be placed on local environments as local producers convert land to industrial uses (e.g. agriculture, forestry and pastureland) in response to phenomena such as desertification (United Nations Development Programme 2010). At stake are cross-cutting issues such as food security, global health, intellectual property, indigenous peoples, equity, justice and human rights.

In some way or form, almost all cultures have recognized the importance of nature and its biological diversity for their societies and have therefore understood the need to maintain it. Yet, power, greed and politics have affected this precarious balance (Shah 2013). There is a need to protect biodiversity with a view to promoting fairness and justice to ensure a resilient and productive future.

Discussion topics

- Explore the links between climate change and biodiversity in relation to aquatic dead zones or some other marine-related topic.
- Identify and explore the role of new technologies in reducing biodiversity.
- What is a 'flex' crop, and what are their implications for biodiversity?
- What is the relationship between biodiversity and crime?
- Biodiversity is essential to resilience. Discuss in relation to responding to climate change.

Further reading

Boekhout van Solinge, T. (2008). 'The Land of the Orangutan and Bird of Paradise Under Threat', in R. Sollund (ed.), *Global Harms: Ecological crime and speciesism*. New York: Nova Science Publishers.

Green, P., Ward, T., and McConnachie, K. (2007). 'Logging and Legality: Environmental crime, civil society, and the state', *Social Justice*, 34(2): 94–110.

Ngoc, A.C., and Wyatt, T. (2012). 'A Green Criminological Exploration of Illegal Wildlife Trade in Vietnam', *Asian Criminology*, 8: 129–42.

South, S., and Brisman, A. (2013). 'Critical Green Criminology, Environmental Rights and Crimes of Exploitation', in S. Winlow and R. Atkinson (eds), *New Directions in Crime and Deviancy*. London: Routledge.

Walters, R. (2011). *Eco Crime and Genetically Modified Food*. London: Routledge.

Chapter 9

Pollution and toxic waste

Introduction

This chapter will discuss the following topics:

- pollution of air, land and water;
- hazardous and toxic waste;
- environmental justice and toxic sites; and
- resource extraction and pollution.

Pollution affects us all, particularly given the propensity for contaminants and waste to circulate around the world in air and sea currents, for the world's waste to leach into air, water and soil, and for the growing mountain of discarded e-waste to be transferred around the world assisted by the globalization of trade on both licit and illicit markets. The landscapes of pollution and waste are interconnected and serve as a poignant reminder that, despite differences, we are all citizens of a single planet.

Pollution of air, land and water

Pollution refers to the contamination of soil, water or the atmosphere by the discharge of harmful substances that adversely affect the environment. A range of activities collectively contribute to the pollution of the planet. Deville and Harding (1997: 27) categorize the main activities which produce threats to the environment as:

- obtaining resources – either extracting non-renewable minerals and energy or harvesting and managing 'renewable' resources such as fish or forest timbers;
- transforming or using these resources – constructing buildings, bridges and other infrastructure, manufacturing products or burning fossil fuels;
- disposing of unusable 'by-products' – managing, reusing, recycling or disposing of waste materials from obtaining and transforming resources.

Each of these specific areas of activity produces environmental harms, and each embodies risks for particular human populations and biotic communities.

The problem of pollution is directly related to how humans use and dispose of natural resources in systemic processes of production and consumption. For instance, the industrial revolution in Europe was accompanied by massive increases in air, land and water pollution as coal was burned and industrial chemicals were discharged. With an integrated global economic system churning out all manner of consumer products and waste materials, the extent of pollution has reached epic planetary proportions. Few places on earth are free from some type of pollutant and foreign contaminant, whether this is in the Arctic or the middle of the central Australian desert.

While the political economic system as a whole – global capitalism – is inherently polluting, given the scale and reach of transnational chains of production and consumption, nonetheless some industries are more 'dirty' than others. It is notable for example that 'Just 122 corporations account for 80 per cent of all carbon dioxide emissions. And just five private global oil corporations – Exxon Mobil, BP Amoco, Shell, Chevron and Texaco – produce oil that contributes some ten per cent of the world's carbon emissions' (Bruno, Karliner and Brotsky 1999: 1).

Air, land and water pollution negatively affect humans and community life (see Meško, Dimitrijevic and Fields 2010). Smog hanging over a city is one of the most visible sign of pollution (it can be seen clearly by the human eye and, aside from the fact that it blocks out the sun and stars, there are health effects, especially for those predisposed to respiratory disease). But many types of pollution, particularly to land and water are less visible and as a result likely to be less visible than the problem of smog. The practice of burying waste in subterranean spaces (under the earth) is one issue that comes to mind here.

Air pollution stems from the release of chemicals and particulates into the atmosphere, including such substances as carbon monoxide and sulphur dioxide, and is clearly evident in the form of city smog. Indoor air pollution is also a concern, particularly in developing countries where cooking and heating with biomass fuels (agricultural residues, dung, straw, wood) or coal, produces high levels of indoor smoke that contain a variety of pollutants damaging to health (World Health Organization 2013). Space debris is also on the horizon (30,000 items greater than 10cm in size), although the major concern here is the propensity for collision.

Land (or soil) pollution occurs when chemicals are released into the soil, including heavy metals such as lead and cadmium and pesticides, which can kill living bacteria in the earth or contaminate all life within the soil (including plants and non-plant creatures). Agriculture and mining stand out as two of the most polluting activities here, along with the burgeoning extractive and resources industries and the use of chemicals. We are increasingly mining ever deeper into the earth to extract mineral reserves (see Australian Centre for Geomechanics 2013) and burying some of the world's most hazardous waste deep in the ground (e.g. radioactive waste).

Water pollution occurs when contaminants, such as untreated sewerage waste and agricultural run-off containing chemical fertilizers, poison and alter existing surface and ground waters. Surface run-off transfers contaminants from one place to another, and harmful chemicals which are suspended in the air get dissolved in rainwater and pollute the soil when they come to the earth's surface in the form of acid rain (Naik 2010). The scope of water pollution extends from small-scale ponds to inland waterways, to estuaries, lakes and rivers, to the world's oceans. Sea currents transfer pollutants and wastes around the globe – in the world of nature there are no borders – a poignant reminder that we all live on one planet, regardless of human-centred divisions.

Mangroves and swamps are a special case, where land and water pollution issues overlap (e.g. dumping of domestic and industrial waste, discharges from passing watercraft). Port activities around the world can also be a major source of water pollution through waste-water discharges, bilge and ballast water as well as storm-water run-off from industrial activities associated with or surrounding ports.

Pollution may result from natural events such as volcanic activity that spew particulate matter into the atmosphere. However, the main causes of pollution are due to humans and directly linked to existing techniques and processes of production (e.g. agriculture, mining, manufacturing), consumption (e.g. waste disposal), transportation (e.g. internal combustion engines in cars, trucks and buses) and war (e.g. use of depleted uranium in armaments). As such, pollution is generally ingrained in everyday practices and systems, although these, in turn, are frequently subject to regulation. Industry and citizens are generally free to pollute, but the law stipulates under what conditions and to what extent.

Pollution is now occurring in every part of the planet and across many different types of terrain, although local responses vary greatly. The problem of air pollution, for example, is of growing concern and is basically one that impacts upon humans in ways that fundamentally undermine their health and well-being, as evidenced in millions of premature deaths worldwide each year (Walters 2009, 2010, 2013a). Importantly, it is the victimization of people that frequently generates the original concern with activities that cause systematic pollution. Sometimes public and governmental action is called for under the activist banner of environmental justice insofar as some groups may be disproportionately affected by air pollution (see Hurley 1995; Bullard 2005a and b). In other cases a ubiquitous problem (pollution clouds over Beijing or London) may call forth action linked to special events such as the summer Olympics.

Ecological destruction is not limited to the air or the land. It also finds its place within the planet's waters. Inland rivers, oceans and seas are also filling up with highly toxic pollutants. In the specific case of international waters pollution has no respect for national borders or national interests. The pollution affects all. Of particular concern is the accumulation of plastics in the world's oceans (see White 2013c).

The plastic debris deposited in the planet's oceans is generating increasing concern because of the potential impact of releases of persistent bio-accumulating and toxic compounds (PBTs). Much of the plastic takes the form of microplastics, plastic particles smaller than 5 millimetres in diameter. This also means that the plastic debris in the ocean may not be distinguishable on satellite images where concentrations consist of fragments that are small in size.

The environmental harm stemming from plastics in the ocean varies according to size and composition of the material. Threats to biodiversity and individuals manifest in physical damage through ingestion and entanglement in plastic and other debris, and through chemical contamination by ingestion. The importation of alien species can also alter endemic community structures of animals. In general, 'potential chemical effects are likely to increase with a reduction in the size of plastic particles while physical effects, such as the entanglement of seals and other animals in drift plastic, increase with the size and complexity of the debris' (UNEP 2011: 25). Fish, seabirds, sea turtles and marine mammals have all been affected by ingestion of plastics.

A key concern is the biochemical and physiological response of organisms to ingested plastics contaminated with PBTs. Not only are there issues associated with the potential impacts of the releases of chemical additives that were part of the plastics' original formulation, but as plastic breaks down into fragments (plastic particles of small size) it accumulates PBTs that are already present in seawater and sediments. Many of these specific pollutants cause chronic effects such as endocrine disruption, affecting reproduction, increases in the frequency of genetic mutations (mutagenicity) and a tendency to cause cancer (carcinogenicity). The world's oceans, and the creatures within them, are under serious threat from a variety of negative influences.

Hazardous and toxic waste

Chemicals and other toxic waste such as persistent organic pollutants (POPs) have proliferated over the past 60 years. Specifically, the rise of the chemical industries means that many different types of toxic waste are produced, gathered up and put together into the same dump sites (e.g. rivers and lakes and ocean outlets, landfills). This has been accompanied by new problems and complexities in waste disposal, especially in relation to toxicity as well as the extent of waste (Field 1998; Klenovsek and Mesko 2010).

The emergence of e-waste (computers, mobile phones, etc.) has only added further to existing waste management problems (White 2008a; Gibbs *et al*. 2010a and b, 2011; Interpol 2009). Indeed, 'The electronics industry is the world's largest and fastest growing manufacturing industry, and as a consequence of this growth, combined with rapid product obsolescence, discarded electronics or E-waste, is now the fastest growing waste stream in the industrialized world' (Basel Action Network and Silicon Valley Toxics Coalition 2002: 5). According to the United Nations, about 20 million to 50 million tons of e-waste is generated

160 Transgression and victimization

> **Box 9.1 E-waste facts and figures**
>
> - Every year around 40 to 50 million tonnes of electronic waste is generated worldwide (Schwarzer *et al.* 2005; Lundgren 2012: 11) and the mountain is growing at the rate of around 4 per cent a year (Deng *et al.* 2006).
> - E-waste contains more than a thousand difference substances, many of which are toxic, including lead, mercury, arsenic, cadmium, selenium, hexavalent chromium and flame retardants (Widmer *et al.* 2005) and 22 per cent of the yearly world consumption of mercury is used in electronics manufacture (Realff, Raymond and Ammons 2004).
> - Lead solder from e-waste has been linked to lead-contaminated children's jewellery (Weidenhamer and Clement 2007).
> - Of the e-waste in developed countries that is sent for recycling, 80 per cent ends up being shipped (often illegally) to developing countries such as China, India, Ghana and Nigeria for recycling (Lundgren 2012: 9).
> - A hidden aspect of e-waste is that the loss of scarce metals present in e-waste has to be compensated for by intensified mining activities, and it is well known that the rapid increase in demand for raw materials used in electronic products has given rise to conflicts over resources worldwide (Lundgren 2012: 12).
> - A study commissioned by the US Environmental Protection Agency (EPA) revealed that it was ten times cheaper to export e-waste to Asia than it was to process it in the United States (Lundgren 2012: 14).
> - Analysis of data also shows that the trade in e-waste has grown not only between the developed and developing countries but also among the developing countries themselves, reflecting a continuous growth and tolerance for cross-border movement (Ray 2008 cited in Lundgren 2012: 14).

worldwide annually (UNEP 2006). The waste contains toxins such as lead and mercury or other chemicals that can poison waterways if buried or release toxins into the air if burned. Much of this waste ends up as transfers from rich countries to the poor.

Production and disposal of waste is a matter of significant concern to green criminologists interested in questions of environmental harm. Systematic analysis in this area is evident in a range of studies, many of which are directly linked to environmental justice concerns. Examples include:

- the role of organized criminal syndicates in the dumping of waste, including toxic waste (Block 2002; Ruggiero 1996);

- inequalities associated with the location of disadvantaged and minority communities near toxic waste sites (Saha and Mohai 2005; Pellow 2007; Pinderhughes 1996);
- the use of medical and epidemiological evidence in demonstrating the nature and dynamics of toxic crimes (Lynch and Stretesky 2001);
- the global trade in electronic waste as a form of environmental crime that is of particular concern at the present time (Gibbs *et al.* 2010b; Interpol 2009);
- the social and cultural context within which local residents come to perceive what it is that pollutes their neighbourhoods and local rivers (Natali 2010);
- environmental racism linked to the social status of being poor, part of a minority group or indigenous community (Bullard 1994; Brook 1998);
- specific incidents in which toxic materials have been dumped into developing countries by unscrupulous companies (White 2009c).

Social and environmental harm is being caused by both legal and illegal transfers of hazardous waste, and it is the poor and vulnerable of the world's population who are paying the price (Clapp 2001). Particular environments are being denuded, and human and animal health is suffering, as toxic materials permeate specific areas and become embedded in local landscapes.

The definition of waste is itself highly contentious, because substances can change in content, form and impact over time. In part this is reflected in waste management strategies that talk about the need to reduce, reuse, recycle, recover waste by physical, biological or chemical processes, and to make use of landfill, incineration or other disposal methods (Meyers, McLeod and Anbarci 2006). Things change over time – and what is considered waste today, or in one manifestation, may well be considered a 'resource' tomorrow or in another social application.

Consider as well the diverse categories of waste, as indicated by the following list from a European Commission publication (see Meyers, McLeod and Anbarci 2006: 506):

- production or consumption residues not otherwise specified below;
- off-specification products;
- products whose date for appropriate use has expired;
- materials spilled, lost or having undergone another mishap, including any materials, equipment, etc., contaminated as a result of the mishap;
- materials contaminated or soiled as a result of planned actions (e.g. residues from cleaning operations, packing materials, containers, etc.);
- unusable parts (e.g. reject batteries, exhausted catalytic converters, etc.);
- substances which no longer perform satisfactorily (e.g. contaminated acids, contaminated solvents, exhausted tempering salts, etc.);
- residues of industrial processes (e.g. slags, still bottoms, etc.);

- residues from pollution abatement processes (e.g. scrubber sludges, baghouse dusts, spent filters, etc.);
- machining/finishing residues (e.g. lathe turnings, mill scales, etc.);
- residues from raw materials extraction and processing (e.g. mining residues, oil field slops, etc.);
- adulterated materials (e.g. oils contaminated with polychlorinated biphenyls, etc.);
- any materials, substances or products whose use has been banned by law;
- products for which the holder has no further use (e.g. agricultural, household, office, commercial and shop discards, etc.);
- contaminated materials, substances or products resulting from remedial action with respect to land; and any materials, substances or products which are not contained in the above categories.

In addition to this list, categories of waste that deserve further reflection include medical or clinical waste, and radioactive waste. Both these waste streams can leave a toxic legacy for present and future generations.

Waste production and economic growth feed off one another. The obvious implication of an expanding system, one based upon ever-increasing production and consumption, is for constant and escalating pressures on the world's non-renewable resources. Waste is both a by-product of production and the refuse left over from consumption. The raw materials that go into making goods and into the provision of services are fundamentally determined by the producers, not end consumers. This involves exploitation of environments, human and non-human animals alike. Similarly, the waste by-products of production and the refuse left over from consumption are ultimately determined according to the dictates of profit-making interests. For example, plastic wrappers entice consumers to buy, and then become part of the waste which must be disposed of afterwards.

A key moment in the history of waste is its commodification on a large scale, which is linked to the growth of waste-removal companies in the post-World-War-Two period (Field 1998). One consequence of this trend is that waste becomes an aggregate rather than specific substance. Many different and specific wastes are brought together by the one company or brought to a single depot. That is, specific waste from specific sites is mixed up together, and the cash-nexus arrangement means that waste is sought after and collected in bulk. Waste disposal was previously linked to immediate production sites, such as around a factory, and affected all classes who lived in proximity to the site, including workers, managers and owners. But its commodification allows for two outcomes: first, the amalgamation of many wastes into an indistinguishable generalized waste, and secondly, the transportation of waste off-site to new and specific places for waste disposal, which, in some cases, simply includes dumping at sea; later, it includes transference to less developed countries in the Caribbean, Africa and Asia (see Pellow 2007). In other words, there is a separation of waste product from the producer of waste.

For a specific example of the consequences of the commodification of e-waste in a particular country, see Joines (2012) on how China has used the trade in e-waste for its own economic development. The author notes that 'globalization in effect hides the gravity of the e-waste trade. Because manufacturing, production, consumption and disposal all take place in different areas, it is hard to see the true consequences of such a trade'. The case vignette provides one account of just such consequences.

Case vignette 9.1 The river runs black in Guiyu

In the city of Guiyu in southern China, home to one of the world's largest e-waste dumps, the river runs black (Greenpeace International 2005). Water, land and air are polluted as a result of the dismantling and processing of e-waste, including the burning of PVC components in the open. The city supports thousands of businesses that process discarded electronics. There are 'diseases of the skin, stomach, respiratory tract and other organs', and drinking water has to be trucked in from a neighbouring province. The industry is driven by dumping from developed countries as well as the growth of domestically generated e-waste. E-waste is 'a double-edged sword', providing reclaimable materials on the one hand and toxic compounds like antimony, lead, cadmium, mercury, PVC and brominated flame retardants on the other (see Lundgren 2012). The most high-profile sites are in China, India and Africa. But less-investigated locations include the Philippines, Indonesia and Pakistan (Siegel 2011; Lundgren 2012). Given the tightening of regulations in Asia, there is a trend for 'more e-waste to flow into West African countries'. Expanding technologies continue to shrink the average life-span of electronic devices, and the e-waste mountain continues to grow. Whether deposited to landfill or recycled, e-waste remains an ongoing topic of concern for green criminologists, not only because of its growing volume and toxicity but also because of the crime, criminality, social and ecological injustices associated with its location and disposal (see Pellow 2007). From a criminological perspective the problem of e-waste provides a number of angles for potential study: the illegal trafficking of electronic waste across borders; analysis of an environmental risk that is not necessarily criminalized (Gibbs *et al.* 2010b, 2011); and the security implications associated with the mining of end-of-life computer hard drives for sensitive personal information and bank account details, providing opportunities for fraud (Lundgren 2012: 17). Law-enforcement agencies such as Interpol are also increasingly concerned about the links between organized crime and electronic waste.

The specific mechanisms for the transfer of hazardous waste from the North to the South vary, and are ostensibly governed by international conventions and protocols. However, the dynamic nature of hazard transfer is enabled both by the in-built limitations of domestic or national laws (Collins 2010) and through the sidestepping of existing international regulation through strategies such as renaming the process as recycling (Clapp 2001).

There is often overlap between the harmful actions of legitimate businesses and those of criminal syndicates. The dearth of adequate regulatory, enforcement and prosecution agencies and resources at local, regional and international levels means that from a cost-benefit perspective there is little disincentive to desist from illegal dumping, however it is organized. Yet much of the criminality associated with waste disposal has its origins in the regulatory apparatus of the state. Several interrelated issues have a bearing on this.

First, waste disposal is a lucrative money-making business. Huge profits are there to be made in cases where waste is a product with an inelastic price – that is, an increase in price does not equally reduce demand for the service (Van Daele, Vander Beken and Dorn 2007: 35). This has made waste disposal attractive to organized criminal syndicates while simultaneously opening the door for some legitimate waste-management companies to increase their profits by utilizing illegal practices:

> Available estimates indicate that profits from illegal waste management are about three to four times higher than those for legal activities. For hazardous wastes, the profit differential is even higher. It is possible that commercial entities' creative cost reduction beyond what is allowed is encouraged by these factors and that corporate culture considers the environment less important than profits. Beyond this, the growing use of subcontractors may decrease transparency, reducing the risks of detection of illegal waste management practices.
> (Van Daele, Vander Beken, T., and Dorn 2007: 36)

Secondly, the impetus to bend rules and merge practices stems from the costs of waste disposal themselves. These are comprised of two major components (Dorn, Van Daele and Vander Beken 2007):

- high costs of legal waste management – related to industry standards, international conventions, government regulation, application of suitable technologies;
- high costs of compliance – traceability, labelling, automation and book-keeping procedures.

Sub-contracting the transport and disposal of hazardous waste is one means to be legal and also be the beneficiary of illegal waste management. Criminality is in many ways built into the dynamics and structures associated with waste as an industry and as a multi-jurisdictional problem, as indicated in Box 9.2.

Box 9.2 Interfaces and hazardous waste

Hazardous waste moves across jurisdictions and is covered by many different laws and statutes administered at different jurisdictional levels. Each interface can involve different stake-holders and actors. What occurs at each particular level has impacts and flow-through effects for other levels and jurisdictions. For instance, the presence or absence of a suitable treatment facility will determine the movement and transport history of specific kinds of waste. This, in turn, influences the potential for criminal (e.g. breaking the law in a criminally harmful way) or illegal (e.g. breaching the law through non-compliance with a licensing regime) disposal of the waste. Intergovernmental interfaces may be bogged down by inadequate information-sharing and/or inter-agency protocols that create bureaucratic 'red tape'. Conversely, criminal organizations and individuals engaged in illegal activity often have the advantage of speed and flexibility in decision-making and actions. The nature of the interfaces – including their complexity and questions relating to boundary ambivalence – that is, who precisely is responsible for what and when? – can work against systematic and coherent responses to illegal disposal threats.

If problems like waste and pollution are to be adequately addressed, then it is imperative to understand the nature, extent and dynamics of the problem. This can be more complicated than it sounds. For example, the scale of the problem of waste (and pollution more generally) can be measured in a number of ways: from the volume of waste generated, to how much waste is transferred intrastate, interstate or offshore; who is generating the waste; different types of hazardous wastes; the biological, social and environmental impacts of hazardous wastes; through to the present and future impact of landfills for current and intergenerational health and environmental well-being. Defining the problem is not only a technical task, but can also involve active contests over evidence of contamination and evidence of wrongdoing.

Environmental justice and toxic sites

Toxic towns periodically make headlines as local residents and businesses come to the realization that where they live and work, and where their children play, is contaminated. The experience of toxicity and contamination is not new, nor is it confined to any one particular geographical area. Toxic towns are residential areas – small villages, rural towns or suburbs of larger cities – that are located near contaminated physical sites (such as polluted waterways, hazardous landfills or legacy wastes from past industrial activities) and/or are affected by contaminated soil or polluted air and water that permeates their specific geographical locations. Given the health and well-being implications stemming from such environmental harms, and the fact that they appear to be ubiquitous, it is important for the social sciences to take an interest in these matters.

The environmental justice movement originated in the United States in the late 1970s as a result of community mobilization around issues of contamination. Up to this time specific government efforts to curb pollution and preserve endangered landscapes reflected the differential capacity of population groups to win space for reforms and to protect their immediate amenities and interests. This was to change as minority communities began to mobilize around their particular interests in places such as Warren County, North Carolina and Gary, Indiana (Brisman 2007; Hurley 1995; Edwards 1998; Pellow 2007).

The focus of the environmental justice movement is on environmental injustice, on discrimination and demands for equitable treatment in the face of disproportionate environmental disadvantage for some groups relative to others (Bullard 2005a and b; Agyeman and Carmin 2011). Much attention has been directed towards site-specific environmental hazards, such as waste dumps and the proximity of certain groups to these facilities.

According to Stretesky and Hogan (1998), environmental justice researchers try to do at least two things: first, analyse the placement of active waste facilities in minority and poor areas and, secondly, analyse the social and political processes that shape racial, ethnic and economic demographic patterns around existing hazardous waste sites. Discrimination in this context takes two forms: direct and indirect. Direct discrimination relates to the 'prejudice leads to discrimination' model, in which there is express intent to deny or harm another individual or group based on some characteristics that the targeted individual or group possesses (e.g. put the hazard where 'certain' people do not find it so offensive). Indirect discrimination relates to practices that result in negative and differential impact on minorities even though the policies or regulations guiding those actions were established and carried out with no intent to harm (e.g. economic and social forces may serve to constrain the choices of minorities and the poor when compared to the choices available to whites and the affluent – that is, what school to attend, where to live, and what kind of work is available).

The social impact of environmental harm can be both immediate, as in the case of respiratory problems or increased probability of disease outbreak, and long-term (e.g. lower quality of life, alteration of physiological functioning). Temporal considerations also are relevant to analysis of discrimination relating to environmental harm. For example, environmental justice researchers deal with temporal issues by considering when and why poor or minority communities end up living near toxic waste facilities. A key question is whether or not the proximity between pollution and certain communities is the result of the placement of the facility in that community (direct discrimination), or whether the placement of the facility attracts these communities because housing values become depressed (indirect discrimination). By physically mapping out environmental harms, over time and in relation to population characteristics, it is possible to determine what kind of discrimination is in fact at play (see for example, Stretesky and Hogan 1998; Lynch, Stretesky and McGurrin 2002). Did the pollution come to the people, or did the people come to live near the pollution? This is answerable through temporal analysis.

'Environmental racism' is a term that that has been applied to the ways in which, in the United States context in particular, minority communities comprised of people of colour (e.g. African Americans) have suffered denial of basic human rights and environmental protection, and have generally and disproportionately had to live and work close to polluting industries and toxic dumping grounds. As a concept, environmental racism refers to 'any policy, practice, or directive that differentially affects or disadvantages (whether intended or unintended) individuals, groups, or communities because of their race or colour' (Bullard 2005b: 32). Those who live in proximity to contaminated land, air and water tend to be those with less overall social and economic power, and this, in turn is associated with 'race' and ethnicity (Hurley 1995; Bullard 2005a).

The environmental justice movement seeks to prevent environmental threats and is premised upon a series of interlinked propositions and principles (see Bullard 2005b). These principles emphasize values such as social equity (in which all individuals should have a right to be protected from environmental degradation) and harm prevention (which focuses on eliminating a threat before harm occurs). Each of these areas requires considerable resources be devoted to measuring effects such as human exposure to environmental chemicals, and to sociological analysis of harm and risk distributions among diverse population groups.

Intervention in this area is generally premised upon ideological and practical support for the adoption of the precautionary principle. The precautionary principle refers to the idea that official action be taken to protect people and environments in cases where there is scientific uncertainty as to the nature of the potential damage or the likelihood of risk. This principle has been integrated into the regulatory and legal frameworks of the European Union, but has been less popular in the United States. From an environmental justice perspective the preferred emphasis when it comes to precaution is to err on the side of human safety and well-being rather than industrial development. As Bullard (2005b: 28) observes:

> It asks 'How little harm is possible?' rather than 'How much harm is allowable?' This principle demands that decision makers set goals for safe environments and examine all available alternatives for achieving the goals, and it places the burden of proof of safety on those who propose to use inherently dangerous and risky technologies.

Moreover, this framework requires that those

parties applying for operating permits for landfills, incinerators, smelters, refineries, chemical plants, and similar operations must prove that their operations are not harmful to human health, will not disproportionately affect racial and ethnic minorities and other protected groups, and are non-discriminatory.

(Bullard 2005b: 28–9)

The focus of environmental justice movements has tended to be on human populations, at the local level, living in urban or semi-rural environments (see also Chapter 3). In studying issues pertaining to contamination and toxicity the features of any particular site need to be examined from the point of view of:

- *The past*: legacy issues in relation to storage of toxic materials (e.g. radioactive and hazardous waste) and long-term presence of substances such as mining sludge.
- *The present*: current claims to injury and harms arising from contemporary practices such as pesticide spraying and mining procedures that pollute the air, water and land.
- *The future*: potential transference issues (e.g. as a result of floods) and accumulation issues (e.g. increases in toxicity hazard over time as with the stockpiling of car and truck tyres).

Importantly, it can be envisaged that unexpected weather events linked to climate change will impinge upon towns and surrounding areas in particularly damaging ways, in that they increase the possibility of transference of toxic harm across physical boundaries and regardless of ordinary preventive barriers.

Resource extraction and pollution

Resource extraction industries are the economic lifeblood of many countries around the world. Mining, forestry and petroleum (involving drilling at sea as well as on land) constitute major sources of revenue and profit for states and corporations alike. They employ many people across a broad range of occupations and types of paid work. They also demand huge expenditure from the point of view of investment, exploration, operations and rehabilitation. Resource extraction is not cheap. It also has its environmental and social costs.

The harms resulting from extractive industries like mining are and should be an issue of major public concern (Carrington, Hogg and McIntosh 2011; Munro 2012). These include harms stemming from environmental degradation and contamination. In some circumstances mining ventures create toxic sites and thus produce the conditions for contaminated communities, with significant detrimental consequences for local habitats and human residents. The negative impact of the mining industry on the environment is well-known and readily acknowledged, not only by conservation bodies and environmental activists, but by governments and the mining industry itself (see for example, Australian Bureau of Statistics 2003; Australian and New Zealand Minerals and Energy Council and Minerals Council of Australia 2000; Thomson and Joyce 2006; Lacey, Parsons and Moffat 2012). Indeed, public pressure has ensured that recent years have seen considerable industry attention being paid to improving standards of environmental management and ensuring the rehabilitation of mined-out areas.

Nonetheless, significant questions remain about the environmental and social consequences of mining, particularly the huge open-cut mining projects, mountain-top mining, and new forms of mining such as coal-seam fracking. Resource extraction has a long history and extensive geographical reach. It is also tied to who has the power to do what, where, how cost effectively, and for whose benefit. Detrimental environmental impacts associated with mining are intrinsic to mining itself. This being the case, the crucial question is basically how best to weigh up specific types of environmental harm in relation to economic and social benefit. In other words, mining inevitably involves a trade-off between ecological considerations and economic gain. There is nothing particularly profound about this; nor is this trade-off confined solely to mining. It also pertains to other extractive industries, such as forestry and fishing.

The operational aspects of mining (that is, methods and technologies used in extraction) and the net consequences of mining (that is, the overall impact on particular extraction sites) are the bread and butter of environmental impact assessment and the basis for the construction of a community 'social license to operate' (SLO) (see Thomson and Boutilier 2011). In other words, short of banning mining altogether, the project of environmental justice (and ecological sustainability) is one of equity and ecological well-being, within the overarching framework of nature–human interaction. The point is not necessarily to stop mining (although this may be warranted in some instances), but to ensure the least harm when doing it.

The pollution accompanying mining is a matter of growing concern among those who live and work in coal-mining areas, who are experiencing the shattering effects on community and health from industry practices such as 'fracking' and open-cut mining (Munro 2012). The scale of the harm and how mining operations are organized and carried out is also highly relevant in considerations of the anthropocentric causes of climate change. Mining can have substantial impact in regard to greenhouse gas emissions. For example, the Alberta Tar Sands project in Canada is notorious for its huge contribution to greenhouse gas emissions, because of the enormous size and the open-cut methods of the mining operations (Klare 2012). In Australia, recent legal action against extensions to existing open cut coal mining operations in Queensland have highlighted the environmental impact, including greenhouse gas emissions, resulting from such extensions (Millner and Ruddock 2011).

Case vignette 9.2 Coal seam fire

In Jharia in eastern India over a million people live and work atop a coal seam that has been burning for several decades, one of thousands of coal-seam fires said to be burning across the globe. According to a *Sixty Minutes* documentary, 60 square kilometres (an area the size of 12,000 football fields) is on fire. Presenter Allison Langdon describes what she sees and hears.

> It's when the sun drops and the fires raging just below the surface break through at countless points right across the countryside that this place really becomes a vision of hell. As the coal underground burns to ash, the ground above completely collapses. The gas spewing from countless cracks and vents is a deadly toxic cocktail of carbon dioxide, carbon monoxide, sulphur dioxide, methane, even mercury. The air is thick with the smell of sulphur, and the ground itself is radiating heat.
> (*Sixty Minutes*, Australia 2012)

The stories of personal tragedy are poignant – a mother describes how her son was killed by gases from the fire below.

> It was winter ... we did not have enough warm clothes, which is why they were sleeping in the room that was slightly warm because of the gases ... and he just didn't wake up.
> (*Sixty Minutes*, Australia 2012)

Opened in 1896, the Jharia mines in Dhanbad district, around 270 km from Ranchi, have huge deposits of coal. Shortly after 1971 the coal mines were nationalized. Since then, their operator has been Bharat Coking Coal Limited (BCCL), which now controls one of the biggest coal deposits in India and the whole of Asia. Before 1973 coal mining was done underground, but after 1973 BCCL decided to shift to opencast (Zipfel 2012).

> The coalfield of Jharia is, on the one hand, India's biggest coal mining area and, on the other, the area with the most coal seam fires. Coal seam fires are not only one of the biggest causes of environmental pollution locally, but also globally. These blazes spout enormous quantities of carbon dioxide into the air, in India alone 1.4 billion tons a year. As a result, India has become the fourth biggest producer of greenhouse gas worldwide.
> (Zipfel 2012)

Coal mining is, in some places, literally setting the world on fire.

Importantly, the search for increasingly scarce natural resources is taking companies to new frontiers of mineral and gas exploration and technical exploitation. This carries with it several problematic risks. First, there are hazards and dangers associated with activities such as drilling in deep-offshore locations (as evidenced by the demise of the BP oil rig in the Gulf of Mexico); that is, new methods of extraction carry with them new dangers and new potential harms. Second, the more remote and marginal the areas that are exploited, and the more reliant on mining those communities become for their local economy, the less likelihood of adequate regulation of mining activities. In either case, issues pertaining to extensive production of greenhouse gas emissions remain of general concern.

In addition to issues surrounding the contribution of mining to global warming (because of scale and method of operations, regardless of where they are located), there are other specific environmental issues associated with application of new methods of operation. For instance, in developed countries there is presently much consternation and controversy over the environmental impact of 'fracking', a technique that involves using chemicals to extract coal-seam gas. In the United States, as with Australia, a major concern is that hydraulic fracturing fluids used to fracture rock formations contain numerous chemicals harmful to human and environmental health, especially if they enter drinking-water supplies. A recent US report found that:

> Between 2005 and 2009, the oil and gas service companies used hydraulic fracturing products containing 29 chemicals that are (1) known or possible human carcinogens, (2) regulated under the Safe Drinking Water Act for their risks to human health, or (3) listed as hazardous air pollutants under the Clean Air Act.
> (United States House of Representatives Committee on Energy and Commerce 2011: 1)

It was also noted that in many instances the companies were injecting fluids containing chemicals that they themselves could not identify.

Similar problems have been identified in Australia, where public risk assessment of the chemicals being used is urgently needed (Cleary 2012). Prime agricultural land in eastern Australia is being dotted by an increasing number of coal-seam gas wells, with major implications for people and environments. The industry has the potential to:

> contaminate underground aquifers; produce billions of litres of unmanageable saline waste water that will yield millions of tonnes of salt and threaten farmland, river systems and wetlands; overlay an extensive network of access roads and pipelines; accelerate climate change by leaking methane gas into the atmosphere; trigger earthquakes; depress land values; and impose a crippling cost across the economy by doubling or even tripling the price of domestic gas.
> (Cleary 2012: 23–4)

In Australia, the main protagonists in the fracking debate are, on the one side, coal and gas companies and, on the other, farmers, tourism operators and environmentalists. Profit and power are the key determinants in these debates, as is the extent of community mobilization and politicization of the issues. Consistent with the general pattern of environmental injustice, it is the most vulnerable who are likely to suffer from both take-over of land and radical alterations to existing land uses (Borras and Franco 2010; Boekhout van Solinge 2008a and b).

Resource extraction is certainly not a new phenomenon. Indeed, the history of the modern world is based precisely upon resource extraction and conflicts over natural resources (Klare 2001; Stretesky *et al.* 2013). One aspect of these conflicts is seen in the processes of colonization, a phenomenon that has affected many different indigenous peoples in places such as South America, North America and Australasia, as well as the native inhabitants of Africa, Asia and beyond (White 2011a). In countries such as Australia, indigenous territories were considered frontier lands that were unowned, underutilized and therefore open to exploitation. The prior ownership rights, interests and knowledge of indigenous inhabitants were treated as irrelevant by the European invaders. Environmental victimization of this sort is central to dispossession and maltreatment of indigenous peoples across many continents and over a period of several centuries.

In the 'race for what's left' traditional and indigenous people worldwide are especially vulnerable to the imposition of corporate power (Klare 2012). In Canada, for example, governments are eager to allow extraction industries to enter into and fully work lands occupied by indigenous peoples, regardless of the wishes of the local people – as particularly evidenced by the exploitation of the Alberta Tar Sands (Rush 2002; Smandych and Kueneman 2010).

What is at threat is not simply the immediate physical needs of indigenous and traditional peoples, but a whole way of life and livelihood that frequently includes hunting, fishing and small-scale agriculture. In the United States, for example, the Chippewa people have fought against mining operations on their lands, knowing that mining on their ceded lands would lead to environmental destruction of the land and water, thereby destroying their means of subsistence (Clark 2002; Schlosberg 2007). As with similar events elsewhere in the world, such contamination of the natural world constitutes an assault that goes to the heart of indigenous culture and identity.

There is no doubting the national and regional economic importance of the natural resource and extractive industries. But mining of oil, gas and minerals in particular generates considerable amounts of hazardous materials and contaminants. Yet, due to issues such as remoteness, political largesse and the trend toward self-regulation (in some industries), questions can be asked about how adequate the regulation of potential hazards and harms are in relation to the big economic players. For instance, more concrete data is needed with regard to the extent of mining-related contamination in rural and remote areas, in cities and towns, and on private lands, public lands, and in waterways. The damage is being done; we need to know to what extent and how far-reaching it is. What we know so far is certainly not encouraging (Munro 2012). Environmental justice also demands that workers, residents and key stake-holders be included as participants in data-collection processes, and that their specific vulnerabilities as victims or potential victims of environmental harm be prioritized for analysis and action.

Air, land and water are directly affected by the extraction (mining) and processing (smelting) of mined substances. So, too, the world's climate is being altered by the emission of greenhouse gases to which mining is a major contributor. Recent developments such as mega-mines and coal-seam fracking will exacerbate these harms due to the scale and nature of the methods used.

Conclusion

One consequence of unsustainable environmental practices is to put more pressure on companies to seek out new resources (natural and human) to exploit, in the face of dwindling reserves due to over-exploitation and the contamination of nature from already produced waste. Nature itself is used as a dumping ground, particularly in the invisible spaces of the open seas and less developed countries. Waste is both a driver and an outcome of the production process. The social consequences of no work, no income, and no subsistence livelihood for significant numbers of people worldwide means that waste-producing and toxic forms of production (including recycling) are more likely to be accepted by the economically vulnerable. Their victimization is thus embedded in the wider systemic pressures associated with global capitalism. Profitability very often means adopting the most unsustainable practices for short-term gain. The global financial crisis and subsequent recessions potentially exacerbate this trend. Ultimately the disconnection between production and consumption, and the implicit distinction between well-being in the North and well-being in the South, ensures the continuation of global environmental degradation that places all in peril.

As this chapter has discussed, it is the poor and minorities worldwide who bear the brunt of waste disposal practices, whether these are legal or illegal. There is ample evidence that globalization is seeing the transfer of dirty industries and dirty waste to the Third World (Schmidt 2004; Harvey 1996; Pellow 2007). Characteristically, the biggest polluters and generators of waste – such as the United States and the European Union – are also the most likely to export their waste to less-developed counties. There is also strong evidence within particular national contexts, such as the USA, and internationally that those who are forced to live close to polluting industries and waste disposal sites are the poor and are frequently people of colour and indigenous people (Brook 1998; Bullard 1994; Simon 2000). The same people have to put up with the worst and most hazardous kinds of pollution and waste, regardless of whether these come to them through legal or illegal means. In other words, from the point of view of equality, equity and fairness, it is clear that pollution and waste is basically a problem for the poor, and something that is generally avoided by the rich. The most disadvantaged sections of the community are the ones who live in closest proximity to legal landfill sites and garbage dumps. They are also the most susceptible to illegal dumping, whether it is in Abidjan or Chicago (see Pellow 2004).

Discussion topics

- What is 'pollution' and why does it matter?
- What are the methods by which waste is transferred, transformed and trafficked (e.g. the mixing of toxic wastes into 'legitimate' waste streams; the labelling of some waste as 'recycle' material)?
- What is the role of transnational criminal organizations and corruption in the phenomenon of illicit trafficking, and dumping, of waste?
- What is the nexus between legal and illegal waste disposal, and how are the costs of compliance and expensive methods of disposal drivers for some legitimate companies to utilize illegal means to offload waste and/or contract out to criminal organizations?
- Pollution and waste are just the normal environmental costs of doing business. Discuss.

Further reading

Bisschop, L. (2012a). 'Is It All Going To Waste? Illegal transports of e-waste in a European trade hub', *Crime, Law and Social Change*, 58(3): 221–49.

Clapp, J. (2001). *Toxic Exports: The transfer of hazardous wastes from rich to poor countries*. Ithaca, NY and London: Cornell University Press.

Collins, C. (2010). *Toxic Loopholes: Failures and future prospects for environmental law*. Cambridge: Cambridge University Press.

Lundgren, K. (2012). *The Global Impact of E-Waste: Addressing the challenge*. Geneva: International Labour Organization.

Pellow, D. (2007). *Resisting Global Toxics: Transnational movements for environmental justice*. Cambridge, MA: MIT Press.

Chapter 10

Environmental victims

Introduction

This chapter will discuss the following topics:

- environmental victimology;
- humans and environmental victimization;
- eco-justice and non-human environmental victims; and
- victim mobilization.

In a report that maps the contours of environmental crime and victimization, Skinnider (2011: 2) observes that 'historically, research on environmental crime has lacked the theoretical and methodological depth applied to other traditional crimes'. In part this is the result of perceptions of environmental crimes as 'victimless', to the extent that 'they do not always produce an immediate consequence, the harm may be diffused or go undetected for a lengthy period of time' (ibid.). This is further compounded by the condoning of environmentally harmful activities by governments, industry and in some cases particular communities and society as a whole. As a result, 'victims of environmental harm are not widely recognized as victims of "crime" and thus are excluded from the traditional view of victimology which is largely based on conventional constructions of crime' (ibid.).

Questions of inequality, disadvantage and subordination are never far from the surface in debates about environmental victims. Likewise, green criminology places such questions at the centre of research and analysis in the context of an eco-justice framework.

Environmental victimology

Environmental victimization refers to specific forms of harm which are caused by acts or omissions leading to the presence or absence of environmental agents which are associated with human injury (Williams 1996). According to Williams (1996: 21) environmental victims are 'those of past, present, or future generations who are injured as a consequence of change to the chemical, physical, microbiological, or psychosocial environment, brought about by deliberate or reckless, individual or collective, human act or act of omission'. In response to a growing body of literature on non-human victims, within green criminology and other disciples, this definition of 'victim' now needs to be extended to include animals, plants and eco-systems. In other words, the 'environment' itself should be counted as a possible victim of crime.

As our collective knowledge of global environmental harm increases, there is an appreciation that those who suffer environmental victimization deserve sustained analysis and strategic interventions in their own right (see Hall 2013a and b). This is not a straightforward task and the complexity of the issue is further compounded when we include the non-human in addition to the human as victim.

As with 'conventional' victims within criminal justice, there are persistent issues of recognition, acknowledgement, participation, redress, compensation and restoration. It is vital to gain a picture of how such harms are or could be dealt with within existing criminal laws, and of the potential for human-rights law to offer protection and newly conceptualized rights in relation to the environment. What is to be done with and for victims and survivors of environmental harm takes us into the realms of restitution, compensation and restoration, and is likewise in need of illumination.

The notion of environmental victim implies that someone or something is being harmed through the conscious or neglectful actions of another. From a green criminology perspective, environmental harm is best seen in terms of justice, based upon notions of human, ecological and animal rights (see Chapters 1 and 3). The key issue is weighing up different kinds of harm and violation of rights within a broad eco-justice framework, and stretching the boundaries of conventional criminology to include other kinds of harm than those already deemed illegal.

In the specific area of environmental victimology, the literature to date has tended to focus on humans as victims rather than other species or particular environments (see for example, Williams 1996; Jarrell and Ozymy 2012; Hall 2013a and b). Moreover, the complexities and development of victimology as a specific sub-discipline or associated discipline of criminology has primarily been due to attention given to the dynamic nature of relationships between human actors as perpetrators, as victims, and as observers (Rock 2007; Fattah 2010).

Environmental victimology, as such, has been less concerned with non-human animals and specific biospheres than with the interests and well-being of humans in specific circumstances. In this regard we might well heed the lessons of mainstream victimology, that being and becoming a victim is never socially neutral. This holds true for environmental victimization as it does for other sorts of victim-making. Fattah (2010: 46) makes the comment that:

> In most instances victims are not chosen at random, and in many cases the motives for the criminal act develop around a specific and non-exchangeable victim. Therefore, an examination of victim characteristics, of the place the victim

occupies, and the role the victim plays in these dynamic processes is essential to understanding why the crime was committed in a given situation, at a given moment, and why a particular target was chosen.

This should not be interpreted as suggesting that somehow the victim is responsible in some way for their targeting. Rather, it is an acknowledgement that the more one examines specific actions that produce and involve environmental victims, the greater the consensus that those who suffer harm do so because of their specific proximity and/or relationship to perpetrators of the harm. Largely these consist of relations of power, domination and exploitation. It is the social, economic and political characteristics of victim populations that make them vulnerable to victimization in the first place. This extends to the non-human as well as the human.

Consider for example the choices made (by humans) about which species receive human protection and which do not (see Sollund 2012a, 2013). Endemic species (that is, those which have an historical relationship with particular ecosystems, in particular geographical areas) are not always the species that are most valued and most likely to gain support from human backers when it comes to situations of species competition. In this context, human decisions trade-off one species against another. The galaxia fish is a case in point. A number of types of this species of fish are unique to the island state of Tasmania in Australia. However due to the destruction of habitat and the introduction of non-native species they are now under serious threat.

The key problem is introduced trout species. Galaxias are not only forced to compete for food (insects that fall or land on the surface of the water), but are also preyed upon by non-native predators such as the Brown and Rainbow trout (Threatened Species Unit, Parks and Wildlife Service Tasmania 1998). Trout were introduced into Tasmania in the mid-1800s, primarily for the purposes of recreational fishing. Today they are also a valued part of the aquaculture industry. Almost all of government and private attention has been on protecting the trout, regardless of the consequences of this for the galaxia. This is because the trout is deemed a valued and valuable species (for tourism, for commercial food markets), while the plight of the galaxia is ignored, since it has no economic value. Laws have been designed to protect the trout (e.g. catch limits, closed seasons, licences). While officially the galaxia is classified as 'protected', the fact is that its main predator has been encouraged to flourish regardless of ecological outcome and its impact on the future viability of the galaxia species.

The significance of this story of the victimization of the galaxia fish is that it alerts us to the fact that not all species are 'valued' in the same way and the realization that they too can be 'victims' (of policy, of introduced predators) but not recognized as such. Hence, the status and value of animals, of particular species, and of individual animals varies greatly according to circumstance and larger ecological patterns and trends (see White 2013c). Likewise, our appreciation of rivers, mountains and oceans is contingent upon how these are conceptualized in popular discourse and legal opinion (Stone 1972). Whether and how the non-human is viewed as victim is a relatively new area of investigation within green criminology. Environmental victimology cannot afford to omit such considerations as it develops further.

The significance of scholarship in this area is demonstrated by a growing body of literature in green criminology and forums devoted to reconceptualizing the notion of environmental victims (for example, a 2012 conference in Delft, the Netherlands was entirely devoted to environmental crime and its victims). As the study of environmental victimology develops, it must be inclusive of different notions of who is a victim, what is a victim and how processes of denial (indifference, oversight, ignorance) influence who and what is considered a victim, as well as the impacts of these variables on the experience of victimization and suffering (e.g. recognized or unrecognized; heard or unheard) and the meting out of justice in terms of compensation (immediate, delayed, denied).

Humans and environmental victimization

The majority of human victims of environmental degradation – stemming from industrial and commercial activities, global warming, loss of biodiversity and increased waste and pollution – are the poor and the dispossessed. While all are threatened by global environmental disaster, there remain large social differences in the likelihood of exposure and subsequent resilience to injury, harm and suffering. For those who disproportionately bear the brunt of global patterns of environmental transformation, degradation and victimization, big questions arise as to who will compensate them for their often prolonged suffering, now and into the future.

When it comes to measuring the value of human life some people count more than others and in some circumstances the health and well-being of certain people will be sacrificed on the altar of business profits and 'national' interests. This can be quantified in terms of United Nations figures on world poverty, on disease, on illnesses related to indoor and outdoor air pollution, on life expectancy and other similar data sets. Victimization is also measurable in terms of production processes worldwide in which destruction of local environments is part and parcel of resource extraction and the recycling of commodities.

> The open burning, acid baths and toxic dumping pour pollution into the land, air and water and exposes the men, women and children of Asia's poorer peoples to poison. The health and economic costs of this trade are vast and, due to export, are not born by the western consumers nor the waste brokers who benefit from the trade.
> (Basel Action Network and Silicon Valley Toxics Coalition 2002: 1)

In this example, the atrocity and suffering related to environmental harm is linked to a basic denial of human rights. This is not only evident in disparities in access to resources or in environmental living conditions; it is also found in the activities of regimes and companies that use violence against those who dare to threaten their economic and political interests. This has led some to argue that, since environmental injustice and human rights are inextricably interwoven, the former should be recognized as a major component of the latter (Adeola 2000: 687).

This story is familiar the world over, including within developed countries. It is a story of lack of care for those who are culturally and socially constructed as 'other' and therefore relieved of the obligations of compassion and compensation. Denial of harm on the part of the advantaged and socially privileged is easier when stereotypes, denigrating images and self-interest are mobilized in order to ignore such harms. This has long been the substantive concern of environmental justice movements (see Bullard 2005a and b; see also Hall 2013a and b). Environmental injustice is accomplished precisely through the devaluing of those who suffer the consequences of environmental harms not of their own making but stemming from decisions made by someone else, elsewhere in the world, in the interests of those who will never share their environmental risks and harms.

As extensive work on specific incidents and patterns of victimization demonstrate, some people are more likely to be disadvantaged by environmental problems than others. For instance, studies have identified disparities involving many different types of environmental hazards that especially adversely affect people of colour, ethnic minority groups and indigenous people in places such as Canada, Australia and the US (Bullard 1994; Pinderhughes 1996; Langton 1998; Stretesky and Lynch 1999; Brook 1998; Rush 2002; Robyn 2011). In the context of discussions on differential environmental victimization it is also important to consider how particular substances (e.g. chemicals, heavy metals) differentially victimize by sex (e.g. different impacts for male and female in humans; feminization of marine species) and age (the developing foetus, the developing child; the infirm, the very elderly).

People from poor and non-English-speaking backgrounds may also suffer disadvantages through their lack of participation in decision-making forums, as well as lack of information about potential hazards and risks. For example, methylmercury is a potent neurotoxin that can have serious health impacts, particularly for foetal growth. Apparently a large proportion of canned tuna fish sold in the United States contains unsafe levels of methylmercury. Yet, the populations at risk of overconsumption – namely minorities and low-income groups – are most likely to be uninformed of the risks and less likely to be aware of fish advisories and to change consumption habits (Pallo and Barken 2010).

The subjective disposition and consciousness of people is crucial to perceptions of threat, risk and imminent danger. The unequal distribution of exposure to environmental risks, whether in relation to the location of toxic waste sites or proximity to clean drinking water may not always be conceived as an 'environmental' issue, nor indeed as an environmental 'problem'. For instance, Harvey (1996) points out that the intersection of poverty, racism and desperation may occasionally lead to situations where, for the sake of jobs and economic development, community leaders actively solicit the relocation of hazardous industries or waste sites to their neighbourhoods. On the other hand the underlying reasons may be cultural, as noted by Waldman (2007), who describes a local community in South Africa that saw the contamination effects of asbestos as 'natural'. This was due to a combination of religious beliefs (that stressed a passive stance to the world around them) and the fact that often harms that are imperceptible to the senses only exist as a problem if they are constituted as such in public discourse (and, in particular, the public discourse of the village community). Sometimes too, governments and regulatory agencies alike ignore near misses and early warnings, despite strong evidence for precaution.

Consciousness of risk can also be studied from the point of view of differential risk within at-risk populations. In others words, a particular suburb or city may be placed in circumstances that heighten risks to well-being and health for everyone (e.g. dumping toxic waste in Abidjan, Ivory Coast; spraying chemical pesticides in New York City). However, particularly where heightened risk is deemed to be 'acceptable' in terms of cost-benefit analysis, as in the use of pesticides to prevent the spread of disease borne by mosquitoes, there are 'hidden' costs that may not be factored in. For instance, children and those with chemical sensitivities will suffer disproportionately if chemicals are sprayed, since they are more vulnerable than others to ill effects arising from the treatment. In such circumstances, the crucial questions are not only 'how many will be harmed' but also 'who will be harmed'? (Scott 2005a: 56). To appreciate this, we need to be conscious of differences within affected populations.

To take another example of how distribution of risk impacts upon different groups within at-risk populations, consider the case of Environmental Protection Agency (EPA) standards in the United States that limit the level of dioxin releases from paper mills into rivers and streams.

> These releases are known to contaminate fish, and so the EPA based its release levels on the average consumption of such fish. Yet Native American consumption is well known to be higher than the average American, making the dioxin release a much greater health risk to native Americans.
> (Schlosberg 2007: 60)

Vulnerability to environmental harm, therefore, is also due to social differences in how people utilize or interact with nature based on certain perceptions. All those who consume fish under the above circumstances may be at risk of dioxin poisoning (or methylmercury poisoning in the case of canned tuna) but certain groups are more vulnerable because of their particular cultural prescriptions and traditions.

Who is a victim is also reflective of differing degrees of harm, injury and suffering. Death from environmental catastrophe is only one example of how victimization manifests. Whether the affliction is or incorporates a disease or permanent injury or prolonged mental illness and psychological distress, a large proportion of 'victims' are simultaneously 'survivors'. They sometimes sustain injuries that significantly alter the course and quality of their lives and that are economically onerous in terms of health care. So too, the breaking up of communities, the displacement of individuals, the loss of economic livelihood and dispossession of land all constitute varying forms and degrees of harm and victimization of human populations.

Box 10.1 Mapping victim issues

In mapping out the issues faced by victims of environmental crime, Skinnider (2011:77) identifies the following issues for further study, based on the needs and challenges for victims arising from a Canadian scoping study. These include:

- *Measuring the extent of victimization.* Determining whether and how these types of crime can be included in studies of victimology and victim surveys. How to enhance our knowledge of the many ways in which environmental crime affects victims, victim vulnerabilities, etc.
- *Mapping trends and patterns.* Patterns of victimization can be related to broader patterns of global, socio-economic, gender and age inequalities. This has significance for attempts to develop a critical victimology of environmental crime.
- *Examining the concept of harm*, how it is defined and applied across different statutes, including a comparative study of regulatory schemes and strategies (within Canada and internationally).
- *Analysing the similarities and differences* of the position of the various kinds of victims under criminal/regulatory administrative/civil regimes (including access to justice mechanisms, sentencing trends, remediation, etc.). Particularly the issue of 'future generations' as victims and how to ensure such interests are represented in the process and the modalities of compensation.
- *Conducting comparative studies* of enforcement methods and their impact on victims. This could explore methods and best practices of promoting compliance with regulations; analyse the methods of promoting compliance with environmental protection regulations; and examine issues around civil and criminal liability of corporations.
- *Studying the impact of criminalizing* certain environmentally dangerous practices.
- Studying and evaluating the *relative effectiveness of various regulatory, education and awareness-raising methods* for the protection of the environment.

The pragmatic questions of who and what is victimized, when, where and why victimization occurs, and how things can be different continue to resonate, as do the social, political and economic flow-on effects. Victimization is about all species, their places of habitation and the elements that sustain planetary life.

Eco-justice and non-human environmental victims

For green criminology the notion of eco-justice signifies an active concern with both the human and the non-human (see Chapter 3). More expansive definitions of rights and justice extend the definition of 'victim' to include the non-human in the moral equation. This means that animals and eco-systems can under certain circumstances be considered 'victims', too. This is reflected in Box 10.2.

Acknowledgement of 'victim' status is crucial to understanding the ways in which environmental harm affects both human and the non-human. This means locating creatures and environments within their unique ecological niche and context. It also means examining events and contemporary human practices from the vantage point of history and geography.

Consider, for example, the way in which humans attribute 'value' to non-human animals, and the judgements made by humans as to their 'worth' as living creatures (see also Chapter 7). In strict legal terms, it is pointed out that:

> Animals have for centuries been characterized by the common law as the property of humans and, in accordance with the law governing such property, they could be treated in any way their owners saw fit. Humans could breed them, sell them, kill them – even torture them – without running afoul of any law.
>
> (Sankoff and White 2009: 1)

Box 10.2 Eco-justice and victims

- *Environment justice* – **the victim is humans:** environmental rights are seen as an extension of human or social rights so as to enhance the quality of human life, now and into the future.
- *Ecological justice* – **the victim is specific environments:** human beings are merely one component of complex ecosystems that should be preserved for their own sake.
- *Species justice* – **the victim is animals and plants:** animals have an intrinsic right to not suffer abuse, and plants the degradation of habitat to the extent that threatens biodiversity loss.

Recent commentary and research on animal rights and animal welfare directs attention to the changing nature of 'animal law' and the ways in which animals as property are being challenged by alternative conceptions of animals as 'persons' and/or as rights-holders in their own right (Sankoff and White 2009; Beirne 2009). Radical positions declare much of current practice and attitudes towards animals as fundamentally immoral and wrong, as a form of non-human oppression (see Svard 2008). From the point of view of species justice, each animal ought to be given opportunity as far as possible to fulfil its potential as a sentient being.

Be this as it may, if the non-human is to be acknowledged as a 'victim' then the non-human must be able to convey, in some way, the nature of their victimization. In other words, they need a human translator to speak on their behalf about the nature and consequences of the harms that they suffer. In practice, this basically means that there must be advocates to give voice to the concerns of those who cannot articulate what is happening to them such as trees, soil, bees, orchids, rivers, lakes. Some observe that this should also involve active listening, by humans, to the non-verbal cues from nature, the signals emanating from the natural world and its inhabitants, that denote things are not quite right such as the impacts of climate change (e.g. oceans warming, insect eggs hatching earlier) (see Schlosberg 2007; Besthorn 2013). It is argued that there is much to learn by bringing the non-human into the dialogue about ecological health and well-being that affects all.

At a pragmatic level, and in the context of decision-making processes in an environmental court, Preston (2011b: 143) describes how future generations or non-human biota may be considered victims:

> Environmental harm may require remediation over generations and hence the burden and the cost of remediation is transferred to future generations. Remediation of contaminated land and restoration of habitat of species, populations and ecological communities are examples of intergenerational burdens passed from the present generation to future generations. Where intergenerational inequity is caused by the commission of an environmental offence, the victims include future generations. ... The biosphere and non-human biota have intrinsic value independent of their utilitarian or instrumental value for humans. When harmed by environmental crime, the biosphere and non-human biota are also victims. The harm is able to be assessed from an ecological perspective; it need not be anthropocentric.

As it stands, the law (in some countries) already allows for a modicum of protection for the non-human as well as the human. The definition of 'victim' is however evolving and expanding. Public interest law, for example, has been utilized to give standing to human representatives of non-human entities such as rivers and trees. For example, a river was represented at a restorative justice conference in New Zealand by the chairperson of the Waikato River Enhancement Society (Preston 2011b: 144, fn53). In some cases there are 'surrogate victims' who are recognized as representing the community affected (including harms to particular biotic groups and abiotic environs) for the purpose of court determinations.

Case vignette 10.1 A river gets 'rights'

On 30 August 2012, the *New Zealand Herald* reported that 'for the first time a river has been given a legal identity'. Under a preliminary agreement between Whanganui River iwi [extended kinship group] and the New Zealand Government, the Whanganui River (and its tributaries) in the North Island was to 'become a legal entity and have a legal voice'. A spokesman for the Minister of Treaty Negotiations said Whanganui River will be recognized as a person when it comes to the law – 'in the same way a company is, which will give it rights and interests' (Shuttleworth 2012).

The agreement forms the basis of long-standing claims by the Whanganui River iwi dating back to 1873 and resulting in one of the longest-running court cases in New Zealand. The agreement recognizes the status of the river as Te Awa Tupua (an integrated living whole) and the inextricable relationship of iwi (the local Maori community) with the river. The key elements agreed so far include:

- Recognition of the status of the Whanganui River (including its tributaries) as Te Awa Tupua, an integrated, living whole from the mountains to the sea.
- Recognition of Te Awa Tupua as a legal entity, reflecting the view of the River as a living whole and enabling the River to have legal standing and an independent voice.
- Vesting of the Crown-owned parts of the river-bed in the name of Te Awa Tupua.
- Appointment of two persons (one by the Crown and the other by the River iwi) to a guardianship role – Te Pou Tupua – to act on behalf of Te Awa Tupua and protect its status, health and well-being.
- Development of a set of Te Awa Tupua values, recognizing the intrinsic characteristics of the River and providing guidance to decision-makers.
- Development of a Whole of River Strategy by collaboration between iwi, central and local government, commercial and recreational users and other community groups. The strategy will identify issues for the River, consider ways of addressing them, and recommend actions. The

> goal of the strategy will be to ensure the long-term environmental, social, cultural and economic health and well-being of the River.
>
> Christopher Finlayson, Attorney-General and Minister for the Treaty of Waitangi Negotiations, said: 'This agreement recognizes Whanganui Iwi's commitment to place the interests of the river at the centre of the settlement. Whanganui Iwi have not sought to have their relationship with the river defined in these settlement negotiations in terms of ownership of the riverbed or water, but have focused on recognizing the mana of the river from which the iwi's mana flows, and on its future health and well-being' (Finlayson 2012).

In the context of environmental harm as this pertains to humans, eco-systems and animals, to maximize liberty is to maximize general functioning, the 'to be' and the 'to do' of life (White 2013c; see also Chapter 3). This depends to a large degree on being recognized as being of worth and significant status (from the point of view of humans, since it is we who confer 'value' upon ourselves and elements of the world around us).

This concern with the idea that all things have the right 'to be' and 'to do' in ways that reflect a core defining trait or characteristic has also been extended to the abiotic or non-living. For example, consider the following conception of 'rights' applied to a river.

> A fundamental river right (i.e. the riverine equivalent of a human right) would be the right to flow. If a water body couldn't flow it wouldn't be a river, and so the capacity to flow (given sufficient water) is essential to the existence of a river. Therefore, from the perspective of the river, building so many dams across it and extracting so much water from it that it ceased to flow into the sea, would be an abuse of its Earth rights.
>
> (Cullinan 2003: 118)

Eco-justice is thus an inclusive concept that deals with transgressions against humans and the non-human.

Putting justice principles into a victim context carries with it certain implications. For example, addressing victim needs and entitlements incorporates the notion of justice as fairness or equality. For the non-human this could mean establishment of support services for victims and survivors of environmental crime that include harmed animals. There will be instances of shared victimization, as in the case of climate change, illegal fishing and air pollution, in which everyone is affected, somehow. There will also be instances of specific victimization, as in the case of some plant and animal species being vulnerable to harm although this may be unrecognized or unacknowledged due to remoteness of location or general human devaluing of species. As with humans, there will be differing degrees and durations of harm, injury and suffering as this pertains to animals.

The absence of animal considerations within mainstream victimology is due in part to the absence of legal status as 'persons' and thus the treatment of non-human animals as outside the usual realms of ordinary law and legal decision-making. The difference in analytical approach is also due to species differences in the exercise of agency, relating to issues of consciousness, response and social dynamics (including for example victim-precipitation). Humans may be treated like animals (i.e., treated badly), but traditional victimology would nonetheless see human victims less in terms of objects of harm (e.g. victims of cruelty) than subjects with rights (i.e., victims of human-rights violations). Again, the distinction between and among species, and their relative status in legal and philosophical terms has ramifications for who or what is defined as a victim.

Environmental victimization from the point of view of human victims has an additional dimension that requires additional discussion. The concern is not only with analysis of the harm done to particular individuals and groups but also the ways in which these individuals and groups respond to this victimization. Here the question of human agency looms large, because it is this agency that creates space for political responses to environmentally harmful activity more generally. In other words, the study of human victims is important not only to assess the damage and the social processes behind victimhood but for the potential for change embodied in some instances of victimization. This, too, is vital to green criminology: namely, the necessity of not only understanding the world, but analysing ways in which it can be transformed in positive directions.

Victim mobilization

Just as environmental victimization differs concretely in its manifestation, so too victim responses vary greatly. In broad terms, different events, in different countries, have given rise to responses that vary from the passive to the confrontational, and from those involving collaborative activities aimed at redress to those based upon violence (Williams 1996; Hall 2013a).

Detailed analysis of specific events, over time, has revealed that there may be stages in the struggle for justice by victims, involving spontaneous and organized actions. The issues may be centred upon justice and/or on relief. The effectiveness of specific struggles, such as those related to events in Bhopal, India or the Cape region in South Africa (Waldman 2007) can also be analysed in terms of who defines the issues, who fights for or against the issues, who owns the struggle and how the struggle is shaped and carried out in regard to local and international participants (see Sarangi 1996; Waldman 2007; Engel and Martin 2006). Examination of victim responses needs to take into account the type and extent of networking and coalition-building, but also the lack of participation and marginalization of some victim groups within a wider victim movement (Waldman 2007).

Non-violence and co-operative negotiation with authority figures may be privileged over mass mobilizations and public demonstrations. What is effective, however, depends very much upon the immediate political struggles and social contexts in question. For instance, in Bolivia there were mass demonstrations, at times violent, against privatization of the drinking water supply. The result was to forestall such privatization. Moreover, it ultimately contributed to the election of a progressive government, one with the first ever indigenous President.

On the other hand, what works in environmental activism should not be reduced to the formula that 'local' equals 'best'. The effectiveness of activism stemming from environmental victimization largely depends upon going beyond localism as such, to forge links and allies outside the immediate locale of an event, disaster or situation. Union Carbide, the scourge of the Bhopal disaster in India, had a presence in some 137 different countries. What the company did in any one country has implications for what it is doing and may potentially do in other countries; likewise, how victims respond in their own country to environmental victimization has ramifications for what happens in other countries. The form of transnational corporations (with a presence in many different countries) reinforces the notion of taking activism beyond local borders as a way of providing a moral or ethical barometer for companies.

Activism usually occurs in a moral climate in which certain justifications are claimed in support of particular actions. This opens the door to some interesting observations and debates over how the moral high ground is constructed, by whom and with what consequences. Williams (1996: 36), for instance, has noted that:

> If, between states and between state and citizen, the need to ensure human security 'must prevail' over justice norms as reflected in international or domestic law, and we accept the inference that military force may then legitimately be used against the entity posing the threat to human security, do we then accept that the principle extends to violence by community activists against the threat posed by the lead smelter down the road?

The degree to which the aims justify certain means, and the precise relationship between means and ends, is subject to intense scrutiny and debate within environmental social movements. Different groups will construe their activities as 'righteous' and as 'appropriate under the circumstances' according to the philosophical criteria and ideological leanings peculiar to the group at hand. How particular nation-states respond to environmental issues also influences action on the ground. This too shapes local, regional and transnational campaigns. For instance, different jurisdictions view and respond to acts of environmental 'resistance' in different ways. In the United States a recent tendency has been to brand damage-causing acts of protest as forms of ecotage or environmental terrorism, and to prosecute and sanction offenders heavily (Rovics 2007; Brisman 2008). By contrast, a court case in England that involved six Greenpeace activists charged with criminal damage after being involved in scaling and defacing a chimney at a plant at Kingsnorth, saw the jury deciding that the activists had been justified in causing damage to the coal-fired power station due to the larger threat of global warming (McCarthy 2008). How nation-states respond to activism provides impetus for the adoption of different kinds of tactics and strategies.

Activists, states and corporations use both confrontational and conciliatory tactics in their interaction with one another (see Table 10.1). When it comes to confrontation, activists engage in measures such as mass mobilization, protest demonstrations, trespass and breaking and entering, and even eco-sabotage. For their part, states (at varying levels, up to national) may utilize tactics such as abrogation of regulation (de-regulation), entering into no discussions with those who dissent, cracking down on activists and relying upon arrest and imprisonment to quell resistance. Corporations engage in reluctant rule compliance, economic blackmail (e.g. jobs versus the environment), the threat of capital flight (e.g. take our business elsewhere) and suing protesters (e.g. for financial losses due to disruption). Confrontation is not the preserve of any one party.

Nor is conciliation limited to selected participants. Activists are known to engage in closed-door negotiations, to undertake their own investigations of illegal activity, and to lobby politicians and corporate bosses. The state may be open to negotiation with diverse parties, including NGOs and community groups, to enact particular forms of environmental regulation, to promote 'green' campaigns (e.g. around recycling) and to, in effect, lobby and rely upon NGOs. Likewise, corporations can be drawn into community negotiations, engage in 'green' public

Table 10.1 Types of engagement between activists, the state and corporations

Activists	State	Corporations
Confrontational		
Mass mobilization	Deregulation	Reluctant rule compliance
Protest actions	No discussion	Job blackmail
Trespass and break-in	Crackdown on dissent	Threat of capital flight
Eco-sabotage	Arrest, imprisonment	Lawsuit
Conciliatory		
Closed-door co-operation	Negotiation	Negotiation
Petitions	Enviro-regulation	Green public relations
Information website	Green campaigns	Green industries
Lobbying politicians	Lobbying NGOs	Alliances with NGOs

Source: White 2013d

relations, form alliances with certain NGOs and seek business opportunities in developing 'green' industries.

Another aspect of environmental activism is that frequently activists and victims alike become targets in their own right – the more they press their claims and engage in concerted efforts to gain compensation or reform existing practices, the greater the risk. This pitting of David (the little person) against Goliath (the big company; or in some cases the state) is one of the more disconcerting aspects of corporate/state/activist interaction. In the case of the Bhopal disaster, for example, the Indian state actively prosecuted actual victims and activist supporters who operated outside narrowly defined state-sanctioned forms of response.

> In 1985, police raided a medical clinic for victims, confiscated medical records and arrested six volunteer doctors. At least 10 criminal cases have been lodged against 7,100 activists, including charges for violating the Official Secrets Act. In 1991, police attacked activists from a local victims' organization, ironically while they were trying to submit a plea to the governor asking for protection from police brutality.
> (Engel and Martin 2006: 488)

Recent reports from Central and South America likewise highlight the increasing number of incidents in which environmental activists and victims are subject to detention, beatings, rape and homicide. It is alleged in many cases that governments and corporations are colluding to violate the rights of activists who work to protect the natural environment (Clark 2009), and certainly analysis of mining and logging in this part of the world reveals deepening rifts between the powerful and the less powerful over exploitation of natural resources (Boekhout van Solinge 2010a and b). Organizations such as the Sierra Club and Amnesty International are simultaneously reaching the conclusion that environmental and human rights are in fact closely linked (Clark 2009; see also Hall 2013a).

It is 'people power' that gives shape to and helps construct certain issues as significant or important enough to warrant some kind of state response (see Hannigan 2006). One consequence of certain issues coming to the fore as bona fide social problems is that governments have been forced to enact laws relating to air, water, toxic waste, use of public lands, endangered species, and the list goes on. The relationship between public policy and government strategic action is also of course shaped by contingency – specific events, situations and disasters tend to shake things up rapidly and with immediate effect.

Environmental victims vary greatly in terms of attitude, behaviour and the capacity to respond. From an activist point of view, it is also possible to draw out which elements of victim activism seem to have more purchase than others when it comes to obtaining resources and a semblance of justice (see also Engel and Martin 2006). An activist framework broadly based upon ecological citizenship provides a potential meeting point for a variety of actors. For victims, the promise is one of solidarity and support; for other activists there is the potential to harness the emotions and energy of victims (the lived experience of suffering) so as to collectively forge a new, and better, world. For victims – especially, those who consider they have having 'nothing left to lose' – can make ferocious fighters and tenacious enemies, and thus powerful allies in the struggles for social and environmental justice.

The transition between simply responding to special instances of environmental injustice and broader movements towards ecological citizenship hinges upon that vital link between social inequality and environmental degradation. This link is evident in cases of structural exploitation of humans (and surrounding environments), as with the location of factories on the Mexican side of the US–Mexican border, where businesses can take advantage of much less stringent environmental regulations than exist in the United States. It is also apparent in any analysis of the disproportionate consequences of 'accidents' such as Chernobyl or Bhopal for poor and dispossessed peoples and for those workers who live and work close to potentially dangerous sites. In other words, environmental harm is unevenly distributed in geographical and social terms, and this is evident in which population groups generally constitute the bulk of environmental victims (Cifuentes and Frumkin 2007; Pellow 2007; Faber 2009; White 2010b).

From the point of view of ecological citizenship, then, what is required is a shift in consciousness and activities in ways that can materially further the cause of victims, while simultaneously tapping into existing networks of transnational activism (including global social networks). As Kamenetz (2010) notes in a headline on the Gulf of Mexico spill 'social media is providing a "voice" – six months after the BP oil spill it's clear that in the age of social media a company can't spin and rebrand its way out of a mess like it used to'.

In other circumstances community groups are now standing up to their polluters. Bullard (1990), for instance notes the emergence of networks of black activists working against environmental damage in their communities. In Australia, a community in the Hunter Valley, a rich grape-growing region of Australia, stood up to a company seeking to extend their coal-mining activities, a protest recently validated by a controversial decision of the New South Wales Land and Environment Court denying the company's right to expand, or, as the media put it, 'placing grapes above coal'.

Environmental justice focuses predominantly on the impacts of particular social practices and environmental hazards on specific *human* populations (as defined on the basis of geography, class, gender, occupation, age, ethnicity and race). It is about social inequality. Environmental victimization focuses predominantly on those acts and omissions that harm specific groups (and, ideally, specific ecosystems and specific non-human animals). In summary, an environmental justice approach to victimization encapsulates the following elements:

- emphasis on harm as experienced in the here and now (e.g. death and disability caused by toxic dumping in local area);
- human-centred conceptions of harm and justice (e.g. social inequality and questions of social equity);
- differing demands amongst those most affected are constructed around human self-interests (e.g. compensation, rights);
- specific locality (i.e., territory) and particular issues (e.g. event) provide for a local conceptualization of the key problem that warrants action.

The perennial question is, how can environmental victimization be addressed most effectively, in the interests of the victims and their communities?

In summary, an ecological citizenship approach to victimization encapsulates the following elements:

- recognition of the global nature of specific phenomena (e.g. disposal of toxic waste in Third World involves transnational forces);
- acknowledgement of the global effects of localized practices and victimization (e.g. logging and climate change, radiation poisoning and wind currents);
- emphasis on the pursuit of social and ecological justice (i.e., humans, biospheres, non-human animals);
- acknowledgement that NIMBY (including carbon-emission trading schemes) puts the problem into someone else's backyard.

What is needed, therefore, is the movement from singular and narrowly defined interests and localities, to more universalizing and global concerns that acknowledge the intrinsic commonalities across borders and a shared moral universe amongst political activists. Having said this, it is important not to lose sight of the fact that many of the impacts of environmental harms and crimes (despite being generated by global institutions and activities) are experienced most acutely at the level of the 'local' (the people of Bhopal, the citizens of the Gulf of Mexico, the people of Fukushima living in proximity to the nuclear power plant).

From the point of view of activism, five key observations and assertions are important:

- The *impetus for action* by victims stems from the event and impact of specific environmental harms. Activism is born of direct experience.
- The *strategic effectiveness* of victim action is bolstered by the movement from specific environmental justice concerns to general ecological citizenship concerns. Activism is born of a shared global voice.
- The *commitment and powerful voice* offered by environmental victims is enhanced insofar as victim action is *connected* to the actions of New Social Movements. But their specific self-interests, as survivors and victims, must be acknowledged. Activism is born of solidarity.

- *Transnational environmental activism* demands participation of both the committed 'ideological' activist and those activists created in the crucible of 'suffering' caused by environmental harm and the fight for human survival. Activism is born of reciprocal empathy.
- *Appropriate tactics of dissent* will continue to evoke debate, especially in light of the labelling of certain actions as eco-terrorism rather than civic engagement. Those with less to lose may be more inclined to push the boundaries of legality when it comes to social protest. Activism is born of dissent over strategies.

These observations about victim mobilization and activism also need to be discussed in relation to the role of the state, and the paradoxical situation presented by the state as both perpetrator of environmental crime and central player in dealing with environmental harm. The particular relation of the victim to the state depends, however, on the specific issues, the specific tactics and the specific social environment within which the state-activist relationship is forged. Repressive measures against activists (including environmental victims) in some countries may not be mirrored in what happens in other countries. Resistance to state intrusions, and to state policies, may be more successful in some countries, depending upon the timing and the issue, than in others.

Conclusion

This chapter illustrates how environmental victimization is not a solely human experience and how 'the biosphere and non-human biota have intrinsic value *independent* of their utilitarian or instrumental value for humans' (Preston 2011b: 143). Discerning who or what is an environmental victim is partly subjective ('in the eyes of the beholder') and partly objective (based upon evidence of some kind). Ultimately the construction of victimhood is a social process involving dimensions of time and space, behaviours involving acts and omissions, and social features pertaining to power and collectivities. The human and the non-human can be included among 'victims', and frequently the exploitation of each, with associated and resulting harms, stem from the same sources (namely, corrupt governments and profit-seeking corporations).

Advocates are needed, whether this refers to human or non-human victims, so that the plight and suffering of environmental victims is given the emphasis it deserves. Only then can potential action be taken to compensate and repair the harm to such victims.

Discussion topics

- Who/what is or should be acknowledged as a victim of environmental crime?
- Environmental victimization represents a violation of basic human rights. Discuss.

- What are agencies of social control doing about environmental victimization?
- How is or should victimhood be addressed by courts and the criminal justice system?
- How is or could compensation for victims and reparation of harms be achieved?

Further reading

Hall, M. (2013). *Victims of Environmental Harm: Rights, recognition and redress under national and international law*. London: Routledge.

Jarrell, M., and Ozymy, J. (2012). 'Real crime, Real Victims: Environmental crime victims and the Crime Victims' Rights Act (CVRA)', *Crime, Law and Social Change*, 58(4): 373–89.

Skinnider, E. (2011). *Victims of Environmental Crime – Mapping the issues*. Vancouver: International Centre for Criminal Law Reform and Criminal Justice Policy.

Sollund, R. (2012). 'Speciesism as Doxic Practice Versus Valuing Difference and Plurality', in R. Ellefsen, R. Sollund, and G. Larsen (eds), *Eco-global Crimes: Contemporary problems and future challenges*. Farnham: Ashgate.

Williams, C. (1996). 'An Environmental Victimology', *Social Justice*, 23(4): 16–40.

Part III

Intervention and prevention

Chapter 11

Environmental regulation

Introduction

This chapter will discuss the following topics:

- reasons for environmental regulation;
- models of environmental regulation;
- approaches to compliance and enforcement;
- self-regulation and Environmental Management Systems;
- limits and opportunities of regulation.

The role of the state in dealing with environmental harm is much more circumscribed than the policing and regulation of social harms such as street crime. When it comes to environmental issues, the tendency has been to emphasize efficiency and facilitation, rather than control. At a practical level the costs of monitoring and enforcement and compliance, in relation to traditional regulatory standards-setting and the role of government can be expensive. The complexity of procedures, and complaints, particularly by businesses about 'green tape' (akin to bureaucratic 'red tape'), has been accompanied by efforts to streamline processes and to decrease formal regulatory controls as much as possible.

The state nevertheless has a formal role and commitment to protect citizens from the worst excesses or worst instances of environmental victimization. Hence, the introduction of extensive legislation and regulatory procedures designed to give the appearance of active intervention, and the implication that laws exist which actually do deter such harms. The existence of such laws may be encouraging in that they reflect historical and ongoing struggles over certain types of business and communal activity. But what is actually happening on the ground?

The concern of this chapter is to examine regulatory approaches to dealing with environmental harm and wrongdoing. It outlines the ways in which environmental regulation is theorized and how it is implemented, and the limitations of environmental regulation.

Reasons for environmental regulation

There are diverse rationales for social intervention on environmental matters. There is, at times, a basic incompatibility of regulatory projects. Some of the motivations for regulation include:

- evidence of extreme forms of direct and indirect environmental harm that makes it politically undeniable and problematic;
- a moral basis for action, especially around the themes of ecological justice and preserving or protecting nature;
- a concern stemming from consideration of local communities and equity, so that distributions of harm/safety are fairer;
- protection of the 'value' of natural resources, from the point of view of economic baselines;
- the notion of universal human interests in the case of trends and processes seen to be a threat to global life;
- an agenda informed by social justice and equality considerations, focusing on the exploitation of humans and of nature.

The bottom line is that the task of environmental regulation is simultaneously analytical, political and moral.

Intervention on environmental matters depends in part upon how risk is conceived and whether assessment of risk subsequently leads to action. Responding to environmental harm is not only about reacting to specific events or incidents. It also includes evaluation of potential threats or risks into the future. Taking precaution is central to protecting the planet from projected harms. This involves weighing up and recognizing which risks actually exist, and for whom.

Risk is a multidimensional concept generally incorporating several key elements. One notion of risk sees it as a prediction or expectation that involves: a hazard (the source of danger), uncertainty of occurrence and outcomes (expressed by the probability or chance of occurrence), adverse consequences (the possible outcome), a time frame for evaluation, and the perspectives of those affected about what is important to them (Leiss and Hrudey 2005: 3). In law, risk of environmental harm is an important component of what constitutes harm (rather than ordinary tort law, which requires actual injury as a prerequisite to recovery). This is because preventative environmental regulation is intended precisely to regulate the risk of harm occurring: that is, to prevent environmental harm before it occurs. Risk incorporates notions of both probability and harm (Lin 2006: 961), thereby raising issues relating to the certainty of knowledge (about environments, about harms) and how best to measure or ascertain likely outcomes. Intervention is premised upon taking the right precautionary measures to suit the perceived risk of harm. Assessment of risk is not solely based upon probability, since the potential magnitude of harm must also be taken into account.

Typically, environmental risks as scientifically construed are based upon processes and examples such as (Deville and Harding 1997; White 2008a):

- global warming (for example, due to excessive discharges of carbon dioxide);
- biodiversity loss (for example, due to release and establishment of non-native plant and animal species);
- stratospheric ozone depletion (for example, due to use of CFCs);
- desertification and land degradation (for example, due to land clearing for unsustainable agricultural practices);
- marine ecosystem health (for example, due to oil spills);
- freshwater ecosystem health (for example, due to discharge of pollutants);
- atmospheric pollutants (for example, due to acid rain);
- damage to specific ecosystems (for example, due to overfishing and overlogging);
- damage to human and non-human physical and mental health (for example, due to chemical residues in food).

Responding to these risks can take a variety of institutional and community forms, of which environmental regulation is of major importance.

For instance, three broad approaches in responding to environmental harm have been identified – a socio-legal approach, a regulatory approach, and a social-action approach (White 2008a). In the socio-legal approach the emphasis is on use of criminal law as presently constituted, and with attempts to improve quality of investigation, law enforcement, prosecution and conviction on illegal environmentally related activity. A regulatory approach places the emphasis on social regulation, using many different means, as the key mechanism to prevent and curtail environmental harm, and attempts to reform existing systems of production and consumption through adoption of a constellation of measures, including enforced self-regulation and bringing non-government groups directly into the regulatory process. A social-action approach emphasizes the need for fundamental social change, and attempts to engage in social transformation through emphasis on deliberative democracy and citizen participation, and support for radical as well as other wings of social movements.

The main focus of this chapter is the second approach, one that emphasizes regulatory strategies that might be utilized to improve environmental performance, including 'responsive regulation' (Ayres and Braithwaite 1992; Braithwaite 1993) and 'smart regulation' (Gunningham and Grabosky 1998). These approaches attempt to recast the state's role by using non-government, and especially private sector, participation and resources in fostering regulatory compliance in relation to the goal of 'sustainable development'. Increasingly important to these discussions is the perceived and potential role of third-party interests, in particular non-government environmental organizations, in influencing policy and practice (Braithwaite and Drahos 2000; O'Brien et al. 2000; Gunningham and Grabosky 1998).

The main concern of this kind of approach is with reform of existing methods of environmental protection. The overall agenda of writers in this genre has been summarized as follows: 'Generally speaking, environmental reformers are optimistic about the possibilities of addressing environmental harms without fundamentally changing the status quo. Either implicitly or tacitly, minimization ("risk management") rather than elimination of environmental depredation is conceived as the reformist object' (Chunn, Boyd and Menzies 2002: 12).

The regulatory field is made up of many different stake-holders and participants. These include, for example, businesses, employees, government agencies, communities, shareholders, environmentalists, regulators, the media, trade customers, financial institutions, consumers and the list goes on. There are also myriad laws, rules and regulations that guide how the regulatory project is meant to be carried out in practice (for concrete illustration of this see Kluin 2013).

As with most crimes that traverse jurisdictional levels, there are various levels of regulation and legal convention in relation to environmental crime. For the purposes of illustration we concentrate on the problem of waste and waste disposal, and the regulations and laws pertaining to these in the Australian context. These are summarized in Figure 11.1.

The role and influence of various people and agencies is determined by factors such as resources, training, information, skill, expertise and legislation. These are also affected by the type of regulation that is the predominant model at any point in time.

Models of environmental regulation

There are several ways to analyse issues pertaining to environmental regulation and the prevention of environmental harm. For example, there has been burgeoning interest in corporate regulation, including in relation to environmental matters, in the 'regulation' literature (see for example, Haines 1997; Braithwaite and Drahos 2000). At a theoretical level, much of this work has attempted to present regulation as lying on a continuum from direct command control on the part of the state through to voluntary compliance on the part of companies and individuals. The emphasis varies according to the theoretical position of the writer.

It has been observed that the broad tendency under neo-liberalism (or free-market capitalism) has been toward deregulation (or, as a variation of this, 'self-regulation') when it comes to corporate harm and wrongdoing (Snider 2000). In the specific area of environmental regulation, the general trend has been away from direct governmental regulation and toward 'softer' regulatory approaches. The continuum of regulation, from strict regulation through to no regulation, is illustrated in Table 11.1 (White 2008a). Measures include Environmental Impact Assessments (EIAs) and Environmental Management Systems (EMSs) through to voluntary adoption of good environmental practices.

Laws and legal instruments

TIER 1
- **International Instruments**
  Conventions, protocols, agreements
- e.g. Basel, Rotterdam, Stockholm, London, Vienna, Kyoto

TIER 2
- **Regional Instruments – External & Foreign Territories**
  Conventions, legislation, regulation
- e.g. Norfolk Island, Antarctica; eg East Timor, Forum Islands (Waigani)

TIER 3
- **Commonwealth Instruments**
  Legislation, regulations, standards, evidentiary certificates
- e.g. Hazardous Waste (Regulation of Exports & Imports) Act and Regulations; Standards

TIER 4
- **National Instruments**
- Measures, national policy
- e.g. Movement of controlled waste NEPM; National Waste Policy (2010)

TIER 5
- **State and Territory instruments**
  Legislation, regulations, strategies, policies, guidelines, fact sheets
- e.g. Environmental Protection Acts; Waste-specific State and Territory legislation and regulations

TIER 6
- **Municipal Instruments**
- By-Laws, regulations, policies, guidelines, fact sheets
- e.g. Local by-laws, planning regulations, legislation governing landfills

Focus of regulation

INTERNATIONAL MANAGEMENT AND MOVEMENT
- **Concern is with transboundary movement and management of hazardous waste**
- Interpol; Department of Sustainability, Environment, Water, Population and Communities
- e.g. Basel Convention. Waigani Convention

REGIONAL MANAGEMENT AND MOVEMENT
- **Concern is with regional border control**
- Department of Sustainability, Environment, Water, Population and Communities; Australian Customs and Border Protection Service
  e.g. East Timor, Forum Islands, Antarctica

NATIONAL MANAGEMENT AND MOVEMENT
- **Concern is with border control – movement in (imports) and out (exports) of Australia**
- Department of Environment, Sustainability and Water; Australian Customs and Border Protection Service; Australian Federal Police
- e.g. Hazardous Waste Regulation of Exports and Imports

INTERSTATE MANAGEMENT AND MOVEMENT
- **Concern is with interstate movement of wastes**
- State Environmental Protection Agencies; Key stake-holders in the waste management chain
- e.g. Controlled Waste NEPM – Basel framework informs hazard characteristics and lists of hazardous substances and materials

INTRASTATE MANAGEMENT AND MOVEMENT
- **Concern is with intrastate movement of wastes**
- State Environmental Protection Agencies; Key stake-holders in the waste management chain
- e.g. State hazardous waste-specific legislation – Basel framework informs hazard characteristics and lists of hazardous substances and materials

MUNICIPAL MANAGEMENT AND MOVEMENT
- **Concern is with domestic hazardous wastes in major waste streams at local level**
- Councils; Water Authorities; Planning Authorities
- e.g. Local By-Laws and planning legislation; legislation governing landfills – Annex II of the Basel Convention lists "other wastes" – e.g. household waste

Figure 11.1 Tiers and types of regulation: Australia.

Table 11.1 The environmental regulation continuum

Strict regulation		No regulation
Command and control regulation	Self-regulation	Deregulation
Direct regulation	Strong or weak codes of practice	Indirect or no regulation
Licences and permits	Standard setting	Voluntarism
Setting of standards	Industry-based compliance	Property-rights
Environmental Impact Assessments (EIA)	Environmental Management Systems (EMS)	Incentive-based

Source: White 2008a

Two general models stand out when it comes to regulation overall and environmental regulation in particular. The first is Ayres and Braithwaite's notion of 'enforced self-regulation' (1992). This is based upon a regulatory pyramid (see Figure 11.2). The usual pyramid of sanctions has an extensive base, with the emphasis on persuasion that rises to a small peak of harsh punishment. In the case of business transgressions, to take an example, the progression up the pyramid might include persuasion, a warning letter, a civil penalty, a criminal penalty, licence suspension, and licence revocation. By combining different forms of regulation, Ayres and Braithwaite (1992) reconstitute the usual regulatory pyramid so that the bottom layer consists of self-regulation, the next layer of enforced self-regulation (via government legislation), the next layer of command regulation

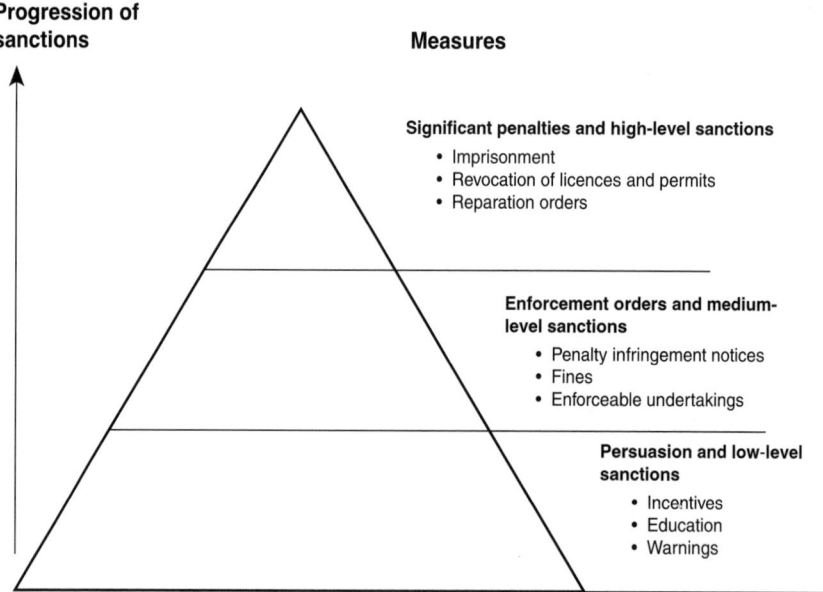

Figure 11.2 The regulatory pyramid.

with discretionary punishment, and at the top, command regulation with non-discretionary punishment.

Building upon the insights of these and other writers, Gunningham and Grabosky (1998) argue that what is needed is 'smart regulation'. This refers to the design of regulation that still involves government intervention, but selectively and in combination with a range of market and non-market solutions, and of public and private orderings. The central thesis of 'smart regulation' is that recruiting a range of regulatory actors to implement complementary combinations of policy instruments, tailored to specific environmental goals and circumstances, will produce more effective and efficient policy outcomes. Essentially this means incorporating into the regulatory field the full schedule of regulatory options, from direct regulation associated with command-and-control approaches through to voluntary schemes and economic incentive approaches (see Gunningham and Grabosky 1998).

A number of issues arise in relation to how measures linked to the enforced self-regulation pyramid and smart regulation are utilized in practice. Questions can be asked regarding:

- the standards of what is deemed to be acceptable;
- the flexibility required in devising appropriate safeguards and strategies at local/site level;
- how to enact total management planning;
- what constitutes adequate monitoring;
- who is to do enforcement and compliance;
- what penalties and consequences are to consist of;
- how a plurality of instruments rather than a single approach is to be co-ordinated;
- how to deal with a culture of reluctance to use punitive measures against corporate misconduct;
- the general corporate immunity from prosecution and penalty; and
- why and how the extent of regulation varies according to size of firm.

What detailed examination of particular forms of regulation show, and what explorations of different approaches to environmental regulation acknowledge, is that how regulation is carried out in practice, and whose interests are reflected in specific regulatory regimes, is basically an empirical question. That is, regulatory performance cannot be read off from an abstract understanding of regulation theory as such. Nevertheless, environmental-regulation models directly influence the scope and possibilities of environmental regulation as it gets translated into practical measures at the ground level. The adoption of particular environmental regulation models thus helps to shape the methods and behaviour of regulators. In ideal terms, the two key models of regulation discussed here would incorporate a range of actors and measures in order to 'keep things honest', presumably in ways that would be to the advantage of all stake-holders.

However, the continuing degradation of the environment today is linked to the dominant regulation and enforcement framework itself, one that puts the stress on self-regulation and deregulation. This is reflected in state policies and practices. For instance, very often the preference on the part of state authorities is for education, promotion and self-regulation, rather than imposition of directive legislation and active enforcement and prosecution (White 2008a). Yet, to be effective, those in charge of regulation and enforcement must be willing to utilize the 'big stick' and to monitor compliance systematically and diligently. Systematic review of empirical evidence concerning environmental monitoring and enforcement finds that traditional regulatory structures are most effective in ensuring good environmental outcomes (Gray and Shimshack 2011). For example, persistent and continuous inspections, accompanied by substantive operational powers (including use of criminal sanctions), can in fact lead to rapid positive changes in polluting practices (see Commission for Environmental Co-operation 2001; White 2011a).

Snider (2000) describes how in Canada, despite policy directives specifying 'strict compliance', a permissive philosophy of 'compliance promotion' has reigned. Given the tone of mainstream regulation literature (that offers a theoretical justification for enlisting private interests through incentives and inducements), it is hardly surprising that persuasion is favoured at the practical level. Close examination of self-regulation models, however, finds evidence of regulatory failures, and this in turn indicates that governments cannot totally abdicate responsibility when a regulatory problem requires a state response (see Priest 1997–98). Certain conditions are necessary if self-regulation, as such, is going to offer an effective form of regulation (see Ayres and Braithwaite 1992). The tendency, however, is for governments to shed regulatory functions and responsibilities and to rely upon the rhetoric and cost savings afforded by self-regulation (including at the international level, as illustrated by the powerful role of the International Standards Organization in driving government policy responses vis-à-vis environmental regulation).

It is essential to consider the financial and political environment within which regulators are forced to work. For example, while never before in history have there been so many laws pertaining to the environment, it is rare indeed to find extensive government funding, resources and personnel being put into enforcement and compliance activities. The fiscal crisis of the state, as manifest in massive budget cuts in Greece, Italy, Spain, Portugal, Ireland, Britain and the United States, also bears with it a crisis in the regulatory field. Environmental Protection Agencies struggle with inadequate monies and demoralized officers as departmental belts are tightened and priorities are placed elsewhere.

Many contemporary regulatory approaches attempt to recast the state's role by using non-government (especially private-sector) participation and resources in fostering regulatory compliance in relation to the goal of 'sustainable development'. Analyses of these new regulatory regimes, however, offer equivocal results in terms of effectiveness. For example, analysis of Canadian environmental law and policies reveals a patchwork of legislative and regulatory measures that fundamentally fail to protect the environment (Boyd 2003). At its broadest level, the ways in which regulation works or does not work are fundamentally shaped by systemic imperatives and philosophical vision. For instance, Boyd (2003) contrasts a model of regulation based upon an effort to mitigate the environmental impacts of an energy- and resource-intensive industrial economy with that based upon ecological principles that are oriented to decreasing the consumption of energy and natural resources. However complex the laws and regulations in the first scenario, they cannot succeed in achieving sustainability, because the system as a whole is inherently geared to growth in energy and resource consumption. In the latter case, the emphasis is on restructuring the economy to incorporate ecological limits, and thus to reduce environmental harm over time.

Approaches to compliance and enforcement

Issues of compliance and enforcement are at the heart of the regulatory project. The intent of legislation and regulation is to shape behaviour in particular directions. When this does not occur, it sometimes signals a failure in regulatory practices. It is important, therefore, to study why regulation fails as well as under what conditions it works. To illustrate this we can consider a review conducted by the Queensland Department of Environment and Resource Management (DERM) in Australia, which examined the motivations for non-compliance in the waste industry (Greenfield 2009: 8). The study found three main reasons for non-compliance:

- *Economic motivations* – money to be made from non-compliance, and the cost of compliance.
- *Lack of enforcement* – the legislation is not enforced; they don't think they will get caught.
- *Ignorance* – people don't understand how to obey; people don't know about the laws.

The study found that these reasons for non-compliance translated to more than 88 per cent of the non-compliant population intentionally, knowingly and willingly breaking the law.

In the light of the regulatory pyramid presented earlier (Figure 11.2), it is interesting to note that, in this case, the 'shape' of the compliance pyramid in relation to waste issues was found to be inverse, as shown in Figure 11.3 (Greenfield 2009: 11). In other words, the bulky portion of the pyramid was at the top (66 per cent intentional non-compliance) and the slim portion at the bottom (23 per cent opportunistic non-compliance).

Not surprisingly, general commentary in this field has pointed out that, due to their dual functions as regulators and enforcers, Environmental Protection Agencies and their equivalents have been charged in the past with adopting too conciliatory a relationship with the entities they are meant to be scrutinizing (Bricknell 2010: 47).

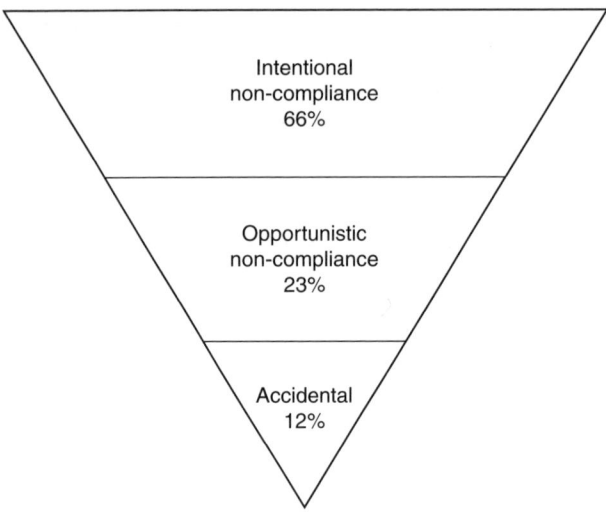

Figure 11.3 Understanding non-compliance in the Australian waste sector. Source: Greenfield 2009: 11.

In response to this charge, as well as issues pertaining to regulatory capture, Hayman and Brack (2002: 22) advocate a number of measures could help improve the effectiveness of domestic enforcement programmes including:

- a clear national control regime;
- effective national capacity-building;
- targeting flagrant violators;
- increasing sanctions and introducing probation penalties;
- improving case processing times;
- encouraging compliance through positive incentives;
- involving supply and processing chains in the enforcement process.

According to Hayman and Brack (2002: 22) 'criminal profiling is vital for focused enforcement efforts'. But this may be easier said than done. This is because of the inherent tensions and contradictions within the environmental regulatory field itself over its central mission and how to achieve it.

Compliance means the state of conformity with the law. The mandate of most environmental protection agencies is not only to enforce compliance through use of criminal prosecutions, but to forge strategic alliances and working partnerships with industries, local governments and communities in support of environmental objectives. Often these are framed in terms of economic objectives, and perhaps social ones as well. However, as emphasized in a Western Australian review of environmental protection:

'Speak softly and carry a big stick' is an appropriate aphorism for today's environmental regulator, but to be effective there must be certainty that the big stick can and will be used and the how, why and where of its use. It is the anticipation of enforcement action that confers the ability to deter

(Robinson 2003: 11)

Bearing these sentiments in mind, it is instructive to briefly consider recent findings from a review of EPA practices in the Australian state of Victoria. In 2011, EPA Victoria commissioned an independent review of its regulatory approach and compliance and enforcement activities. The Review found that:

- The EPA had become confused as to the role of compliance and enforcement and had reduced the importance and prominence of these activities. This had limited EPA's ability to act strategically and resulted in the organization becoming fractured, reactive and inconsistent. It had also resulted in a loss of confidence from community and business in EPA's ability to protect the environment (EPA Victoria 2011: 2).
- The Review also found that there was a significant underinvestment in the number of authorized officers and their training and support. A reactive strategy, limited procedures and lack of accredited training meant that EPA had not adequately supported authorized officers to consistently and effectively apply and explain the law (EPA Victoria 2011: 2).

After the review a number of organizational and cultural changes were proposed. These were presented as alternatives to the purely risk-based model that had driven previous EPA policies and practices (which is akin to the traditional regulatory pyramid discussed earlier). Basically it was argued that the severity of the EPA's enforcement response should be proportionate to any environmental harm or potential harm, and that the nature and characteristics of the perpetrators likewise be taken into account.

The Victoria Review argued that there should be an escalating regulatory intervention that would correspond with the level of environmental risk (including consequence) posed by a particular breach or incident (Krpan 2011). The net result of matching sanctions with estimates of harm and risk is a model based upon a sliding scale of intervention.

We have reconceptualized this approach as being akin to a 'toolbox' (see Figure 11.4). The standard approach to regulation has tended to rely upon the regulatory pyramid (as shown earlier in Figure 11.2). The assumption is sometimes made that the sanctions of the pyramid ought to be based upon a progression that moves from the base of the pyramid to the top. This translates into a regime in which offenders are frequently treated leniently, especially if they are 'first offenders', almost regardless of the harm caused or the reasons behind the harm occurring. By contrast, the toolbox approach says that regulatory tools ought to be applied when and as needed, to fit the *circumstances* (low through to

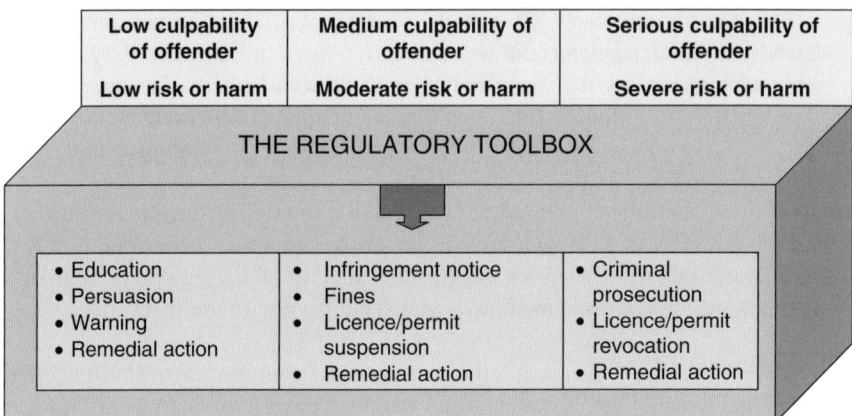

Figure 11.4 The regulatory toolbox. Source: Adapted from Krpan 2011.

severe risk and harm) and the *offender* (low to serious levels of culpability). There is no 'progression' over time up the pyramid. Rather, each case is dealt with on its own merits, and if the 'big stick' is appropriate (given the nature of the risk, harm and offending), then it will be used. The toolbox approach allows for the tailoring of measures and sanctions that best fit the nature of the case before the regulators.

The Victoria Review also recommended that the EPA target enforcement effort on the most significant harm to the environment, by considering consequence and likelihood:

- *Consequence* – the risk or harm to health and environment. This is categorized into low, minor, moderate, major and severe. Consequence takes into account actual or potential impacts on human health, environment and amenity. It considers the scale and duration of any harm or impact and the level of public concern (EPA Victoria 2011: 5).
- *Likelihood* – the chance that non-compliance will occur. This also has five categories; low, unlikely, possible, likely and certain. Likelihood takes into account objective elements of: (a) the track record of the business – past incidents, inspections, enforcement and pollution reports; (b) systems in place to identify and manage environmental risk; (c) capability of the business and its operators; and (d) the level of resources dedicated to environmental management, compliance and maintenance.

To put the enforcement issues slightly differently, and as Robinson (2003) argues, prosecution ought to be an equal partner in the enforcement toolbox, and should be neither the first nor the last resort, but the appropriate response to a particular set of circumstances.

> **Box 11.1 Exploratory research on environmental compliance and enforcement**
>
> As a student exercise, undertake the following:
> Define the scope of the Environmental Protection Agency or equivalent in your local area – does it involve harm to the natural environment, to humans, to animals and plants?
> Identify:
>
> - relevant legislation;
> - relevant penal provisions;
> - relevant civil enforcement proceedings;
> - the responsible government agencies.
>
> Ascertain whether each relevant agency collates data in relation to the following:
>
> - number of prosecutions or other enforcement proceedings undertaken by the agency;
> - data on conferences, mediation and agreements undertaken by the parties under the various Acts;
> - extent to which (1) and (2) above are recorded, monitored and/or followed up by agency.

The specifics of environmental regulation would entail such things as:

- assessing a firm's environmental record;
- preparation of an environmental improvement plan;
- conducting periodic environmental audits;
- implementation of an Environmental Management System;
- examination of the intensity of the administrative and resource burden;
- analysis of the risks of regulatory capture by firms;
- consideration of the public right to know about contracts; and
- examination of the firm's history.

Consider, for example, the notion of regulatory capture. The concept of regulatory capture refers to the situation where a government agency is dominated by the very agencies it is meant to be regulating. For example, Simon (2000) details many instances in which the US Environmental Protection Agency seemed to be more concerned with protecting corporate interests than protecting the environment. An example of this was a study that showed that the EPA devoted more of its resources in terms of time and money in the early 1990s to exempting corporations from its regulations than it did to enforcing the regulations. EPA activity had also extended its activities to opposing congressional attempts to pass tougher environmental regulations. Meanwhile, many former officials within the EPA ended up taking jobs as waste-industry executives. In terms of both activities and exchange of personnel, such situations serve private rather than public interests.

In a study of self-policing in relation to the US Environmental Protection Agency, Stretesky (2006) found that there is a wide range of specific issues that require further examination, including how corporate culture affects compliance with environmental regulatory efforts through to possible impacts of sanction severity on deterring potential offenders. A key point emphasized in this study is that, if the policy shift from direct regulation to market-based incentives is so important to policy-makers, then much more research about the dynamics and consequences of this shift is warranted. As indicated above, where the 'big stick' is not actively used, and where compliance is basically left up to the firm or industry, then regulation generally falls down.

Self-regulation and Environmental Management Systems

Nonetheless, the idea of encouraging trustworthiness ('virtue') by individual companies and by industry associations – of promoting regulation by 'consent' – continues to find favour amongst politicians and business leaders alike. In part this is reflected in the notion of corporate social responsibility, an idea that locates being virtuous (and monitoring virtue) in the hands of the company rather than the state (Gilmour 2002; Rix 2002).

In the specific area of environmental regulation, there has long been support for the idea that persuasion, not coercion, is or ought to be the key regulatory mechanism. This is usually associated with the ideology of 'self-regulation' (see, for example, Grabosky 1994, 1995). Here it is argued that corporate regulation should be informed by the idea of enlisting 'private interests' in regulatory activity via 'inducements', such as adopting waste minimization programmes which translate into more efficient production, or earning a good reputation among consumers for environmental responsibility.

The privatization of regulation has been accompanied by at least five different models of self-regulation, ranging from those reliant primarily on voluntary codes of conduct through to those that are strictly monitored by specialized government agencies (Priest 1997–98).

A popular form of self-regulation is adoption of Environmental Management Systems (EMS). This describes attempts at the firm and industry levels to build environmental valuation and risk analysis into core activities (such as accounting practices, insurance, public image, standards, liability, audits and reporting). As part of this, emphasis is placed on improving environmental awareness amongst employees, adopting clean technologies and engaging in activities such as recycling, and closely managing the supply and waste chain in order to minimize potential environmental harm.

In practical terms, a number of barriers to EMS have been identified (see Kirkland and Thompson 1999). Some of these include:

- *Awareness* – lack of recognition of need, lack of awareness, lack of concern, belief of current adequacy, denial of need, avoidance of the unknown, reluctance to use relatively new solutions.
- *Perceived costs* – related to lack of experience of firms and consultants, longer-term forward financial planning, underestimation of benefits via reduced waste, enhanced public image and avoidance of fines, civil damages, etc.
- *Implementation* – resistance to complexity, concerns about use of EMS in relation to legal compliance issues, resources (money, time, skills, knowledge), loss of commitment, inappropriate and/or limited application within organization.
- *Personnel* – lack of skills, knowledge, expertise and examples to implement process, reluctance to use external assistance such as consultants, no delegated responsibility or delegated responsibility with no resources or power to implement change.

A specific issue that stands out is that 'Innovation may be particularly difficult in the case of small- and medium-sized companies where absorptive capacity is limited and where a failure in an innovation could result in the failure of the business' (Kirkland and Thompson 1999: 134). In other words, for such firms there may be neither expertise nor understanding, but lots of fear.

At a more abstract level, the embracing of Environmental Management Systems (EMS) by many firms and corporations has been interpreted in several different ways. At the centre of changes to environmental regulation has been the movement toward 'corporate ownership' of the definitions, and responses to, environmental problems. This has taken different forms. One type of response has been to adopt the language of EMS and to assert that regulation is best provided by those industries and companies directly involved in production processes. This occurs at both particular firm levels, and in relation to the setting of international standards for environmental management, as in the case of the ISO 14000 (the International Organization for Standardization, or ISO – a private body – sets standards in relation to the environment).

As explained, there are various dimensions to EMS, relating to environmental valuation and risk analysis, product design, corporate culture and environmental awareness, supply and waste-chain management, and so on (see Kirkland and Thompson 1999). While EMS may be seen as progressive and a positive step forward in environmental regulation by some, embedded within EMS ideology are certain assumptions that imply 'more of the same' rather than system transformation. This is acknowledged in literature that is more sceptical and critical of what EMS appears to offer, as discussed in Box 11.2.

Box 11.2 Differing views of Environmental Management Systems

- *Traditionalist* – as far as possible (in the light of regulatory and compliance obligations) ignores impact of business activities on the natural environment, or, due to perceived barriers, will not implement EMS procedures, or displaces activity to areas where unfettered firm activity is profitable/possible: i.e., decisions to not adopt EMS are economic-based and contingent upon immediate business strategic market concerns.
- *Reformist* – sees value in development and implementation of EMS insofar as economic and environmental interests seen to be in harmony, attempts to offer a managerialist approach to limit human economic activity within bounds set by the ecosystem framework of environmental sustainability: i.e., decisions to adopt EMS are economic-based and values-based.
- *Radical* – dismisses EMS as tokenistic and as doing little to deal with the root causes of environmental degradation, in that dominant systemic pressures are inherently destructive to the environment in terms of ever-growing production, consumption, depletion of resources and waste generation: i.e., decisions to adopt EMS are essentially a form of ideological greenwashing that masks production and pollution as usual.
- *Strategic* – sees EMS as addressing some of the worst environmental excesses (i.e., real material consequences in specific cases), but at ideological and symbolic level EMS serves to construct products and companies as 'green' and legitimizes corporate management as the primary societal agent responsible for addressing environmental issues: i.e., decisions to adopt EMS are part of a political, practical and ideological response to the threat to corporate hegemony.

Source: drawing upon Levy 1997

According to the critics, the key message of EMS is that corporations have the 'know how' to best protect the environment (on our behalf), in that they have the technical means and managerial strategies to do so. As Levy (1997) points out, and as echoed in the 'smart regulation' literature (see Gunningham and Grabosky 1998), EMS is presented as a win-win opportunity in which the potential structural conflicts between profit maximization and environmental goals are avoided.

This needs to be demonstrated empirically, however, and such processes nonetheless represent another way to circumvent direct government regulation. Much the same has been argued in relation to the 'standards' put forward by the

International Organization for Standardization (ISO). Thus, the ISO 14000 standards (relating to environmental impacts) constitute a private-sector initiative that allows for the state to divest itself of regulatory functions and simultaneously remove regulation and standards-setting from the democratic process and beyond the reach of citizens and social movements (Wall and Beardwood 2001). The issue of who regulates what, and who controls the process, is central to any discussion of how best to respond to environmental harm.

Limits and opportunities of regulation

There is a need to deconstruct notions such as 'self-regulation' by examining the real world of corporate activity and the persisting damage caused by systemic exploitation of humans and the natural environment. This involves identifying and explaining the transformations in regulation along a number of dimensions, taking into account the specific role of international institutions such as the World Trade Organization, the International Monetary Fund and the World Bank, and accounting for the shifts in regulatory emphasis away from the state and toward private business interests (see for example, Goldman 1998; O'Brien et al. 2000; Beder 2006).

In the context of neo-liberal policies and globalized capitalist relations, the relationship of the state to private interests is ultimately contingent upon baseline economic criteria. Recent arguments that what we need to do is to adopt forms of 'smart regulation' (that involve a wide constellation of policy measures) tend to assume that improved environmental performance is possible at a price acceptable to both business and community. This can be achieved simply through adoption of the right mix of policy prescriptions (see Gunningham and Grabosky 1998). The emphasis is on efficiency and effectiveness of regulation; specific problems are presented primarily as technical matters, rather than as residing in the realm of politics. In the end, the appeal to 'pragmatic' multi-dimensional sorts of regulation conflate the idea of feasible forms of regulation with forms of regulation that currently predominate in the here and now.

Yet, as Snider (2000: 172) points out with regard to corporate crime, of which environmental harm is one manifestation, the broad trend has been for it to 'disappear'. This occurs through decriminalization (the repeal of criminal law), through deregulation (the repeal of all state laws, criminal, civil and administrative) and through downsizing (the destruction of the state's enforcement capability). A vital part of this disappearance has been the demise of 'command-and-control' legislation – that is, direct and systematic state intervention undertaken in the public interest in opposition to specific private interests. The thing about the regulatory pyramid is that it is not actually a pyramid if the peak is never attained (that is, if the 'big stick' is never or rarely used) (see especially Gray and Shimshack 2011). Likewise, the contingencies of decision-making are such that the public interest is liable to disappear when the key voices in regulation are those of the industries themselves.

The mandate of most state-directed environmental protection agencies today is not only to enforce compliance through use of criminal prosecutions, but also to forge strategic alliances and working partnerships with industries, local governments, and communities in support of environmental objectives. These are often explicitly framed in terms of economic, as well as environmental, objectives. In many cases, the multiple demands on EPAs from different sections of government, business and community, and the varied tasks in which they participate, may lead to a dilution of their enforcement capacities and activities. Important questions can be asked therefore in regard to the number of investigators and inspectors responsible for enforcing environmental law, and the philosophical framework that underpins their work. Budget cuts, reductions in personnel and loss of agency status all contribute to reducing ability of state regulators to actually do their job. These are political decisions and deliberate policy choices.

Yet in the midst of such decisions and choices there are principles and practices that alert us to the potentials and possibilities of good environmental regulatory systems. The Review of the Victoria EPA cited earlier, for example, proposed eight principles by which the EPA should undertake its regulatory role. The principles provide a benchmark against which the community can judge the EPA's performance. They also provide a basis for the EPA to measure its own effectiveness as a regulator. The principles and their regulatory impact are:

- *Targeted*: compliance and enforcement activities will be targeted at preventing the most serious harm.
- *Proportionate*: regulatory measures will be proportional to the problem they seek to address.
- *Transparent*: regulation will be developed and enforced transparently, to promote the sharing of information and learning. Enforcement actions will be public, to build the credibility of EPA's regulatory approach and processes.
- *Consistent*: enforcement should be consistent and predictable. EPA aims to ensure that similar circumstances, breaches and incidents lead to similar enforcement outcomes.
- *Accountable*: to ensure accountability, duty-holders' compliance, enforcement decisions and the conduct of authorized officers will be explained and open to public scrutiny.
- *Inclusive*: EPA will engage with community, business and government to promote environmental laws, set standards and provide opportunities to participate in compliance and enforcement.
- *Authoritative*: EPA will be authoritative by setting clear standards, clarifying and interpreting the law and providing authoritative guidance and support on what is required to comply. EPA will be prepared to be judged on whether individuals and business understand the law and their obligations. EPA will also be an authoritative source of information on the state of the

environment, the level of compliance with the laws it regulates, key risks and new and emerging issues.
- *Effective*: enforcement will seek to prevent environmental harm and impacts to public health, and improve the environment. Enforcement action will be timely, to minimize environmental impacts and enhance the effectiveness of any deterrence.

(EPA Victoria 2011: 3)

Identification of such principles simultaneously raises issues as to why they are or are not adopted. They also bolster the argument that good regulation ultimately rests upon the backbone of professional regulators, and that the professionalization of environmental regulation provides one means to counteract its inherent politicization (White and Heckenberg 2013).

Collaborations, culture and training are interlinked. It has been suggested that the mandate of protecting the environment needs to be highlighted at an organizational level, and that agencies and individuals need to earn respect through assessment across three broad areas:

- being held accountable for outcomes by the wider community, through performance measures relating to air, water and land quality;
- being transparent in relation to an assumed intelligent audience (e.g. affected community, the general public), by acknowledging both successes and failures; and
- ensuring that statutory duties are performed well, which in turn opens up space for innovation.

These can be seen as vital elements of professionalized and accountable practices, and as reinforcing a positive regulatory and enforcement culture at the organizational level.

Conclusion

As the discussion of regulatory systems, pyramids, issues and approaches in this chapter demonstrates, there are ongoing matters that require both theoretical consideration and practical application. The institutional culture surrounding regulation, compliance and enforcement activities has a great bearing on how work to monitor, investigate and prosecute environmental crimes is carried out in practice. There appear to be regular 'pendulum swings' in which activity oscillates between hardening, with greater use of a 'big-stick' approach, and the relative relaxation of controls and the shift toward self-regulation by industry.

Simultaneously, there is a push in some jurisdictions toward professionalizing environmental law enforcement, a move which would help institutionalize a more consistent approach to environmental regulation. Acknowledgement of different types of expertise and the importance of multi-disciplinary teams may be aligned with the movement toward professionalization of environmental law enforcement (White and Heckenberg 2013). Clearly defined areas of expertise, supported by ongoing training and education, can instil a strong sense of mission and independent critical thinking when it comes to regulating environmental crimes.

Discussion topics

- Which firms or industries have the most leverage to influence legislation and 'negotiate' compliance?
- How do regulators balance over-implementation and enforcement of legislation with minimizing harm to the environment?
- How do different size firms respond to regulation (e.g. transnational corporations, small and medium-sized businesses)?
- Do self-reports, predominantly relating to less serious environmental breaches, actually mask more serious breaches?
- Environmental Protection Authorities work an eight-hour day, many transnational corporations work a twenty-four-hour day. What are the implications of this for 'good practice' regulation?

Further reading

Ayres, I., and Braithwaite, J. (1992). *Responsive Regulation: Transcending the deregulation debate*. New York: Oxford University Press.

Braithwaite, J., and Drahos, P. (2000). *Global Business Regulation*. Cambridge: Cambridge University Press.

Gray, W., and Shimshack, J. (2011). 'The Effectiveness of Environmental Monitoring and Enforcement: A review of the empirical evidence', *Review of Environmental Economics and Policy*, 5(1): 3–24.

Gunningham, N., and Grabosky, P. (1998). *Smart Regulation: Designing environmental policy*. Oxford: Clarendon Press.

Snider, L. (2010). 'Framing E-waste Regulation: The obfuscating role of power', *Criminology and Public Policy*, 9(3): 569–77.

Chapter 12

Environmental law enforcement

Introduction

This chapter will discuss the following topics:

- environmental law enforcement;
- undertaking environmental law enforcement;
- networks and collaborative practices;
- NGO engagement in environmental law enforcement; and
- valuing environmental law enforcement.

Intervention on environmental harm occurs within a complex legislative environment that incorporates different laws, regulations, conventions and guidelines that relate to local, national, regional and international jurisdictions. Many different issues and trends are covered, relating to air, land and water use, biodiversity, the transport and use of hazardous waste, and carbon emissions. Much of the formal state intervention involves regulatory engagement, rather than criminal-justice proceedings. Moreover, not all harms are criminalized or subject to state prohibition, leaving a space for non-state actors to take part in activities that challenge the lack of state intervention in protecting certain environments (e.g. campaigns against deforestation) or species (e.g. anti-whaling campaigns).

It is rare that the state uses coercion solely, or even as the key lever of compliance, with regard to environmental laws. Rather, a wide variety of measures are used, frequently in conjunction with each other, as a means of dealing with environmental harm. Likewise, a range of agencies is assigned the task of ensuring compliance and enforcing the law vis-à-vis environmental protection. The *fusion of administrative, civil and criminal remedies* has major implications for how environmental enforcement agencies see their primary roles, and how they carry out their work, including how they define serious harm and environmental crime. Even where a tightening up of regulation occurs (as opposed to deregulation and self-regulation), this can have a negative flow-on effect insofar as, for example, European Union (EU) regulations surrounding disposal of hazardous waste may have the unintended consequence of encouraging (both legal and illegal) transfer of waste to non-EU countries which have less stringent regulatory regimes.

Environmental law enforcement

Environmental harm, as construed by official law-enforcement agencies, is essentially about the violation of national and international laws put in place to protect the environment. What is legally deemed to be 'bad' or criminal, therefore, is the main point of attention, whether this is illegal trade in wildlife and plants, or pollution of the air, water and land.

There are many diverse agencies engaged in some form of environmental law enforcement. Many jurisdictions have specialist agencies to tackle particular sorts of crime. An Environmental Protection Agency (EPA), for example, may be given the mandate to investigate and prosecute environmental crimes. The police may play only an auxiliary role in relation to the work of these agencies. In other circumstances and for other purposes, members of the police service may be specially trained as law-enforcement officers in defined areas of work. Some agencies are engaged in both regulation and enforcement, and individual agencies may be charged with either or both. Agencies dealing with environmental matters work in and across different jurisdictions and deal with myriad issues. This is illustrated in Table 12.1, which outlines different tiers of governance involving various bodies engaged in environmental law enforcement.

More generally, the central mandate of an agency tends to be driven by the specific type of crime. For example, Environmental Protection Agencies (or their equivalent) often focus on 'brown' issues pertaining to pollution and waste. Forestry Commissions or National Parks Authorities (or equivalent) tend to concentrate on 'green' issues, and so deal with matters of conservation, animal welfare and land use. Bodies such as the Royal Society for the Prevention of Cruelty to Animals (or equivalent) are charged with the responsibility to intervene in cases of harsh treatment of, particularly, domesticated animals (such as companion animals or those destined to be food). A Customs service typically investigates trade in illegal fauna and flora, as well as the international shipment of toxic wastes and banned substances. Police services may have a general duty to protect animals and monitor the environment, while in some cases being vested with the lead role in wildlife offences. The regulation and policing of fisheries may involve specific fisheries management authorities and specially trained fisheries officers. Health departments may be the key authorities when it comes to the management and disposal of radioactive and clinical waste. Park rangers could be tasked with the job of preventing the poaching of animals from national parks and private reserves. The list of agencies that have some role in environmental law enforcement is extensive.

Table 12.1 Environmental enforcement agencies at different tiers: Australia

Geo-political scale	Examples at the operational level
Local Councils	Urban and metropolitan councils
	Regional or rural (shires)
State	Environmental Protection Agencies
	Local Government Association
	State Police services
	Royal Society for the Prevention of Cruelty to Animals (RSPCA)
	Parks and Wildlife Service
National	Australian Fisheries Management Authority
	Australian Federal Police
	Australian Customs Service
	Office of Consumer Affairs
	Department of Sustainability, Environment, Water, Population and Communities
National/state bodies	Australian Crime Commission
	National Pollution Inventory
	The Australasian Environmental Law Enforcement and Regulators Network (AELERT)
International	Interpol
	International Network of Environmental Enforcement and Compliance (INECE)

Source: White 2011a

Who precisely is going to deal with which type of crime is partly a function of the alleged offence, since this will often dictate the agency deemed to be responsible for a particular area – whether this is drug enforcement, counter-terrorism or environmental crime. Specialist agencies and specialist police can also wear more than one hat. For example, in the United States 'conservation police' (a term that broadly refers to fish and wildlife officers, wildlife management officers, game wardens, park rangers, and natural resources police) have authority to deal with conventional crime as well as environmental crime. This means that in addition to investigating and enforcing laws relating specifically to fish and wildlife issues, their activities can incorporate more generalist policing concerns, including those involving things such as drug law enforcement and human trafficking (Shelley and Crow 2009).

Within a particular national context there may be considerable diversity in law-enforcement agencies and personnel, and there are myriad bodies that in some way or another are charged with policing functions (see Haberfeld and Cerrah 2008). For example, in the United Kingdom there are specialist policing bodies such as state security services (e.g. MI5 and MI6), regulatory authorities such as the Environment Agency, municipal police such as Royal Parks Police, as well as the usual Home Office police – all of whom may be called upon to play a role in combating crime (Crawford 2008). Periodically these kinds of agencies might be brought together in the form of environmental crime task forces, as in some instances in the United States, which may also include participation from non-law-enforcement agencies (Dighe and Pettus 2011; see also Spapens 2011).

Police will have quite different roles in environmental law-enforcement depending upon the city or state/province or region within which they work, and the agency within which they are employed. In a federal system of governance, for example – as in the USA, Canada and Australia – there can be great variation in enforcement practices depending upon whether police operate at the local municipal level (such as the Toronto Police Service), provincial or state level (Ontario Provincial Police) or the federal level (Royal Canadian Mounted Police). In dealing with specific crimes and particular sorts of criminality, lines of authority will be dictated by inter-jurisdictional protocols (such as federal laws overriding local laws or national security legislation that supersedes state laws) and in some instances Court decisions (that establish the limits of legal encroachment by diverse authorities).

Looking farther afield, who is doing what is further complicated by geographical proximity of countries – as in Europe – which facilitates the transfer of crime problems across national borders. This can be compounded by political arrangements, such as a common European passport and currency that makes it easier to move within the boundaries of the European Union as a whole. From a domestic policing perspective, this means that there is a need for both vertical connections within any particular national context (around particular crime issues), and horizontal connections with relevant agencies outside that specific country (given the relative ease of cross-over into other jurisdictions). In some instances – as with the Task Force on Organized Crime in the Baltic Sea Region (which includes representatives from Denmark, Estonia, the European Commission, Finland, Germany, Latvia, Lithuania, Poland, Russia and Sweden) – specific organizational structures are set up in order to share intelligence, on environmental crime in this instance, and to develop co-operative enforcement structures to deal with offenders.

At the international level, agencies such as Interpol are central players in global environmental law enforcement. In 2010, at the 79th Interpol General Assembly, the Chiefs of Police from 188 countries adopted an Environment Enforcement Resolution. This resolution acknowledges that:

> Environmental law enforcement is not always the responsibility of one national agency, but rather, is multi-disciplinary in nature due to the complexity and diversity of the crime type which can encompass disciplines such as wildlife, pollution, fisheries, forestry, natural resources and climate change, with reaching effect into other areas of crime
>
> (Interpol and UNEP 2012: 2)

Reflecting concern over environmental issues, a summit of International Chiefs of Environmental Compliance and Enforcement was held in March 2012. This forum provided an opportunity for national leaders of environment, biodiversity and natural resources agencies to meet and discuss action around issues such as investigative assistance and operational support, information management, capacity-building standards and effective networks, and there were also commodity-specific side-meetings covering fisheries, forestry, pollution and wildlife. A summary of this forum pointed out:

- the scale of environmental crime and the connection with organized transnational crime, including issues of smuggling, corruption, fraud, tax evasion, money laundering, and murder;
- the interconnectivity of environmental crime with other forms of criminal activity requiring co-operation and collaboration across all levels of law enforcement in order to combat and prevent the illegal activities;
- the current scale of environmental crime involves very similar approaches, means and severity to other forms of crime, but is aggravated and exacerbated further by the direct serious implications it has on the development goals of many countries;
- the sheer scale of environmental crime including, but not limited to, illegal logging and deforestation, illegal fisheries and smuggling of toxic waste, and the severe implications of this not only on the environment, but also on human security and economic development.

(Interpol and UNEP 2012: 2)

It is not only issues which have been highlighted in such summits, but operational policies and practices as well. This is reflected in efforts to link up agencies and personnel across jurisdictions and across substantive enforcement areas. Several different consortiums have been forged internationally to deal with specific types of environmental crime. For instance, the International Consortium on Combating Wildlife Crime is comprised of five intergovernmental organizations working to bring co-ordinated support to the national wildlife law-enforcement agencies and to the sub-regional and regional networks that act in defence of natural resources:

1 the Convention on International Trade in Endangered Species of Wild Fauna and Flora (CITES);
2 Secretariat, Interpol;
3 the United Nations Office on Drugs and Crime (UNODC);
4 the World Bank; and
5 the World Customs Organization (WCO).

This collaborative group is chaired by the CITES Secretariat (CITES 2012).

On another front, Project Leaf (Law Enforcement Assistance for Forests) is an Interpol and United Nations Environment Programme (UNEP) climate-initiative consortium that is directed against illegal logging and related crimes. The objectives of this Project are to:

- form National Environmental Security Task Forces (NESTs) to ensure institutionalized co-operation between national agencies, Interpol NCBs [National Central Bureaux], and international partners;
- conduct operations to suppress criminality, disrupt trafficking routes, and ensure the enforcement of international and national legislations on sustainable forestry;
- expand the project through awareness-raising making a real contribution to global-emissions goals, protecting biodiversity, and preventing environmental destruction.

(Interpol 2012)

A NEST is a task force of a firmly established team of experts who work together to address a specific issue. It is comprised of senior criminal investigators, criminal analysts, training officers, prosecutors, financial specialists, forensic experts and others, drawn from police, customs, environmental and other specialized enforcement agencies, and also involving non-government and regional organizations as appropriate.

Environmental policing thus is carried out in the light of both considerable variations in policing functions and agencies, and in relation to different levels of government. To put it differently, those who do 'policing' work may not be *the* police, and the police are not necessarily involved directly in all types of environmental law-enforcement work. Environmental law enforcement includes officials working for local municipal councils (and rural shire councils) through to those working on behalf of Interpol in Thailand. It also includes a wide range of NGOs that operate in various official and unofficial capacities. For instance, animal welfare may be deemed to be the official responsibility of organizations such as the Royal Society for the Prevention of Cruelty to Animals (RSPCA), who then investigate and prosecute cases of animal abuse. Other NGOs, such as Greenpeace Amazon, may not have an 'official' role per se, but nonetheless gather evidence of activities such as illegal logging, which can then be passed on to relevant police and judicial authorities.

Undertaking environmental law enforcement

The nature of environmental crime poses a number of challenges for effective policing and hence prosecution. Environmental crimes may have local, national, regional and global dimensions. They may be difficult to detect (as in the case of some forms of toxic pollution undetectable to human senses). They may demand intensive cross-jurisdictional negotiation, and even disagreement between nation-states about specific events or crime patterns. Some crimes may be highly organized and involve criminal syndicates, such as illegal fishing. Others may include a wide range of criminal actors, ranging from the individual collector of endangered species to the systematic disposal of toxic waste via third parties.

These various dimensions of environmental crime pose particular challenges for environmental law enforcement, especially from the point of view of police inter-agency collaborations, the nature of investigative techniques and approaches, and the different types of knowledge required for dealing with specific kinds of environmental harm. Moreover, many of the operational matters pertaining to environmental crimes are inherently international in scope and substance. The scope and complexity of environmental crime means that greater investment in enforcement policy, enforcement capacity and performance management is sorely needed in most jurisdictions (see Akella and Cannon 2004; Dobovsek and Pracek 2010: 148).

The special challenge for agency responses to transnational environmental harms is that many different jurisdictions have to be mobilized simultaneously around the same aims and objectives. Enforcement practices in these circumstances must be inclusive, comprehensive and well-organized. This is achievable provided there is enough consensus and political support among partner nation-states. Some of the issues that influence the manner and dynamics of global governance include the scale at which regulation and enforcement takes place (e.g. local council of York, nation-state of Britain, regional group of European Union, international sphere of Interpol); the type of collaboration, networks and partnerships established in a particular area; the extent of harmonization of laws, enforcement practices and communication strategies; and the sort of NGO involvement allowed, encouraged and/or resisted in particular jurisdictional contexts.

The plethora of players and laws demands an approach to environmental law enforcement and compliance that necessarily must be collaborative in nature. Dealing with global environmental harm will demand extraordinary efforts to relate to each other across distance, time, language and cultural borders; to understand specific issues; to co-ordinate actions; to enforce international laws and conventions; and to gather and share information and intelligence. These are domestic policing issues as well as international.

Environmental regulation and enforcement frequently only finds effective purchase within particular jurisdictions and national contexts. Thus, for example, new forms of intervention, such as 'environmental enforcement sweeps', are now being applied where a specific community faces multiple environmental burdens. Such sweeps involve the use of administrative, civil, and criminal enforcement tools in tandem to address the problems in a comprehensive fashion (Dighe and Pettus 2011). Factory pollution, for example, might be be met by examination of the permit-compliance history of companies, investigation of violations of different environmental laws, and involvement of multiple agencies alongside community input. This model seems to present an ideal method of responding to environmental problems. Whether or not resources are put into this kind of intervention, however, is ultimately dictated by political and economic considerations.

One of the many issues pertaining to the proliferation of agencies dealing with environmental crime is that each may be driven by different aims and objectives, different methods of intervention, with different powers, and exhibiting different levels of expertise and collaboration with others. Another issue relates to the need to distinguish between organizational affiliation (which may be formal and policy-oriented) and inter-agency collaboration (which refers to actual operational practices and linkages). In some cases, there is a clear need for capacity-building in order for collaboration – and, especially, rapid response – to be successfully institutionalized as part of normal agency practice. There can also be agency differences in defining and interpreting just what the crime is and how it should be responded to – as in the case of breaches versus crime, customs offences versus fisheries offences, and so on.

In a scoping analysis of law-enforcement practices and institutions in Brazil, Mexico, Indonesia and the Philippines, in relation to a variety of environmental issues, Akella and Cannon (2004: 19) identified the following common problems across different sites:

- poor inter-agency co-operation;
- inadequate budgetary resources;
- technical deficiencies in laws, agency policies and procedures;
- insufficient technical skills and knowledge;
- lack of performance monitoring and adaptive management systems.

In a national study of crime in the Australian fishing industry, Putt and Anderson (2007: 54) likewise found 'the survey of fisheries officers as highlighting insufficient sharing of information by agencies and of collaboration across jurisdictions'. They observed that:

- the lack of formal agreements was seen as a major problem;
- protocols to enable the sharing of information that does not breach privacy provisions would clearly be of benefit (subject to some degree of agreement on the purpose of sharing the information and what the expected benefits are to all parties);
- differing priorities will continue to affect the success of joint operations, as well as the willingness of agencies to collaborate with information and resource commitments.

Tomkins (2005) also clearly identified the need to share intelligence and to develop co-operative enforcement structures to deal with environmental offenders. Who does what, and how, remain important practical issues.

The criminalization of environmental harm does not necessarily equate with the prosecution and punishment of environmental offenders. This is because of a range of issues relating to detection, arrest, prosecution and sentencing of those who violate environmental laws. Many factors affect the determinants of the quality of environmental law enforcement, and the enforcement chain has a number of interdependent links, as seen in Box 12.1.

Box 12.1 The enforcement chain

- Probability of *detection* is correlated to the incentives given to park guards, rangers, and forest and fishery environment protection agents (e.g. pay levels and other rewards); to availability of equipment; to number of personnel charged with detecting environmental crimes; and to technical knowledge and skill of personnel.
- Probability of *arrest*, given detection, is correlated to police pay and reward structure, to availability of equipment, to quality of evidence, and to social perceptions about the crime.
- Probability of *prosecution*, given arrest, is correlated to rewards for prosecutors, to capacity of the justice system and those in it to prosecute environmental crimes, to whether the illegal act is a criminal or civil offence, to social attitudes toward the crime, and to quality of evidence.
- Probability of *conviction*, given prosecution, is correlated to rewards for judges and magistrates, to capacity of the justice system, to nature of the crime, to social attitudes toward the crime, and to quality of evidence.

Source: Akella and Cannon 2004: 10

All these factors impinge upon environmental law enforcement, regardless of whether or not enforcement is undertaken by government or non-government agencies.

Networks and collaborative practices

To be effective, agencies need to be able to harness the co-operation and expertise of many different contributors and liaise with relevant partners at the local through to the international levels. In its most basic sense, collaboration simply refers to people or agencies working together for a shared purpose. However, the meaning and social processes pertaining to collaboration-in-practice can be complicated and variable. This is because it often involves forms of collaboration that extend both vertically (within institutional hierarchies) and horizontally (across institutional settings).

Collaboration is not only about whom one works with, it also implies a temporal element. For instance, the notion of engagement hinges upon working with other agencies and other personnel over *a defined period of time*. Over the course of a specific collaboration environmental law-enforcement officers need to be conscious of many different issues regarding their own roles and expertise:

- conflicts of interest;
- capacities and levels of competence;
- mechanisms to deal with potential harm or wrongdoing;
- knowledge of codes of conduct;
- consideration of the social composition of the collaborating team;
- storage of materials and data associated with the collaboration;
- confidentiality and anonymity;
- fair, honest, comprehensive and accurate reflection and reporting on the collaboration process.

Working on specific environmental issues means engaging with different people with a wide variety of experience and expertise. It also means involvement in processes that should build a sense of coalition or shared purpose through heightened transparency and consultation. This is about building collaborative alliances (Pink and Lehane 2012).

Another useful concept relevant to improving environmental law-enforcement practice is that of networking. A network approach to environmental law enforcement focuses on sets of relationships and the forging of informal and formal ties between relevant agencies and people. In regard to transnational environmental crime, the International Network of Environmental Compliance and Enforcement (INECE) provides a case in point, as does the Interpol Environmental Crimes Committee. Regional and national networks of enforcement personnel and regulatory agencies are further examples of grounded collaboration involving diverse sets of players (see Pink 2010). For example, the Australasian Environmental Law Enforcement and Regulators Network (AELERT) has been very active since its inception less than a decade ago and is quickly growing into a significant professional forum for practitioners.

This formal networking is essential in several different ways. It allows for sharing of ideas and information about 'best practice'. It enables participants to gain a perspective on environmental crimes that occur within specific local and regional contexts and those that are more global in scope. It fosters cross-agency co-operation and intelligence exchanges within specific national contexts (horizontal connections that bring together EPA, police, customs and other agency personnel), as well as internationally (vertical connections that bring together national representatives from different parts of the world, including United Nations personnel).

The combination of networks, whether internal or external, informal or formal, and involving law-enforcers, non-law-enforcers and environmental enforcers, is perceived to have resulted in superior efficiencies in enforcement efforts in countries such as Australia (Pink 2010). Networking provides a practicable basis for intervention in areas that are by their nature complex and multifaceted. For example, the need for environmental enforcement and regulation is growing rapidly (in the light of climate change and massive environmental degradation generally), yet the resources for this are shrinking (as the hard economic times continue and due to government choice in priorities). This makes networking even more essential insofar as it can help to reduce costs, cut red tape and enhance law-enforcement capabilities (Pink and Lehane 2012).

In addition to questions of resources, staffing, recruitment of the right people, and training, a big factor affecting agency performance is how well it interacts with other relevant agencies in the field. Related to organizational matters, the dynamics of environmental crime are such that new types of skills, knowledge and expertise need to be drawn upon as part of the law-enforcement effort. For example, crimes related to toxic waste and pollution require the sophisticated tools and scientific know-how associated with environmental forensics (Murphy and Morrison 2007; Dobovsek and Pracek 2010; White 2012a). Investigatory methods and powers, particularly in relation to the gathering of suitable evidence for specific environmental crimes, will inevitably be shaped by state and national laws and regulations, and influenced by regional and international conventions and protocols. The availability of local expertise, staff and resources will determine how investigation is carried out in practice.

Greater numbers of training packages are starting to be produced in the specific area of environmental law enforcement. For example, in South Africa a recent training manual for law-enforcement agencies provides an outline of the key legal principles of environmental law, the types of environmental crime, issues relating to criminal prosecution (including consideration of strict liability and vicarious liability), environmental inspection and investigation, the gathering of evidence (including different types of evidence), factors relevant to prosecution and the nature of the trial process (Akech and Mwebaza 2010).

At a practical level, a productive strategy for harmonizing enforcement efforts is to focus on consistency in delivering regulatory and enforcement tasks, rather than focusing on uniform legislation as such. For instance, international networks of law-enforcement officers (e.g. Interpol and organizations such as the International Network of Environmental Enforcement and Compliance) provide valuable forums for the exchange of information and knowledge transfer about 'best practice' and 'what works' in which situations. Participation in common training programmes and attendance at conferences and workshops provides opportunities to enhance overall law-enforcement capabilities as well as contributing to shared understandings and values in regard to specific types of criminal activity. Agencies such as Interpol provide a forum where criminal investigators from around the globe meet to discuss issues such as determining the role of organized crime in specific types of criminal enterprises (e.g. people-smuggling), and developing training and enforcement actions to combat particular sorts of criminal activity (e.g. illegal oil pollution into oceans, seas and inland waterways).

Importantly, the use of regional case studies and reference to local experiences both reaffirms the importance of acknowledging specific jurisdictional differences and creates opportunities for adopting a more balanced view of what constitutes the most productive law-enforcement approaches and strategies.

Understanding the complexities of global issues is a vital step in forging a transnational value system protective of collective social interests, ecological well-being and human rights (see Interpol and UNEP 2012). The risks, harms and threats posed by and accompanying climate change add further impetus to think creatively about near and over-the-horizon challenges when it comes to environmental law enforcement. Climate change has massive implications for policing, and recent commentary has suggested that it will profoundly affect the core business of policing, not just the work of those directly engaged in environmental law enforcement (Bergin and Allen 2008; see also Pink and Lehane 2012).

In the end, to be effective, agencies need to be able to harness the co-operation and expertise of many different contributors and to liaise with relevant partners at the local through to the international levels. A 'joined-up' approach also means that links can be made between different forms of crime as well as between different agencies, and different parts of the world. For instance, illegal fishing (an important environmental crime) has been tied to trafficking of persons, smuggling of migrants and the illicit traffic in drugs. This is due to the influence of transnational organized crime in the fishing industry worldwide (UNODC 2011). International co-operation is also necessitated by the sophistication and transnational nature of the crimes as well. In response, the International Monitoring, Control and Surveillance Network has been formed and is dedicated to preventing and deterring illegal, unreported and unregulated fishing. It has participation from over 50 countries.

NGO engagement in environmental law enforcement

The dearth of adequate controls and regulatory actions within official criminal justice and state offices on matters pertaining to environmental harm is nevertheless still a problem of considerable proportions. To put it simply, not enough is being done to detect, prevent, prosecute and respond to environmental crime (see White 2011a). Accordingly, it is very often transnational environmental activists who have stepped into the breach, exposing instances of ecological and species harm, providing details of poor regulation and enforcement practices, and contributing both formally and informally to crime reduction and prosecution processes. As increasingly important players in the world of environmental protection, conservation and management, environmental activists frequently have both to confront powerful social, economic and political interests, and to work with and alongside powerful groups, organizations and state apparatus.

For example, at the Interpol Conference on International Environmental Crime in Lyon, France, in September 2010 there were representatives from both official environmental law-enforcement agencies, and from a wide range of non-government agencies such as Greenpeace Amazon. From the discussions, it was clear that, while government agencies may be constitutive of the official networks, they frequently lack adequate resources and staff. Conversely, the Non-Government Organizations are not only actively engaged with environmental issues, but they are often well-resourced. As a consequence, there are now different types of partnerships emerging. In one instance, there is direct sharing of resources, as in the case of an American NGO funding individual staff within Interpol's Environment Crime section. In another instance, NGOs are directly engaged in sharing evidence collected through their own independent investigations (into illegal wildlife trade or illegal logging for example) with trusted authorities in places such as Brazil. There is also the interesting case of a criminal syndicate trading in illegal wildlife in Russia that was in fact headed by senior police. This made it difficult for other state police to intervene. The ring was eventually busted with the assistance of NGO activists posing as buyers and secretly filming the transactions.

The complex nature of environmental harms covering many different issues relating to air, land and water use, biodiversity, the transport and use of hazardous waste, and carbon emissions demands expertise and personnel across a wide range of areas and extensive networks of surveillance. With regard to this, Non-Government Organizations can and do play a significant role in investigating and exposing environmental harm and offender wrongdoing (see for examples, Environmental Investigation Agency 2008).

NGOs can have both formal and informal roles in environmental regulation and law enforcement (Nurse 2013c; Stretesky and Knight 2013). So called 'wildlife' NGOs, such as the RSPCA, may be granted official status and legal rights in regard to investigation and prosecution of animal abuse. Local environmental groups may be given a supplementary regulatory role, officially supported and partially funded by the state to, for example, monitor water quality at the regional or municipal level. For those agencies and groups contracted to do this kind of work, issues of resources, specialist equipment and staff/volunteer training are important, as are questions concerning the effectiveness of NGO participation in securing good regulatory outcomes.

Other organizations and agencies may combine key activities so as to include campaign work as well as direct 'policing' of related activities. For example, Greenpeace engages in both public campaigns (that may occasionally push the limits of the law) as well as collecting evidence of ecological wrongdoing that can be used in a court of law to prosecute environmental offenders. The specific role of agencies such as the Environmental Investigation Agency may be to investigate environmental crimes and to channel resources into protection and prosecution across a range of environmental areas (including, for example, pollution issues as well as illegal trade in endangered species). Other NGOs may have a more specific mandate, whether it is to expose the social and ecological harms associated with e-waste (as with the Basel Action Network) or illegal trafficking of animals (such as the Freeland Foundation).

Environmental activism deals with acts and omissions that are already criminalized and prohibited, such as illegal fishing or illegal dumping of toxic waste. But it also come to grips with events that have yet to be designated officially as 'harmful' but that show evidence of exhibiting potentially negative consequences. It thus deals with different kinds of harms and risks, as these affect humans, local and global environments, and non-human animals. Not surprisingly, very often the target for action, and the object of change, is the state. In part this is because much environmental destruction globally is supported by particular nation-states in collusion with powerful corporations. Specific types of transnational environmental crime are basically linked in some way to the nature and extent of state intervention (or non-intervention), which in turn depends on the geographic location and political-economic importance of the specific activities in question. In response to these trends, NGOs use both confrontational and conciliatory tactics in pursuing their objectives (White 2011a, 2012b).

For NGOs involved in environmental law-enforcement activities there are two separate sets of practical issues: ones that parallel those of conventional official environmental law-enforcement agencies, and those that stem directly from the status and ideological orientation of the NGO itself (for elaboration see White 2012c). These are summarized in Box 12.2.

Box 12.2 NGOs compared with official environmental law enforcement

Issues in common

Expertise: Skills related to gathering evidence for the purposes of court; knowledge and marshalling of forensic and other technical knowledge; investigatory skills.

Training: Needs to be continuous, with training resources constantly updated and refreshed, in the light of the complexities and changing nature of environmental crime, as well as innovations in crime detection, investigation, networking and technological development.

Morale: What happens in the public sphere and governmental domain affects the morale and work activities of all those engaged in environmental enforcement law activities, and this can influence the confidence of activists in formal system outcomes, including court outcomes.

Collaboration: Forging links between police and non-police environmental enforcement agencies, and between official and NGO agencies, with appropriate rules of engagement.

Areas of divergence

Legality and social constructions of harm: NGOs may be among the biggest critics of existing rules and conventions, and this puts NGOs at loggerheads with those whose official environmental law-enforcement brief is dictated by international and national laws over which the NGOs may disagree.

Illegal actions in support of a cause: Some NGOs justify taking illegal action around environmental and animal rights issues, based on the premise that many presently legal activities constitute a crime against nature, and this can make collaboration between NGOs and official environmental law-enforcement agencies complicated, at the very least, if not impossible.

Intervention powers: For NGO investigators, legally mandated powers of investigation will vary (e.g. RSPCA versus Greenpeace), as will their legal standing in relation to questioning witnesses, initiating prosecutions and collecting evidence.

Displacement of roles: In some countries the active engagement of NGOs around environmental matters is accompanied by the displacement of a formal authority role on the part of governments, especially where NGOs end up doing what should be done by formal state agencies, aided and abetted by the same governments that find it cheaper and easier to have NGOs do the work than funding such activities themselves.

Accountability: This is partly determined by ideology and ideals (e.g. save whales, save forests) and one's record of activism in relation to these ideas. While acting outside the usual restrictions of law and bureaucratic structures offers a degree of 'real-world' flexibility in responding to actual environmental harms, it also will engender difficulties in forming alliances with official environmental law-enforcement agencies and their personnel.

Source: White 2012c

There are many ways in which transnational environmental activist groups can work with official agencies and personnel to achieve similar goals, including sharing intelligence and joint efforts to gather evidence against wrongdoers. On the other hand, in countries and regions where legal and illegal logging is built into the fabric of state-corporate collusion, it may well be the policing of anti-logging activists that predominates. The specific status and role of NGOs will thus vary depending upon immediate social and political circumstances.

There are a number of issues, problems and dilemmas that shape the precise role and contribution of NGOs to environmental law enforcement. Acknowledgement of these by both sides, plus a willingness to engage in dialogue with various stake-holders, would provide space in which to build upon the positive aspects of NGO engagement, and to minimize the potential conflicts between NGO and official agencies in their pursuit of social and ecological justice. For example, for both official agencies and NGOs there is a need to develop new and sophisticated skills of investigation. Effective collaboration likewise has to be a hallmark of engagement in this area because of the plethora of agencies, stake-holders and organizations generally involved, and the fact that much environmental crime crosses borders. It is increasingly clear that government and non-government agencies and actors need to work together in a wide range of ways for the sake of better environmental governance generally.

Valuing environmental law enforcement

The damage caused by environmental crime ultimately must be realized in the form of greater sanctions and judicial commitment if environmental law-enforcement efforts are to be justly rewarded and valued in their own right. However, as pointed out earlier in this book, environmental crime frequently embodies a certain ambiguity. This is because it is not only located in frameworks of risk (e.g. precautionary principle) or evaluated in terms of actual harms (e.g. polluter pays), but is also judged in the context of cost-benefit analysis (e.g. license to trade or to pollute or to kill or capture). Philosophically, therefore, some types of harm are seen as less damaging than others, and thus to warrant different treatment from those perceived to be more serious. The notion of trade-off implicit within a cost-benefit approach immediately undermines the potential seriousness of the harm in question.

In law, this is generally reflected in how particular acts or omissions come to be legally defined as serious or not. As discussed in Chapter 1, some are deemed to be *malum in se* – as inherently wrong and evil – whilst others are deemed to be *malum prohibitum* – not seen as inherently bad, but as wrong simply because they breach regulation. It is notable in this regard that Environmental Protection Agencies are mainly and primarily concerned with compliance activities – that is, how individuals, firms and corporations comply with rules. This can reinforce the general idea that environmental crimes are essentially less serious than others.

Accordingly, most offences involving the environment are prosecuted in lower courts (or dealt with by civil and administrative penalties), and most penalties are on the lower rather than higher end of the scale (see Chapter 14). Unsurprisingly, one of the complaints among those engaged in environmental law enforcement (both government and non-government actors) is that all their hard work too frequently ends up being for nought. The dilemma is twofold. On the one hand, the valuing of environmental harm (by courts especially) is essential if eco-crime is to garner the resources needed to fight it. On the other hand, to the extent that sanctions are viewed as inadequate (especially relative to law-enforcement efforts), then this will negatively impact upon the enforcement process, leading to demoralization and in some instances vigilantism.

How the chain of enforcement evolves at a practical level is vital to the effectiveness of environmental law enforcement. The nature of court decisions in relation to environmental crimes and the harm they generate is as important as the resources put into enforcement efforts at the front end of the enforcement process. Thus, each part of the enforcement chain affects the recognition and validity of this work as 'real' law enforcement dealing with 'real' crimes. How justice is played out in practice is in fact vital to the morale and effectiveness of environmental law-enforcers. The effect of court decisions on environmental law-enforcement officers continues to be a matter of substantial concern. As much as anything, it impacts upon the recognition and validity of this work as 'real' law-enforcement activity dealing with 'real' crime.

Conclusion

If environmental crime is to be adequately dealt with now and into the future, then new technologies and new collaborations are required, as well as extensive additions to agency resources. Moreover, networks are a key form of collaboration, as the sharing of intelligence and information is crucial to effective law enforcement. How contemporary law-enforcement agencies are presently responding to transnational environmental crime also provides insights and lessons about 'what works' in this field. Current practice shows the importance of formal global networks in relation to collaboration. This is evident not only in the transfer of ideas, techniques and technologies through networks such as the International Network of Environmental Compliance and Enforcement. Such collaborations also provide for the reinforcement of cultures that place value on environmental harm and on what environmental law-enforcement officers do.

A common problem in the area of environmental law enforcement is the lack of political will and financial resources being directed to environmental protection. Thus, while formal environmental law-enforcement agencies and the like struggle with meagre budgets and low staff numbers, and NGOs do what they can to highlight environmental degradation and species harm, much remains to be done. For this to occur, the 'environment' must come to the fore as an issue of significant public interest and public standing. It is the politics of the environment, therefore, that ultimately determines the extent and effectiveness of environmental regulation and law enforcement.

Discussion topics

- Environmental harm is facilitated by the state as well as corporations and other powerful actors. What are the implications of this for officers and agencies engaged in environmental law enforcement?
- What agencies and actors are involved in environmental law-enforcement activities in your particular jurisdiction and/or country?
- The police are not the only ones engaged in environmental law enforcement, nor should they be. The complexity of issues and scope of intervention means that expertise and experience from many quarters will need to be drawn upon in combating environmental crime. Discuss.
- There are different models of how to organize environmental law enforcement. In some cases there are specific environmental police units, in others specially put together 'flying squads' comprised of personnel from different

agencies. Should the specific type of crime determine the organizational response to it? Provide concrete examples of different types of policing practice.
- The establishment of international eco-police, with dedicated specialist skills and capacities to investigate and prosecute environmental crime, could be an important innovation at the global level. What are the arguments for and against the notion of an international 'green police' service?

Further reading

Akella, A., and Cannon, J. (2004). *Strengthening the Weakest Links: Strategies for improving the enforcement of environmental laws globally*. Washington, DC: Conservation International.

Nurse, A. (2013). 'Privatising the Green Police: The role of NGOs in wildlife law enforcement', *Crime, Law and Social Change*, 59(3): 305–18.

Pink, G., and Lehane, J. (2012). 'Environmental Enforcement Networks: Their role in climate change enforcement', in R. White (ed.), *Climate Change from a Criminological Perspective*. New York: Springer.

Wellsmith, M. (2011). 'Wildlife Crime: The problems of enforcement', *European Journal on Criminal Policy and Research*, 17(2): 125–48.

White, R. (2011). 'Environmental Law Enforcement: The importance of global networks and collaborative practices', *Australasian Policing: A Journal of Professional Practice and Research*, 3(1): 2–16.

Chapter 13

Environmental forensic studies

Introduction

This chapter will discuss the following topics:

- science, knowledge and uncertainty;
- environmental forensic science;
- environmental forensic studies;
- stake-holders and stake-holder discourses
- the politics of knowing and knowledge; and
- evidence and investigation.

The field of environmental forensic studies combines science – both the natural and social sciences – with investigation. The key term and variable is that of 'evidence', and the purpose of forensic study is to ensure that the gathering and interpretation of information conforms to the highest levels of scientific rigour and validity. This requires critical scrutiny of sources of data, the yardsticks by which to measure harm, and close consideration of who is saying what and for what reasons. As this chapter indicates, effective environmental forensic study involves a wide number of stake-holders and types of information. It is a complex area in which to work.

Science, knowledge and uncertainty

Doing science is both a social and a technical activity, in that social contexts influence scientific interpretation of what the 'facts' convey. That is, the vital role of science in bringing problems to public attention, and in devising methods to monitor or curb environmental hazards, is contingent upon how scientists are integrated into the policy-making process.

On the one hand, even where there is consensus among scientists about what is scientifically correct, comparison between how scientists deal with scientific certainty and uncertainty in specific cases (e.g. greenhouse gas and global temperatures, radiation doses and cancer) indicate that scientists' application of precaution as a policy recommendation is dependent on context – it is directly linked to the nature of the specific issue at hand (Silva and Jenkins-Smith 2007). Popular understandings and existing policy initiatives shape how scientific knowledge is translated into judgements about appropriate policy.

On the other hand, the relationship between scientific advice and institutional decisions means considerable variation in how different governments deal with the same issue (even if scientists largely agree on the basic nature of the phenomenon). For example, the United States and the European Union have major policy differences regarding the use of genetically modified organisms (GMOs). This is not simply a dispute over the science involved in study of GMOs; it reflects differences in the vested interests associated with GMO production and distribution. Policy differences are apparent in other areas as well, as with the assessment of pesticide hazards in the United States, Britain and the European Union (see Irwin 2001). Whatever the specific science involved, it has been observed that 'institutions do not simply follow broad and established principles, but must instead tread a sensitive path between scientific evidence, social pressures and commercial anxieties' (Irwin 2001: 116).

It is rare that scientific evidence is uncontested and that proof of environmental harm is simply a matter of 'let the facts decide'. What counts as 'science', what counts as 'evidence', who counts as being a 'scientific expert' and what counts as 'sensible' public policy are all influenced by factors such as economic situation, the scientific tradition within a particular national context, the scientific standards that are used in relation to specific issues, and the style and mode of government. Thus, science is one of the backbones of discovery, measurement and explanation of environmental harm, but it, too, is embedded in particular social processes and decision-making frameworks. In this respect, science is inherently social. This is probably most apparent today in the attacks on science and scientists by the climate-change contrarians (Brisman 2012a).

There is no doubt that scientific knowledge claims must be critically scrutinized, but then again this is in the nature of the scientific method itself. That is, science demands testing and retesting of propositions in the light of evidence and ongoing theoretical developments. Determining the extent and nature of any specific environmental problem demands scientific testing and diagnosis at some stage. The definition of 'clean air', for example, may be subject to legal and political wrangling in terms of what level of pollution regulators are willing to accept. But it is the scientist who will tell us what is actually in the air at any point in time.

Scientific knowledge thus also has a social context. It is produced in socially patterned ways, and is not socially neutral in application. Again, it is important to consider the ways in which scientific knowledge is applied in practice, and the effects of different applications on specific population groups. Consider for example the risk-assessment process by which 'safe levels' of exposure to chemicals and other pollutants are assessed. This area of work can be highly problematic, and incorporate a range of ideological and moral assumptions. As Field

(1998: 90) comments, 'The use of the apparently reasonable scientific concept of average risk, for example, means that data from the most sensitive individuals, such as children, will not be the basis for regulation, but rather data from the "statistically average" person'. Thus, science provides grounds upon which we may base judgements, but these grounds are not necessarily neutral in terms of social impact. The interplay between scientific finding and social objective is of vital importance.

Whilst one can be properly sceptical of 'science' – especially when allied to particular social interests (e.g. the corporation medical officer or toxicologist) – this does not mean dismissing science altogether. Rather, it means corroborating information from as many sources as possible, and making sure that the scientific method has been rigorously applied. The idea of peer-review was introduced precisely to 'keep things honest', which is also why many science journals today also require disclosures by reporting scientists regarding who funded their research and whether it can be considered independent of the funding bodies.

It is also useful to acknowledge here that for many green criminologists not only is conventional scientific expertise essential to understanding what is happening to the environment, but, in addition, there is recognition of 'expertise from below' – as in the case of farmers who 'know' their land, indigenous people who 'know' their country, and so on. The concept of 'indigenous ecological knowledge', for example, refers to the unique, traditional local knowledge existing within and developed around the specific conditions of women and men indigenous to a particular geographical area. Such IEK systems, including management of the natural environment, have been a matter of survival to the peoples who generated these systems. Simultaneous to this is the concept of 'indigenous technology', which is defined in terms of hardware (equipment, tools, instruments and energy sources) and software (a combination of knowledge, processes, skills and social organization) that focus attention on particular tasks (Robyn 2002). Fire-burning amongst indigenous Australians, for example, constituted an informed and conscious means to work in and with certain types of local environment (Langton 1998).

The use of science and technology as part of researching transnational environmental crimes and harms is crucial. This means that criminologists need to be aware of and work with a variety of sciences. By drawing upon multiple scientific studies and knowledge-production techniques, composite socio-ecological accounts of harm can be compiled. Environmental forensics provides a case in point.

> Environmental forensics as a subject is developing apace, with new legal instruments and regulations to spur on investigations. New tools are becoming available which are providing ever more sensitive methods to identify chemicals or changes in biological communities. Key to successful participation in expert witness cases involving the environment is good, scientifically defensible data from a wide range of approaches which all point to the same

outcome. These data may need to be presented to lay members of a jury or magistrates bench, so clear, concise figures are usually best. However, if you cannot defend it scientifically, it is of no benefit to anyone.

(Mudge 2008: 14)

Environmental forensic study is essentially about the nature of 'truth claims'.

In investigation of environmental harm, science is marshalled in order to substantiate or repudiate certain claims about the world. Fundamental to this process is the idea of 'proof'. The *burden of proof* is directed at the question of who has to make the case for safety (that is, the originator of the potential harm, or someone else, such as a Non-Government Organization). The *standard of proof* asks whether we are confident that the case for safety has been made adequately (that is, what level of confidence we have in the data available in regard to a particular phenomenon). Encapsulated within these phrases are a series of interlinked issues relating to definitions of seriousness, thresholds and knowledge certainty. In other words, there need to be criteria pertaining to degrees of sufficient evidence that, in turn, establish the point at which decisions can be made based upon the available evidence.

The fact that knowledge is frequently uncertain, however, can impede decision-making in various ways. Indeed, action or inaction on environmental threats has been legitimated one way or the other by claims of scientific uncertainty. The uncertainty has been due to both lack of data, and a more general problem of indeterminacy. For example, 'For pollution issues uncertainty may cause even greater problems: it may not be clear what the cause of a polluted ecosystem is, and, since those actors causing pollution will frequently not directly benefit from preventing it, they will resist action as long as the cause can be questioned' (DeSombre 2006: 5). Indeterminacy refers to processes and systems that cannot readily be captured by the methods of science as such, as with specific eco-systems that suddenly undergo qualitative change after a period of relative stability (e.g. algae blooms in river systems).

Environmental forensic science

'Forensic science' generally refers to specific areas of technical and vocational expertise. Training in chemistry, ballistics, fingerprint analysis, DNA testing, computer forensics, and so on can be highly specialized. So, too, crime scene investigation (including specific types of crime scene, such as arson and bush-fire arson cases) demands the development of particular skills, capacities and expertise. Dealing with the human element of crime that can draw upon the expertise of biology, bio-mechanics, psychology and social work, likewise is oriented toward hands-on or practical types of intervention.

Environmental forensic scientists use a range of instruments and tools to determine where, for instance, environmental pollution has occurred, how it has occurred and who is responsible.

In the handling of environmental claims, these forensic applications can be useful, especially in identifying the source of pollution; determining when the release of a pollutant into the environment occurred; segregating and identifying multiple contaminant plumes; allocating investigation and remedial costs; recovering remediation costs from responsible parties; defending third-party lawsuits of environmental trespass and defending toxic tort claims.

(Zechman 2002)

Techniques relevant to green criminology include DNA testing of fish, animals, timber and soils to track their illegal movement; chemical fingerprinting in relation to oil spills; toxicology and chemical analysis of contaminated landfill sites and factory outlets; satellite surveillance and remote sensing in connection with land clearance and deforestation; and site analysis and mapping in relation to air and water pollution. Diverse investigatory methods can be used to build a composite picture of specific types of environmental harm.

The use of forensic techniques in dealing with environmental crime is an expanding and ever more sophisticated area of work within environmental law-enforcement agencies and networks (including for example, Environmental Protection Agencies, Wildlife Protection and Natural Resource Management bodies, and the Interpol Environmental Crime groups). Typically, at an applied level, international environmental crime refers to such things as the trans-border movement and dumping of waste products, the illegal traffic in real or purported radioactive or nuclear substances, and the illegal traffic in species of wild flora and fauna. These concerns are reflected institutionally as well. For example, Interpol has three key working groups that are actively involved in investigatory and operational work in regard to environmental crime: *pollution*, *wildlife* and *illegal fishing*. The Pollution Crimes Working Group, for instance, is an active forum in which criminal investigators from around the globe meet to discuss issues such as determining the role of organized crime in environmental crime and identifying trends and patterns in trans-border shipments of hazardous waste.

The area of wildlife forensics deals with the application of scientific knowledge to a range of species protection, law-enforcement and wildlife verification challenges that face policy-makers, investigation and enforcement officers, and commercial stake-holders. These challenges include the illegal capture or killing of animals, birds, reptiles and plants in contravention of domestic or international law; the illegal harvesting of living resources from protected areas and the trade in those resources, a problem of particular relevance for fisheries and forestry sectors; and the illegal trade in raw and processed parts of protected animals, birds, reptiles and plants and in goods manufactured from such parts (see, for example, Alacs and Georges 2008; Cooper and Cooper 2012).

There are major and continuing challenges in undertaking environmental forensic investigations. Consider, for example, the complexities involved in environmental crime scene investigation. Issues here include first responder safety in regard to hazardous waste and pollutants, the scientific skills and knowledge of environmental crime scene investigators and forensic specialists, the availability of environmental forensic technologies to crime scene investigators, and emerging technologies that may assist with investigations (Ramer 2007).

Acknowledgement of the complexities of the issues is but a first step in recognizing the limitations of such work. For example, in one study it was found that investigation of environmental pollution situations in Brazil is a complex environmental contamination situation, but *few analytical resources* were available to accomplish the necessary comprehensive evaluation, and thus to provide material proof for the situation and to determine whether it was an environmental crime according to the law (Barbieri, Schwarzbold and Rodriguez 2007). The methods included:

- data from quarterly monitoring reports sent to authorities as part of the landfill operation permit requirements;
- monitoring lead and chromium exposure of nearby residents;
- testing of fish in nearby artificial pond;
- groundwater analysis;
- sediment analysis.

Putting the pieces together (of pollution, of perpetrators) is both the problem and the basis for achieving suitable outcomes. Moreover, there are always additional considerations to take into account in attempting to determine wrongdoing when it comes to specific types of environmental harm such as pollution. These include, for example, the issue of background values: 'Before jumping to conclusions related to contamination sources, we should always consider evaluating background values and remember that high contamination values are not necessarily associated with spilled product. Natural sources are less obvious and yet ubiquitous and sometimes significant' (Petrisor 2007: 198).

There is now a broad spectrum of activity associated with the doing of environmental forensic studies. In drawing upon multiple scientific studies and knowledge production techniques, composite socio-ecological accounts of harm can be compiled, although the questions 'compiled by whom, and for what purposes?' remain of major interest and contention. Recent technical developments in the area include the following.

DNA testing

Illegal fishing and illegal logging can be tracked through the employment of DNA testing at the point of origin and at the point of final sale. Work done on abalone DNA, for example, demonstrates that particular species within particular geographical locations can be identified as having specific (and thus unique) types of DNA (Roffey *et al.* 2004; see also Ogden 2008). The use of phylogenetic DNA profiling as a tool for the investigation of poaching also offers a potential deterrent in that regular testing allows for the linking of abalone species and/or subspecies to a particular country of origin. This increases the chances of detection and thus may have relevance to crime prevention as such. The use of DNA testing to track the illegal possession and theft of animals and plants can thus serve to deter would-be offenders, if applied consistently, proactively and across national boundaries.

Satellite surveillance

Illegal land clearance, including the cutting down of protected trees, can be monitored through satellite technology. Compliance with or transgression of land clearance restrictions, for example, can be subjected to satellite remote sensing in ways that are analogous to the use of closed-circuit television (CCTV) in monitoring public places in cities. Interestingly, the criminalization of land clearance, which primarily affects private landholders, was due in part to images of extensive rates of land clearance provided through satellite remote sensing studies. Use of such technologies also embeds certain notions of 'value' and particular relations between nature and humans, issues that warrant greater attention in any further development of this kind of technological application (Bartel 2005).

Automated video monitoring

New software and digital hardware technologies combined with utilization of Ethernet, the Internet Protocol, and wireless mesh-based networks provides the opportunity for monitoring activity in almost any location in the world from any other location in the world (Hayes, Porteous and Zhou 2008). Intelligent video monitoring embraces automation of much of the monitoring activity and the archival of only those incidents identified to be of interest – e.g. motion detection. Intelligent video analysis can facilitate the audits of large-scale, 24/7 monitoring operations, contributing to both deterrence and evidence-gathering in environmentally sensitive locations.

Contamination forensics

The contamination of land, water and air can be prevented by proactive testing of specific sites, movement routes and currents, by the establishment and collection of benchmark data, and by regular monitoring. To do this requires utilization of methods that might include chemical analysis, study of documentary records, use of aerial photographs, and application of trend techniques that track concentrations of chemical substances over space and/or time (Murphy and Morrison 2007; Brookspan, Gravel and Corley 2007). Bearing in mind that some contaminations, such as nuclear radiation, are not easily visible to human detection, both alternative methods of science and communal reflexivity over potential risks are needed (Macnaghten and Urry 1998).

A vast array of techniques and approaches to environmental forensics are now available (see United States Environmental Protection Agency 2001). For example, forensic sciences are now able to track the chemical signature of oil spills (Pasadakis *et al.* 2008) and to use sophisticated chemical and biological analyses to track such spills (as well as illegal disposal of waste) to their source (Mudge 2008). In addition, the forensic sciences are now actively turning their attention toward climate change, with a view to contributing to monitoring efforts and identifying emerging environmental issues (Petrisor and Westerfield 2008).

Exploration of the use of new technologies, such as 'data dots', allows for particular hazardous waste vehicles and materials to be identified and then re-identified at a later date. 'Data dots' are small markers that can be unobtrusively placed on hazardous materials and transportation vehicles and used to track where waste has been and where it has ended up. In a similar vein, electronic (rather than paper-based) tracking systems provide an immediate record of movement, storage and disposal.

Other methods of investigation include specific techniques such as identification of wildlife through footprints, scats (faeces), bones, fur, claws, blood; use of chemical analysis in relation to certain benchmark data and established allowable thresholds (which is used in relation to toxic outfalls, water and land sites); creation of topographic (elevation) maps and thematic maps (e.g. land-disposal activity, population distribution, vegetation communities, land use); monitoring of relevant internet sites for exposure of wrongdoing and illegal activity (e.g. Facebook, YouTube, MySpace, Twitter, activist sites); and surveillance of local markets through to eBay (e.g. sites and places where ivory, antlers, rare plants, etc. are bought and sold).

Environmental forensic studies

'Environmental forensic studies' refers to the study of forensics as a social phenomenon. Typically, the question here is less to do with 'how to' (e.g. laboratory science and crime-scene techniques), than with the overall implications of forensics for society as a whole. In this respect, the concern is to learn about how science and technology shape the work of the justice system (Fradella, Owen and Burke 2007). The main emphasis of forensic studies is on providing a generalist understanding of the field as a whole, including how developments across the field might feed into particular criminal justice processes (for example, in combating environmental crimes). The intent, as well, is to provide space for critical reflection on specific forensic practices (for example, the expanded use of DNA testing), and to inquire into the effectiveness or otherwise of forensics in relation to how the police, the courts and corrective services undertake their basic roles. A key element of this is how 'evidence' is socially constructed within legal and scientific discourses, and how different players within the criminal justice system conceptualize the nature of criminal investigation, criminal procedure, criminal evidence and courtroom practices.

An emergent strand of environmental forensic studies is attempting to broaden the type of work and impact of social science contributions to this field. Rather than viewing forensic studies solely through the lens of sociological examination of how harms are viewed and subjected to scientific scrutiny (i.e., critical analysis of forensic science), the intention is to illustrate potential application of social science methods *as part of* forensic examination (i.e., the incorporation of social science methods directly into the investigative process). At the heart of this is a combination of stake-holder analysis and examination of the social construction of knowledge. The concern is to undertake research that involves identification of stake-holders and specific stake-holder interests, scrutiny of the narratives around 'risk' and 'harm' from the different stake-holders, and the types of knowledge produced about environmental harm in specific circumstances.

Social science methodologies can be mobilized as part of investigations into environmental harm across several different topic areas. These include the nature of and contests over 'evidence' when it comes to forensic toxicological studies; the inadequacy of regulatory mechanisms in cases where 'denial' is driven by potential threats of liability (health department, municipal council, environmental protection agency, industry and specific companies); and the role of grassroots activists and experts in the context of the politicization of local environmental issues. The main concern of this kind of research is to provide insight into and analysis of stake-holder interests and to raise questions regarding the criteria used to assess the quality and robustness of evidence in relation to the specific problem at hand.

The point of this kind of research is to examine the ways in which 'evidence' surrounding environmental harm is gathered, presented and mobilized by diverse stake-holders. It thus shares similarities with work done on disputes that are characterized by multi-layered conflict about knowledge, rights and development, as evident for example in the multidimensional character of the aquaculture controversy in Canada (Young and Matthews 2010). Such research is about how different stake-holders construct evidence about harm, how meaning is mobilized by different groups, the process whereby different types of evidence are constructed, and how researchers might form definitive judgements about the alleged harm.

The innovative nature of this contribution by social science lies in the key proposition that, from an investigatory point of view, the quality of decision-making and of policy responses is radically enhanced by formation of *multidisciplinary taskforces*, rather than relying on sole expert opinion and decision-making by government fiat. Environmental issues may be socially constructed (see Hannigan 2006), but 'truth' is comprised of interlinked and multidimensional layers that, collectively, ought to determine whether or not precaution is taken, preventative measures enacted and compensation granted. In other words, there is a need to not only acknowledge and discuss social divisions in regard to 'evidence' of environmental harm, but to utilize such discursive frames as the basis for informed decisions about what to actually do about perceived or alleged environmental harms. The risks and harms in fact may well be real, and it is the role of social science to contribute to judgements as to how this might be determined in a practical, concrete manner and how best to respond in each case.

Stake-holders and stake-holder discourses

Ideally there should be wide scale community involvement in risk assessment processes and in after-the-fact diagnosis of alleged environmental harms. If evaluation of environmental harm is to be free from corrupted processes, then a wide range of stake-holder interests and views need to be incorporated into the investigation of alleged harms. From a positive affirming perspective, for example, research has demonstrated that participation is not only important from the point of view of the legitimacy of environmental decision-making, but that it also can enhance problem-solving (Steele 2001; Scott 2005a and b). If sustainability is the goal, if precaution requires thinking about multiple courses of action, and if community involvement is to be of benefit, then it is clear that citizens ought to be engaged as deliberators and contributors in their own right. As indicated in Box 13.1, there is ample scope for community involvement at all stages of environmental risk assessment.

Box 13.1 Community risk assessment in relation to chemical hazards

Issue identification: Here community involvement can provide information about the site, including weather patterns, local environmental information, health concerns and potential value conflicts. Community input can be sought on what risks deserve priority attention and what information may be available in the general community.

Hazard identification: Here the community may provide information about previous studies and/or data gaps, local perceptions of hazards and the applicability of assumptions to that particular community.

Dose-response relationships: Providing information about community attitudes towards the range and type of technical data and selected tests, as well as the assumptions made in the interpretation of the data.

Exposure assessment: Providing information about the community's attitude to biological monitoring and health monitoring; local knowledge of the range and nature of exposures, relevant exposure settings; the community's attitudes to sampling design and environmental monitoring and to the uncertainties and assumptions in the exposure assessment phase.

Risk characterization: Providing information on the community's concepts of risk and safety.

> *Evaluating actions taken*: Community involvement will affect how environmental monitoring may be undertaken to ensure that the best decisions are made.
> *Risk management*: Providing information of communities' concepts of acceptable risk and safety.
>
> Source: drawn from National Toxics Network Inc. n.d. (accessed July 2005)

Table 13.1 Discourses and the languaging of environmental issues

---

Legal discourses
- how the law defines the issues (e.g. crime, liability, responsibility, culpability);
- different pieces of legislation covering different aspects of the environment (e.g. health, environment, water, occupational health and safety).

Policing and regulatory discourses
- including Environmental Protection Agencies (e.g. proof of wrongdoing);
- assigning institutional responsibility for doing something;
- Non-Government Organizations, watchdogs and advocates.

Scientific discourses
- including competing expertise (e.g. toxicology versus medical practitioners);
- in-house science and independent scientific review;
- industry experts and scientists.

Community/lay discourses
- competing claims regarding the 'best interests of the community';
- including local 'experts' (e.g. general practitioners, local residents, indigenous people);
- social network sites and communication (e.g. Facebook, Twitter, YouTube).

Tradition-based discourses
- indigenous understandings of nature and social life;
- traditional ways of doing things and seeing things based upon longer-term settlement history;
- inter-generational acceptance of the way things are and ought to be.

Occupation discourses
- related to specific types of activities (e.g. farmers, fishers, loggers, oyster farmers);
- activities related to traditional and indigenous living and subsistence practices.

Litigation discourses
- claims over damages from environmental victims (e.g. repairing the harm);
- claims over damages to reputation and production by industry (e.g. strategic lawsuits against public participation).

Media discourses
- investigative journalism;
- current-affairs shows and sensationalist accounts;
- internet sites, including blogs;
- live chat-rooms associated with documentaries (e.g. *Sixty Minutes* in Australia and USA).

(Continued)

Table 13.1 Discourses and the languaging of environmental issues *(Continued)*

Victim discourses
- narratives of the victimized (men, women and children);
- narratives of indirect victims (families, friends, overseas relatives);
- human accounts on behalf of affected non-humans such as animals.

Rescuer discourses
- narratives of rescuers (police, fire-fighters, emergency services);
- international NGOs (Médicins sans Frontières, Amnesty International).

Corporate discourses
- annual reports and sustainability reports on websites;
- environmental and civic awards;
- media statements.

International agency discourses
- health and wellbeing (e.g. World Health Organization);
- economic issues and international development (e.g. International Monetary Fund, World Bank);
- regulation, security and human rights (e.g. United Nations).

Activist discourses
- environmental NGOs (e.g. Animal Liberation, Earth First!, Greenpeace, Sea Shepherd);
- progressive radical movements (e.g. socialist, ecological, feminist);
- reactionary social movements (e.g. religious fundamentalist, neo-Nazi).

Source: drawing from and adding to White and Heckenberg 2011: 96

However, when environmental harm is contested – conceptually and evidentially – and there are major specific social interests at play (governments, companies, workers, consumers, environmentalists, residents), then those with the power to do so tend to shape public debate in ways that diminish participation and deliberation. It then becomes important to identify how different groups use different language and concepts to express their views and interests.

Knowledge is always tied to someone and somewhere, and it reflects particular interests and relations of power. Accordingly, one task for green criminology is to identify the diverse and multiple discourses that collectively describe the world around us, in the context of particular environmental issues. These competing discourses are many and varied. Table 13.1 provides an outline of different types of discourse that we consider are useful to study in greater depth.

The issues associated with analysing the discourses and interests that underpin who is saying what (in this case about environmental harms and crimes) are especially pertinent to working with vulnerable population groups or groups outside the centres of world power. For instance, layperson, practitioner and indigenous knowledge is frequently subject to undue dismissal and even ridicule. Yet from the point of view of measurement, scientific and other sorts of knowledge are crucial to determining different kinds of environmental harm. The incorporation of diversity of values and of different kinds of expertise into public dialogue is part and parcel of the democratization of environmental issues.

The politics of knowing and knowledge

At the heart of investigations of environmental crime is the question of whose knowledge of 'wrong' is right? In other words, whose voices are going to be heard, and to what kinds of evidence do we lend credibility? In responding to environmental harm and victimization there are inevitably a range of vested interests and 'discourses' that contribute to the shaping of perceptions and issues (see Hannigan 2006). This implies differences in perspective and a certain contentiousness of knowledge about the nature of the harm or crime.

Assessment of victimization usually involves responding to a series of interrelated questions (see Heckenberg and White 2013):

- How are 'harm' and 'risk' defined, and by whom?
- How do we distinguish 'risk' (potential outcome) from 'harm' (actual outcome)?
- At what point does 'risk' or 'harm' actually occur?
- At what point does 'risk' or 'harm' occur to an extent warranting action or intervention?
- What is the origin and fate of the harm?
- What are the histories of 'risk' or 'harm'?
- Why and how did the harm occur?
- Who are the perpetrators and why and how did they do it?
- Is responsibility for responding in the hands of those harming, or of those being harmed?
- Who has responsibility for proof?
- What is acceptable as evidence?
- What were the triggers for the harm?
- What were the immediate signs of 'danger' or 'harm'?
- What strategies were invoked to diminish or mitigate the harm?
- How do we stop the harm from occurring again?

Answers to these questions frequently vary depending upon stake-holder perspective. Consider, for example, the variety of players who might be associated with disputes over toxic landfill or stockpiled mining tailings in a residential community adjacent to a mining operation. Because victimization is a contestable social process that involves a wide range of individuals, it is important to identify stake-holders and their specific interests (e.g. workers and jobs; residents and amenity). It is useful to explore the diverse and often conflicting discourses around 'risk' and 'harm' by different stake-holders (e.g. medical practitioners' consciousness of risk in relation to the health department; loss of livelihood in the case of farmers; limited perception that there is a problem from local miners).

Moreover, the marshalling of particular types of evidence is typically driven by very specific criteria requirements (and forms of evidence) dictated by institutions and groups. Who says what and why is linked to specific social purposes and interests, and particular discursive domains. The language of crime and victimization is reflective of how an environmental problem (in this case toxic landfill) is socially constructed depending upon how it is being considered and by whom, and who is potentially affected and how.

For example, recent work undertaken by the authors has been able to distinguish three sources of error and/or limited knowledge that impinge upon the assessment of alleged toxicity in relation to various sites within Tasmania, as shown in Table 13.2. These are the problems associated with *partial* knowledge (i.e., knowledge that is incomplete, since it is limited to only one kind of domain expertise, such as soil testing); *skewed* knowledge (i.e., knowledge that is in some way biased, even if accurate within its own terms of reference, such as reliance upon patient records from one medical practice); and *distorted* knowledge (i.e., knowledge that is more akin to propaganda, being ideologically based, as in *ad hominem* attacks against specific protagonists). Each sort of knowledge presents problems in regard to the accumulation of necessary and sufficient knowledge to assess the relevant contamination issues. However, they also suggest relatively straightforward solutions, revolving around, for example, the combining of different knowledge sources, deployment of diverse forms of sampling, and emphasizing substantive empirical evidence over ideological statement.

In terms of potential sources of knowledge, it may well be that it is local residents, local workers and laypeople generally who are more conscious of environmental risk than the scientist or the politician. Some indication of this is provided in a study of interaction between scientists and English sheep farmers in the wake of the 1986 Chernobyl nuclear accident in Ukraine (Wynne 1996). The study highlighted the accurate, detailed and contextual knowledge of the local farmers, even though the scientists considered this layperson knowledge to be lacking in precision. Those who are closer to the 'coal face' and who have lived and worked in the same area for years, are frequently those who notice the small changes that are the harbingers of things to come.

Consciousness of risk is also influenced by the visibility of the potential harm. For example, Beck (1992) observes that many risks in contemporary society are largely invisible to human senses. Radioactivity, for example, cannot be smelt, seen, touched or tasted. Often we do not really know what is in our drinking water. Nevertheless, over time many people have come to appreciate the risks associated with radioactivity, and indeed nuclear energy generally, as well as to be suspicious about everyday consumables such as water (hence, the huge and growing market in bottled water). This reflexivity about risk has been made possible by mediated sources of knowledge, whereby people draw upon multiple sources in order to assess potential threats (e.g. TV programmes, government statements, campaigns by environmental groups). They also draw upon their own experiences, as indicated above (see also Macnaghten and Urry 1998). There are more ways in which to 'know' than simply through the direct senses per se. Exposure to risk scenarios is an integral part of raising consciousness about risk. In recent years this has occurred in ways that have seen the globalization of risk

Table 13.2 Challenges to necessary and sufficient knowledge in assessing toxic towns

Partial knowledge

Description:	• knowledge that is limited to particular domains of expertise • associated with specific kinds of testing and evidence collection • examples include water testing, soil testing, analysis of medical records
Problem:	• reliance upon only one kind of domain knowledge provides only a partial picture of the whole situation • issue is one of incomplete knowledge
Solution:	• combine different knowledge sources into an integrated or composite picture of the whole

Skewed knowledge

Description:	• knowledge that is in some way biased, although nonetheless accurate within its own terms of reference • associated with method of data collection, including sampling techniques • examples include water testing at optimum non-toxic outflow times or reliance upon particular medical practice patient records that may involve an element of self-selection (i.e., similar clientele attend the same clinic)
Problem:	• skewed results due to sampling techniques that involve narrow temporal, spatial and client bases • issue is not one of reliability or accuracy as such, but the bias in data collection method leads to inadequate general findings and/or misinterpretation of the actual overall situation
Solution:	• utilize a sophisticated array of methods and techniques, particularly in regards to sampling procedures, in order to render a more balanced (and thereby realistic) picture of the whole

Distorted knowledge

Description:	• knowledge that is more akin to propaganda than evidence as such • associated with specific ideological and political interests that shape public claims • examples include use of ad hominem attacks on experts or activists (i.e., for who they are and the impact of what they are saying) on the basis of perceived threat to sectoral interests (e.g. business trade, community reputation, state liability)
Problem:	• displaces attention away from discussion of the nature and veracity of the objective evidence available • issue is one of ideological interests prevailing over scientific and other forms of valid evidence (e.g. such as 'elder knowledge' of what has been, and what is now)
Solution:	• expose and separate ideological statements from statements of fact (i.e., those premised upon substantive empirical evidence)

(Macnaghten and Urry 1998) through the actions of environmental activists in many different cities and countries around the world.

Interestingly, the Tasmanian toxic towns project also revealed the importance of one other source of knowledge, information and data that we ignore at our peril. This is *elder knowlege*. There is much to learn from older members of our community when it comes to environmental landscapes of the past and the beliefs, values and environmental histories and practices of former generations. An example of 'elder knowledge' is provided by David Suzuki (2010: 61), who recounts the following anecdote:

> A documentary on fishing, *Empty Oceans, Empty Nets*, shown on PBS in 2002, featured an interview with a young skipper on a swordfish boat from Boston who stated that there are still plenty of swordfish. Based in Boston, she travels to Newfoundland, where she reported hearing that a 200-pound swordfish had been caught. 'There are still big ones', she said. The film then cut to an interview with a grizzled fisherman who must have been in his eighties. He recounted that he used to fish just 5 or 6 miles out of Boston and would throw back anything under 200 pounds! Two fishers with radically different baselines. To the young skipper, a trip all the way to Newfoundland was standard procedure, while a 200-pounder was a big fish. (In fact, the average size of swordfish before 1963 was 266 pounds; it had fallen to 133 pounds in 1973, and to 90 pounds in 1996).

In one of the Tasmanian case studies, elder knowledge related to a former waste tip that had been converted into a sports and recreation ground. At the age of 73 a local resident, Poppy Lopatniuk, took up the reins of the struggle about the actual harms (deaths and illnesses) linked to streets close to the former tip site. From her time spent living in the area, she knew that something was wrong. Her story is described in Box 13.2.

Box 13.2 Elder knowledge about toxic legacy in Tasmania

Chemicals and toxic materials of various kinds had been systematically dumped into the old Howrah tip. Today, this would be considered a criminal 'hot spot', a place where illegal activity is regularly carried out. Persistent and serious illegalities that knowingly cause harm are meant to be criminalized. Not so in the mid-1960s to mid-1970s. The dumping of contaminates was par for the course, and little was done about it at the time.

Poppy Lopatniuk began to agitate around these issues when she noticed people in her street, and her household, were falling ill at seemingly disproportionate rates, and from unusual illnesses. Poppy made a link between the old rubbish tip and the health of local residents. Who got ill was generally restricted to several streets abutting the rubbish dump. People were sick because they were affected by what had gone into the tip. Or so Poppy thought.

> However, those in power felt that the 'evidence' did not support Poppy's claims and concerns. In a series of developments over a period of several years:
>
> - The Cancer Register was used by the Health Department to dismiss the problem (there is not an unusual pattern of cancer types and rates over the locality as a whole) *rather than* to suggest the need for more precise analysis of the clustering of local cancers and other ills (Poppy found in excess of 40 cancer diagnoses mostly in the two small streets on either side of the landfill area).
> - The URS (a Victoria consultancy firm) investigation of the recreational grounds was used to dismiss the problem as ongoing (the bores were dug in places in the park least likely to find contamination) *rather than* to locate the flow of toxicity over time and the actual movement and locations of contaminants (Poppy argued for testing of actual tip sites and the lower grounds where the leachate would have drained).
>
> In other words, official examination of the issues was oriented toward general conclusions that legitimized inertia on the issues. Accordingly, these interventions failed to address the specific nature of the problem (its precise geographical manifestation, and the transference of contamination over time and space). No action was the action plan.
>
> But elder knowledge cannot be dismissed or discounted quite so easily.
>
> Poppy 'knew' that something was wrong. This was embedded in her actual life experiences, her relationships with real live, flesh-and-blood family members and neighbours, and her time spent living in the area. Indeed, the test of time has demonstrated that people have died, that people have been ill, that something was indeed wrong about this idyllic place that everyone simply wanted to call home.
>
> In 2012 Poppy published her story in a book titled *Tomorrow's Children*. She was 85 at the time.
>
> The key message of Poppy's book is that we ignore our elders and elder knowledge at our collective peril. The lack of transparency, the ambiguities of knowledge, the failures to act, the efforts to cut costs and avoid liability – all of these point to one inescapable conclusion: what is dumped where and how, are vital questions that ought to be of interest to all people regardless of where they live. The issues – and the toxic and health legacies – are not going to go away.

Analysis of the politics of knowledge reveals the importance of casting the net wide when it comes to defining issues and determining the nature of harms. Key questions in relation to these discourses have included whose voices are heard, how and when the voices are heard, and the gender (class, race, etc.) bias in those voices.

Evidence and investigation

The study of stake-holder discourses has direct investigatory implications. For instance, the nature of participation and engagement is relevant in respect to several different considerations:

- *intervention strategy* (e.g. task force approach versus specific experts);
- *methodologies* (e.g. multiple forensic methods and testing regimes, such as testing of soils, site histories, testing of local residents, flora and fauna analysis);
- *context bias* (e.g. objective or subjective approaches, depending upon whether we need to know local context, or whether the science demands that we do not know local disputes or context);
- *determining expertise* (e.g. questioning the credentials of the expert; questioning the findings of the expert);
- *retrospective research* (e.g. social forensics as investigative tool, for things such as hazardous waste disposal); and
- *prospective research* (e.g. social impact assessment concerned with risk and precautionary principle, in regard to things such as proposed radioactive waste storage).

Environmental forensic studies is interested in who is saying what and why, as well as who the audience is and why. Fundamentally, however, the focus of research is on the ways in which debate occurs over what constitutes evidence. With respect to this, analysis of stake-holder discourses can provide interesting insights into the social construction of 'evidence' according to specific understandings and the meanings given to particular ways of knowing. Indeed, this approach to environmental forensic studies has had an intrinsic interest in unpacking the evidence assessment process.

Specifically, matters of evidence can be considered from the point of view of definitions (e.g. how is 'risk' or 'harm' defined?), thresholds (e.g. at what point does 'risk' or 'harm' occur to an extent warranting action or intervention?), burden of proof (e.g. who has the responsibility for proof?) and nature of the evidence (e.g. what is acceptable as evidence?).

Future work associated with this kind of environmental forensic study involves examination of factors that affect investigation generally, and the gathering of information, intelligence and evidence. Among others, issues of concern include critical analysis relating to:

Resources

- number of agents available, from particular government and non-government agencies (e.g. staffing);
- expertise of those carrying out the investigation (e.g. training, credentials);

- ability and capacity to use multi-methods (e.g. resources, funding and expertise);
- leadership and accountability structures (e.g. management).

Potential limitations of investigation

- testing of local areas (e.g. epidemiological testing when those who are ill or die are no longer part of the tested community; geographical concentration of illness);
- testing of human subjects (e.g. age-related differences in susceptibility);
- testing for environmental harm (e.g. tipping points; accumulation of harm over time, such as dioxins in fish).

Complicating factors

- multiparty sites, sites with previous uses and users to current parties, and sites in which wastes are commingled over a period of time (e.g. assigning liability);
- threat of lawsuit by powerful protagonists (e.g. companies suing researchers who conclude with negative findings);
- politicization of issues (e.g. politicians, local residents, media).

Values and valuations

- need to be able to provide a dollar value of costs of commission/omission (with possible regulation through fines) (i.e., costs of crime);
- cost-benefit analysis of investigation and intervention in relation to compliance costs (that require agency resources, formation of expertise, and monitoring work) and environmental benefits (e.g. what is protected and preserved) (i.e., costs of crime control);
- issue of how to put a value on specific species, environments and human-related outcomes (e.g. value of destruction of fish hatchery).

Evidence-gathering and analysis also has other technical sides as well, and these, too, need to be considered. For example, Mandiberg (2009: 1185–6) describes the difference between technology-based limits, and quality-based limits in the context of pollution regulation and notions of environmental harm.

- *Technology-based limits* focus on pollution emerging from a particular source. They require a source to adopt the best mechanisms practically available to reduce or eliminate the pollution. ... These limits do not, however, reflect an assessment of how the pollutants in question affect a particular water body or air quality control region.

- *Quality-based limits*, on the other hand, are more stringent and do focus on the health of the water body or air quality control region in question. In setting these limits, the agency begins with quality goals and works backwards to impose limits on all sources contributing pollution to that water body or air quality control region.

Each approach implies a different starting point for analysis, and each has different implications for any conclusions that are made in relation to the extent and nature of harm. While there is benefit to be gained in drawing upon each approach, the nature and extent of environmental harm nonetheless requires a contextual interpretation based upon specific trends and incidents: 'For example, a discharge that is slightly over a water-quality-based limit might not actually harm the health of the water body, depending upon discharges from other point sources. On the other hand, a discharge that is significantly over a technology-based limit might cause substantial environmental harm' (Mandiberg 2009: 1186). Hence, the importance of 'thresholds' in relation to the level of environmental harm deemed acceptable or allowable.

Conclusion

This chapter has demonstrated how both natural science and social science methodologies can be mobilized as part of the applied study of environmental harm. Toward this end, the substantive contribution of environmental forensic studies is to identify knowledge that is partial, skewed and distorted, with a view to assembling the most robust evidence possible in assessing environmental harms. This implies several things on the part of the researcher. Firstly, an acceptance that some knowledge is more reliable and valid than other kinds (the question of 'truth'); and secondly, that the contest over knowledge is not socially neutral (but a question of vested 'interests').

As the history of the environmental justice movement shows (see for example, Pellow 2007; Bullard 2005a), research into environmental harm is inevitably political and contentious, bringing into play powerful actors and major industries. For the researcher this demands not only integrity of method, but integrity of purpose. Criminological investigation into environmental harms inevitably means locating oneself within wider struggles for social and environmental justice. The complexity of the problem – environmental harm – demands responses that are multi-pronged but are simultaneously prioritized and get to the core of the matter. That is, research and investigation of environmental harm is performed for a purpose – namely, to help address issues of pressing concern that are destroying environments, non-human species and human lives in the here and now. In the face of this, the process of research is ongoing. So, too, intervention, even based upon uncertain knowledge, must likewise proceed apace.

Discussion topics

- What is the difference between forensic science and forensic studies?
- Information, intelligence and evidence mean different things, yet all are related to each other. Discuss.
- Different stake-holders may hold different views regarding what is harmful or not. Discuss with reference to a local environmental issue.
- Why are multi-disciplinary taskforces preferred when it comes to investigation of contaminated communities and toxic towns?
- What is 'elder knowledge' and why is it important?

Further reading

Barbieri, C., Schwarzbold, A., and Rodriguez, M. (2007). 'Environmental Crime Investigation in Arroio do Meio, Rio Grande do Sul, Brazil: Tannery and shoe factory waste landfill case study', *Environmental Forensics*, 8: 361–9.

Burns, R., Lynch, M., and Stretesky, P. (2008). *Environmental Law, Crime, and Justice*. New York: LFB Scholarly Publishing.

Cooper, J.E., and Cooper, M.E. (2012). *Wildlife Forensic Investigation: Principles and practice*. Boca Raton, FL: CRC Press.

Mandiberg, S. (2009). 'Locating the Environmental Harm in Environmental Crimes', *Utah Law Review*, 4: 1177–222.

Murphy, B., and Morrison, R. (eds) (2007). *Introduction to Environmental Forensics*. Amsterdam: Elsevier.

Chapter 14

Environmental courts

Introduction

This chapter will discuss the following topics:

- environmental crime and justice;
- the value of environmental harm;
- specialist environmental courts; and
- problem-solving methods.

Environmental crime involves transgressions against humans, specific environments and animals. Not all environmental harm is seen to be criminal, however. Moreover, even when harm has been criminalized, sanctions and remedies have tended to be inadequate and insufficient. How justice is played out in practice is vital to the morale and effectiveness of environmental law enforcers. Lots of hard police work goes into gathering evidence and building cases against polluters, illegal fishers, transporters of toxic waste, and so on. New technologies and new collaborations with non-police agencies may be required, as well as extensive police resources, time and energy (see Chapters 12 and 13).

However, what happens when cases get to court? Here the immediate concerns are which courts the cases are heard in (e.g. magistrates' or a superior court), what kind of court (e.g. generalist or specialist), what types of penalties are assigned to offenders (e.g. fines or action orders), and what remedies are invoked for the harm caused (e.g. remediation). An important question is whether environmental harm or crime is 'valued' sufficiently by the law, a critical factor in garnering the resources needed to fight it. Central to this process are the decisions made in and by the court. Typically, until recently, the usual pattern of judicial decision-making was marked by the following features:

- environmental crime is not viewed as a 'real' crime;
- devolving environmental crimes to lower courts;
- poor judicial knowledge about environmental crimes;

- few case precedents, due to low prosecution rates;
- placing a low 'value' on environmental crimes and harms;
- few well-trained people on the ground.

This chapter addresses issues such as what kind of court is best suited to dealing with environmental crime, and which approaches to justice are most appropriate to this project. As the central fulcrum upon which 'justice' hinges, the nature and dynamics of the court have a major bearing on what occurs prior to a case and what happens after a case has been officially processed.

Environmental crime and justice

In the legal framing of environmental crime, the nature of the harm is generally expressed in the following kinds of terms:

> An unauthorized act or omission that violates the law and is therefore subject to criminal prosecution and criminal sanctions. This offence harms or endangers people's physical safety or health as well as the environment itself. It serves the interests of either organizations – typically corporations – or individuals.
>
> (Situ and Emmons 2000: 3)

Such crime violates existing environmental laws, and the victims can include people and the environment. It has also been pointed out that, although corporations are the chief environmental offenders, other organizations (e.g. criminal combines or government agencies) as well as individuals also commit environmental crimes (Situ and Emmons 2000).

Different countries have different laws and frequently quite different approaches to dealing with environmental crime. It is important, therefore, that study be able to drill down to national and sub-national legislative and juridical particulars. Case law and legislation, as well as institutions and institutional processes, will vary depending upon whether one is talking about the United States, Canada, individual member states of the European Union, Russia, India, Argentina, Ecuador, Angola or China (see for example, Boyd 2003; Burns and Lynch 2004). Detailed exploration of one jurisdiction can provide useful concepts and benchmarks by which to compare environmental laws cross-nationally. Nonetheless, there are concerns and issues that overlap jurisdictional differences and these are worth noting in socio-legal analysis

In many jurisdictions, for example, the primary regulatory authority for the control of environmental crime is the Environmental Protection Authority (or equivalent: for example, the Environment Agency in the United Kingdom). Such agencies may operate at federal or state/provincial levels, and their mandate generally includes such things as:

- regulating environmental crime through administration of environmental protection legislation;
- educating the community about environmental issues;
- monitoring and researching environmental quality;
- reporting on the state of the environment to state/provincial or national legislature and other relevant bodies.

Implementing this mandate includes protecting and conserving the natural environment, promoting the sustainable use of natural capital, ensuring a clean environment and reducing risks to human health.

Environmental Protection Agencies are typically in the business of 'compliance' where this refers to the state of conformity with the law (see Chapter 11). Agencies usually secure compliance through two types of activity:

Promotion

- communication (e.g. environmental registry);
- publication of information (e.g. technical information);
- consultation with parties affected by the Act (e.g. industry groups);
- creation of environmental codes of practice and guidelines (e.g. stewardship programmes);
- promotion of environmental audits.

Enforcement

- inspection to verify compliance;
- investigation of violations;
- measures to compel compliance without resorting to formal court action, such as directions by authorized enforcement officers, warnings, ticketing and environment protection compliance orders by enforcement officers;
- measures to compel compliance through court action, such as injunctions, prosecution, court orders upon conviction and civil suit for recovery of costs.

The regulatory apparatus of the state thus relies upon remedies such as administrative measures, civil proceedings and criminal prosecution (usually in this order) as the means to foster and enforce conformity with existing environmental laws.

From the point of view of environmental courts, the 'big stick' of prosecution generally refers to sentencing regimes that include custodial sanctions and fines, and, as discussed below, a wide range of alternative sentencing options. What gets into court are those environmental harms that have already been established to be serious enough to warrant court action, rather than administrative penalties (such as an on-the-spot fine) and low-level regulatory intervention (such as a warning delivered by a park ranger).

The overall aim of criminal law is to prevent certain kinds of behaviour regarded as harmful or potentially harmful. But the purposes of criminal law vary, and involve a constant weighing up of moral wrongness, individual autonomy and community welfare (Findlay, Odgers and Yeo 1994). What falls within the ambit of criminal law (and what does not) is the outcome of a social process that is ongoing and inherently political, since it embodies basic principles and visions of the kind of society people prefer to live in.

A primary task of criminal law is to stipulate the degree of seriousness of criminal conduct. This involves assessing such factors as the physical impact of the conduct on the victim, psychological trauma, the monetary value of property crimes, and so forth. Yet in the case of environmental crime, concern has long been expressed that such crimes are not taken seriously by the courts. This is manifest in the kinds of sanctions generally and usually meted out for environmental crimes.

The value of environmental harm

Is environmental harm or crime 'valued' sufficiently by the law? The short answer is, probably not. In part this is due to the fact that penalty regimes themselves generally reflect prevailing attitudes and perceptions within the criminal justice system regarding the nature of the harm, and the particular courts that deal with environmental crime reflect these prevailing attitudes and perceptions.

There is also the problem that environmental crime itself frequently embodies a certain ambiguity (see Chapter 1). As discussed previously, it is not only located in frameworks of risk (e.g. precautionary principle) or evaluated in terms of actual harms (e.g. polluter pays), but is also judged in the context of cost-benefit analysis (e.g. license to trade or to pollute or to kill or capture). Translated into a court setting this has important ramifications.

> Criminal law is normally reserved for the punishment of socially unacceptable behaviour. Harm to the environment is, in many situations, considered to be acceptable (for example, in certain circumstances we are prepared to allow such pollution under license or authorization) because it is an inherent consequence of many industrial activities which provide significant benefits. This is the rationale for having a system of regulation which defines the framework for determining whether such benefits outweigh the harm caused. The criminal law is not suited to such a balancing process, and thus is mainly used to address clearly unacceptable behaviour or to reinforce the regulatory system.
> (Bell and McGillivray 2008: 281)

Philosophically, therefore, some types of harms are seen as less damaging than others, and thus to warrant different treatment from those perceived to be more serious. The notion of trade-off implicit within a cost-benefit approach immediately undermines the potential seriousness of the harm in question.

We can also relate this to the fact that more often than not Environmental Protection Agencies are mainly and primarily concerned with compliance activities – that is, how individuals, firms and corporations comply with the terms of their licences (see Chapter 11). This reinforces the general idea that environmental crimes are essentially less serious than others. It also ties into the notion that environmental protection is less about crimes against the environment and more about balancing economic and environmental interests.

In the light of these observations it should not be surprising to find that most offences involving the environment are prosecuted in lower courts (or dealt with by civil and administrative penalties), and most penalties are on the lower rather than higher end of the scale. This applies to how courts approach animal cruelty as well as to environmental offences relating to pollution and land clearance (Markham 2009).

Similar trends are apparent across diverse jurisdictions. For example, over 90 per cent of all environmental crimes in the United Kingdom are dealt with in the magistrates' courts, where the most common sanction is fines, and these are low-level (see Bell and McGillivray 2008). A comparison of European states in regard to environmental prosecution and sentencing found that the fine is the criminal penalty most commonly used in legal practice, and that the amounts imposed are apparently relatively low on average (Faure and Heine 2000). In the United States, there is the anomaly that at the same time that appellate courts have interpreted environmental guidelines so as to provide for increasingly severe sentences, the district courts have actually been imposing increasingly lenient sentences. Prison time is the exception not the norm. Moreover, it seems that low-culpability defendants may receive harsher sanctions than high-culpability defendants, given how appellate courts have ignored culpability considerations when interpreting ambiguous provisions under environmental sentencing law guidelines (O'Hear 2004).

On the other hand, even where there are severe penalties available, they may not be applied by the judiciary, especially if they are not familiar with environmental crime and its consequences (Hayman and Brack 2002; see also O'Hear 2004). The experience in the United Kingdom has been that the trivialization of environmental offences in the courtroom serves to impede enforcement as a whole, and to diminish the threats posed by prosecution (de Prez 2000a; see also de Prez 2000b). Specifically, the level of sentences given in courts, principally magistrates' courts, for environmental crimes has been seen to be too low for them to be effective either as punishment or deterrent.

The application of environmental sanctions can also be analysed sociologically. Here the concern is less with available legal remedies than how such remedies are applied, depending upon the perpetrators or victims involved. For example, research undertaken in the United States has shown that the penalties relating to hazardous waste sites in areas with large white populations are higher than those with minority or indigenous populations. Furthermore, there is less environmental enforcement of facilities in communities with higher minority and low-income populations (Pinderhughes 1996; Lynch, Stretesky and Burns 2004; Konisky 2009). Criminal justice needs to be applied equitably and fairly if social justice is to be the outcome.

Without assigning a value to environmental harm, courts are hamstrung in dealing adequately with perpetrators of the harm. Until recently, this deficiency has been more than evident in the light sentences handed down for environmental crime generally (White 2011a). There is a need for both quantitative measures (e.g. monetary values) and qualitative recognition (the intrinsic 'worth' of something in its own right).

Achieving consistency in sentencing for environmental offences has been a special concern of the Chief Judge of the Land and Environment Court of New South Wales. The Honourable Justice Brian Preston has been at the forefront of work to establish an environmental crime sentencing database in New South Wales (Preston and Donnelly 2008a and b). This database provides detailed sentencing information including judgements, recent law, publications, conferences, notes on evidence, and so on. The statistical analysis is comprised of sentencing statistics for environmental offences dealt with by the Land and Environment Court. It includes data on offences, penalty types, characteristics that relate to the objective seriousness or gravity of the offence, and subjective characteristics that relate to the particular offender. Such a tool should have a major impact on judicial practice. It will help shape the way judges and magistrates sentence environmental offenders insofar as it provides a public account of sentencing practices, as these are practically linked to the principles and purposes of sentencing, and it provides a useful indicator of the penalties that generally obtain in specific circumstances. In essence, the database provides a platform for judicial decision-making that treats environmental harm seriously and with suitable sanctions.

As an example, in April 2013 Judge Preston handed down a decision in the New South Wales Land and Environment Court regarding a rich wine-growing region in Australia threatened by the expansion of a transnational mining corporation. He was dubbed in the media as the judge who chose 'grapes over coal', and it remains to be seen how the mining giant Rio Tinto will ultimately respond to the decision. In the meantime the company is pulling out the time-worn threats of economic blackmail (e.g. 1,300 jobs at risk) and the flow-on effects to other industries; the company warned the decision would seriously impact the region's economy. The expansion of Rio Tinto's existing coal mine was successfully opposed by a local community group, in the neighbouring town of Bulga, a significant wine-growing region of Australia in an area known as the Hunter Valley (Hernandez 2013).

Specialist environmental courts

Environmental crime has typically been assigned low value by magistrates and judges, as reflected objectively in sentencing outcomes (i.e., sentencing patterns over time in relation to various environmental offences). These kinds of issues are being addressed in various ways, most of which involve, in one form or another, specialist knowledge or the establishment of specialist courts.

The notion of 'special expertise' in dealing with environmental harms and crimes does not refer solely to the establishment of specific and separate environmental courts as such. Such developments are not always needed or desirable, particularly in jurisdictions which have experienced the recent consolidation of a wide range of criminal matters (including environmental) into generalist courts (as opposed to the development of crime-specific and client-specific specialist tribunals, courts and agencies). What *is* vital, however, is the development and growth of specific expertise in environmental matters, incorporating elements pertaining to valuation of the harm, degrees of seriousness, extent and nature of victimization, and remedies suited to the nature of the crime and its perpetrator(s). Analysis of instances where such expertise has been institutionalized within criminal justice – as in the case of specialist environmental courts – nonetheless can provide insight into the types of expertise and dynamic understandings now being required in this area of law (see for example, Westerhuis 2013; Walters and Westerhuis 2013).

Interpol, for example, provides information to support the work of prosecutors of environmental crimes, while in England a substantial toolkit has been prepared to guide magistrates in assessing the seriousness of environmental offences, determining sentencing criteria for environmental offences and working through specific types of cases (Interpol Pollution Crime Working Group 2007; Magistrates' Association UK 2009). The work of ecological economics is also essential in this regard. This kind of analysis provides multiple criteria by which to evaluate the value of natural resources, wilderness, animals, fish and other species (see Orr 1991; Richardson and Loomis 2009). In the context of courts, both economic and non-market valuation is a vital part of deliberation over the nature of harm and potential damage claims against perpetrators (Duffield 1997).

From a legal perspective, the value of environmental harm is linked to the seriousness of environmental offences. Box 14.1 outlines key criteria suggested by magistrates in England and Wales for assessing the seriousness of environmental offences.

Box 14.1 Criteria to determine seriousness of environmental offences

Immediate and direct impact of the environmental crime

- environmental impact (e.g. dead fish from polluted water);
- social impact (e.g. air pollution and health problems);
- economic impact (e.g. crops damaged by pollution).

Wider effects in environmental, social and economic terms

- global, transboundary (e.g. pesticides into watercourses);
- diffuse impact (e.g. water pollution in rivers, the sea and on beaches);
- cumulative effects (e.g. multiple sources of pollution);
- long-term effects (e.g. health impact from radiation).

Human fatality, serious injury or ill health

- human fatality;
- serious injury (e.g. loss of limb or loss of sight);
- ill health (e.g. persistent respiratory problems).

Health of flora and fauna

- animal health (e.g. endangered species killed or poisoned);
- flora health (e.g. air pollution affecting crops and plants).

State of mind of the defendant

- intentional (deliberate breach of the law) (e.g. collecting wildlife);
- reckless (behaviour might lead to an offence) (e.g. pollutant run off);
- carelessness/lack of awareness (mitigates offence) (e.g. unaware).

Assessing the potential harm and risks taken

- negligence (e.g. risk/potential harm to workers);
- characteristics of pollutant (e.g. radioactivity and threat to health).

Relationship with regulatory authorities

- advice from enforcing authority (e.g. complete disregard when an enforcing authority advises how to abate pollution);
- warnings from enforcing authority (e.g. failure to take notice when warned of committing an offence);
- warnings from workforce (e.g. workforce notifying the employer of unsafe work methods);
- disregarding an abatement notice (e.g. polluter does nothing);
- lack of co-operation (e.g. failure to turn up for interview).

Licensing/permit

- breach of licence;
- no licence;
- fraudulent papers.

Economic gain for the defendant

- profit (e.g. collecting money for waste and dumping it illegally);
- cost saving (e.g. disposing of waste illegally to avoid disposal costs);
- neglecting preventative methods (e.g. failure to use air filters);
- avoiding licence fees (e.g. carrying out an act regardless);
- tax and duties evasion (e.g. avoiding import and/or export duties).

Offence pattern

- re-offending (e.g. previous conviction for same offence);
- repeat offender (e.g. broken the law but not received formal sanction from the court);
- unrelated previous offences;
- isolated incident.

Abatement and reparation

- any necessary reparation, clean-up and restoration work.

Mitigation

- isolated incident (e.g. good past record of the defendant);
- awareness (e.g. genuinely and reasonably lacked awareness);
- guilty plea;
- co-operation;
- role in the offending activity (e.g. relatively minor);
- personal position (e.g. genuine hardship or adverse social circumstances of the defendant);
- tackling the problem (e.g. steps taken to remedy the problem);
- public contrition and remorse.

Source: drawing from Magistrates Association UK 2009

This information provides a guiding template for determining the seriousness of environmental offences and sentencing environmental offenders. Court databases likewise provide a 'living' record of how judges and magistrates are treating different environmental offences in the courts. These are important jurisprudential tools insofar as a perennial problem in regard to those cases that do get to court has been the apparent under-valuing of environmental crimes.

The concept of environmental harm is built into various statutes and guidelines pertaining to environmental crime and justice. In general, distinctions are made on the basis of seriousness, material environmental harm and level of nuisance. In commenting on Australian environmental laws, Bricknell (2010: 13) points out that:

> There is some variation in how harm is defined but 'serious' and 'material' environmental harms are basically distinguished by the intensity and extent of the environmental impact and the actual or potential loss of (or damage to) property. The harm incurred is referenced to a predetermined monetary threshold and further differentiated as to the wilfulness or intentional nature of the act.

Research into US legal systems has demonstrated that environmental criminal statutes and environmental sentencing guidelines represent two very different ways of defining and assessing the social harm addressed by environmental crimes (Mandiberg 2009). Federal environmental crimes contained in legislation such as the Clean Water Act, Clean Air Act, and Resource Conservation and Recovery Act tend to utilize criminal provisions mainly to punish failure to abide by these regulatory systems. The point of each regulatory system is to manage contact between a pollutant and the air, water or soil, not to prevent it. The net result is that the focus is not on environmental harm as such, but rather on unacceptable (or significant) environmental harm – as measured by predetermined technical and administrative thresholds.

By contrast, US federal environmental crime sentencing guidelines focus more on matters of actual harm, rather than risk-reduction concerns. There is evidence here of the importance of graduated punishments based on the seriousness of the social harm being addressed, and support for increased punishment for violators who actually harm the environment. Interestingly, in both sets of legal instruments there is little formal definition of 'environmental harm', and the lack of clarity gives rise to different interpretations of what this might refer to. There are also difficulties with conceptualizations of 'seriousness' and 'causality' (see Mandiberg 2009).

Greater consistency in approach and outcome can be achieved by specialist agencies that deal with environmental crimes, harms and issues on a regular basis. It is notable, therefore, that today there are over 350 environmental courts and tribunals (ECTs) authorized in some 41 countries, and the number is growing (Pring and Pring 2009). In part, the growth in the number of ECTs has mirrored the increasing importance of environmental matters in international forums and law. The impetus of specialist judicial forums stems from continual pressures worldwide for effective resolution of environmental conflicts and/or expanding recognition of the need for procedural and substantive justice vis-à-vis environmental matters.

For instance, the 1992 United Nations Conference on Environment and Development adopted a series of principles. Principle 10 of the Rio Declaration, in mandatory terms, specifies that 'Effective access to judicial and administrative proceedings, including redress and remedy, shall be provided' by states in environmental matters. Pring and Pring (2009: xiii) explain that effective 'access to justice' can be seen in 'three basic stages – at the beginning, middle and end of the adjudication process: (1) access to get to and through the ECT door; (2) access within the ECT to proceedings which are fair, efficient and affordable; and (3) access to enforcement tools and remedies that can carry out the ECT's decision and provide measurable outcomes for preventing or remedying environmental harm'. Among the building blocks for an effective environmental court or tribunal are the mobilization of scientific and technical expertise and the competence of judges and decision-makers.

With regard to the latter, the establishment of courts with special expertise in environmental matters provides an institutional setting within which judicial training can find most purchase. The United Nations Environment Programme (2007b) for example has put resources into judicial training on environmental law. These documents are underpinned by the idea that we need to take environmental crime seriously, and to do so we need sanctions that reflect the seriousness of the crime. However, a defined environment court reaffirms and concretizes the importance of these ideas. It does so by providing a ready forum for the development of specialist expertise aided by the availability of technical experts within the court itself (see Preston 2011a). Moreover, such courts and tribunals provide a ready platform for the further extension of environmental jurisprudence and coherent sanctioning processes.

The multiple demands placed upon specific environmental protection agencies by different sections of government, business and community, and the varied tasks they are required to juggle (e.g. compliance, education, enforcement), may lead to a dilution of their enforcement capacities and activities in both the national sphere and the international arena. The expense of fighting cases in higher courts is itself a deterrent for agencies that are cash-strapped yet have to assume the legal costs associated with prosecution. Special environmental courts and tribunals offer the hope of lower costs and an array of alternative dispute-resolution procedures (Pring and Pring 2009). Accordingly, the establishment of such agencies may well have a positive ripple effect throughout the environmental law-enforcement and prosecution landscape.

It may well be that an International Environment Court (or equivalent) with requisite United Nations support is required as well (see Higgins 2012, but also see Hinde 2003). This is especially so if we are to adequately deal with environmental matters such as, for example, those pertaining to the international spaces of our oceans (e.g. pollution, concentrations of plastic, illegal fishing, transference of toxic materials). Such a court could draw together transboundary expertise from the various environmental law-enforcement networks to assess environmental crimes and harms that have international or global consequences.

There are other reasons to support an International Environmental Court as well, relating to potential developments within law itself. The main emphasis in regulation and criminal justice approaches is how to best utilize existing legal and enforcement mechanisms to protect environments and creatures within specific environments (e.g. illegal fishing). For those who view environmental harm through a wider lens than provided by criminal law, this approach has clear limitations. In particular, the focus on criminal law, regardless of whether or not the analysis is critical or confirming, offers a rather narrow view of 'harm' that can obscure the ways in which the state facilitates destructive environmental practices and environmental victimization. In other words, a strictly legal definition of harm belies the enormous harms that are legal and 'legitimate' but nevertheless negatively impact on people, environments and animals (Lynch and Stretesky 2003).

In responding to this circumstance, activists and green criminologists argue that either the law itself must be radically altered, or action should be directed to crime prevention, regardless of the existing laws that allow environmental harms to continue. With respect to the first course of action, there is growing momentum behind the idea of embedding the crime of ecocide as one of the five 'crimes against humanity' (see Chapter 3).

Problem-solving methods

In addition to proposed legal developments, a range of penalty types, approaches and mechanisms have emerged in relation to environmental sanctions. These fall broadly into the categories of civil, administrative and criminal justice responses. Recent developments in this area include the following types of sanctions and remedies (White 2010d):

- prosecution as a central tool in enforcement and compliance activities, which means using the full application of criminal laws and criminal sanctions strategically and in proportion to the nature of the offence, including the use of imprisonment;
- alternative sentencing mechanisms which involve the compulsory contribution of offenders to an environmental project that requires restoration or enhancement of the environment;
- civil penalties for less serious breaches of environmental law, which ensure timely and efficient application of sanctions appropriate to the nature of the offence;

- imposition of stricter-liability regimes (and use of nominated accountability), given the technical and resource difficulties in prosecuting large companies, which criminalize actions in ways that allow courts to sidestep some issues of *mens rea* in cases of corporate crime;
- tailored enforcement approaches that take into account organization type, which means that sanctions such as fines are suited to the type of firm, rather than the offence committed;
- as a prosecution alternative, restorative justice and enforceable undertakings approaches that can involve the offender, victim and community mutually discussing the nature of the offence and suitable remedies, and which are aimed at repairing the harm at a substantive level.

The sanctioning process for environmental offences presently covers a broad range of strategies, with new possibilities on the horizon. Bell and McGillivray (2008), for instance, mention the use of cumulative penalties, as in the case of points systems in motoring offences, so that a penalty infringement notice (PIN) does not become 'routine' or permit wealthy operators the 'right' to pollute. The more often you cause harm, the greater the penalty each time. Ensuring that the enforcement hammer is brought down hard enough on violators is also seen by Eastern African judges as essential to countering the idea that low fines are merely the cost of doing business (Mwebaza 2010). The United Nations Environment Programme's 'Global Judges Programme' includes reference to the imposition of deterrent fines based upon 'economic benefit of noncompliance' (EBN). This takes into account the value to the violator of deferred compliance: that is, the money that should have been spent on environmental improvements that was presumably invested elsewhere, earning a rate of return on an annual basis (UNEP 2007b). Financial sanctions with bite are at least on the agenda, if not yet fully realized in practice.

Meanwhile, the recent trend in countries like Australia toward alternative sentencing options reflects both the difficulties of prosecution, especially in relation to corporations, and a shift in thinking away from the offender toward addressing the nature of the offence. For instance, the range of sentencing options available across Australia, while they vary from jurisdiction to jurisdiction, includes an increasing number and type of orders (Preston 2007):

- orders for restoration and prevention;
- orders for payment of costs, expenses and compensation;
- orders to pay investigation costs;
- monetary benefits penalty orders;
- publication orders;
- environmental service orders;
- environmental audit orders;
- payment into environmental trust or for other purposes;

- order to attend training;
- order to establish training course;
- order to provide financial assurance.

How this burgeoning range of sentencing options translates into particular sentencing outcomes warrants ongoing and close scrutiny. Importantly, it also points us in the direction of problem-solving, rather than punishment per se, as a key objective of courts dealing with environmental harm.

For instance, the application of suitable sanctions for particular offences and offenders likewise demands sensitivity to, and flexibility based upon, the social and economic context of the perpetrators of environmental crime. This is not simply a matter of tailoring sanctions to suit the offender, as in the case of small versus large firms that commit acts of environmental crime. Rather, it is to also recognize that different classes or categories of environmental 'criminal' will respond quite differently to the sanctioning process. The wildlife poacher who acts as an individual, but one located within a particular cultural setting that legitimates wildlife theft (such as abalone poaching), sees and acts in the world differently to the organized crime syndicate stealing animals from the wild for global markets. Each type of offender and each sort of offence demands a nuanced and carefully weighed-up response that best contributes to forestalling environmental harms into the future (see Chapter 7). Again, this is best achieved when courts adopt a problem-solving rather than solely punishment-oriented regime. Databases such as the one being maintained by the New South Wales Law and Environment Court provide a valuable resource for researchers interested in analysing how well this approach to dealing with environmental harms and crimes is working out in practice for different groups (e.g. individuals, small to medium companies, large corporations).

The power of companies and elite individuals to resist prosecution or avoid criminal proceedings is an issue. There are clear social differences in the ability of the powerful, in relation to the less powerful, to protect and defend their interests. This is evident in how the powerful are able to manipulate rules of evidence, frustrate investigatory processes, confuse notions of accountability and to forestall potential prosecution by ostensibly abiding by and complying with record-keeping procedures (Gunningham, Norberry and McKillop 1997; Hughes 2004). The expense of legal remedies in dealing with environmental harm is further complicated by the ways in which companies contest the domains of contractual and legal responsibility, and by the notions of 'privileged information' as a means to restrict access to needed evidence (White 2010d).

Related to the question of dealing with different offenders, is the matter of combining different strategies of intervention and enforcement. For example, some jurisdictions now employ what is called an 'environmental enforcement sweep' to deal with instances where a community faces multiple environmental burdens. This involves using administrative, civil and criminal enforcement tools in tandem to address the problems in a comprehensive fashion (Dighe and Pettus 2011). Typically this kind of intervention model will deal with a variety of violations of different environment laws. Having a dedicated environment court, one capable of dealing with multiple agencies dealing collectively with particular investigations and prosecutions, means less fragmentation at the prosecution and implementation stages, a more holistic understanding of events and issues, and a more coherent adjudication process.

A problem-solving court must not only deal with competing and overlapping legal principles, and ecological, social and economic objectives. It must not only deal with a highly variable offender list, involving individual persons, communities and corporations. It must also consider the question of 'victimization' and the ways in which victimhood is construed within the domains of environmental law and ecological realities. For example, research undertaken in the United States has shown that the penalties relating to hazardous waste sites in areas with large white populations are higher than those with minority or indigenous populations. Furthermore, there is less environmental enforcement relating to facilities in communities with higher minority and low-income populations (Pinderhughes 1996; Lynch, Stretesky and Burns 2004; Konisky 2009). Criminal justice needs to be applied equitably and fairly if social justice is to be the outcome. Here, key considerations pertain to repairing the harm, acknowledging and compensating victims, rehabilitating specific bio-spheres and ensuring the survival of particular plant and animal species. Considerable expertise is a must if any or all of this is to be achieved.

A problem-solving court has the potential to expand the boundaries of 'good practice' in resolving conflicts over environmental matters. As part of this, it provides an opportunity to develop further the specific area of environmental jurisprudence. This is evident in New South Wales, for example, where the Land and Environment Court has concretely addressed a number of intersecting 'justice' considerations (Preston 2011a: 30–31):

- *Substantive justice*: the Court has been a leader in developing jurisprudence in relation to principles of ecologically sustainable development (principle of integration, precautionary principle, inter- and intra-generational equity, conservation of biological diversity and ecological integrity and internationalization of external, environmental costs including the polluter pays principle), environmental impact assessment, public trust, sentencing for environmental crime.
- *Procedural justice*: access to justice including removal of barriers to pubic interest litigation in relation to standing, interlocutory injunctions, security for costs, laches and costs.
- *Distributive justice*: inter- and intra-generational equity, polluter pays principle, balancing public and private rights and responsibilities.

- *Restorative justice*: victim–offender mediation and polluter pays principle for environmental crime.
- *Therapeutic justice*: adopting court practice and procedure to improve welfare of litigants, including improving accessibility.

Institutionalization of specialist expertise thus reinforces and embellishes the further development of innovative practice and practical implementation of the law in relation to what have often formerly been simply abstract declarations of principle and emergent rights with little applied substance.

Weighing up diverse information, conflicting principles and appropriate responses demands a sophisticated court able to sift through complex evidence and which can be confident in its application of sanctions and remedies. In other words, there is a need for specialist environmental courts (or at the very least, generalist courts with specialist expertise in environmental matters).

> An environmental court is better able to address the pressing, pervasive and pernicious environmental problems that confront society (such as global warming and loss of biodiversity). New institutions and creative attitudes are required to address these problems. Specialization enables use of special knowledge and expertise in both the process and the substance of resolution of these problems. Rationalization enlarges the remedies available.
> (Preston 2011a: 29)

These specialist courts, in turn, must be based upon problem-solving models of intervention, especially given the nature of the tasks at hand. The particular contours, resources and capacities of such courts will vary greatly depending upon national context (Pring and Pring 2009). Their presence, however, allows the possibility of global networking and collaborations that can bolster the fight against environmental crime in the most effective and creative ways.

One emergent aspect of environmental courts as specialist problem-solving courts is the increasing attention being paid to the notion of 'restorative justice' as applied to this area of jurisprudence (Preston 2011b). The restorative justice perspective is informed by concepts such as those of harm reparation, social restoration, community harmony and problem-solving. A retributive system of justice is essentially punitive in nature, with the key focus on using punishment as a means to deter future crime and to provide 'just deserts' for any harm committed. A restorative approach is concerned with promoting harmonious relationships by means of restitution, reparation, and reconciliation involving offenders, victims and the wider community (White, Haines and Asquith 2012). A restorative justice approach seems to be ideally suited to dealing with environmental crimes insofar as they hold the promise that things will be done to rehabilitate or repair the harms that have occurred.

There are other issues and constraints as well. The prosecution and sentencing of environmental crime really only finds purchase within particular jurisdictions and national contexts. The problem, however, is that frequently the key actors involved in such crimes are global creatures, able to take advantage of different systems of regulation and legal compliance (Braithwaite and Drahos 2000). If a global company, for example, is bound by rules in one country but not in another, its behaviour is likely to differ in each setting and across jurisdictions (see for example Hughes 2004).

Harm is not necessarily the same as victimization, especially if the latter is interpreted as applying strictly to humans. For example, environmental victimization has been defined as specific forms of harm which are caused by acts (e.g. dumping of toxic waste) or omissions (e.g. failure to provide safe drinking water) leading to the presence or absence of environmental agents (e.g. poisons, nutrients) which are associated with *human* injury (see Williams 1996). Management of these forms of victimization is generally retrospective (after the fact), and involves a variety of legal and social responses (Hall 2013a). Importantly, the central actor in this definition is humans (not non-human animals or eco-systems). Much the same can be said of reconceptualizations of environmental rights as 'human rights', in that the self-same concept is premised upon notions of humanity.

Nonetheless, the law does allow for a modicum of protection for the non-human as well as the human. This is reflected in legislation pertaining to endangered species (e.g. particular animals such as tigers) and to conservation more generally (e.g. in the form of national parks). Harm is central to these forms of social regulation as well; however, whether 'harm to the environment' is of consequence *unless* it is measured with reference to human values (e.g. economic, aesthetic, cultural) is of ongoing concern in regard to legal decision-making (see Lin 2006). In essence, natural objects (such as trees and forests) lack legal rights (and agency or volition) and so must rely upon humans to bring actions to protect them. Some argue that the inherent interests of 'natural objects' ought to be protected through legal actions by the objects themselves, with humans serving as their guardians or trustees (Stone 1972; Lin 2006).

A creative interpretation and implementation of restorative justice principles allows for recognition of particular categories of victims that may not normally be considered to be victims (see Chapter 10). From the point of view of green criminology, this provides an opening for the extension of justice across the human, environment and animal domains. Who speaks for who is nevertheless still controversial; especially when it comes to natural objects such as trees, rivers and specific bio-spheres (see Besthorn 2004, 2013).

In 2003 South Africa opened its first environmental court in Hermanus, specifically devoted to combating environmental crime. In 2006 the court was closed along with other specialist courts that lacked legislative mandates. The lessons learned are worth reiterating.

Case vignette 14.1 Lessons from a defunct South African environment court

The impetus for the introduction of an environment court was the political recognition of the need for stronger deterrence of poachers in an effort to protect the valuable natural resources in South Africa, especially abalone. Ironically it would be a political decision that would cause the court's demise. The 'court's primary purpose was to prosecute abalone poachers, although cases relating to other environmental issues such as the illegal trade in rhinoceros horns, water pollution and other marine offences were also heard. In its first year the court heard 74 cases, 51 of which resulted in successful prosecutions, translating into a 70% success rate, dramatically increasing the number of convictions for environmental crimes' (Stop Illegal Fishing Programme, Case Study Series 02, n.d.: 2).

In 2006 a high-level political decision was taken to close a number of specialist courts that lacked legislative mandates, including the environmental court in Hermanus. Those charged with environmental offences were transferred back into the general court system.

The following observations from this experience are worth noting and are paraphrased below under three key headings identified in the case study:

Key features and outcomes

Having a specialized court and prosecutors allowed for *building of expertise and experience* in South African environmental law; *collaboration and sharing of expertise* between law-enforcement agencies, the *development of a training manual* detailing the proper application of South African marine regulations including information necessary to successfully prosecute cases; environmental cases were given *prioritized attention* resulting in the rapid hearing of cases and the prosecution of an unprecedented number of criminals; increases in poaching convictions *boosted the morale* of environmental enforcement officers and validated the dangerous actions required to apprehend offenders.

Challenges

Limited availability of specialist prosecutors and magistrates in environmental law; lack of environmental jurisdiction to provide full geographical coverage of the abalone fishery; lack of training for enforcement officials in legislation, policy and procedure; lack of a legislative mandate for the Hermanus Court.

> **Lessons learned**
>
> *Increasing the level of deterrence* through the high probability of conviction and severe punishments contributes to the reduction of environmental crimes; *sharing of knowledge* among prosecutors and other law-enforcers both formally and informally is vital; *providing high penalty jurisdiction* to courts is important, and this can be achieved through, for example, giving environmental courts regional status; *utilizing the media* to draw attention to, and help attract public support against, environmental crimes is a strong tool. The media was briefed on high-profile convictions, and the resulting publicity increased public faith in the system, encouraging bystanders to report crimes and come forward as witnesses.
>
> Source: The Stop Illegal Fishing Programme, Case Study Series 02 n.d.: 1–3

The politics of court funding and legislative mandates can make it difficult to establish, sustain and increase the purview of specialist environmental courts. Yet, as this South African case demonstrates, such courts provide precisely the type of forum for the requisite development of expertise, a critical mass of specialist practitioners and heightened public awareness of the seriousness of the issues.

Conclusion

The continued degradation of specific environments, ongoing extinction of plant and animal species, and the devastating consequences of climate change will inevitably feed into the general mix of where law reform and judicial practice will go over the next period. Effective environmental law enforcement will require collaboration and knowledge-sharing between different nation-states and environmental law-enforcement agencies. The capacity of perpetrators to move across borders, and to use differences between jurisdictions to their advantage, has to be matched by the flexibility of law-enforcement agencies and environment courts in undertaking their respective tasks (Pink and Lehane 2012). The establishment of an International Environment Court is one approach to addressing these complexities at a global level. In the meantime existing environment courts at the domestic level have an important part to play in responding to environmental harms and crimes in new and innovative ways.

From the point of view of jurisprudence and the operation of the court, specialist environmental knowledge and specialist environment courts that operate on the basis of problem-solving methods would appear to be factors most likely to positively contribute to the mission of eco-justice. Progressive methods of institutionally dealing with environmental crime and harm are currently in train, although how far these develop is an open-ended question.

Much depends upon extraneous factors, such as funding for such courts and such approaches, and the politics of intervention in a period of fiscal restraint and economic downturn.

Discussion topics

- What are the pros and cons of establishing specialist environmental courts?
- A major purpose of any court dealing with environmental issues should be to repair the environmental harm. Discuss.
- What are the key debates and issues surrounding the establishment of an international environment court?
- How might environment courts address the issue of indigenous and other types of knowledge in their processes?
- Humans often 'speak' on behalf of the voiceless. Justice in practice demands that there be advocates who can provide a sense of what the non-human – an animal, a river – requires for justice to be achieved. Is this possible?

Further reading

Bricknell, S. (2010). *Environmental Crime in Australia*, AIC Reports Research and Public Policy Series 109. Canberra: Australian Institute of Criminology.

Preston, B. (2011). 'The Use of Restorative Justice for Environmental Crime', *Criminal Law Journal*, 35: 136–45.

Pring, G., and Pring, C. (2009). *Greening Justice: Creating and improving environmental courts and tribunals*. The Access Initiative. <http://www.accessinitiative.org/sites/default/files/Greening%20Justice%20FInal_31399_WRI_0.pdf>.

Situ, Y., and Emmons, D. (2000). *Environmental Crime: The criminal justice system's role in protecting the environment*. Thousand Oaks, CA: Sage.

Walters, R., and Westerhuis, D.S. (2013). 'Green Crime and the Role of Environmental Courts', *Crime, Law and Social Change*, 59(3): 279–90.

Chapter 15

Environmental crime prevention

Introduction

This chapter will discuss the following topics:

- environmental crime prevention;
- dealing with illegal fishing;
- illegal wildlife crime and crime prevention;
- perpetrators and organized crime; and
- dilemmas and issues for environmental crime prevention.

The best way to respond to crime is to prevent it before it occurs. Especially for environmental harm, foresight and prudence is needed in order to modify present activities in the light of future potential harms. For environmental crime prevention, the precautionary principle is crucial. So, too, is learning from the approaches and techniques of conventional criminology that may be usefully employed to prevent environmental crime.

This chapter provides a brief survey of crime-prevention initiatives that have been designed and applied around environmental crimes. The main focus for this discussion is those crimes linked to illegal trade in wildlife and illegal fishing, in part reflecting the amount of work currently being undertaken in these areas.

Environmental crime prevention

Environmental crime prevention encompasses a range of substantive considerations. It must deal with acts and omissions that are already criminalized and prohibited, such as illegal fishing or illegal dumping of toxic waste. It must also come to grips with events that have yet to be designated officially as 'harmful' but that show evidence of exhibiting potentially negative consequences. Environmental crime prevention likewise has to negotiate different kinds of harms, as these affect humans, local and global environments, and non-human animals.

The aims and objectives of environmental crime prevention are inseparable from eco-philosophy. That is, what it is we are trying to prevent is inherently linked to how human interests, the needs and requirements of specific eco-systems, and the rights of non-human animals are viewed. Environmental crime prevention also therefore necessarily encapsulates particular visions of 'the good society'. Crime prevention of any kind always has ramifications for the kind of world within which we live, and the balance we make between liberty and social control (Sutton, Cherney and White 2013). For instance, a strong ecological stance could well justify the *prohibition* of people from going into any wilderness area whatsoever, on the basis of preventing human interference in such areas. Whether or not alternatives are possible or should be made available is exactly what the political deliberations over crime prevention would have to grapple with. The answer very much depends upon the specific vision – the perceived relationship between 'nature', society and animals – that is seen as ideal at any particular point in time (see White 2013c).

If humans are allowed into specific wilderness areas, then the next question is, under what conditions? To prevent possible environment harms perpetrated by the presence of humans in these areas, *rules and regulations* are needed (e.g. on burying human waste, on taking litter out of areas with you as you go). Creative architecture and strategic planning can also ameliorate the impact of humans. For instance, boardwalks and well-marked pathways can channel human traffic in certain directions and through certain areas. Provision of toilets and look-outs might have a 'honey-pot' effect in drawing tourists and bush walkers into particular settings and thus away from more pristine wilderness locations. Once general decisions about the human–nature interface are made, provisions to prevent or minimize damage can be introduced.

Theoretically, good environmental crime prevention ought to be as inclusive of human, environment and animal interests as possible. In order to achieve this, however, we need to be clear as to what 'crime prevention' is actually intended to do. For example, balancing diverse human and non-human interests still means assigning some type of 'value' to the potential harm. Consider oil for instance. Is environmental crime prevention best served by ensuring that oil tankers are ship-shape and tightly regulated in their transportation of oil? This would ensure a modicum of *harm minimization*. Or, should we eliminate the threat of oil spill by banning oil tankers outright? This would entail *harm eradication*. Clearly the type and extent of environmental crime prevention will be dictated by notions of human self-interest, as well as potential threats to eco-systems, animals and livelihoods.

One of the mandates of green criminology is to foster greater attention, analysis and action in regard to environmental harm. From the point of view of environmental crime prevention, the tasks are both instrumental and *symbolic*. We want to put into place strategies that protect certain peoples, places and creatures. At the same time, we want to signal to the community as a whole that this particular project is significant and that it expresses our collective values about 'what counts'. For instance, the establishment of 'green zones' in the Great Barrier Reef Marine Park is important, not only because it secludes certain areas from human interaction, but it sends a strong message that ecological well-being does count in human calculations of marine interests. The choice of words is important, as is publicity surrounding these protected areas.

One of the key lessons from conventional crime prevention is that it ought to be based largely on a *problem-solving*, rather than a policy-prescribed, model of intervention. Different kinds of places lend themselves to different sorts of environmental harms and different kinds of intervention. Perceptions and consciousness of harm are in part linked to proximity of human habitation to the sources of harm themselves. A toxic spill in the middle of a major city, or contamination of Sydney Harbour, is much more likely to capture public attention, and government action, than something that happens in a remote wilderness area of Tasmania or on the high seas.

In regard to environmental crime, great purchase has been derived from the application of 'situational crime prevention' approaches and techniques. Situational crime prevention is based upon the idea that for someone who is capable of, and not averse to, offending, the decision whether or not to commit a specific crime will be a function of both whether an opportunity presents itself and whether the likely rewards from exploiting that opportunity are sufficient to offset the perceived efforts and risks (Sutton, Cherney and White 2013). Situational prevention revolves around identifying modifiable conditions that are susceptible to intervention, and which can reduce or pre-empt perceived opportunities for crime (Clarke 1980, 2005; Clarke and Homel 1997; Tilley 2006). Table 15.1 outlines the broad approaches and specific techniques of situational crime prevention (see also Sutton, Cherney and White 2013).

Situational crime prevention is about removing the opportunity to commit crime and increasing the likelihood of apprehension. This approach is particularly useful and effective in that different kinds of harm tend to call forth different kinds of responses. As demonstrated in the sections below, situational prevention has entailed identification of specific actors, circumstances and exchanges in relation to particular kinds of environmental crime. Once these have been adequately scoped, then appropriate crime-prevention measures can be put into place. Importantly, a focus on 'what works' in the here and now does not preclude adoption of wider social prevention measures – those meant to enhance community well-being over time, and which are designed to bring about systemic changes at social, economic, cultural and political levels.

Much criminal and environmentally destructive behaviour is highly contingent upon particular factors and specific social circumstances. The problem of toxic waste disposal, for example, cannot be divorced from how and why toxic waste is produced in the first place and the consequences of the commodification of waste that has occurred in the last 50 years. Accordingly, to deal with the

Table 15.1 Approaches and techniques of situational prevention

Broad approaches	Specific techniques
Increase the effort of crime	harden targets control access to facilities screen entries and exits deflect offenders control tools/weapons
Increase the risks	extend guardianship facilitate natural surveillance reduce anonymity utilize place managers strengthen formal surveillance
Reduce the rewards	conceal targets remove targets identify property disrupt markets deny benefits
Reduce provocations	reduce frustration and stress avoid disputes reduce emotional arousal neutralize peer pressure discourage imitation
Remove excuses	set rules post instructions alert conscience assist compliance control access to drugs, alcohol and other facilitators

Source: Clarke and Eck 2005

harms associated with toxic waste disposal, a specific crime-prevention plan is needed: one that fits the nature and dynamics of this specific type of environmental harm (see also Crofts *et al.* 2010). The same goes for other forms of harm, whether this is in regard to illegal fishing or the illegal traffic in flora and fauna (see Smith and Anderson 2004; Halstead 1992).

A problem-solving approach to crime prevention therefore demands a certain level of specificity. That is, general pronouncements about the nature of harm need to be accompanied by particular site or harm analysis. To illustrate how this might occur, we can consider the issue of illegal fishing. Before doing so, it is important to point out that fishing – both legal and illegal – is associated with a wide range of potentially harmful activity (White 2008a). Legally provided fishing, such as aquaculture and the 'scientific' harvesting of whales, can engender great harm. The distinction between legal and illegal may in fact not be the best way to conceptualize environmental harm or responses to harm (see Chapter 1).

Dealing with illegal fishing

Conventional crime-prevention approaches provide useful insights into how environmental crimes might be prevented or minimized. Typically, such approaches entail systematic analysis of the issues and analysis of the specific problems in the first instance. This is accompanied by the development of particular interventions across the diverse crime-prevention areas that match the problem at hand (see Sutton, Cherney and White 2013). When it comes to the harms associated with fishing, several different approaches can be identified.

Social crime-prevention methods might introduce school children to programmes that reshape their concepts of 'the environment', 'fish' and 'fishing'. This could include strategic solutions ranging from 'catch and release' as an imperative for recreational fishing, through to doing assignments on the effects of climate change on fish species. Young people who are known to, or who seem likely to, degrade environments or abuse animals could be encouraged to participate in programmes and projects aimed at challenging and changing attitudes and behaviour.

Environmental crime-prevention methods might educate and advise boating enthusiasts and fishers generally about how best to minimize their impact on fisheries, through measures such as knowledge of marine park boundaries through to the use of suitable receptacles for waste products while at sea. At a practical level, regular patrols of coastlines, and the use of satellites, can facilitate surveillance and monitoring of fishing 'hot spots' and areas where environmental transgressions are known to occur frequently. The point is that, whether legal or illegal, various activities can be responded to in a manner that positively reduces their harmful consequences. On the other hand, there are occasions when official reaction is driven solely on the basis of the legal/illegal distinction.

For the sake of simplicity, only instances of illegal fishing will be considered here. Even so, there are major variations in the specific nature of that illegality. Consider for example, the following types of illegal fishing (White 2008a):

- commercial fishing which involves catches in excess of quota, false declarations, destruction of by-catch linked to marine pollution;
- recreational fishing which involves unlicensed fishing and fishing excess to quota;
- indigenous fishing, which may involve fishing in traditional but foreign waters and fishing without a permit;
- large-scale illegal fishing, which also involves super-exploitation of particular species such as sharks;
- specialist illegal fishing which is designed to exploit endangered species specifically for private fish collections or for medicinal purposes;
- foreign illegal fishing, which involves illegal, unreported and unregulated fishing in foreign oceans.

Different scales, motivations and techniques underpin each of these types of illegal fishing. Environmental crime prevention thus has to address the specific nature of the phenomenon in question if it is to be appropriate to the circumstances. Different kinds of illegality in fact require quite different kinds of responses, since they stem from quite different origins.

Conventional crime prevention emphasizes the importance of undertaking scoping analysis before developing an intervention plan (Sutton, Cherney and White 2013). As applied here, it is useful, for example, to assess the key relationships and agencies involved in shaping targets, places and offending, as this occurs in a marine environment (e.g. fisheries management, marine park authorities, customs, navy, consumers). While the general contours of illegal fishing can be mapped out in this way, the structural or underpinning reasons for different types of illegal fishing still require close analysis. The case of indigenous or traditional fishing provides some indication of the complexities of the issues (see White 2008a).

Different types of human behaviour require different responses. While incentives might be crucial to forestalling illegal fishing by Indonesian traditional fishers in Australian waters, trade-related regulation would be more appropriate as a means to deal with large-scale illegal fishing (see Lack 2007). In other instances, a variety of situational measures can be applied that have a distinct marine application (see Smith and Anderson 2004). Indeed, a wide range of techniques, approaches and strategies to environmental crime prevention in relation to illegal fishing can be envisaged, as shown in Box 15.1.

Box 15.1 Approaches and techniques of crime prevention dealing with illegal fishing

Social

(developmental and communal-oriented)

Incentive schemes

- alternative sources of revenue for traditional fishers;
- rights tied to management responsibilities.

Moral persuasion

- 'catch and release' media advertising;
- education in schools about species decline;
- consumer education and fish identification.

Trade-related measures

- schemes that require documentation to accompany product in order to authenticate its legitimacy (link to DNA testing as well);
- schemes that rely on vessel lists that identify authorized vessels ('white lists') and/or vessels considered to have been fishing in breach of Regional Fisheries Management Organizations (RFMO) ('black lists') as a basis for imposing restrictions on the access of these latter vessels to ports and port services;
- trade bans on particular states/entities (IUU vessels) considered to have failed to co-operate in the implementation of the Regional Fisheries Management Organization's (RFMO's) conservation and management measures.

Community mobilization

- coastal watch schemes and monitoring programmes;
- indigenous coastal patrols;
- confidential phone-in hotlines.

Situational

(immediate situation and technologies-oriented)

Increasing the effort

- fencing off key areas;
- ID badges for users;
- partial park closure;
- no anchor markers;
- vessel and employee registration.

Increasing the risk

- harbour and jetty vessel checks;
- CCTV, satellite photos, vessel monitoring scheme;
- boat and aircraft patrols;
- reporting by public users.

Reducing the rewards

- preventing access to parks, relocating species;
- licensing of vessels, fish tagging;
- disrupting markets/distribution channels;
- issuing permits and licensing.

Inducing guilt or shame

- strengthening moral condemnation of over-fishing;
- facilitating compliance by setting up community hot-lines;
- use of warning signs in ports;
- information pamphlets about the state of fishing stocks.

Sources: Lack 2007; Smith and Anderson 2004; Clarke 1997; White and Perrone 2005

However, while suggestive of possible interventions, such a list only makes sense and 'works' when put into specific fishing contexts. Studies of particular types of illegal fishing, such as abalone, lobster and toothfish, show great variation in motives, techniques, local cultures and scale of operation (Tailby and Gant 2002; McMullan and Perrier 2002; Lugten 2005; Anderson and McCusker 2005). As argued throughout this chapter, the specificity of the harm ought to drive the particular type of intervention that is adopted in any given situation. This, in turn, requires close analysis of the multiple facets of each type of harmful activity.

Illegal wildlife trade and crime prevention

Recent criminological work on illegal poaching of elephants and rhinoceros, and on the illegal trade in parrots, has likewise exposed the conjunction of many different factors that go into why and how such activity takes place. Again, a key lesson from this research is that tailoring responses to the specific context and the specific crime is essential. Box 15.2 presents a variety of measures that have been suggested or adopted in relation to particular types of wildlife crime.

Box 15.2 Crime prevention applied to different types of wildlife crime

Elephant poaching

- closure of logging roads;
- DNA coding of ivory;
- use of pilotless drones;
- banning of international trade in ivory.

Conservation of endangered species

- secure reserves;
- reward vigilance from locals/tourists;
- compensation when endangered species destroy crops or livestock;
- more explicit customs declarations.

Illegal trade in parrots

- protecting the nests of target species during breeding season;
- use of CCTV surveillance;
- active focus on geographical areas where most species are concentrated (hot-spots);
- identification and shutting down of key city markets and road blocks on widely used trafficking roads.

Rhinoceros poaching

- more rangers and military patrols on the ground;
- dehorning animals and other science-based interventions, such as microchipping;
- investment in community-based eco-tourism projects;
- bilateral government agreements to co-operatively curb the illegal trade.

Wildlife skins

- protection of snow leopard in return for supported alternative community enterprise;
- promotion of eco-tourism;
- protection of livestock from predators like the snow leopard;
- certification of skins to the benefit of community-based sustainable management programmes.

Sources: Lemieux and Clarke 2009; Wellsmith 2010, 2011; Pires and Clarke 2011, 2012; Pires and Moreto 2011; Ayling 2013

One of the key areas of interest throughout this extensive and growing literature is that of disrupting markets. That is, systematic and rigorous analysis of poaching is demonstrating the importance of studying harvesting networks and the resilience of these networks to environmental law-enforcement efforts (Ayling 2013). The relationship between specific networks of actors – from the local through to inter-city through to regional and transnational levels – and specific markets and marketplaces (including eBay and other internet mechanisms) allows identification of weak points in the supply chains as well as diverse participant motivations. This means that crime-prevention responses can be contemplated that take into account factors such as specific communal circumstance (such as high levels of poverty and unemployment among local residents) and trade routes (smuggling avenues in remote areas and in cities) among other related criminogenic factors.

In specific terms, such considerations are closely associated with the development of a 'market reduction approach' (MRA). The MRA, as applied to the illicit endangered species trade, seeks to identify the routine patterns of those involved: poachers, handlers, and consumers – those who hunt, transform, transport and buy the wildlife (the *likely offenders*); the precise wildlife being hunted, transformed, transported and purchased (the *suitable targets*); and those whose remit is to actually conserve and protect those species (*conservators, police, customs and wildlife officers*) (Schneider 2008, 2012).

Trade in wildlife, for instance, involves transactions involving the thieves through to those who arrange the sale of the product on the market. This has implications for prevention of such crime as well as for identification of perpetrators as such. This is illustrated in Table 15.2. By understanding the social dynamics pertaining to the particular crime in question it becomes apparent who the perpetrators are (as a class or category of offender) and how they are linked into other stake-holders if a crime is to be successfully achieved.

Such an approach does not preclude careful consideration of why certain actors engage in the wildlife crimes in the way they do. Indeed, recent work is highly conscious of the limitations of narrowly conceived situational prevention measures that do not take into account the social and cultural context of phenomenon such as poaching (Pires and Moreto 2011; Kahler and Gore 2012). As Nurse (2013a: 211) comments, 'Citizens who feel marginalized within society and who lack appropriate life chances or are under economic or social pressure to harm animals, will do so unless they are provided with alternatives'. This observation extends to different communities in different parts of the world.

Table 15.2 Focus for market reduction approach to wildlife crime

Focus	MRA/wildlife
Who	hunter, poacher, handler, consumer
What	animals, plants and/or by-products
Location	country of origin (range area), country of consumption
Date	seasonality, mating season
How	how things are harvested, processed, shipped
Why	demand

Source: drawing upon Schneider 2008: 279

Consider for example the use of wildlife as resources for traditional and indigenous people. Imposing a tough conservation policy 'from above', such as fencing nature reserves and coercively keeping people out, can end up criminalizing activities that are historically imbued and built in to the fabric of long-standing cultures and ways of being, such as foraging for food and collecting wood for cooking fires (see Duffy 2010). Creative responses are needed to foster substantial and positive changes in the lives of these communities. For example, in Canada, the Income Security Program (ISP) established for Cree hunters in north Quebec provides guaranteed income to allow the Cree to hunt:

> With the ISP, production is linked to people's need, and there is no incentive to overexploit wildlife resources. Indeed there is a voluntary decrease in hunting in overused areas, and other wildlife conservation practices, such as monitoring the numbers of certain game, are recognized as hunting-related work under the ISP.
>
> (Altman, Bek and Roach 1996: 89)

Other crime-prevention initiatives are likewise receptive to working with, rather than against, community interests in order to enable a win-win environmental solution (see Pires and Moreto 2011). Multiple interests may need to be accommodated as part of the crime-prevention problem-solving process.

Perpetrators and organized crime

In recent years greater attention has been given internationally to the role of organized crime networks in regard to environmental crime. Organizations such as the United Nations Office on Drugs and Crime, the European Union and Interpol, have each signalled the cross-connections between environmental crime and other crimes, such as corruption, money-laundering, human trafficking and murder (see for example, UNODC 2011; Interpol 2013; Gerbrandy 2013). Criminologists have likewise pointed out the linkages between illicit markets involving trade in wildlife and drugs (South and Wyatt 2011) and a recent Europol report highlighted that those involved in high-level drugs trafficking in Brazil, Colombia and Mexico have established a notable role in the illegal supply of endangered species (Europol 2011). Wildlife crimes have also been linked to the fund-raising activities of terrorist groups and warlords in Africa and Asia. Criminal networks are becoming more sophisticated, in part because the financial rewards are great and the risks relatively minor. Wildlife and pollution crimes pay well, and this has not been lost on organized criminal networks of many different persuasions.

Studying the perpetrators of transnational environmental crime generally involves investigating chains of harm (systems) and the interconnectedness of key players (networks). That is, we need to identify the key players and understand the links between diverse players at different stages in any particular criminal process. This is essentially what the market reduction approach aims to achieve, as illustrated above in relation to the wildlife trade (see specially Pires and Clarke 2011, 2012). The creation of particular markets is also linked to the regulatory environment within which crime emerges or is made manifest. For example, in the waste-disposal arena, the imposition of stricter rules in one jurisdiction (for example, the European Union) may generate efforts to sidestep the costs of compliance by subcontracting to illegal operators (see Chapter 9). Criminality is also related to the complexity of an industry, and the push-pull factors that lend themselves to criminal opportunity.

By understanding the social dynamics pertaining to the particular crime it becomes apparent who the perpetrators are (as a class or category of offender) and how they are linked into other stake-holders if a crime is to be successfully achieved. In other words, for any particular type of crime and particular type of criminality, there is a need to undertake an industry scan in order to identify who the key suspects might be. For example, in regard to illegal logging there are a number of potential players linked to specific kinds of activities (Setiono 2007):

- financial backers of illegal logging activities;
- corrupt forestry officials, police and military officers who allow illegal logging practices to occur;
- international shipping companies which are complicit in the smuggling of illegal logs;
- international timber traders who are engaged in forgery of timber permits;
- international and local timber traders involved in illicit trafficking.

A similar exercise can be undertaken with regard to other types of illegal activity such as IUU fishing, illegal trade in parrots and elephant poaching. The area of carbon trading, likewise, warrants closer attention.

For other sorts of crimes, the investigation may involve other kinds of analysis. For example, the dumping of toxic waste in the Ivory Coast in 2006 involved a sequence of connected events, beginning in Amsterdam harbour and ending up at the Ivory Coast. The main concern of this analysis is not only with networks (across business and government domains), but also temporal developments that link the originator of the problem to the final criminal act (White 2009d). The harm that resulted (in which a number of people died) had its origins in decisions made several months earlier. A vital aspect of this kind of analysis is that it ties criminal action to both direct perpetrators (i.e., dumping of toxic materials) and those whose action (or inaction) allowed the crime to take place (i.e., corrupt government officials).

As with most organized crime, investigation of the 'money trail' is crucial to pinpointing who is doing what with whom and when this occurs. As indicated in Box 15.3, there are a number of issues that also require concerted and systematic attention.

Box 15.3 Key issues relating to organized crime and the environment

- The connection between environmental crime and other serious crimes, and the overlap of players, modus operandi, markets, commodity chains, trade routes, and financial arrangements (e.g. money laundering).
- The role of transnational criminal organizations and the influence of corruption as this relates to environmental crime (e.g. illegal disposal of hazardous waste and e-waste; transnational organized crime in the fishing industry).
- Criminogenic opportunities arising from both institutional changes (e.g. carbon-emission trading schemes and fraud) and social and ecological changes (e.g. climate-induced migration and human trafficking).
- Applicability of United Nations Convention Against Transnational Organized Crime (UNTOC) and the United Nations Convention against Corruption (UNCAC) in combating transnational environmental crime.
- Concrete ways of preventing the involvement of criminal organizations in the phenomenon of environmental crime, including through market reduction approaches, task-force interventions and anti-money-laundering strategies.
- Organized crime is not the same as white-collar or corporate crime. Nonetheless, crimes of the powerful ought to likewise be investigated, especially given the overlap between legal and illegal activity in many industries.

Researching organized criminals and powerful white-collar offenders presents a number of challenges not associated with other types of study. Research may be seen as 'dangerous' to vested interests if corruption of officials is widespread. Criminological interest directed at environmental crimes and harms may well provoke negative reactions on the part of powerful interest groups. Many different methods are used to silence critics, to dampen resistance and to minimize public outcry, including violation of human rights (see White 2011a). Resistance to data collection may go hand in hand with denial of harm on the part of the powerful, and threats of harm from criminal elements are a potential risk. These responses represent a challenge for those dedicated to doing critical green criminology research.

When it comes to tackling organized criminal networks and corrupt officials, a number of strategies can be applied. Foremost among these is the development of a centralized international database and of sophisticated data analysis specifically on organized criminal activity and environmental crime. This database could place particular emphasis on identification of key players, diverse modus operandi, organizational structures and networks, and markets (including overlapping players, networks, markets and commodities).

Case vignette 15.1 Mafia and wind farms

The mafia have attracted attention over many years for infiltration of the hazardous waste industry, particularly in Italy (see for example, Walters 2013b). But recently attention has shifted to their involvement in the wind-power sector in Italy. Italian police reportedly 'seized assets worth 1.3 billion Euros from a Sicilian renewable energy developer in the biggest ever seizure of mafia-linked assets including 43 wind and solar energy companies' (Gearin 2013). Massive government subsidies are said to have led to the mafia fraudulently skimming money from the subsidies, costing the public as much as 35 billion Euros over the past decade (see Tranoris 2012). A recent study by Caneppele, Riccardi and Standridge (2013) examined mafia investment in the wind-power sector in Italy. They concluded in part, that (p. 336):

> high profitability attracted legitimate and illegitimate investors. The absence of clear regulations in wind farm authorizations gave large discretion to public officials. These ingredients, combined with other factors (highest levels of WP potential in Southern regions, where OC groups are stronger and public administration is more corrupt) generated the perfect environment for OC infiltration and for joint-ventures between legal and illegal players.

They also found that (p. 336):

> Analysing the law-enforcement investigations in the wind sector, this study found cases of OC presence in different phases of wind farm constructions. The most vulnerable is the authorization phase. It is possible to say that often legitimate investors delegated to OC groups the role of dealing with (and corrupting) local public administration in order to speed up the authorization process and to avoid delays in wind farm construction. In this scenario developers/consultants played a central role bridging legitimate and criminal interests. However there is also evidence of corruption of public officials without the direct involvement of OC groups.

> In February 2009, eight local officials and businessmen from Sicily, Campania and the northern region of Trentino were charged with offering or receiving money and votes in exchange for turbine permits around the city of Mazara del Vallo (Il Giornale 2009, cited in Oles and Hammarlund 2011: 475). In November 2009, in an investigation code-named 'Gone with the Wind', 15 people were arrested for what officials described as a Ponzi scheme to collect up to €30 million in European Union subsidies (Carvajal 2009, cited in Oles and Hammarlund 2011: 475).

Studying perpetrators, including organized criminal networks, can be approached using a variety of techniques and methods (Heckenberg and White 2013). Among these are:

- *Transaction analysis* – study of markets and understanding the social dynamics pertaining to the particular crime (e.g. illegal wildlife trade).
- *Stake-holder analysis* – study of particular industries and identification of who key suspects might be (e.g. financial backers of illegal logging, shipping companies).
- *Chronological analysis* – study of temporal developments, such as sequences of events, that can link the originator of the problem to the final criminal act (e.g. toxic dumping).
- *Company analysis* – study of specific company profiles in terms of history, activities and relationships to particular local communities (e.g. Trafigura, Monsanto).
- *Modus operandi analysis* – study of mode of operation of perpetrators and how this differs from the mode of operation of regulators (i.e., tends to be loose, transnational, motivated by singular purposes, and involve networks on an ad hoc basis).
- *Horizon-scanning* – study of newly emerging opportunities for organized crime and corruption and innovative responses and solutions, drawing upon crime-prevention strategies including those that promote cross-jurisdictional co-operation and collaboration in bringing offenders to justice.

Environmental justice institutions need to be strengthened at the global level if full effect is to be given to crime-prevention and environmental law-enforcement efforts. Accordingly, consideration needs to be given to the establishment of specialist environmental law-enforcement task forces and prosecutors' offices, as well as specialist international courts and tribunals in dealing with organized crime and corruption. Strengthening collaboration across jurisdictions is needed through regular exchange of information and intelligence, including that sourced from the non-government sector and communities, and networking of personnel within key agencies. The establishment of working parties to undertake systematic horizon-scanning of newly emerging criminogenic opportunities for organized crime and corruption, especially those that relate to climate-change mitigation measures, and the identification of capacities and skills needed to combat emergent crimes, is also important.

A crime-prevention action plan begins by acknowledging that to tackle environmental crime requires urgent action, since the scale, pace and specific nature of the harm means that everyone is affected by it in some way or another. The goal of such intervention is to achieve a robust system of prevention, deterrence, criminalization, enforcement and sanctioning of environmental crime from the local through to global levels. To accomplish this, it is necessary to initiate strategic plans that have immediate effect, that build capacity, and that incorporate staged transitions toward achieving the end-goal, namely the reduction and prevention of environmental crime.

Dilemmas and issues for environmental crime prevention

If preventing harm is the aim, then environmental crime prevention will inevitably have to negotiate the legal–illegal divide, and the distinction between sustainable and unsustainable activity. Likewise, reference to the precautionary principle needs to be more fully articulated in and with crime-prevention principles, practices and policies. In the process of dealing with these issues a number of dilemmas and problems will inevitably be encountered.

Defining the problem

The question of how to define the problem is an intractable and necessary part of the further development of environmental crime prevention. Many areas of harm to humans, eco-systems and non-human animals are presently not criminalized. This includes such destructive, degrading and dehumanizing practices as clear felling of old-growth forests, reliance upon battery-hen forms of egg and poultry production, and use of depleted uranium in weapons. From an analytical point of view, conceptualization of harm ought not to rely upon the legal–illegal distinction per se, especially since some of the world's most environmentally disastrous practices are in fact still legal. Environmental crime prevention may well entail the exposure of negative, degrading and hazardous practices as a prelude to the banning and close control of such practices. New concepts of harm, as informed by ecological sciences and environmental values, will inevitably be developed as part of this process.

Prevention and precaution

The uncertainties surrounding future impacts and consequences means that debate will occur over when preventative measures need to be introduced as a precautionary measure. The politics of ecological sustainability will collide with the interests of economic growth, since greater adherence to the precautionary principle will almost always lead to curtailment of existing profit-making enterprises. Environmental crime prevention has to have a forward-looking component if human, biosphere and non-human interests are to be protected into the future. This means interventions now to guarantee environmental well-being later. Differences in opinion over future consequences means that those who take action now (such as protesting against a large polluting pulp mill) for the sake of up-and-coming generations may well be criminalized in the present. But the history of law reform is built precisely upon such tensions.

Tailoring the responses

While the specificity of the harm demands specificity in response, there are some forms of environmental harm that cannot be contained easily, due to the enormous scope of the problem. For example, the transnational movement and illegal dumping of toxic waste will require international co-operation amongst nation-states and social movement activists. Co-ordination of environmental crime prevention will require free exchange of information and constant surveillance, as well as creative thinking vis-à-vis grappling with issues such as scarcity of water, diminished food sources and expanded need for adequate waste treatment facilities. Climate change and how to deal with it will ultimately require global action. It will also involve the criminalization of what today is considered acceptable practice. For example, the imposition of severe water restrictions and harsher penalties for wasteful water use are just harbingers of things to come.

Problems of displacement

As with conventional crime prevention, displacement may well occur where good environmental crime-prevention measures are introduced. For example, a tightening up of regulation in respect of the shipment of toxic waste in Europe or the US may force companies to relocate their factories to places such as Mexico and Africa, where vulnerable governments have less rigid controls on production and waste treatment. The Not In My Back Yard (NIMBY) syndrome will produce unintended consequences that perpetuate environmental harm. Therefore, a global perspective is essential when it comes to environmental crime prevention. So too, when subsistence fishing, farming and hunting wither due to overexploitation and climate change, then great shifts in human populations and resource use will take place. The environmental refugee poses a whole new set of questions for criminology.

Questions of agency

What the issue of traditional fisheries highlights is that people in different circumstances have different kinds of choices. The small-scale subsistence fisher has much less power, and exercise of agency, than does the large-scale trawler operator. Disparities in power and resources ought not to translate into seeing the more vulnerable and disadvantaged as easy targets for crime prevention (analogous to dealing with 'street crime'), while the criminal actions of corporate polluters and large-scale organizations receive less concerted attention. Moreover, the plight of the dispossessed and disadvantaged means that often any environmental destruction brought about by their actions (cutting down of forests, overfishing) is best remedied by social-justice initiatives rather than criminal-justice interventions, whether these take the form of crime prevention or law enforcement.

Community crime prevention

Environmental crime prevention, as with all good crime-prevention approaches, ought to incorporate the activities of ordinary people as part and parcel of the overall strategy. The involvement of diverse communities in this form of crime prevention likewise raises some interesting issues. For example, some types of engagement may be based upon Neighbourhood Watch models of citizen surveillance and monitoring – as in the case of coastal watch projects intended to alert authorities to changes in environmental conditions or the presence of illegal fishers. The place and status of community members, as volunteers or as paid auxiliary workers, can however be contentious. In Australia's Northern Territory local indigenous people would be ideal coastal watch participants, given their familiarity with the lands and seas of the north. Yet, it is questionable whether indigenous people have been accorded sufficient respect and credibility by law-enforcement officials from agencies such as Customs, much less mainstream police services. In other types of community participation, local residents in urban areas may well play an important and vigilant role in exposing toxic waste spills, release of pollutants into the air, water and land, and illegal harvesting of flora and fauna. How local authorities respond to such groups is crucial to the present and future contours of community crime-prevention initiatives that target environmental harm.

Politics of knowing

Environmental crime prevention ought to be based upon a problem-solving approach, but it is not always easy to discern what is accurate or true when it comes to specific environmental harms. There is a need, therefore, for multi-disciplinary approaches to the study of environmental harm, involving co-operation between different 'experts', including those with traditional and experiential knowledge associated with culture and livelihood (such as indigenous peoples and farmers), as well as sensitivity to ideas and research generated in intellectual domains such as law, zoology, biology, philosophy, sociology and chemistry. On the other hand, we have to be aware that there are major industries of 'denial' of environmental harm, including both corporations and governments, and this places even greater pressure on criminologists to provide affirmative data and interpretations that will bolster specific environmental crime-prevention initiatives.

Conclusion

One of the concerns of this chapter has been to provide a general overview of key elements that together form a central part of environmental crime prevention. These include a vision of the 'good' society; adoption of a problem-solving approach; combination of community crime prevention and situational prevention measures; appreciation of the symbolic as well as instrumental applications of crime prevention; use of a wide range of approaches, techniques and measures; tailoring responses to specific harms and specific types of crime; and acknowledging ongoing dilemmas and challenges for environmental crime prevention. A central tenet of prevention is the notion of precaution. This not only applies to environmental crime prevention, but also to lessons learned. Green criminologists can benefit from applying conventional criminological approaches to current environmental problems. There is much to learn and much yet to do in this area of criminological intervention.

Discussion topics

- Crime prevention is simply the precautionary principle put into practice. Discuss.
- What might a good crime-prevention strategy look like in relation to a specific wildlife crime?
- What might a good crime-prevention strategy look like in relation to a specific pollution crime?
- What measures can be taken to prevent crimes committed by the powerful, including transnational corporations and nation-states?
- What is the relationship between eco-justice and crime prevention?

Further reading

Enticott, G. (2011). 'Techniques of Neutralizing Wildlife Crime in Rural England and Wales', *Journal of Rural Studies*, 27: 200–8.
Lemieux, A., and Clarke, R. (2009). 'The International Ban on Ivory Sales and its Effects on Elephant Poaching in Africa', *The British Journal of Criminology*, 49(4): 451–71.

Pires, S., and Clarke, R. (2011). 'Sequential Foraging, Itinerant Fences and Parrot Poaching in Bolivia', *The British Journal of Criminology*, 51(2): 314–35.

Schneider, J. (2012). *Sold into Extinction: The global trade in endangered species*. Santa Barbara, CA: Praeger.

Wellsmith, M. (2010). 'The Applicability of Crime Prevention to Problems of Environmental Harm: A consideration of illicit trade in endangered species', in R. White (ed.), *Global Environmental Harm: Criminological perspectives*. Cullompton: Willan.

Conclusion

The field of green criminology has grown rapidly in recent years in response to deteriorating environmental conditions. The demise of plant and animal species through both legal and illegal means, the growth in human populations, and the shrinking of natural resources (such as drinking water) and non-renewable resources (such as oil and gas), all add up to enormous pressures on the environment generally. With biodiversity under threat, global resilience to the impacts of climate change is thereby reduced. Yet, the commodification of nature ensures that economic value is, ironically, best realized in conditions of advancing scarcity. For some, environmental degradation and destruction is profitable.

Climate change, in particular, is set to fundamentally transform the present world. The impact of global warming is already being felt, and rises in the Earth's temperature will continue to generate increasingly profound shifts in weather conditions and climatic events. While there is a tendency to attribute extreme-weather-related events to a 'once in a hundred years' experience, the devastation wrought by superstorms like 'Sandy' along the eastern seaboard of the United States in October 2012 was not simply a one-off phenomenon; it marks part of the beginning of regular chaotic events, the predicted result of anthropogenic contributions to greenhouse gas emissions.

Simultaneously, the global pursuit of a Western consumer lifestyle daily adds to the pollution of air, water and land. Factories belch out smoke, as do cars, buses and trucks designed to transport people and goods. The rapid obsolescence of electronic goods not only contributes to the growing waste problem, but also fuels the illegal transference of electronic waste. Vast areas of the planet continue to suffer deforestation in the global scramble for new mega-mines, for coal-seam gas, for land for GMO 'flex' crops, and pastures for cattle and sheep. Changing land uses are creating new toxic towns; while at the same time new forms of recycling of ships and electronic products are producing contaminated communities. And the planet continues to heat up.

For over two decades the study of environmental crime and harm has been the core focus of green criminology. Who is doing what, where and how have been key questions for those working in this area. The main emphasis has been on offenders and perpetrators of harm, and on detailing specific instances of environmental destruction. The pursuit of social and ecological justice has informed much of this work, and in more recent times much greater attention has also been paid to environmental victims.

By its very nature, the development of green criminology as a field of sustained research and scholarship incorporates many different perspectives and strategic emphases. For some, the point of academic concern and practical application is to reform aspects of the present system. Critical analysis, in this context, consists of thinking about ways to improve existing methods of environmental regulation and perhaps to seek better ways to define and legally entrench the notion of environmental crime. It might also involve working with corporations in the hope of encouraging better practices and more benign ways of dealing with the natural environment.

For others, the issues raised by green criminology are inextricably linked to the project of social transformation. From this perspective, analysis focuses on the activities of transnational capitalism, and the interventionist roles of nation-states, and deals with systemic hierarchical inequalities. Such analysis opens the door to identifying the strategic sites for resistance, contestation and struggle on the part of those fighting for environmental, ecological and species justice.

For us, the doing of critical green criminology is about exploring different types of environmental crimes and harms, about putting things into social and ecological context, about challenging the status quo, and about making the world a better place. Responding to environmental harm ultimately requires the testing of existing social and political limits and boundaries. To change the future means changing the institutions of the present. Students of green criminology around the world can play a part in how this future evolves.

Glossary

Term	Explanation
Anthropocentric	Refers to a human-centred view of the world which privileges humans over all other life forms.
Biocentric	Refers to a species-centred view of the world which views humans as just one of a number of beings on the earth, all of which have the same rights, and all of which should be valued equally.
Bio-piracy	The appropriation, mostly by those in the developed world, of the traditional knowledge, technologies and genetic resources of indigenous peoples and those living in developing countries.
Bio-security	The protection of people, animals and ecological systems from the transference of pests and diseases across national and international borders.
Biodiversity	The variety and number of plants, animals, fungi and bacteria within a particular environmental space.
Brown issues	Those environmental issues that impact urban life: for example air pollution and disposal of toxic wastes.
Built environment	Significant sites of human habitation and residency, including urban and rural areas and areas of cross-over, such as major regional concentrations of people, commuter suburbs, zones, etc.
Chlorofluorocarbons	Also known as CFCs. A family of non-toxic, non-flammable chemicals containing carbon, chlorine and fluorine. Used in the manufacture of aerosol sprays, as solvents and to facilitate cooling in refrigerators and air-conditioners. Known to damage the ozone layer; also powerful greenhouse gases.
Climate change	A change of climate which is attributed directly or indirectly to human activity, that alters the composition of the global atmosphere, and which is in addition to natural climate variability observed over comparable time periods.

Commodification	The process by which a resource (e.g. water) is transformed from use-value into exchange-value ('worth' is gauged by how much something will sell for on the commodities market).
Conservation criminology	A specific criminological concern with natural resource conservation and management, based upon legal definitions of environmental crime, and one that seeks to assess and address threats, risks and harms as part of the environmental law enforcement, prevention and regulation processes.
Constructivist green criminology	An approach to the study of environmental harm and crime that emphasizes how categories and labels are socially and politically constructed.
Corporate colonisation	The process by which commercial interests gain control of nature, reflected in varying strategies including genetic changes in food crops, use of plantation forestry, and preference for large-scale technology-dependent and high-yield agricultural and aquacultural methods.
Deep ecology	Views humans as one component of an intricate web of life that includes plants, animals, mountains and rivers, all with rights of their own and whose existence is not simply for human pleasure.
Differential victimization	The disproportionate effect of environmental harms on particular groups based on ethnicity and class. For example, the siting of toxic dumps near people of colour, people in poverty and indigenous communities.
Dioxins	The generic term for a group of environmentally persistent toxic chemicals that can concentrate in body fat and accumulate as they move through the food chain.
Ecocentric	An ecocentric perspective considers issues of social justice to be as important as, and inextricably bound to, issues of ecology. While there is an explicit recognition that humans need to impact upon or utilize non-human nature in order to survive, there is also the realization that humans need to develop ecologically sustainable ways of satisfying their basic needs.
Ecocide	Activities that destroy and diminish the well-being and health of ecosystems and species within these, including humans.
Eco-crime	Intentional acts of harm against the natural environment including ecocide (destruction of the environment on a large scale); geocide (destruction of the earth) and eco-terrorism (terrorism in support of ecological, environmental or animal rights causes).
Eco-feminism	Attempts to connect feminism (a social movement that focuses on issues pertaining to the oppression and rights of women) with ecological perspectives (that focus on various aspects of nature, and the relationship between humans, the biosphere and animals). A key concern is the commonalities between gender oppression and environmental degradation.

Eco-global criminology — A green criminological approach informed by ecological considerations and by a critical analysis that is global in scale and perspective. Based upon eco-justice conceptions of harm, it considers transgressions against humans, non-humans and environments.

Ecological citizenship — Acknowledges that human beings are one component of complex ecosystems that should be preserved for their own sake via the notion of the rights of the environment. It means present generations of humans ought to act in ways that do not jeopardize the existence and quality of life of future generations. It also means we extend the moral community to include non-human nature.

Ecological justice — An approach to the conceptualization of harm within green criminology. Refers to the relationship of human beings generally to the rest of the natural world and includes concerns relating to the health of the biosphere, (and, more specifically, plants and creatures that also inhabit the biosphere). The main concern is with the quality of the planetary environment (that is frequently seen to possess its own intrinsic value) and the rights of other species (particularly animals) to a life free from torture, abuse and destruction of habitat.

Ecological sustainability — Forms of production and consumption that maximize ecological well-being and biodiversity as foundations of the nature/human relationship.
See also **Sustainable development**.

Eco-rights — The reconceptualization of rights to include expanded notions of environmental and community rights, particularly around the concepts of 'common good', 'common property' and sustainable environments.

Ecotage, or ecological sabotage — Acts of sabotage against industries such as forestry and coal-fired power stations, carried out by radical environmental activists to defend the environment.

Eco-terrorism — Refers broadly to violent or illegal acts, such as tree-spiking or damaging laboratories, in support of environmental or animal-rights causes. It is sometimes erroneously applied to legitimate social protests, non-violent forms of civil disobedience and illegal activity that is obtrusive but not violent (such as tree-sitting to protest against logging).

Environmental crime — Environmental harms deemed to be illegal. These includes acts or omissions related to illegal taking of flora and fauna, pollution offences and transportation of banned substances such as radioactive materials.

Environmental criminology — A conventional criminological approach to dealing with environmental crime as legally defined, drawing mainly upon place-based criminology (also known as 'environmental criminology') that concentrates on situational crime prevention.

Environmental harm	Refers to a wide variety of injuries and degradations linked to the use, misuse and poor management of the 'natural environment', including such things as pollution, toxic waste and the killing of plants, soils and animals. Environmental harm can be conceptualized as involving acts and omissions that are both 'legal' and 'illegal'.
Environmental horizon-scanning	A process of looking over the horizon at those issues and trends most likely to involve environmental crime, harm and victimization now and into the future.
Environmental justice	An approach to the conceptualization of harm within green or environmental criminology. Refers to the distribution of environments among peoples in terms of access to and use of specific natural resources in defined geographical areas, and the impacts of particular social practices and environmental hazards on specific populations (e.g. as defined on the basis of class, occupation, gender, age, ethnicity). Concern is with human beings at the centre of analysis, and the focus is on human health and well-being and how these are affected by particular types of production and consumption.
Environmental victimization	The social processes by which specific forms of harm are caused by 'acts' (e.g. dumping of toxic waste) or 'omissions' (e.g. failure to provide safe drinking water), leading to the presence or absence of environmental agents (e.g. poisons, nutrients) that are associated with human injury.
E-waste	Abbreviation for electronic waste. Refers to obsolete, discarded electronic goods such as computers, monitors, televisions, mobile phones and printer cartridges, frequently exported from developed countries to developing countries for the purpose of dismantling and recycling of parts which are often toxic.
Genetically modified organisms	Also known as GMOs. Biological entities created via alteration of the genetic make-up of cells, usually by the insertion, removal or manipulation of individual genes.
Green criminology	Broadly refers to the study by criminologists, of environmental harms, environmental laws and environmental regulations. Within green criminology the three broad approaches to conceptualizing environmental harm are: environmental justice (main focus is on the environment), ecological justice (main focus is on humans) and species justice (main focus is on animals).
Green issues	Refers to the protection and preservation of wilderness areas and conservation issues relating to logging practices, ozone depletion, acid rain and loss of wildlife.
Greenhouse gases	Those gases that contribute to the 'greenhouse effect' contributing to a warming of the atmosphere and the earth's surface. Greenhouse gases on the increase due to human activity include methane, carbon monoxide and nitrous oxide.

Greenwashing	The practice of putting a particular 'corporate spin' on environmental issues and problems. Much of it has to do with image-making, and hence is heavily tied up with public relations and the manipulation of ideas through the mass media.
Indigenous ecological knowledge	The unique, traditional local knowledge existing within and developed around the specific conditions of life for women and men indigenous to a particular geographical area.
Intergenerational equity	The principle of intergenerational equity asserts that future generations have the right to environments that are equal in terms of quality and amenity to that of the present generation.
Malum in se	Refers to conduct that is seen to be inherently wrong by nature, and that is considered serious.
Malum prohibitum	Refers to conduct that is prohibited by law but generally considered less serious than other types of social harm.
Market reduction approach	A crime-prevention strategy designed to disrupt markets in such a way that it reduces opportunities for potential perpetrators to buy, sell and transport illegal commodities.
Not in my backyard (NIMBY)	A political stance that environmentally destructive activities should not occur in one's own local area. Derivatives include NIABY (not in anyone's backyard) and NOPE (not on planet earth).
Persistent organic pollutants	Also known as POPs. Chemicals that remain intact in the environment for long periods, become widely distributed geographically, accumulate in the fatty tissue of living organisms and are toxic to people and wildlife. POPs circulate globally via air and water and are detrimental to human health and the environment.
Precautionary principle	The idea that official action be taken to protect people and environments in cases where there is scientific uncertainty as to the nature of the potential damage or the likelihood of risk.
Privatization	The process of transition from common property to private property, accompanied by a shift toward concentrated private ownership and management, plus greater reliance on market mechanisms (rather than government controls) to distribute goods and services and protect environments.
Radical green criminology	A broad radical orientation towards issues pertaining to environmental harm and crimes against nature, emphasizing questions of power and inequalities related to class, race, ethnicity and gender.
Restorative justice	A way of responding to criminal behaviour through adopting a participatory, problem-solving approach to justice focused on repairing the harm.
Specieist criminology	Refers to a focus on specieism as the main target for criminological research and a critique of anthropocentrism in the construction of environmental issues. Sees species and individual members of species as having intrinsic value and rights.

Glossary

Species justice	An approach to the conceptualization of harm within green criminology represented by those who wish to include consideration of animal rights within the broad perspective. In specific terms, concepts such as speciesism are invoked.
Speciesism	The practice of discriminating against non-human animals because they are perceived as inferior to the human species. In other words, privileging human viewpoints.
Sustainable development	That form of economic development that attempts to minimize environmental damage within the context of existing systems of production and consumption. See also ***Ecological sustainability.***
White issues	Refers to science laboratories and the environmental impact of new technologies, for example genetically modified organisms, food irradiation and nanotechnologies.

References

Aas, K. (2007). *Globalization and Crime*. Los Angeles: Sage.
Adeola, F. (2000). 'Cross-National Environmental Injustice and Human Rights Issues', *American Behavioral Scientist*, 43(4): 686–706.
Agnew, R. (2011). 'Dire Forecast: A theoretical model of the impact of climate change on crime', *Theoretical Criminology*, 16(1): 21–42.
—— (2012). 'It's the End of the World as We Know It: The advance of climate change from a criminological perspective', in R. White (ed.), *Climate Change from a Criminological Perspective*. New York: Springer.
—— (2013). 'The Ordinary Acts that Contribute to Ecocide: A criminological analysis', in N. South and A. Brisman (eds), *The Routledge International Handbook of Green Criminology*. London: Routledge.
Agyeman, J., and Carmin, J. (2011). 'Introduction: Environmental injustice beyond borders', in J. Agyeman and J. Carmin (eds), *Environmental Inequalities Beyond Borders: Local perspectives on global injustices*. Cambridge, MA: MIT Press.
Ahmed, N. (2013). 'The Link Between Intensifying Inequality, Debt, Climate Change, Fossil Fuel Dependency and the Global Food Crisis is Undeniable', *The Guardian*, 6 March 2013. <http://www.guardian.co.uk/environment/blog/2013/mar/06/food-riots-new-normal> (accessed 7 March 2013).
Akech, M., and Mwebaza, R. (2010). *Enforcement of Environmental Crime Laws: A framework training manual for law enforcement agencies*. Pretoria: Institute for Security Studies.
Akella, A., and Cannon, J. (2004). *Strengthening the Weakest Links: Strategies for improving the enforcement of environmental laws globally*. Washington, DC: Conservation International.
Alacs, E., and Georges, A. (2008). 'Wildlife Across Our Borders: A review of the illegal trade in Australia', *Australian Journal of Forensic Sciences*, 40(2): 147–60.
Al-Damkhi, A., Khuraibet, A., Abdul-Wahab, S., and Al-Attar, F. (2009). 'Toward Defining the Concept of Environmental Crime on the Basis of Sustainability', *Environmental Practice*, 11(2): 115–24.
Altman, J., Bek, H., and Roach, L. (1996). 'Use of Wildlife by Indigenous Australians: Economic and policy perspectives', in M. Bomford and J. Caughley (eds), *Sustainable Use of Wildlife by Aboriginal Peoples and Torres Strait Islanders*. Canberra: Bureau of Resource Sciences, Australian Government Publishing Service.
Anderson, K., and McCusker, R. (2005). *Crime in the Australian Fishing Industry: Key issues*, Trends and Issues in Crime and Criminal Justice No. 297. Canberra: Australian Institute of Criminology.

Animal Legal Defense Fund (2007). 'Winning the Case Against Cruelty: Animal bill of rights'. <http://www.aldf.org/billofrights/index/php> (accessed 2 August 2012).

Ascione, F. (2001). 'Animal Abuse and Youth Violence', *Juvenile Justice Bulletin*, September 2001. Washington, DC: Office of Juvenile Justice and Delinquency Prevention, US Department of Justice.

—— (ed.) (2010). *The International Handbook of Animal Abuse and Cruelty: Theory, research, and application*. West Lafayette, IN: Purdue University Press.

Australian Bureau of Statistics (2003). 'Mining and the Environment'. *1301.0 – Year Book Australia, 2003*. Canberra: ABS.

Australian Centre for Geomechanics (2013). 'Deep Mining Brochure 2014'. <http://www.deepmining2014.com/> (accessed 12 June 2013).

Australian and New Zealand Minerals and Energy Council and Minerals Council of Australia (2000). *Strategic Framework for Mine Closure*. Canberra: ANZMEC and MCA.

Ayling, J. (2013). 'What Sustains Wildlife Crime? Rhino horn trading and the resilience of criminal networks', *Journal of International Wildlife Law and Policy*, 16(1): 57–80.

Ayres, I., and Braithwaite, J. (1992). *Responsive Regulation: Transcending the deregulation debate*. New York: Oxford University Press.

Bakan, J. (2004). *The Corporation: The pathological pursuit of profit and power*. London: Constable.

Banerjee, D., and Bell, M. (2007). 'Ecogender: Locating gender in environmental social science', *Society and Natural Resources*, 20: 3–19.

Barbieri, C., Schwarzbold, A., and Rodriguez, M. (2007). 'Environmental Crime Investigation in Arroio do Meio, Rio Grande do Sul, Brazil: Tannery and shoe factory waste landfill case study', *Environmental Forensics*, 8: 361–9.

Bartel, R. (2005). 'When the Heavenly Gaze Criminalises: Satellite surveillance, land clearance regulation and the human–nature relationship', *Current Issues in Criminal Justice*, 16(3), 322–39.

Basel Action Network and Silicon Valley Toxics Coalition (2002). *Exporting Harm: The high-tech trashing of Asia*. Seattle, WA and San Jose, CA: BAN/SVTC.

Baum, M. (2011). '"Room on the Ark?": The symbolic nature of U.S. pet evacuation statutes for nonhuman animals', in C. Freeman, E. Leane, and Y. Watt (eds), *Considering Animals: Contemporary studies in human–animal relations*. Farnham: Ashgate.

Baur, G. (2008). *Farm Sanctuary: Changing hearts and minds about animals and food*. New York: Touchstone.

Beck, U. (1992). *Risk Society: Towards a new modernity*. London: Sage.

Beder, S. (2002). *Global Spin: The corporate assault on environmentalism*, rev. ed. Totnes: Green Books.

—— (2006). *Suiting Themselves: How corporations drive the global agenda*. London: Earthscan.

Beirne, P. (2004). 'From Animal Abuse to Interhuman Violence? A critical review of the progression thesis', *Society & Animals*, 12(1): 39–65.

—— (2007). 'Animal Rights, Animal Abuse and Green Criminology', in P. Beirne and N. South (eds), *Issues in Green Criminology: Confronting harms against environments, humanity and other animals*. Cullompton: Willan.

—— (2009). *Confronting Animal Abuse: Law, criminology and human–animal relationships*. New York: Rowman & Littlefield.

—— (2011). 'Animal Abuse and Criminology: Introduction to special issue', *Crime, Law and Social Change*, 55: 349–57.
Beirne, P., and South, N. (eds) (2007). *Issues in Green Criminology: Confronting harms against environments, humanity and other animals*. Cullompton: Willan.
Bekoff, M. (2010). 'Introduction', in M. Bekoff (ed.), *Encyclopedia of Animal Rights and Animal Welfare*, vol. 1. Santa Barbara, CA: Greenwood Press.
Bell, S., and McGillivray, D. (2008). *Environmental Law*, 7th ed. London: Oxford University Press.
Bell, S., Hampshire, K., and Topalidou, S. (2007). 'The Political Culture of Poaching: A case study from northern Greece', *Biodiversity and Conservation*, 16: 399–418.
Benton, T. (1998). 'Rights and Justice on a Shared Planet: More rights or new relations?', *Theoretical Criminology*, 2(2): 149–75.
—— (2007). 'Ecology, Community and Justice: The meaning of green', in P. Beirne and N. South (eds), *Issues in Green Criminology*. Cullompton: Willan.
Bergin, A., and Allen, R. (2008). *The Thin Green Line: Climate change and Australian policing*, ASPI Special Report, Issue 17. Canberra: Australian Strategic Policy Institute.
Besthorn, F.H. (2004). 'Restorative Justice and Environmental Restoration, Twin Pillars of a Just Global Environmental Policy: Hearing the voice of the victim', *Journal of Societal and Social Policy*, 3(2): 33–48.
—— (2013). 'Speaking Earth: Environmental restoration and restorative justice', in K. van Wormer and L. Walker (eds), *Restorative Justice Today: Practical applications*. Los Angeles: Sage.
Bhattacharjee, B. (2012). 'Threat to Social and Environmental Degradation Embellished: A geographical analysis of Jharia coal-field', *Geo-Analyst*, 2(1): 94–9.
Bisschop, L. (2012a). 'Out of the Woods: The illegal trade in tropical timber and a European trade hub', *Global Crime*, 13(3): 191–212.
—— (2012b). 'Is It All Going To Waste? Illegal transports of e-waste in a European trade hub', *Crime, Law and Social Change*, 58(3): 221–49.
Bisschop, L., and Vande Walle, G. (2013). 'Environmental Victimisation and Conflict Resolution: A case study of e-waste', in R. Walters, D.S. Westerhuis, and T. Wyatt (eds), *Emerging Issues in Green Criminology* (pp. 34–54), Basingstoke: Palgrave Macmillan.
Block, A. (2002). 'Environmental Crime and Pollution: Wasteful reflections', *Social Justice*, 29(1–2): 61–81.
Boekhout van Solinge, T. (2008a). 'Crime, Conflicts and Ecology in Africa', in R. Sollund (ed.), *Global Harms: Ecological crime and speciesism*. New York: Nova Science Publishers.
—— (2008b). 'The Land of the Orangutan and the Bird of Paradise under Threat', in R. Sollund (ed.), *Global Harms: Ecological crime and speciesism*. New York: Nova Science Publishers.
—— (2010a). 'Equatorial Deforestation as a Harmful Practice and a Criminological Issue', in R. White (ed.), *Global Environmental Harm: Criminological perspectives*. Cullompton: Willan.
—— (2010b). 'Deforestation Crimes and Conflicts in the Amazon', *Critical Criminology*, 18: 263–77.
Boekhout van Solinge, T., and Kuijpers, K. (2013). 'The Amazon Rainforest: A green criminological perspective', in N. South and A. Brisman (eds), *Routledge International Handbook of Green Criminology*. London: Routledge.

Borras, S., and Franco, J. (2010). *Towards a Broader View of the Politics of Global Land Grab: Rethinking land issues, reframing resistance*. Initiatives in Critical Agrarian Studies ICAS Working Paper Series No. 001. <http://ramshorn.ca/sites/ramshorn.ca/files/Borras%20%26%20Franco,%20Politics%20of%20Land%20Grab.pdf> (accessed 10 September 2013).

Borras, S., Franco, J., and Wang, C. (2013). 'The Challenge of Global Governance of Land Grabbing: Changing international agricultural context and competing political views and strategies', *Globalizations*, 10(1): 161–79.

Boyanowsky, E. (1999). 'Violence and Aggression in the Heat of Passion and in Cold Blood', *International Journal of Law and Psychiatry*, 22(3–4): 257–71.

Boyd, D. (2003). *Unnatural Law: Rethinking Canadian environmental law and policy*. Vancouver: University of British Columbia Press.

Boyer, P. (2012). 'Wake Up Call from Real World', *The Mercury*, Tasmania, Australia, 23 October 2012: pp. 14–15.

Braithwaite, J. (1993). 'Responsive Business Regulatory Institutions', in C. Coady and C. Sampford (eds), *Business Ethics and the Law*. Sydney: Federation Press.

Braithwaite, J., and Drahos, P. (2000). *Global Business Regulation*. Cambridge: Cambridge University Press.

Braithwaite, J., and Pettit, P. (1990). *Not Just Deserts: A republican theory of criminal justice*. Oxford: Clarendon Press.

Brezina, T., and Kaufman, J.M. (2008). 'What Really Happened in New Orleans? Estimating the threat of violence during the hurricane Katrina disaster', *Justice Quarterly*, 2(4): 701–22.

Brickey, K. (2008). *Environmental Crime: Law, policy, prosecution*. New York: Aspen.

Bricknell, S. (2010). *Environmental Crime in Australia*, AIC Reports Research and Public Policy Series 109. Canberra: Australian Institute of Criminology.

Brisman, A. (2007). 'Toward a More Elaborate Typology of Environmental Values: Liberalizing criminal disenfranchisement laws and policies', *New England Journal on Criminal and Civil Confinement*, 33(2): 283–457.

—— (2008). 'Crime–Environment Relationships and Environmental Justice', *Seattle Journal for Social Justice*, 6(2): 727–817.

—— (2012a). 'The Cultural Silence of Climate Change Contrarianism', in R. White (ed.), *Climate Change from a Criminological Perspective*. New York: Springer.

—— (2012b). 'The Violence of Silence: Some reflections on access to information, public participation in decision-making, and access to justice in matters concerning the environment', *Crime, Law and Social Change*, DOI 10.1007/s10611-013-9416-3.

Brisman, A., and South, N. (2012). 'A Green-cultural Criminology: An exploratory outline', *Crime Media Culture*, 9(1): 1–21.

Brisman, A., Beirne, P., and South, N. (2013). 'A Guide to a Green Criminology', in N. South and A. Brisman (eds), *The Routledge International Handbook of Green Criminology*. London: Routledge.

Brook, D. (1998). 'Environmental Genocide: Native Americans and toxic waste', *American Journal of Economics and Sociology*, 57(1): 105–13.

Brookspan, S., Gravel, A., and Corley, J. (2007). 'Site History: The first tool of the environmental forensics team', in B. Murphy and R. Morrison (eds), *Introduction to Environmental Forensics*, 2nd ed (pp. 23–48). London: Elsevier Academic Press.

Bruno, K., Karliner, J., and Brotsky, C. (1999). *Greenhouse Gangsters vs. Climate Justice*. San Francisco, CA: Transnational Resource & Action Centre.

Bryce, E. (2013). 'Conservationists Warn of an Impending Disaster for Habitats Already Severely Marginalised by Agricultural Change', *The Guardian*, 1 March 2013. <http://www.guardian.co.uk/environment/blog/2013/mar/01/biofuel-habitat-loss-usa> (accessed 2 March 2012).

Bulkeley, H., and Newell, P. (2010). *Governing Climate Change*. London: Routledge.

Bullard, R. (1994). *Unequal Protection: Environmental justice and communities of color*. San Francisco, CA: Sierra Club.

—— (2005a). 'Introduction', in R. Bullard (ed.), *The Quest for Environmental Justice: Human rights and the politics of pollution*. San Francisco, CA: Sierra Club.

—— (2005b). 'Environmental Justice in the Twenty-first Century', in R. Bullard, R. Warren, and G. Johnson (eds), *The Quest for Environmental Justice: Human rights and the politics of pollution*. San Francisco, CA: Sierra Club.

Bullard, R., Warren, R., and Johnson, G. (eds) (2005). *The Quest for Environmental Justice: Human rights and the politics of pollution*. San Francisco, CA: Sierra Club.

Burns, R., and Lynch, M. (2004). *Environmental Crime: A sourcebook*. New York: LFB Scholarly.

Burns, R., Lynch, M., and Stretesky, P. (2008). *Environmental Law, Crime, and Justice*. New York: LFB Scholarly Publishing.

Caneppele, S., Riccardi, M., and Standridge, P. (2013). 'Green Energy and Black Economy: Mafia investments in the wind power sector in Italy', *Crime, Law and Social Change*, 59(3): 319–39.

CapeNature (2007). 'Threats to Biodiversity'. <http://www.capenature.co.za/biodiversity.htm?sm%5Bp1%5D%5Bcategory%5D=602> (accessed 24 August 2010).

Cardwell, P., French, D., and Hall, M. (2011). 'Tackling Environmental Crime in the European Union: The case of the missing victim?', *Environmental Law and Management*, 23(3): 113–21.

Carrabine, E., Cox, P., Lee, M., Plummer, K., and South, N. (2004). *Criminology: A sociological introduction*, 2nd ed. London: Routledge.

Carrington, K., Hogg, R., and McIntosh, A. (2011). 'Resource Boom Underbelly: The criminological impact of mining development', *Australian and New Zealand Journal of Criminology*, 44(3): 335–54.

Cazaux, G. (1999). 'Beauty and the Beast: Animal abuse from a non-speciesist criminological perspective', *Crime, Law and Social Change*, 31: 105–26.

Central Land Council (CLC) (n.d.). 'Caring for Country: Indigenous ecological knowledge'. Alice Springs, Australia. <http://www.clc.org.au/articles/info/indigenous-ecological-knowledge> (accessed 16 June 2013).

Chunn, D., Boyd, S., and Menzies, R. (2002). '"We all live in Bhopal": Criminology discovers environmental crime', in S. Boyd, D. Chunn, and R. Menzies (eds), *Toxic Criminology: Environment, law and the state in Canada*. Halifax, NS: Fernwood.

Cifuentes, E., and Frumkin, H. (2007). 'Environmental Injustice: Case studies from the South', *Environmental Research Letters*, 2: 1–9.

Clapp, J. (2001). *Toxic Exports: The transfer of hazardous wastes from rich to poor countries*. Ithaca, NY and London: Cornell University Press.

Clark, B. (2002). 'The Indigenous Environmental Movement in the United States', *Organization & Environment*, 15(4): 410–42.

Clark, R.D. (2009). 'Environmental Disputes and Human Rights Violations: A role for criminologists', *Contemporary Justice Review*, 12(2): 129–46.

Clarke, R.V. (1980). 'Situational Crime Prevention: Theory and practice', *British Journal of Criminology*, 20(2): 136–47.

—— (ed.) (1997). *Situational Crime Prevention: Successful case studies*, 2nd ed. New York: Harrow & Heston.
—— (2005). 'Seven Misconceptions of Situational Crime Prevention', in N. Tilley (ed.), *Handbook of Crime Prevention and Community Safety*. Cullompton: Willan.
Clarke, R.V., and Eck, J.E. (2005). *Crime Analysis for Problem Solvers in 60 Small Steps*. Washington, DC: US Department of Justice, Office of Community Oriented Policing Services.
Clarke, R.V., and Homel, R. (1997). 'A Revised Classification of Situational Crime Prevention Techniques', in S. Lab (ed.), *Crime Prevention at a Crossroads*. Cincinnati, OH: Anderson.
Cleary, P. (2012). *Mine-Field: The dark side of Australia's resources rush*. Collingwood, VIC: Black Inc.
Clifford, M. (ed.) (1998). *Environmental Crime: Enforcement, policy and social responsibility*. Gaithersburg, MD: Aspen.
Clifford, M., and Edwards, T. (1998). 'Defining "Environmental Crime"', in M. Clifford (ed.), *Environmental Crime: Enforcement, policy and social responsibility*. Gaithersburg, MD: Aspen.
Cohen, S. (1993). 'Human Rights and Crimes of the State: The culture of denial', *Australian and New Zealand Journal of Criminology*, 26(2): 97–115.
Collins, C. (2010). *Toxic Loopholes: Failures and future prospects for environmental law*. Cambridge: Cambridge University Press.
Commission for Environmental Co-operation of North America (CEC) (2001). *Special Report on Enforcement Activities: Report prepared by the North American working group on enforcement and compliance co-operation*. Montreal: CEC.
—— (2005). *Illegal Trade in Wildlife: A North American perspective*. Montreal: CEC. <http://www.cec.org/Storage/58/5059_Illegal-Trade-Wildlife_en.pdf> (accessed 6 September 2006).
Connell, R. (2007). *Southern Theory: The global dynamics of knowledge in social science*. Sydney: Allen & Unwin.
Convention on the Illegal Trade in Endangered Species (CITES) (2012). 'The International Consortium on Combating Wildlife Crime'. <http://www.cites.org/eng/prog/iccwc.php> (accessed 6 September 2012).
Cooper, J.E., and Cooper, M.E. (2012). *Wildlife Forensic Investigation: Principles and practice*. Boca Raton, FL: CRC Press.
Cooper, M. (2002). 'Bush and the Environment: Are the President's policies helping or hurting?', *The CQ Researcher*, 12(7): 865–96.
Cornforth, M. (1976). *Dialectical Materialism: An introduction, vol. 2: Historical materialism*. London: Lawrence and Wishart.
Corporate Watch (2009). 'State Crackdown on Anti-Corporate Dissent: The animal rights movement'. <www.corporatewatch.org/download.php?id=92> (accessed 9 September 2013).
Cottle, S., and Lester, L. (eds) (2012). *Transnational Protests and the Media*. New York: Peter Lang.
Council of Europe (2012). *Manual on Human Rights and the Environment*, 2nd ed. Strasbourg: Council of Europe.
Crawford, A. (2008). 'Plural Policing in the UK: Policing beyond the police', in T. Newburn (ed.), *Handbook of Policing*, 2nd ed. Cullompton: Willan.
Croall, H. (2007). 'Food Crimes', in P. Beirne and N. South (eds), *Issues in Green Criminology: Confronting harms against environments, humanity and other animals*. Cullompton: Willan.

Crofts, P., Morris, T., Wells, K., and Powell, A. (2010). 'Illegal Dumping and Crime Prevention: A case study of Ash Road, Liverpool Council, New South Wales, Australia', *Public Space: The Journal of Law and Social Justice*, 5(4): 1–23.

Crook, S., and Pakulski, J. (1995). 'Shades of Green: Public opinion on environmental issues in Australia', *Politics*, 30(1): 39–55.

Cullinan, C. (2003). *Wild Law: A manifesto for earth justice*. London: Green Books/Gaia Foundation.

Curson, P., and Clark, L. (2004). 'Pathological Environments', in R. White (ed.), *Controversies in Environmental Sociology*. Melbourne: Cambridge University Press.

Dadds, M., Turner, C., and McAloon, J. (2002). 'Developmental Links between Cruelty to Animals and Human Violence', *Australian and New Zealand Journal of Criminology*, 35(3): 363–82.

Davison, A. (2004). 'Sustainable Technology: Beyond fix and fixation', in R. White (ed.), *Controversies in Environmental Sociology*. Cambridge: Cambridge University Press.

Delaney, P., and Shrader, E. (2000). 'Gender and Post-Disaster Reconstruction: The case of hurricane Mitch in Honduras and Nicaragua'. Washington, DC: World Bank.

Deng, W.J., Louie, P.K.K., Liu, W.K., Bi, X.H., Fu, J.M., and Wong, M.H. (2006). 'Atmospheric Levels and Cytotoxicity of PAHs and Heavy Metals in TSP and PM2.5 at an Electronic Waste Recycling Site in Southeast China', *Atmospheric Environment*, 40(36): 6945–55.

de Prez, P. (2000a). 'Excuses, Excuses: The ritual trivialisation of environmental prosecutions', *Journal of Environmental Law*, 12(1): 65–78.

—— (2000b). 'Beyond Judicial Sanctions: The negative impact of conviction for environmental offences', *Environmental Law Review*, 2: 11–22.

DeSombre, E. (2006). *Global Environmental Institutions*. London: Routledge.

Deville, A., and Harding, R. (1997). *Applying the Precautionary Principle*. Sydney: Federation Press.

Dighe, K., and Pettus, L. (2011). 'Environmental Justice in the Context of Environmental Crime', *United States Attorneys' Bulletin*, 59(4): 3–14.

Dobovsek, B., and Pracek, R. (2010). 'Solving Problems Related to Environmental Crime Investigations', in G. Meško, D. Dimitrijević, and C. Fields (eds), *Understanding and Managing Threats to the Environment in South Eastern Europe*. Dordrecht: Springer.

Dodson, L., Piatelli, D., and Schmalzbauer, L. (2007). 'Researching Inequality Through Interpretive Collaborations: Shifting power and the unspoken contract', *Qualitative Inquiry*, 13(6): 821–43.

Dorn, N., Van Daele, S., and Vander Beken, T. (2007). 'Reducing Vulnerabilities to Crime of the European Waste Management Industry: The research base and the prospects for policy', *European Journal of Crime, Criminal Law and Criminal Justice*, 15(1), 23–36.

Duffield, J. (1997). 'Nonmarket Valuation and the Courts: The case of the Exxon Valdez', *Contemporary Economic Policy*, 15(4): 98–110.

Duffy, R. (2010). *Nature Crime: How we're getting conservation wrong*. New Haven, CT: Yale University Press.

Edwards, S. (1998). 'A History of the US Environment Movement', in M. Clifford (ed.), *Environmental Crime: Enforcement, policy and social responsibility*. Gaithersburg, MD: Aspen.

Ellefsen, R., Sollund, R., and Larsen, G. (eds) (2012). *Eco-Global Crimes: Contemporary problems and future challenges*. Farnham: Ashgate.

Elliott, L. (2007). 'Transnational Environment Crime in the Asia Pacific: An 'un(der)securitized' security problem?', *The Pacific Review*, 20(4): 499–522.

Eman, K., Meško, G., and Fields, G.B. (2009). 'Crimes Against the Environment: Green criminology and research challenges in Slovenia', *VARSTVOSLOVJE, Journal of Criminal Justice and Security*, 11(4): 574–92.

Eman, K., Meško, G., Dobovšek, B., and Sotlar, A. (2013). 'Environmental Crime and Green Criminology in South Eastern Europe – Practice and research', *Crime, Law and Social Change*, 59(3): 341–58.

Engdahl, F. (2007). *Seeds of Destruction: The hidden agenda of genetic manipulation*. Montreal: Global Research.

Engel, S., and Martin, B. (2006). 'Union Carbide and James Hardie: Lessons in politics and power', *Global Society*, 20(4), 475–90.

Environmental Investigation Agency (EIA) (2008). *Environmental Crime: A threat to our future*. London: EIA.

Environmental Protection Authority, Victoria (EPA Victoria) (2011). *Compliance and Enforcement Review: Overview of key themes and recommendations for EPA Victoria*. Melbourne: EPA Victoria.

European Environment Agency (2010). *EEA Signals 2010: Biodiversity, climate change and you*. Copenhagen: European Environment Agency.

Europol (2011). Octa 2011: EU Organised Crime Threat Assessment. The Hague: Europol. <https://www.europol.europa.eu/sites/default/files/publications/octa2011.pdf> (accessed 1 June 2013).

Faber, D. (2009). 'Capitalising on Environmental Crime: A case study of the USA polluter-industrial complex in the age of globalization', in K. Kangapunta and I. Marshall (eds), *Eco-Crime and Justice: Essays on environmental crime*. Turin: United Nations Interregional Crime Research Institute (UNICRI).

Farrall, S., Ahmed, T., and French, D. (eds) (2012). *Criminological and Legal Consequences of Climate Change*. Oxford: Hart Publishing.

Fattah, E. (2010). 'The Evolution of a Young, Promising Discipline: Sixty years of victimology, a retrospective and prospective look', in S. Shoham, P. Knepper, and M. Kett (eds), *International Handbook of Victimology*. Boca Raton, FL: CRC Press.

Faure, M., and Heine, G. (2000). *Criminal Enforcement of Environmental Law in the European Union*. Copenhagen: Danish Environmental Protection Agency.

Ferrier, P. (2010). 'The Economics of Agricultural and Wildlife Smuggling', *Trends in Organized Crime*, 13: 219–30.

Field, R. (1998). 'Risk and Justice: Capitalist production and the environment', in D. Faber (ed.), *The Struggle for Ecological Democracy: Environmental justice movements in the US*. New York: Guilford Press.

Findlay, M., Odgers, S., and Yeo, S. (1994). *Australian Criminal Justice*. Melbourne: Oxford University Press.

Finlayson, C. Hon. (2012). 'Whanganui River Agreement Signed', New Zealand Government press release, 30 August 2012. <http://www.beehive.govt.nz/release/whanganui-river-agreement-signed> (accessed 12 June 2013).

Fitzgerald, A., and Baralt, L.B. (2010). 'Media Constructions of Responsibility for the Production and Mitigation of Environmental Harms: The case of mercury-contaminated fish', *Canadian Journal of Criminology and Criminal Justice/La Revue canadienne de criminologie et de justice pénale*, 52(4), 341–68.

Fitzgerald, A.J., Kalof, L., and Dietz, T. (2009). 'Slaughterhouses and Increased Crime Rates: An empirical analysis of the spillover from "the jungle" into the surrounding community', *Organisation and Environment*, 22(2): 158–84.

Flynn, C. (2011). 'Examining the Links between Animal Abuse and Human Violence', *Crime, Law and Social Change*, 55: 453–68.

Food and Agriculture Organization of the United Nations (2011). *State of the World's Forests 2011*. Rome: FAO.

Forni, O. (2010). 'Mapping Environmental Crimes', *Freedom from Fear Magazine*, March 2010: 34–37. Turin: United Nations Interregional Crime Research Institute.

Forsyth, C., Gramling, R., and Wooddell, G. (1998). 'The Game of Poaching: Folk crimes in southwest Louisiana', *Society & Natural Resources: An International Journal*, 11(1): 25–38.

Fortney, D. (2002). 'Thinking Outside the Black Box: Tailored enforcement in environmental criminal law', *Texas Law Review*, 81: 1609.

Foster, J. (2002). *Ecology Against Capitalism*. New York: Monthly Review Press.

Francione, G. (2010). 'Law and Animals', in M. Bekoff (ed.), *Encyclopedia of Animal Rights and Animal Welfare*, vol. 2. Santa Barbara, CA: Greenwood Press.

Franklin, A. (2006). *Animal Nation: The true story of animals and Australia*. Sydney: University of New South Wales Press.

Fraser, D. (2010). 'Animal Welfare', in M. Bekoff (ed.), *Encyclopedia of Animal Rights and Animal Welfare*, vol. 1. Santa Barbara, CA: Greenwood Press.

French, H. (2000). *Vanishing Borders: Protecting the planet in the age of globalization*. New York: Norton.

Friedrichs, D. (2007). 'Transnational Crime and Global Criminology: Definitional, typological and contextual conundrums', *Social Justice*, 34(2): 4–18.

Fussey, P., and South, N. (2012). 'Heading Towards a New Criminogenic Climate: Climate change, political economy and environmental security', in White, R. (ed.), *Climate Change from a Criminological Perspective*. New York: Springer.

Fyfe, N., and Reeves, A. (2009). 'The Thin Green Line? Police perceptions of the challenges of policing wildlife crime in Scotland', in R. Mawby and R. Yarwood (eds), *Policing, Rurality and Governance*. Aldershot: Ashgate.

Gearin, M. (2013). 'Mafia probe nets $1.7 bn in clean energy assets', *ABC News* Australia, 4 April 2013. <http://www.abc.net.au/news/2013-04-03/clean-energy-developer-targeted-over-mafia-links/4608208> (accessed 21 June 2013).

Gedicks, A. (2005). 'Resource Wars against Native Peoples', in R. Bullard (ed.), *The Quest for Environmental Justice: Human rights and the politics of pollution*. San Francisco, CA: Sierra Club Books.

Gerbrandy, G.-J. (2013). 'EU Action Plan Against Wildlife Trafficking'. Presentation at Workshop on Wildlife Crime, Committee on Environment, Public Health and Food Safety. Brussels: D66.

Gibbs, C., Gore, M., McGarrell, E., and Rivers, L. (2010a). 'Introducing Conservation Criminology: Towards interdisciplinary scholarship on environmental crimes and risks', *British Journal of Criminology*, 50(1): 124–44.

Gibbs, C., McGarrell, E., and Axelrod, M. (2010b). 'Transnational White-Collar Crime and Risk: Lessons from the global trade in electronic waste', *Criminology & Public Policy*, 9(3): 543–60.

Gibbs, C., McGarrell, E.F., Axelrod, M., and Rivers, L. (2011). 'Conservation Criminology and the Global Trade in Electronic Waste: Applying a multi-disciplinary research framework', *International Journal of Comparative and Applied Criminal Justice*, 35(4): 269–91.

Gilmour, J. (2002). 'Can Partnerships be an Agent for Change in Corporations?', *Alternative Law Journal*, 27(1): 11–12.

Goldman, M. (1998). 'Inventing the Commons: Theories and practices of the commons' professional', in M. Goldman (ed.), *Privatizing Nature: Political struggles for the global commons*. London: Pluto Press/Transnational Institute.

Grabosky, P. (1994). 'Green Markets: Environmental regulation by the private sector', *Law & Policy*, 16(4): 419–48.

—— (1995). 'Regulation by Reward: On the use of incentives as regulatory instruments', *Law & Policy*, 17(3): 256–79.

Gray, W., and Shimshack, J. (2011). 'The Effectiveness of Environmental Monitoring and Enforcement: A review of the empirical evidence', *Review of Environmental Economics and Policy*, 5(1): 3–24.

Green, E. (2011). 'Telephoning Fish: An examination of the creative deviance used by wildlife violators in the United States', *International Journal of Rural Criminology*, 1(1): 23–39.

Green, P. (2005). 'Disaster by Design: Corruption, construction and catastrophe', *British Journal of Criminology*, 45: 528–46.

Green, P., and Ward, T. (2004). *State Crime: Governments, violence and corruption*. London: Pluto Press.

Greenfield, R. (2009). 'Examining Motivations for Non-Compliance: Waste disposal project'. Queensland: Department of Environment and Resource Management (DERM), November, 2009.

Greenpeace International (2005). *Recycling of Electronic Wastes in China and India: Workplace and environmental contamination*. Amsterdam: Greenpeace International.

Gros, J.G. (2008). 'Trouble in Paradise: Crime and collapsed states in the age of globalization', in N. Larsen and R. Smandych (eds), *Global Criminology and Criminal Justice: Current issues and perspectives*. Peterborough, ON: Broadview Press.

Gullone, E., and Clarke, J. (2010). 'Abuse, Cruelty and Welfare: An Australian perspective', in F. Ascione (ed.), *The International Handbook of Animal Abuse and Cruelty: Theory, research and application*. West Lafayette, IN: Purdue University Press.

Gunningham, N., and Grabosky, P. (1998). *Smart Regulation: Designing environmental policy*. Oxford: Clarendon Press.

Gunningham, N., Norberry, J., and McKillop, S. (eds) (1995). *Environmental Crime, Conference Proceedings*. Canberra: Australian Institute of Criminology.

Haberfeld, M., and Cerrah, I., (eds) (2008). *Comparative Policing: The Struggle for Democratization*. Los Angeles: Sage.

Hackett, S., and Uprichard, E. (2007). *Animal Abuse and Child Maltreatment: A review of the literature and findings from a UK study*. London: National Society for the Prevention of Cruelty to Children (NSPCC).

Haines, F. (1997). *Corporate Regulation: Beyond 'punish or persuade'*. Oxford: Clarendon Press.

Haines, F., and Reichman, N. (2008). 'The Problem that is Global Warming: An introduction', *Law & Policy*, 30(4) 385–93.

Hall, M. (2011). 'Environmental Victims: Challenges for criminology and victimology in the 21st century', *Journal of Criminal Justice and Security*, 4: 371–91.

—— (2013a). *Victims of Environmental Harm: Rights, recognition and redress under national and international law*. London: Routledge.
—— (2013b). 'Victims of Environmental Harms and Their Role in National and International Justice', in R. Walters, D.S. Westerhuis, and T. Wyatt (eds), *Emerging Issues in Green Criminology* (pp. 219–41). Basingstoke: Palgrave Macmillan.
Hallsworth, S. (2011). 'Then They Came for the Dogs!', *Crime, Law and Social Change*, 55: 391–403.
Halsey, M. (2004). 'Against "Green" Criminology', *British Journal of Criminology*, 44(6): 833–53.
—— (2005). *Deleuze and Environmental Damage: The violence of the text*. Farnham: Ashgate.
—— (2013). 'Conservation Criminology and the "General Accident" of Climate Change', in N. South and A. Brisman (eds), *Routledge International Handbook of Green Criminology*. London: Routledge.
Halsey, M., and White, R. (1998). 'Crime, Ecophilosophy and Environmental Harm', *Theoretical Criminology*, 2(3): 345–71.
Halstead, B. (1992). *Traffic in Flora and Fauna*, Trends & Issues in Crime and Criminal Justice No. 41. Canberra: Australian Institute of Criminology.
Hannigan, J. (1995). *Environmental Sociology: A social constructionist perspective*. London: Routledge.
—— (2006). *Environmental Sociology*, 2nd ed. London: Routledge.
Hartman, C., and Squires, G., (eds), (2006). *There is No Such Thing as a Natural Disaster: Race, class and Hurricane Katrina*. New York: Routledge.
Harvey, D. (1996). *Justice, Nature and the Geography of Difference*. Oxford: Blackwell.
Harvey, N. (1998). *Environmental Impact Assessment: Procedures, practice and prospects in Australia*. Melbourne: Oxford University Press.
Hayman, G., and Brack, D. (2002). *International Environmental Crime: The nature and control of environmental black markets*. London: Royal Institute of International Affairs.
Heckenberg, D. (2010). 'The Global Transference of Toxic Harms', in R. White (ed.), *Global Environmental Harm: Criminological perspectives*. Cullompton: Willan.
—— (2011). 'What is a Case Study and What is it Good For?', in L. Bartels and K. Richards (eds), *Qualitative Criminology: Stories from the field*. Sydney: Hawkins Press.
Heckenberg, D., and Johnston, I. (2012). 'Climate Change, Gender and Natural Disasters: Social differences and environment-related victimisation', in R. White (ed.), *Climate Change from a Criminological Perspective*. New York: Springer.
Heckenberg, D., and White, R. (2013). 'Innovative Approaches To Researching Environmental Crime', in N. South and A. Brisman (eds), *Routledge International Handbook of Green Criminology*. London: Routledge.
Herbig, F.J., (2010). 'The Illegal Reptile Trade as a Form of Conservation Crime: A South African criminological investigation', in R. White (ed.), *Global Environmental Harm: Criminological perspectives*. Cullompton: Willan.
Herbig, F.J., and Joubert, S. (2006). 'Criminological Semantics: Conservation criminology – vision or vagary?', *Acta Criminologica*, 19(3): 88–103.
Hernandez, V. (2013). 'Aussie Judge Picks Grapes Over Coal: Thumbs down Rio Tinto's expansion plan in Hunter Valley', *International Business Times*, 16 April 2013. <http://au.ibtimes.com/articles/457451/20130416/aussie-judge-picks-grapes-over-coal-thumbs.htm> (accessed 20 June 2013).

Higgins, P. (2010). *Eradicating Ecocide: Laws and governance to prevent the destruction of our planet*. London: Shepheard-Walwyn.

—— (2012). *Earth is Our Business: Changing the rules of the game*. London: Shepheard-Walwyn.

Higgins, P., Short, D., and South, N. (2013). 'Protecting the Planet: A proposal for a law of ecocide', *Crime, Law and Social Change*, 59(3): 251–66.

Higgins, V., and Natalier, K. (2004). 'Governing Environmental Harms in a Risk Society', in R. White (ed.), *Controversies in Environmental Sociology*. Cambridge: Cambridge University Press.

Hinde, S. (2003). 'The International Environmental Court: Its broad jurisdiction as a possible fatal flaw', *Hofstra Law Review*, 32(2): 727–57

Holtom (2011). 'Shell Case Echoes Call to Eradicate Ecocide', Our World 2.0. United Nations University. <http://ourworld.unu.edu/en/shell-case-echoes-call-to-eradicate-ecocide/> (accessed 25 June 2013).

Homer-Dixon, T. (1999). *Environment, Scarcity and Violence*. Princeton, NJ: Princeton University Press.

Hughes, S.D. (2004). 'The Current Status of Environmental Performance Reporting', *National Environmental Law Review*, No. 4: 41–58.

Hurley, A. (1995). *Class, Race and Industrial Pollution in Gary, Indiana, 1945–1980*. Chapel Hill, NC: University of North Carolina Press.

Ibrahim, D.M. (2006). 'The Anticruelty Statute: A study in animal welfare', *Journal of Animal Law and Ethics*, 1: 175–203.

International Fund for Animal Welfare (2009). 'Fighting Wildlife Trafficking Online'. <http://www.ifaw.org/international/node/680> (accessed 21 June 2013).

International Union for the Conservation of Nature (IUCN) (2011). IUCN Red List of Threatened Species. Glade, Switzerland: IUCN.

Interpol (2009). *Electronic Waste and Organised Crime: Assessing the links*, Phase II Report for the Interpol Pollution Crime Working Group. Lyon: Interpol.

—— (2013) *Environmental Crime Programme: Project LEAF*. Lyon: Interpol. February 2013. <http://www.interpol.int/contentinterpol/search?SearchText=Project+LEAF&x=19&y=8> (accessed 23 March 2013).

—— 'INTERPOL Meeting Aims to Strengthen Cooperation on Environmental Crime Activities' (media release). Lyon: Interpol.

Interpol Pollution Crime Working Group (2007). 'Arguments for Prosecutors of Environmental Crimes', advocacy memorandum, 5 June 2007.

Interpol and United Nations Environment Programme (Interpol and UNEP) (2012). 'Summit Report: International Chiefs of Environmental Compliance and Enforcement'. Lyon: Interpol and UNEP.

Irwin, A. (2001). *Sociology and the Environment: A critical introduction to society, nature and knowledge*. Cambridge: Polity Press/Blackwell.

Israel Police and the Israeli Ministry of Environmental Protection (various dates). See websites <http://www.police.gov.il> and <http://www.sviva.gov.il> (accessed 5 October 2007).

Izzo, V.N. (2009). 'Catastrophes as Crime Scenes: Analysing the legal context', *Law Text Culture*, 13: 108–34.

Jarrell, M., and Ozymy, J. (2012). 'Real Crime, Real Victims: Environmental crime victims and the Crime Victims' Rights Act (CVRA)', *Crime, Law and Social Change*, 58(4): 373–89.

Joines, J. (2012). 'Globalization of E-waste and the Consequence of Development: A case study of China', *Journal of Social Justice*, 2: 1–15.

Julian, R. (2004). 'Inequality, Social Differences and Environmental Resources', in R. White (ed.), *Controversies in Environmental Sociology*. Melbourne: Cambridge University Press.

Kahler, J., and Gore, M. (2012). 'Beyond the Cooking Pot and Pocket Book: Factors influencing noncompliance with wildlife poaching rules', *International Journal of Comparative and Applied Criminal Justice*, 36(2): 103–20.

Kamenetz, A. (2010). 'Why Environmental Activists Embrace Social Media'. FastCompany. com. <http://www.fastcompany.com/1686631/why-environmental-activists-embrace-social-media> (accessed 12 June 2013).

Khagram, S. (2004). *Dams and Development: Transnational struggles for water and power*. Ithaca, NY: Cornell University Press.

Kirkland, L.-H., and Thompson, D. (1999). 'Challenges in Designing, Implementing and Operating an Environmental Management System', *Business Strategy and the Environment*, 8: 128–43.

Klare, M. (2001). *Resource Wars: The new landscape of global conflict*. New York: Owl Books/Henry Holt.

—— (2012). *The Race For What's Left: The global scramble for the world's last resources*. New York: Metropolitan Books/Henry Holt.

Klenovsek, A., and Meško, G. (2010). 'International Waste Trafficking: Preliminary explorations', in G. Meško, D. Dimitrijevic, and C. Fields (eds), *Understanding and Managing Threats to the Environment in South Eastern Europe*. Dordrecht: Springer.

Kluin, H.A. (2013). 'Environmenal Regulation in Chemical Corporations: Preliminary restuls of a case study', in R. Walters, D. Westerhuis, and T. Wyatt (eds), *Emerging Issues in Green Criminology: Exploring power, justice and harm*. Basingstoke: Palgrave Macmillan.

Konisky, D. (2009). 'The Limited Effects of Federal Environmental Justice Policy on State Enforcement', *Policy Studies Journal*, 37(3): 475–96.

Kramer, R. (2013). 'Public Criminology and the Responsibility to Speak in the Prophetic Voice Concerning Global Warming', in E. Stanley and J. McCulloch (eds), *State Crime and Resistance*. London: Routledge.

Kramer, R., and Michalowski, R. (2012). 'Is Global Warming a State-Corporate Crime?', in R. White (ed.), *Climate Change from a Criminological Perspective*. New York: Springer.

Krpan, S. (2011). *Compliance and Enforcement Review: A review of EPA Victoria's approach*. Melbourne: EPA Victoria. <http://epanote2.epa.vic.gov.au/EPA/publications.nsf/2f1c2625731746aa4a256ce90001cbb5/2c81c8735bc744d9ca25783700094c64/$FILE/1368.pdf> (accessed December 2011).

Kuehn, R. (2004). 'Suppression of Environmental Science', *American Journal of Law & Medicine*, 30(2): 333–69.

Lacey, J., Parsons, R., and Moffat, K. (2012). *Exploring the Concept of a Social License to Operate in the Australian Minerals Industry: Results from interviews with industry representatives EP125553*. Brisbane: CSIRO.

Lack, M. (2007). *Catching On? Trade-related measures as a fisheries management tool*. Cambridge: TRAFFIC International.

Lane, P. (1998). 'Ecofeminism Meets Criminology', *Theoretical Criminology*, 2(2): 235–48.

Langton, M. (1998). *Burning Questions: Emerging environmental issues for indigenous peoples in northern Australia*. Darwin: Centre for Indigenous Natural and Cultural Resource Management.

Le Billon, P. (2012). *Wars of Plunder: Conflicts, profits and the politics of resources*. New York: Columbia University Press.

Leiss, W., and Hrudey, S. (2005). 'On Proof and Probability: Introduction to "Law and Risk"', in Law Commission of Canada (ed.), *Law and Risk*. Vancouver: University of British Columbia Press.

Lemieux, A., and Clarke, R. (2009). 'The International Ban on Ivory Sales and its Effects on Elephant Poaching in Africa', *The British Journal of Criminology*, 49(4): 451–71.

Lever-Tracy, C. (2011). *Confronting Climate Change*. London: Routledge.

Levy, D. (1997). 'Environmental Management as Political Sustainability', *Organization & Environment*, 10(2): 126–47.

Liddick, D. (2011). *Crimes Against Nature: Illegal industries and the global environment*. Santa Barbara, CA: Praeger.

Lin, A. (2006). 'The Unifying Role of Harm in Environmental Law', *Wisconsin Law Review*, 3: 898–985.

Lugten, G. (2005). 'Big Fish To Fry – International law and deterrence of the toothfish pirates', *Current Issues in Criminal Justice*, 16(3): 307–21.

Lundgren, K. (2012). *The Global Impact of E-waste: Addressing the challenge*. Geneva: International Labour Organization.

Lynch, M. (1990). 'The Greening of Criminology: A perspective on the 1990s', *The Critical Criminologist*, 2(3): 1–4 and 11–12.

Lynch, M., and Stretesky, P. (2001). 'Toxic Crimes: Examining corporate victimization of the general public employing medical and epidemiological evidence', *Critical Criminology*, 10(3): 153–72.

—— (2003). 'The Meaning of Green: Contrasting criminological perspectives', *Theoretical Criminology*, 7(2): 217–38.

—— (2006). 'Toxic Crimes: Examining corporate victimization of the general public employing medical and epidemiological evidence', in N. South and P. Beirne (eds), *Green Criminology*. Aldershot: Ashgate.

—— (2010). 'Global Warming, Global Crime: A green criminological perspective', in R. White (ed.), *Global Environmental Harm: Criminological perspectives*. Cullompton: Willan.

Lynch, M., Stretesky, P., and Hammond, P. (2000). 'Media Coverage of Chemical Crimes, Hillsborough County, Florida, 1987–97', *British Journal of Criminology*, 40: 112–26.

Lynch, M., Stretesky, P., and McGurrin, D. (2002). 'Toxic Crimes and Environmental Justice: Examining the hidden dangers of hazardous waste', in G. Potter (ed.), *Controversies in White-collar Crime*. Cincinnati, OH: Anderson Publishing.

Lynch, M., Stretesky, P., and Burns, R. (2004). 'Determinants of Environmental Law Violation Fines Against Petroleum Refineries: Race, ethnicity, income, and aggregation effects', *Society and Natural Resources*, 17(4): 343–57.

Lynch, M., Burns, R., and Stretesky, P. (2010). 'Global Warming and State-corporate Crime: The politicalization of global warming under the Bush administration', *Crime, Law and Social Change*, 54: 213–39.

McCarthy, M. (2008). 'Cleared: Jury decides that threat of global warming justifies breaking the law', *The Independent*, 11 September 2008. <http://www.independent.co.uk/environment/climate-change/cleared-jury-decides-that...> (accessed 10 October 2008).

McGrath, M. (2008). 'Extinction Risk Under-Estimated', *BBC News*, 3 July 2008. <http://news.bbc.co.uk/2/hi/science/nature/7487223.stm>(accessed 5 October 2009).

McMullan, J., and Perrier, D. (2002). 'Lobster Poaching and the Ironies of Law Enforcement', *Law & Society Review*, 36(4): 679–720.

Macnaghten, P., and Urry, J. (1998). *Contested Natures*. London: Sage.

MacNair, R. (2002). *Perpetration-Induced Traumatic Stress: The psychological consequences of killing*. Westport, CT: Praeger.

MacLeay Argus (2013). 'Noxious Weed Outbreak Closes Connection Creek', *MacLeay Argus*, 2 April 2013.

Madsen, F. (2009). *Transnational Organized Crime*. London: Routledge.

Magistrates' Association UK (2009). *Costing the Earth: Guidance for sentencers*. London: Magistrates' Association.

Maher, J., and Pierpoint, H. (2011). 'Friends, Status Symbols and Weapons: The use of dogs by youth groups and youth gangs', *Crime, Law and Social Change*, 55: 405–20.

Maier-Katkin, D., Mears, D.P., and Bernard, T.J. (2009). 'Towards a Criminology of Crimes Against Humanity', *Theoretical Criminology*, 13: 227–55.

Mandiberg, S. (2009). 'Locating the Environmental Harm in Environmental Crimes', *Utah Law Review*, 4: 1177–222.

Mapsofworld.com (2011). World Maps in 800 Different Themes. <http://www.mapsofworld.com/> (accessed June 2011).

Mares, D. (2013). 'Climate Change and Crime: Monthly temperature and precipitation anomalies and crime rates in St Louis MO 1990–2009', *Crime, Law and Social Change*, 59(2): 185–208. DOI 10.1007/s10611-013-9411-8.

Markham, A. (2009). 'Animal Cruelty Sentencing in Australia and New Zealand', in P. Sankoff and S. White (eds), *Animal Law in Australasia: A new dialogue*. Sydney: Federation Press.

Massari, M., and Monzini, P. (2004). 'Dirty Business in Italy: A case-study of illegal trafficking in hazardous waste', *Global Crime*, 6(3–4): 285–304.

Mehta, M. (2009). *In the Public Interest: Landmark judgement and orders of the Supreme Court of India on environment and human rights*, vols 1–3. New Delhi: Prakriti Publications.

Melrose, S. (2009). 'Naturalistic Generalization', in A.J. Mills, G. Durepos, and E. Wiebe (eds), *Encyclopedia of Case Study Research*. Thousand Oaks, CA: Sage.

Merchant, C. (2005). *Radical Ecology: The search for a liveable world*. New York: Routledge.

Meško, G., Dimitrijevic, D., and Fields, C. (eds) (2010). *Understanding and Managing Threats to the Environment in South Eastern Europe*. Dordrecht: Springer.

Meyers, G., McLeod, G., and Anbarci, M. (2006). 'An International Waste Convention: Measures for achieving sustainable development', *Waste Management and Research*, 24(6): 505–13.

Mgbeoji, I. (2006). *Global Biopiracy: Patents, plants, and indigenous knowledge*. Vancouver: University of British Columbia Press.

Michalowski, R., and Kramer, R. (2006). *State-Corporate Crime: Wrongdoing at the intersection of business and government*. New Brunswick, NJ: Rutgers University Press.

Mileti, D.S. (1999). *Disasters by Design: A reassessment of natural hazards in the United States*. Washington, DC: Joseph Henry Press.

Millner, F., and Ruddock, K. (2011). 'Climate Litigation: Lessons learned and future opportunities', *Alternative Law Journal*, 36(1): 27–32.

Mitchell, D. (2008). *A Note on Rising Food Prices*, Policy Research Working Paper 4682. Washington, DC: World Bank, Development Prospects Group.

Mjoset, L. (2009). 'The Contextualist Approach to Social Science Methodology', in D. Byrne and C.C. Ragin (eds), *The Sage Handbook of Case-based Methods* (pp. 39–68). Thousand Oaks, CA: Sage.

Mol, H. (2013). '"A Gift from the Tropics to the World": Power, harm and palm oil', in R. Walters, D. Westerhuis, and T. Wyatt (eds), *Emerging Issues in Green Criminology*. New York: Palgrave Macmillan.

Mudge, S. (2008). 'Environmental Forensics and the Importance of Source Identification', in R. Hester and R. Harrison (eds), *Environmental Forensics*, Issues in Environmental Science and Technology No 26. Cambridge: Royal Society of Chemistry.

Munro, S. (2012). *Rich Land, Wasteland – How coal is killing Australia*. Sydney: Pan Macmillan Australia.

Murphy, B., and Morrison, R. (eds) (2007). *Introduction to Environmental Forensics*. Amsterdam: Elsevier.

Mwebaza, R. (2010). *Annual Regional Conference of Judges on Environmental Security in Eastern Africa: Summary of presentations*. Pretoria: Institute for Security Studies.

Naik, A. (2010). Causes of Pollution. *Buzzle*. 22 October 2010. <http://www.buzzle.com/articles/causes-of-pollution.html> (accessed 13 January 2012).

Natali, L. (2010). 'The Big Grey Elephants in the Backyard of Huelva, Spain', in R. White (ed.), *Global Environmental Harm: Criminological perspectives*. Cullompton: Willan.

National Heritage Trust (NHT) (2003). *Weed Management Guide: Salvinia*. National Heritage Trust, Australia. <http://www.environment.gov.au/biodiversity/invasive/weeds/publications/guidelines/wons/pubs/s-molesta.pdf > (accessed 13 June 2013).

National Toxics Network Inc. (n.d.). 'The Precautionary Principle Gets Real'. Rivett ACT: National Toxics Network. <http://ntn.org.au/wp/wp-content/uploads/2010/02/precautionaryprinciplegetreal.pdf>.

Ngoc, A.C., and Wyatt, T. (2012). 'A Green Criminological Exploration of Illegal Wildlife Trade in Vietnam', *Asian Criminology*, 8: 129–42.

Nobo, C., and Pfeffer, R.D. (2012). 'Natural Disasters and Crime: Criminological lessons from hurricane Katrina', in R. White (ed.), *Climate Change from a Criminological Perspective*. New York: Springer.

Nurse, A. (2011). 'Policing Wildlife: Perspectives on criminality in wildlife crime', *Papers from the British Criminology Conference*, 11: 38–53.

—— (2013a). *Animal Harm: Perspectives on why people harm and kill animals*. Farnham: Ashgate.

—— (2013b). 'Perspectives on Criminality in Wildlife', in R. Walters, D.S. Westerhuis, and T. Wyatt (eds), *Emerging Issues in Green Criminology*. Basingstoke: Palgrave Macmillan.

—— (2013c). 'Privatising the Green Police: The role of NGOs in wildlife law enforcement', *Crime, Law and Social Change*, 59(3): 305–18.

O'Brien, G., O'Keefe, P., Rose, J., and Wisner, B. (2006). 'Climate Change and Disaster Management', *Disasters*, 30(1): 64–80.

O'Brien, R., Goetz, A., Scholte, J., and Williams, M. (2000). *Contesting Global Governance: Multilateral economic institutions and global social movements*. Cambridge: Cambridge University Press.

O'Connor, J. (1994). 'Is Sustainable Capitalism Possible?', in M. O'Connor (ed.), *Is Capitalism Sustainable?: Political economy and the politics of ecology.* New York: Guilford Press.

O'Hear, M. (2004). 'Sentencing the Green-collar Offender: Punishment, culpability, and environmental crime', *Journal of Criminal Law & Criminology,* 95(1): 133–276.

Ogden, R. (2008). 'Fisheries Forensics: The use of DNA tools for improving compliance, traceability and enforcement in the fishing industry', *Fish and Fisheries,* 9, 462–72.

Oles, T., and Hammarlund, K. (2011). 'The European Landscape Convention, WindPower, and the Limits of the Local: Notes from Italy and Sweden', *Landscape Research,* 36(4): 471–84. <http://dx.doi.org/10.1080/01426397.2011.582942> (accessed 4 September 2013).

Organisation for Economic Co-operation and Development (OECD) (2009). *OECD Work on the International Futures Programme: Horizons.* Paris: OECD Publications. <http://www.oecd.org/sti/futures/42332642.pdf> (accessed 4 September 2013).

Orr, D. (1991). 'The Economics of Conservation', *Conservation Biology,* 5(4): 439–41.

O'Sullivan, S. (2009). 'Australasian Animal Protection Laws and the Challenge of Equal Consideration', in P. Sankoff and S. White (eds), *Animal Law in Australasia.* Sydney: Federation Press.

Page, T. (1991). 'Sustainability and the Problem of Valuation', in R. Costanza (ed.), *Ecological Economics: The science and management of sustainability.* New York: Columbia University Press.

Pakulski, J., Tranter, B., and Crook, S. (1998). 'The Dynamics of Environmental Issues in Australia: Concerns, clusters and carriers', *Australian Journal of Political Science,* 33(2): 235–52.

Pallo, B., and Barken, M. (2010). 'The Domestic and International Dimensions of Methylmercury Contamination in Tuna: An analysis of the efficacy of the fish advisory standards of two federal agencies', in D. Taylor (ed.), *Environmental and Social Justice: An international perspective,* Research in Social Problems and Public Policy, vol. 18: 179–210. Bingley: Emerald.

Parks and Wildlife Service Tasmania (1998). 'Threatened Species Listing Statement: Swan Galaxias (Galaxias Fontanus)', Hobart: Threatened Species Unit, Parks and Wildlife Service. <http://www.dpiw.tas.gov.au/inter,nsf/Attachments/RLIG-5428GN/$FILE/swan.pdf> (accessed 5 August 2010).

Pasadakis, N., Gidarakos, E., Kanellopoulou, G., and Spanoudakis, N. (2008), 'Identifying Sources of Oil Spills in a Refinery by Gas Chromatography and Chemometrics: A case study', *Environmental Forensics,* 9: 33–9.

Pearce, F., and Tombs, S. (1998). *Toxic Capitalism: Corporate crime and the chemical industry.* Aldershot: Dartmouth Publishing.

Pearse, G. (2012). *Greenwash: Big brands and carbon scams.* Collingwood, VIC: Black Inc.

Pečar, J. (1981). 'Ekološka kriminaliteta in kriminologija', *Revija za kriminalistiko in kriminologijo,* 34(1), 33–45. (See Eman, Meško, and Fields 2009.)

—— (1988). '"Kriminološko" javno mnenje', *Zbornik znanstvenih razprav,* 48: 105–25. (See Eman, Meško, and Fields 2009.)

—— (1996). 'Podjetniška kriminaliteta', *Revija za kriminalistiko in kriminologijo,* 47(3): 203–12. (See Eman, Meško, and Fields 2009.)

Pellow, D. (2004). 'The Politics of Illegal Dumping: An environmental justice framework', *Qualitative Sociology,* 27(4): 511–25.

—— (2007). *Resisting Global Toxics: Transnational movements for environmental justice.* Cambridge, MA: MIT Press.
Peng, C., Xueming, S., Hongyong, Y., and Dengsheng, L. (2011). 'Assessing Temporary and Weather Influences on Property Crime in Beijing, China', *Crime, Law and Social Change*, 55: 1–13.
Petrisor, I. (2007). 'Background in Environmental Forensics: "Raising the awareness?"', *Environmental Forensics*, 8: 195–8.
Petrisor, I., and Westerfield, W. (2008). 'Hot Environmental and Legal Topics: Greenhouse gas regulation and global warming', *Environmental Forensics*, 9: 1–5.
Petrossian, G. (2012). *The Decision to Engage in Illegal Fishing: An examination of situational factors in 54 countries.* Unpublished thesis, October 2012. Rutgers University Community Repository. <http://mss3.libraries.rutgers.edu/dlr/showfed.php?pid=rutgers-lib:38695> (accessed 26 June 2013).
Pezzullo, P., and Sandler, R. (2007). 'Introduction: Revisiting the environmental justice challenge to environmentalism', in R. Sandler and P. Pezzullo (eds), *Environmental Justice and Environmentalism: The social justice challenge to the environmental movement.* Cambridge, MA: MIT Press.
Pinderhughes, R. (1996). 'The Impact of Race on Environmental Quality: An empirical and theoretical discussion', *Sociological Perspectives*, 39(2): 231–48.
Pink, G. (2010). 'Governmental Co-ordination to Enforce Environmental Laws: The experiences of an Australian environmental regulator'. Canberra: Compliance and Enforcement Branch, Department of the Environment, Water, Heritage and the Arts.
Pink, G., and Lehane, J. (2012). 'Environmental Enforcement Networks: Their role in climate change enforcement', in R. White (ed.), *Climate Change from a Criminological Perspective.* New York: Springer.
Pires, S.F. (2012). 'The Illegal Parrot Trade: A literature review', *Global Crime*, 13(3): 176–90.
Pires, S., and Clarke, R. (2011). 'Sequential Foraging, Itinerant Fences and Parrot Poaching in Bolivia', *The British Journal of Criminology*, 51(2): 314–35.
—— (2012). 'Are Parrots CRAVED? An analysis of parrot poaching in Mexico', *Journal of Research in Crime and Delinquency*, 49(1): 122–46.
Pires, S., and Moreto, W. (2011). 'Preventing Wildlife Crimes: Solutions that can overcome the "tragedy of the commons"', *European Journal on Criminal Policy and Research*, 17(2): 101–23.
Plumwood, V. (2005). 'Gender, Eco-Feminism and the Environment', in R. White (ed.), *Controversies in Environmental Sociology.* Melbourne: Cambridge University Press.
Pollan, M. (2007). 'Unhappy Meals', *New York Times Magazine*, 28 January: 38–47: 65–70.
Pollard, R. (2008). 'Animals, Guardianship and the Local Courts: Toward a practical model for advocacy', Animals theme, *Reform.* Sydney: Australian Law Reform Commission.
Preston, B. (2007). 'Principled Sentencing for Environmental Offences – Part 2: Sentencing considerations and options', *Criminal Law Journal*, 31(3): 142–64.
—— (2011a). 'Operating an Environment Court: The experience of the Land and Environment Court of New South Wales and 12 benefits of judicial specialisation in environmental law', Keynote address at *Renewing Environmental Law: A Conference*

for Public Interest Environmental Law Practitioners. Vancouver: University of Victoria Environmental Law Centre, West Coast Environmental Law and Ecojustice.
—— (2011b). 'The Use of Restorative Justice for Environmental Crime', *Criminal Law Journal*, 35: 136–45.
Preston, B., and Donnelly, H. (2008a). *Achieving Consistency and Transparency in Sentencing for Environmental Offences*, Monograph 32, June 2008. Sydney: Judicial Commission of New South Wales.
—— (2008b). 'The Establishment of an Environmental Crime Sentencing Database in New South Wales', *Criminal Law Journal*, 32: 214–38.
Priest, M. (1997–8). 'The Privatization of Regulation: Five models of self-regulation', *Ottawa Law Review*, 29(2): 233–302.
Pring, G., and Pring, C. (2009). *Greening Justice: Creating and improving environmental courts and tribunals*. Washington, DC: The Access Initiative.
Purvis, N., and Busby, J. (2004). 'The Security Implications of Climate Change for the UN System', in *Environmental Change and Security Project Report*. Washington, DC: Woodrow Wilson International Center for Scholars.
Putt, J., and Anderson, K. (2007). *A National Study of Crime in the Australian Fishing Industry*, Research and Public Policy Series, No. 76. Canberra: Australian Institute of Criminology.
Realff, M.J., Raymond, M., and Ammons, J.C. (2004). 'E-waste: An opportunity', *Materials Today*, 7(1): 40–45.
Regan, T. (2004). *Empty Cages: Facing the challenge of animal rights*. Lanham, MD: Rowman & Littlefield.
Richardson, L., and Loomis, J. (2009). 'The Total Economic Value of Threatened, Endangered and Rare Species: An updated meta-analysis', *Ecological Economics*, 68(5): 1535–48.
Rix, S. (2002). 'Globalisation and Corporate Responsibility', *Alternative Law Journal*, 27(1): 16–22.
Robin, M.-M. (2010). *The World According to Monsanto: Pollution, corruption and the control of our food supply*. New York: New Press.
Robinson, B. (2003). 'Review of the Enforcement and Prosecution Guidelines of the Department of Environmental Protection of Western Australia'. Perth: Communication Edge.
Robyn, L. (2002). 'Indigenous Knowledge and Technology', *American Indian Quarterly*, 26(2): 198–220.
Rock, P. (2007). 'Theoretical Perspectives ON Victimisation', in S. Walklate (ed.), *Handbook of Victims and Victimology*. Cullompton: Willan.
Rodriguez, H., Quarantelli, E., and Dynes, R. (eds) (2007). *Handbook of Disaster Research*. New York: Springer.
Rolston, H. (2010). 'Wild Animals and Ethical Perspectives', in M. Bekoff (ed.), *Encyclopedia of Animal Rights and Animal Welfare*, vol. 2. Santa Barbara, CA: Greenwood Press.
Rosen, G., and Smith, K. (2010). 'Summarizing the Evidence on the International Trade in Illegal Wildlife', *EcoHealth*, 7: 24–32.
Rosoff, S., Pontell, H., and Tillman, R. (1998). *Profit Without Honor: White-collar crime and the looting of America*. Upper Saddle River, NJ: Prentice Hall.
Rotton, J., and Cohn, E. (2003). 'Global Warming and US Crime Rates: An application of routine activity theory', *Environment and Behavior*, 35(6): 802–25.

Rovics, D. (2007). 'Pivotal Moment in the Green Scare', *Capitalism Nature Socialism*, 18(3): 8–16.
Rowe, R. (2007). 'Wanted: More bio-detectives', Higher Education, *The Australian*, 17 January, p. 26.
Ruggiero, V. (1996). *Organized and Corporate Crime in Europe: Offers that can't be refused*. Aldershot: Dartmouth.
Ruggiero, V., and South, N. (2010). 'Critical Criminology and Crimes Against the Environment', *Critical Criminology*, 18(4), 245–50.
Rush, S. (2002). 'Aboriginal Resistance to the Abuse of Their National Resources: The struggles for trees and water', in S. Boyd, D. Chunn, and R. Menzies (eds), *Toxic Criminology: Environment, law and the state in Canada*. Halifax, NS: Fernwood Publishing.
Ryder, R. (2010). 'Specieism', in M. Bekoff (ed.), *Encyclopedia of Animal Rights and Animal Welfare*, vol. 2. Santa Barbara, CA: Greenwood Press.
Saha, R., and Mohai, P. (2005). 'Historical Context and Hazardous Waste Facility Siting: Understanding temporal patterns in Michigan', *Social Problems*, 52(4): 618–48.
Sankoff, P., and White, S. (eds) (2009). *Animal Law in Australasia: A new dialogue*. Sydney: Federation Press.
Sarangi, S. (1996). 'The Movement in Bhopal and Its Lessons', *Social Justice*, 23(4): 100–8.
Schaedla, W. (2007). 'Wildlife Smuggling: Augmenting Southeast Asia's intergovernmental response', in L. Elliott (ed.), *Transnational Environmental Crime in the Asia-Pacific: A workshop report* (pp. 42–51). Canberra: Australian National University.
Schlosberg, D. (2007). *Defining Environmental Justice: Theories, movements and nature*. Oxford: Oxford University Press.
Schmidt, C. (2004). 'Environmental Crimes: Profiting at the earth's expense', *Environmental Health Perspectives*, 112(2): A96–A103.
Schneider, J. (2008). 'Reducing the Illicit Trade in Endangered Wildlife: The market reduction approach', *Journal of Contemporary Criminal Justice*, 24(3): 274–95.
—— (2012). *Sold into Extinction: The global trade in endangered species*. Santa Barbara, CA: Praeger.
Schwarzer, S., De Bono, A., Giuliani, D., Kluser, S., and Peduzzi, P. (2005). 'E-waste, the hidden side of IT equipment's manufacturing and use', Environment Alert Bulletin No. 5. Geneva: UNEP/DEWA/GRID.
Scott, D. (2005a). 'When Precaution Points Two Ways: Confronting "West Nile Fever"', *Canadian Journal of Law and Society*, 20(2): 27–65.
—— (2005b). 'Shifting the Burden of Proof: The precautionary principle and its potential for the "democratization" of risk', in Law Commission of Canada (ed.), *Law and Risk*. Vancouver: University of British Columbia Press.
Secretariat of the Convention on Biological Diversity (2010). *Global Biodiversity Outlook 3*. Montreal: SCBD.
Setiono, B. (2007). 'Fighting Illegal Logging and Forest-related Financial Crimes: The anti-money-laundering approach', in L. Elliot (ed.), *Transnational Environmental Crime in the Asia-Pacific: A workshop report*. Canberra: Australian National University.
Serpell, J. (2010). 'Companion Animals', in M. Bekoff (ed.), *Encyclopedia of Animal Rights and Animal Welfare*, vol. 1. Santa Barbara, CA: Greenwood Press.
Shah, A. (2013). 'Biodiversity', *Global Issues: Social, political, economic and environmental issues that affect us all*. 3 March 2013. <http://www.globalissues.org/issue/169/biodiversity> (accessed 16 June 2013).

Shelley, T., and Crow, M. (2009). 'The Nature and Extent of Conservation Policing: Law enforcement generalists or conservation specialists?', *American Journal of Criminal Justice*, 34(1): 9–27.

Shiva, V. (2008). *Soil Not Oil: Environmental justice in an age of climate crisis*. Brooklyn: South End Press.

Shuttleworth, K. (2012). 'Agreement Entitles Whanganui River to Legal Identity', *The New Zealand Herald*, 30 August 2012. <http://www.nzherald.co.nz/nz/news/article.cfm?c_id=1&objectid=10830586> (accessed 12 June 2013).

Siegel, L.J. (2011). 'Enterprise Crime: White-collar and green-collar crime', in *Criminology*, 11th ed., Stamford Connecticut: Cengage Learning: 441–74.

Silva, C., and Jenkins-Smith, H. (2007). 'The Precautionary Principle in Context: US and EU scientists' prescriptions for policy in the face of uncertainty', *Social Science Quarterly*, 88(3): 640–64.

Simon, D. (2000). 'Corporate Environmental Crimes and Social Inequality: New directions for environmental justice research', *American Behavioral Scientist*, 43(4): 633–45.

Situ, Y., and Emmons, D. (2000). *Environmental Crime: The criminal justice system's role in protecting the environment*. Thousand Oaks, CA: Sage.

Sixty Minutes, Australia (2012). 'Firestorm'. Reporter Allison Langdon. 27 September 2012. <http://sixtyminutes.ninemsn.com.au/article.aspx?id=8539564> (accessed June 2013).

Skinnider, E. (2011). *Victims of Environmental Crime – Mapping the issues*. Vancouver: International Centre for Criminal Law Reform and Criminal Justice Policy. <http://www.icclr.law.ubc.ca/files/2011/Victims%20of%20Environmental%20Crime.pdf> (accessed 14 October 2012).

Smandych, R., and Kueneman, R. (2010). 'The Canadian–Alberta Tar Sands: A case study of state-corporate environmental crime', in R. White (ed.), *Global Environmental Harm: Criminological perspectives*. Cullompton: Willan.

Smandych, R., and Larsen, N. (2008). 'Introduction: Foundations for a global criminology and criminal justice', in N. Larsen, and R. Smandych (eds), *Global Criminology and Criminal Justice: Current issues and perspectives*. Peterborough, ON: Broadview Press.

Smith, D., and Vivekananda, J. (2007). *A Climate of Conflict: The links between climate change, peace and war*. London: International Alert.

Smith, R., and Anderson, K. (2004). *Understanding Non-compliance in the Marine Environment*, Trends & Issues in Crime and Criminal Justice No. 275. Canberra: Australian Institute of Criminology.

Snider, L. (2000). 'The Sociology of Corporate Crime: An obituary (or: Whose knowledge claims have legs?)', *Theoretical Criminology*, 4(2): 169–206.

—— (2010). 'Framing E-waste Regulation: The obfuscating role of power', *Criminology & Public Policy*, 9(3): 569–77.

Snyder, R.A. (2013). 'Two Years On: The legacy of BP-Deepwater Horizon oil spill', *The Conversation*, 27 March 2013, Conversation Media Group. <http://theconversation.com/two-years-on-the-legacy-of-the-bp-deepwater-horizon-oil-spill-12754> (accessed September 2013).

Solano, J., and Ferrero-Waldner, B. (2008). *Climate Change and International Security*, paper from the High Representative and the European Commission to the European Council. Brussels: European Union.

Sollund, R. (2008). 'Causes for Speciesism: Difference, distance and denial', in R. Sollund (ed.), *Global Harms: Ecological crime and speciesism*. New York: Nova Science Publishers.
—— (2011). 'Expressions of Speciesism: The effects of keeping companion animals on animal abuse, animal trafficking and species decline', *Crime, Law and Social Change*, 55: 437–51.
—— (2012a). 'Speciesism as Doxic Practice Versus Valuing Difference and Plurality', in R. Ellefsen, R. Sollund, and G. Larsen (eds), *Eco-global Crimes: Contemporary problems and future challenges*. Farnham: Ashgate.
—— (2012b). 'Oil Production, Climate Change and Species Decline: The case of Norway', in R. White (ed.), *Climate Change from a Criminological Perspective*. New York: Springer.
—— (2013). 'Animal Trafficking and Trade: Abuse and species injustice', in R. Walters, D.S. Westerhuis, and T. Wyatt (eds), *Emerging Issues in Green Criminology* (pp. 72–92). Basingstoke: Palgrave Macmillan.
South, N. (1998a). 'A Green Field for Criminology? A proposal for a perspective', *Theoretical Criminology*, 2(2): 211–33.
—— (1998b). 'Corporate and State Crimes Against the Environment: Foundations for a green perspective in European criminology', in V. Ruggiero, N. South, and I. Taylor (eds), *The New European Criminology*. London: Routledge.
—— (2007). 'The "Corporate Colonisation of Nature": Bio-prospecting, bio-piracy and the development of green criminology', in P. Beirne and N. South (eds), *Issues in Green Criminology: Confronting harms against environments, humanity and other animals*. Devon: Willan.
—— (2010). 'The ecocidal tendencies of Late Modernity: Transnational crime, social exclusions, victims and rights', in R. White (ed.), *Global Environmental Harm: Criminological Perspectives* (pp. 228–47). Devon: Willan.
—— (2012). 'Climate Change, Environmental (In)security, Conflict and Crime', in S. Farrall, D. French, and T. Ahmed (eds), *Climate Change: Legal and criminological implications*. Oxford: Hart.
South, N., and Beirne, P. (2006). *Green Criminology*, International Library of Criminology, Criminal Justice & Penology (second series). Aldershot: Ashgate.
South, N., and Brisman, A. (eds) (2013a). *The Routledge International Handbook of Green Criminology*. London: Routledge.
—— (2013b). 'Critical Green Criminology, Environmental Rights and Crimes of Exploitation', in S. Winlow and R. Atkinson (eds), *New Directions in Crime and Deviancy*. London: Routledge.
South, N., and Wyatt, T. (2011). 'Comparing Illicit Trades in Wildlife and Drugs: An exploratory study', *Deviant Behaviour*, 32: 538–61.
Spapens, T. (2011). 'Cross-Border Police Cooperation in Tackling Environmental Crime', INECE Conference Proceedings, pp. 237–49.
Spencer, D.C., and Fitzgerald, A. (2013). 'Three Ecologies, Transversality and Victimization: The case of the British Petroleum oil spill', *Crime, Law and Social Change*, 59: 209–23.
Stanley, E. (2008). *Torture, Truth and Justice: The case of Timor-Leste*. London: Routledge.

Steele, J. (2001). 'Participation and Deliberation in Environmental Law: Exploring a problem-solving approach', *Oxford Journal of Legal Studies*, 21(3): 415–42.

Stephens, S. (1996). 'Reflections on Environmental Justice: Children as victims and actors', *Social Justice*, 23(4): 62–86.

Stone, C. (1972). 'Should Trees Have Standing?: Toward legal rights for natural objects', *Southern California Law Review*, 45: 450–87.

Stop Illegal Fishing Programme (n.d.). 'Environmental Courts Prove to be Effective', Stop Illegal Fishing Case Study Series 02. <http://www.stopillegalfishing.com/doc/environmental_courts_prove_to_be_effective.pdf> (accessed 11 September 2013).

Stretesky, P. (2006). 'Corporate Self-Policing and the Environment', *Criminology*, 44(3): 671–708.

Stretesky, P., and Hogan, M. (1998). 'Environmental Justice: An analysis of superfund sites in Florida', *Social Problems*, 45(2): 268–87.

Stretesky, P., and Knight, O. (2013). 'The Uneven Geography of Environmental Enforcement NGOs', in R. Walters, D. Westerhuis, and T. Wyatt (eds), *Emerging Issues in Green Criminology: Exploring power, justice and harm*. Basingstoke: Palgrave Macmillan.

Stretesky, P., and Lynch, M. (1999). 'Corporate Environmental Violence and Racism', *Crime, Law and Social Change*, 30: 163–84.

—— (2009). 'A Cross-National Study of the Association Between Per Capita Carbon Dioxide Emissions and Exports to the United States', *Social Science Research*, 38: 239–50.

Stretesky, P., Long, M., and Lynch, M. (2013). *The Treadmill of Crime: Political economy and green criminology*. London: Routledge.

Sunstein, C., and Nussbaum, M. (2006). *Animal Rights: Current debates and new directions*. Oxford: Oxford University Press.

Sutherland, W.J., and Woodroof, H.J. (2009). 'The Need for Environmental Horizon Scanning', *Trends in Ecology and Evolution*, 24(10): 523–7.

Sutherland, W.J., Clout, M., Cote, I., Daszak, P., Depledges, M.H., Fellman, L., Fleishman, E., Garthwaites, R., Gibbons, D.W., De Lurio, J., Impey, A.J., Lickorish, F., Lindenmayer, D., Madgwick., J., Margerison, C., Maynard, T., Peck, L.S., Prior, S., Redford. K.H., Schalemann, J.P.W., Spalding, M., and Watkinson, A.R. (2009). 'A Horizon Scan of Global Conservation Issues for 2010', *Trends in Ecology and Evolution*, 25(1): 1–7.

Sutton, A., Cherney, A., and White, R. (2013). *Australian Crime Prevention: Principles, policies and practices*. Melbourne: Cambridge University Press.

Suzuki, D. (2010). *The Legacy: An elder's vision for our sustainable future*. Vancouver: Greystone Books.

Svard, P.-A. (2008). 'Protecting the Animals? An abolitionist critique of animal welfarism and green ideology', in R. Sollund (ed.), *Global Harms: Ecological crime and speciesism*. New York: Nova Science Publishers.

Sykes, G.M., and Matza, D. (1957). 'Techniques of Neutralization: A theory of delinquency', *American Sociological Review*, 22(6): 664–70.

Tailby, R., and Gant, F. (2002). *The Illegal Market in Australian Abalone*, Trends & Issues in Crime and Criminal Justice No. 225. Canberra: Australian Institute of Criminology.

Takemura, N. (2012). 'Uncontrollable Nuclear Power Accidents and Fatal Environmental Harm: Why we have not been ready for the impacts of climate change', in R. White (ed.), *Climate Change from a Criminological Perspective*. New York: Springer.

Teclaf, L.A. (1994). 'Beyond Restoration: The case of ecocide', *Natural Resources Journal*, Fall: 933–56.
Thomson, I., and Boutilier, R. (2011). 'Social License to Operate', in P. Darling (ed.), *SME Mining Engineering Handbook*. Littleton, CO: Society for Mining, Metallurgy and Exploration.
Thomson, I., and Joyce, S. (2006). 'Changing Mineral Exploration Industry Approaches to Sustainability', in M. Doggett and J. Parry (eds), *Wealth Creation in the Minerals Industry: Integrating science, business and education*. Littleton, CO: Society of Economic Geologists.
Thornton, W.E., and Voigt, L. (2007). 'Disaster Rape: Vulnerability of women to sexual assaults during hurricane Katrina', *Journal of Public Management & Social Policy*, 2007: 23–49.
Tilley, N. (2006). 'Knowing and Doing: Guidance and good practice in crime prevention', in J. Knutsson and R. Clarke (eds), *Putting Theory to Work: Implementing situational crime prevention and problem-oriented policing*, Crime Prevention Studies, Vol. 20. New York: Criminal Justice Press.
Tomkins, K. (2005). 'Police, Law Enforcement and the Environment', *Current Issues in Criminal Justice*, 16(3): 294–306.
Tranoris, P. (2012). 'Needed Reform in Italian Wind Energy Policy', *EK130Wind: Introduction to Wind Energy*, 12 March 2012. <http://blogs.bu.edu/ek130 wind/2012/12/03/needed-reform-in-italian-wind-energy-policy/> (accessed 4 September 2013).
Tranter, B. (2004). 'The Environment Movement: Where to from here?', in R. White (ed.), *Controversies in Environmental Sociology*. Cambridge: Cambridge University Press.
Tsing, A. (2005). *Friction: An ethnography of global connection*. Princeton, NJ: Princeton University Press.
UNISDR (2007). *Environment and Disaster Risk: Emerging perspectives*. Prepared on behalf of the ISDR Working Group on Environment and Disaster Reduction. Geneva. <http://postconflict.unep.ch/publications/env_vulnerability.pdf> (accessed October 2010).
United Nations Development Programme (2010). Biodiversity Conservation and Sustainable Land Management. Website information, UNDP (accessed 11 January 2010).
United Nations Environment Programme (UNEP) (1992). *Rio Declaration on the Environment and Development*. New York: UN.
—— (2006). 'Call for Global Action on E-waste'. New York: UNEP.
—— (2007a). *Global Environment Outlook 4*. Nairobi: UNEP.
—— (2007b). *Judicial Training Modules on Environmental Law: Application of environmental law by national courts and tribunals*. Nairobi: UNEP.
—— (2010). Fact Sheet 'Disasters and Conflicts'. Geneva: UNEP. <http://www.unep.org/pdf/brochures/DisastersAndConflicts.pdf> (accessed 4 September 2013).
—— (2011). *UNEP Year Book: Emerging issues in our global environment 2011*. Nairobi: UNEP.
—— (2012). *Global Environment Outlook 5*. Nairobi: UNEP.
—— (2013). 'Threats to Biodiversity'. <http://www.unep-wcmc.org/threats-to-biodiversity_52.html> (accessed 4 September 2013).
United Nations Office for Drugs and Crime (UNODC) (2011). *Transnational Organized Crime in the Fishing Industry: Focus on: Trafficking in persons, smuggling of migrants, illegal drugs trafficking*. Vienna: United Nations.

United States Environmental Protection Agency (2001). *Report Prepared for 13th Interpol Forensic Science Symposium, Lyon, France, October 16–19*. Washington, DC: USEPA Office of Criminal Enforcement, Forensics, and Training Environmental Crime.

United States House of Representatives Committee on Energy and Commerce Minority Staff (2011). *Chemicals Used in Hydraulic Fracturing*. Washington, DC: US House of Representatives.

Van Daele, S., Vander Beken, T., and Dorn, N. (2007). 'Waste Management and Crime: Regulatory, business and product vulnerabilities', *Environmental Policy and Law*, 37(1): 34–8.

Van Dijk, J. (2008). *The World of Crime: Breaking the silence on problems of security, justice, and development across the world*. Los Angeles and Vancouver: Sage and University of British Columbia Press.

Vidal, J. (2013). 'Shell to Resume Niger Delta Oil Spill Compensation Talks', *The Guardian*, 20 June 2013. <http://www.guardian.co.uk/environment/2013/jun/19/shell-niger-delta-oil-spill-talks> (accessed 25 June 2013).

Volpe, M.R. (2007). 'Restorative Justice in Post-Disaster Situations: Untapped potential', *Cardozo Journal of Conflict Resolution*, 8: 611–22.

Waldman, L. (2007). 'When Social Movements Bypass the Poor: Asbestos pollution, international litigation and Griqua cultural identity', *Journal of Southern African Studies*, 33(3): 577–600.

Wall, E., and Beardwood, B. (2001). 'Standardizing Globally, Responding Locally: The new infrastructure, ISO 14000, and Canadian agriculture', *Studies in Political Economy*, 64: 33–58.

Walter, M. (ed.) (2013). *Social Research Methods*. South Melbourne: Oxford University Press.

Walters, B. (2005). 'Let the People Speak', *Current Issues in Criminal Justice*, 16(3): 340–50.

—— (2011). 'Enlarging Our Vision of Rights: The most significant human rights event in recent times?', *Alternative Law Journal*, 36(4): 263–68.

Walters, R. (2004). 'Criminology and Genetically Modified Food', *British Journal of Criminology*, 44(1): 151–67.

—— (2005). 'Crime, Bio-Agriculture and the Exploitation of Hunger', *British Journal of Criminology*, 46(1): 26–45.

—— (2009). 'Crime Is in the Air: Air pollution and regulation in the UK', 'What is crime?' project, Briefing 8. London: Centre for Crime and Justice Studies.

—— (2010). 'Toxic Atmospheres: Air pollution, trade and the politics of regulation', *Critical Criminology*, 18: 307–23.

—— (2011). *Eco Crime and Genetically Modified Food*. London: Routledge.

—— (2013a). 'Air Crimes and Atmospheric Justice', in N. South and A. Brisman (eds), *The Routledge International Handbook of Green Criminology*. London: Routledge.

—— (2013b). 'Eco Mafia and Environmental Crime', in K. Carrington, M. Ball, E. O'Brien, and J. Tauri (eds), *Crime, Justice and Social Democracy: International perspectives*. Basingstoke: Palgrave Macmillan.

Walters, R., and Martin, P. (2013). 'Crime and the Commodification of Carbon', in R. Walters, D.S. Westerhuis, and T. Wyatt (eds), *Emerging Issues in Green Criminology*. Basingstoke: Palgrave Macmillan.

Walters, R., and Westerhuis, D.S. (2013). 'Green Crime and the Role of Environmental Courts', *Crime, Law and Social Change*, 59: 279–90.

Walters, R., Westerhuis, D., and Wyatt, T. (eds) (2013). *Emerging Issues in Green Criminology*. Basingstoke: Palgrave Macmillan.

Warchol, G. (2004). 'The Transnational Illegal Wildlife Trade', *Criminal Justice Studies*, 17: 57–73.

Warchol, G., Zupan, L., and Clarke, W. (2003). 'Transnational Criminality: An analysis of the illegal wildlife market in Southern Africa', *International Criminal Justice Review*, 13: 1–26.

Webster, J. (2010). 'Sentience and Animal Protection', in M. Bekoff (ed.), *Encyclopedia of Animal Rights and Animal Welfare*, vol. 2. Santa Barbara, CA: Greenwood Press.

Weidenhamer, J.D., and Clement, M.L. (2007). 'Leaded Electronic Waste is a Possible Source Material for Lead-Contaminated Jewelry', *Chemosphere*, 69(7): 1111–15.

Wellsmith, M. (2010). 'The Applicability of Crime Prevention to Problems of Environmental Harm: A consideration of illicit trade in endangered species', in R. White (ed.), *Global Environmental Harm: Criminological perspectives*. Cullompton: Willan.

—— (2011). 'Wildlife Crime: The problems of enforcement', *European Journal on Criminal Policy and Research*, 17(2): 125–48.

Westerhuis, D. (2013). 'A Harm Analysis of Environmental Crime', in R. Walters, D.S. Westerhuis, and T. Wyatt (eds), *Emerging Issues in Green Criminology*. Basingstoke: Palgrave Macmillan.

White, R. (2002). 'Environmental Harm and the Political Economy of Consumption', *Social Justice*, 29(1&2): 82–102.

—— (2003). 'Environmental Issues and the Criminological Imagination', *Theoretical Criminology*, 7(4): 483–506.

—— (2005a). 'Environmental Crime in a Global Context: Exploring the theoretical and empirical complexities', *Current Issues in Criminal Justice*, 16(3): 271–85.

—— (2005b). 'Stifling Environmental Dissent: On SLAPPS and Gunns', *Alternative Law Journal*, 30(6): 268–73.

—— (2007). 'Green Criminology and the Pursuit of Social and Ecological Justice', in P. Beirne and N. South (eds), *Issues in Green Criminology: Confronting harms against environments, humanity and other animals*. Devon: Willan.

—— (2008a). *Crimes Against Nature: Environmental criminology and ecological justice*. Cullompton: Willan.

—— (2008b). 'Depleted Uranium, State Crime and the Politics of Knowing', *Theoretical Criminology*, 12(1): 31–54.

—— (ed.) (2009a). *Environmental Crime: A reader*. Cullompton: Willan.

—— (2009b). 'Climate Change and Social Conflict: Toward an eco-global research agenda', in K. Kangaspunta and I. Marshall (eds), *Eco-Crime and Justice: Essays on environmental crime*. Turin: United Nations Interregional Crime Research Institute (UNICRI).

—— (2009c). 'Researching Transnational Environmental Harm: Ethical issues, technical problems and political dilemmas', *International Journal of Comparative & Applied Criminal Justice*, 33(2): 229–48.

—— (2009d). 'Toxic Cities: Globalising the problem of waste', *Social Justice*, 35(3): 107–19.

—— (ed.) (2010a). *Global Environmental Harm: Criminological perspectives*. Devon: Willan.

—— (2010b). 'Transnational Environmental Crime and Eco-Global Criminology', in S. Shoham, P. Knepper, and M. Kett (eds), *International Handbook of Criminology*. New York: Taylor and Francis.

—— (2010c). 'Environmental Law Enforcement: The importance of global networks and collaborative practices', *Australasian Policing: A Journal of Professional Practice and Research*, 3(1): 2–16.

—— (2010d). 'Prosecution and Sentencing in Relation to Environmental Crime: Recent socio-legal developments', *Crime, Law and Social Change*, 53(4): 365–81.

—— (2011a). *Transnational Environmental Crime: Toward an eco-global criminology*. London: Routledge.

—— (2011b). 'Environmental Law Enforcement: The importance of global networks and collaborative practices', *Australasian Policing: A Journal of Professional Practice and Research*, 3(1): 2–16.

—— (2012a). 'The Criminology of Climate Change', in R. White (ed.), *Climate Change from a Criminological Perspective*. New York: Springer.

—— (ed.) (2012b). *Climate Change from a Criminological Perspective*. New York: Springer.

—— (2012c). 'Climate Change and Paradoxical Harm', in S. Farrell, D. French, and T. Ahmed (eds), *Legal and Criminological Consequences of Climate Change*. London: Hart.

—— (2012d). 'NGO Engagement in Environmental Law Enforcement: Critical reflections', *Australasian Policing: A Journal of Professional Practice and Research*, 4(1): 7–11.

—— (2012e). 'Environmental Forensic Studies and Toxic Towns', *Current Issues in Criminal Justice*, 24(1): 107–21.

—— (2013a). 'Eco-global Criminology and the Political Economy of Environmental Harm', in N. South and A. Brisman (eds), *Routledge International Handbook of Green Criminology*. London: Routledge.

—— (2013b). *Environmental Harm: An eco-justice perspective*. Bristol: Policy Press.

—— (2013c). 'Environmental Crime and Problem-solving Courts', *Crime, Law and Social Change*, DOI 10.1007/s10611-013-9414-5.

White, R., and Graham, H. (2010). *Working With Offenders: A guide to concepts and practices*. Cullompton: Willan.

White, R., and Habibis, D. (2005). *Crime and Society*. Melbourne: Oxford University Press.

White, R., and Heckenberg, D. (2011). 'Environmental Horizon Scanning and Criminological Theory and Practice', *European Journal of Criminal Policy and Research*, 17(2): 87–100.

—— (2013). 'Key Issues in the Policing of Hazardous Waste Disposal', *Australian Environmental Review*: 28(5): 604–8.

White, R., and Perrone, S. (2005). *Crime and Social Control*, 2nd ed. Melbourne: Oxford University Press.

White, S. (2009). 'Animals in the Wild: Animal welfare and the law', in P. Sankoff and S. White (eds), *Animal Law in Australasia: A new dialogue*. Sydney: Federation Press.

Whyte, D. (2004). 'All That Glitters Isn't Gold: Environmental crimes and the production of local criminological knowledge', *Crime Prevention and Community Safety: An international journal*, 6(1): 53–63.

Williams, C. (1996). 'An Environmental Victimology', *Social Justice*, 23(4): 16–40.

—— (2009). 'An Environmental Victimology', in R. White (ed.), *Environmental Crime: A reader* (pp. 200–22). Cullompton: Willan.

Wise, S.M. (2001). 'A New Species of Rights Rattling the Cage: Toward legal rights for animals', *California Law Review*, 89: 207–29

—— (2004). 'Resources on Animals and the Law', *Reference Librarian*, 41(86): 36–42. <http://dx.doi.org/10.1300/J120v41n86_04> (accessed 6 September 2006).

World Health Organization (2013). 'Children's Environmental Health: Air pollution'. <http://www.who.int/ceh/risks/cehair/en/> (accessed 22 June 2013).

Wright Mills, C. (1959). *The Sociological Imagination*. New York: Oxford University Press.

Wyatt, T. (2012). *Green Criminology and Wildlife Trafficking: The illegal fur and falcon trades in Russia Far East*. Saarbrücken: Lambert Academic Publishing.

—— (2012b). 'Agricultural Harm and the Missed Opportunity of Rio + 20: Tanya Wyatt considers the environmental and social impacts of Western Demands', *Criminal Justice Matters*, 90(1): 8–9.

—— (2013). *Wildlife Trafficking: A deconstruction of the crime, the victims, and the offenders*. Basingstoke: Palgrave Macmillan.

Wynne, B. (1996). 'May the Sheep Safely Graze? A reflexive view of the expert/lay knowledge divide', in S. Lash, B. Szerszynski, and B. Wynne (eds), *Risk, Environment and Modernity: Toward a new ecology*. London: Sage.

Yates, R. (2007). 'Debating "Animal Rights" Online: The movement–countermovement dialectic revisited', in P. Beirne and N. South (eds), *Issues in Green Criminology: Confronting harms against environments, humanity and other animals*. Cullompton: Willan.

—— (2011). 'Criminalizing Protests About Animal Abuse: Recent Irish experience in global context', *Crime, Law and Social Change*, 55: 469–82.

Young, J. (2011). *The Criminological Imagination*. Cambridge: Polity Press.

Young, N. and Matthews, R. (2010). *The Aquaculture Controversy in Canada: Activism, policy, and contested science*. Vancouver: University of British Columbia Press.

Zechman, M. (2002). 'Forensics Come to Environmental Claims: Forensic tools used in the medical field are now being applied to solve environmental problems and to investigate claims', *Risk & Insurance Online*, 14 October 2002.

Zehr, H. (1990). *Changing Lens: A new focus for crime and justice*. Scottdale, PA: Herald Press.

Zhang, Li, Hua, N., and Sun, S. (2008). 'Wildlife Trade, Consumption and Conservation Awareness in Southwest China', *Biodiversity Conservation*, 17: 1493–516.

Zimmerman, M.E. (2003). 'Black Market for Wildlife: Combating transnational organized crime in the illegal wildlife trade', *Vanderbilt Journal of Transnational Law*, 36: 16–57.

Zipfel, I. (2012). 'The Fiery Coalfields of Jharia', *The Global Journal*, 9 July 2012. <http://theglobaljournal.net/article/view/772/> (accessed 14 March 2013).

Index

[*Note*: page numbers in **bold** refer to tables, page numbers in *italics* refer to figures, page numbers in ***bold italics*** refer to boxes.]

abatement 264
abuse of animals 14, 117–136; animals and criminology 117–119; conclusion 136; and cruelty 124–128; human categorization of animals 119–123; introduction 117; wildlife crime/illegal trade 128–136
accountability 214, 216, 231
accountable regulation 214
acid rain 37, 154, 158, 199
acknowledgement 51
action evaluation 245
activism 46, 52, 61, 63–64, 118, 123, 158, 186–192, 229, 242, 250–251
ADLF *see* Animal Defense League Fund
advocacy 51, 95, 119, 135, 183, 192
AELERT *see* Australasian Environmental Law Enforcement and Regulators Network
affective elements 63–64
Africa 14, 33, 37, 62, 68, 94–95
agency 293
Agent Orange 12, 54
aggression 108
Agnew, Robert 42, 110–111
agribusiness 141–143
air pollution 9, 30, 113, 156–159, 185, 296
Akella, A. 224
algae blooms 238
alteration in human behaviour 108
alternative data sources ***91***
ambiguity 9, 62, 128, 232, 259
American Pet Products Association 135
Amnesty International 189

analytical framework of green criminology 46–48
Anderson, K. 224
Animal Defense League Fund 135
animal liberation movements 46
animal rights 30, 46–47, 117, 123, 130–131, 133–136
animal-assisted therapy 119
animals and criminology 117–119
Antarctic ozone hole 107
anthropocentric perspective 19–20, 42, 46–47, 57, 66, 75, 113–114
anti-privatization 107
anti-social behaviour 117–118
appearance of 'green criminology' 7
appendices to CITES ***139***
applying notions of justice 50–53; justice as acknowledgement 51; justice as engagement 51; justice as fairness 50; justice as functioning 51–53
approaches to compliance 205–210
aquaculture 243, 279
Arctic 40, 72, 76, 104, 141
arms trafficking 39, 140
arrest 225
arson 238
asbestos poisoning 75, 94, 180
assault 77, 91
assisted colonization 152
asylum seeking 108
Athabasca tar sands 56, 112–113, 169, 172
Australasian Environmental Law Enforcement and Regulators Network 226

Australia 12, 37–38, 54, 56, 75, 85, 94, 104, 118, 120, 124, 130–132, 141, 145, 150, 168–172, 177, 190, 219
authoritative regulation 214–215
automated video monitoring 241
autonomy 259
awareness raising 181–182, 211
Axelrod, M. 19
Ayres, I. 202

banned dogs 118–119
Basel Action Network 229
Basel Convention on the Control of Transboundary Movements 10, 36
basic survival 109
basis of horizon-scanning *41–42*
BCCL *see* Bharat Coking Coal Limited
Beck, U. 61, 248
Beirne, P. 20, 128, 131
Bell, S. 268
best practice 226–227
bestiality 118
Bharat Coking Coal Limited 170
Bhopal 186–191
bio-insecurity 140–143, 149
bio-mechanics 238
bio-piracy 17, 107, 141, 143, 148–149
bio-security 142, 149–150
bio-technology 107
biocentric perspective 66
biocentrism 65
biodiversity 26, 28, 31, 33, 58, 137–155; exploitation of nature 140–143; flex crops, GMOs 146–150; importance of 138–140; protecting 150–154; reductions in 143–146; threats to 137–155
biofuels 145–147
biomass 146
black marketeering 57, 108
Boyd, D. 205
BP Amoco 157
BP Horizon oil spill 74, 171, 190
Brack, D. 205–206
Braithwaite, J. 202
bribery 144
Bricknell, S. 265
Brisman, A. 19
'brown' environmental crime 14–15
'brown' issues 70
built environment 68, 76, 86
Bullard, R. 167–168, 190

burden of proof 238
bush broker 150
bush meat trade 37
bush medicine 141
bush tender 150

Canada 37, 56, 81, 102, 113, 130–131, 140, 143–144, 172
cancer 235, 251
Caneppele, S. 289
Cannon, J. 224
capability 51–53
capitalism responsibility for environmental degradation 22
capitalism and transformation of nature *34*
carbon emission trading 54, 56, 105, 108–109, 288
carbon tender 150
Carrabine, E. 14
case studies: BP Horizon oil spill 74; city of Guiyu 163; coal seam fire 170; green criminology in Slovenia 15–16; horizon-scanning 42; Mafia 289–290; Niger Delta 55; river 'rights' 184–185; salvinia 151–152; South African environmental court 273–274
categorization of animals 119–123, *120–121*
categorizing environmental harm 67–70, *67*; focal considerations 68; geographical considerations 68; locational considerations 68–69; temporal considerations 69
causality 265
cause 41
censorship 63
CFCs *see* release of chlorofluorocarbons
chain of enforcement *225*
chains of causation 12
chaotic events 296; *see also* disasters
characteristics of harm 97
chemical fingerprinting 239
chemical hazards 244–245
Chernobyl 37, 190, 248
Chevron 157
child abuse 117
chronological analysis 290
CITES *see* Convention on International Trade of Endangered Species
city of Guiyu 163
clean air 236, 265
clear felling 9, 11–13, 27, 38, 66, 130, 291

334 Index

climate change 3, 30, 42–43, 57–58, 76, 95, 101–116; conclusion 115; ecocide 112–114; and global warming 101–111; introduction 101; state–corporate crime 112–114
climate-induced migration 106–107, 109
climate-related disaster 28
cloning of human tissue 70
coal seam fire 169–170, 296
coercion 217
collaborative practices 215–216, 225–228, 230, 290–291
collapse of public order 110
collective security 108, 134
collusion 113, 131, 230
colonialism 79–80
colouring environmental issues *70*
commitment 192
commodification of nature 12, 32, 296–297
commodity chains 71–72
communities and change analysis 108
community crime prevention 293
community risk assessment ***244–245***
companion animals 118, 121–122, 127, 134–135, 218
company analysis 290
comparative criminology 39
compensation 56, 115, 176, 268–269
compliance 204–210, 214, 220–221, 223, 241, 257–259, 272, 283
complicating factors 253
concept of balance 75
concept of ecocide 54–58
concept of harm 181
conceptual foundations 5–98; dimensions of environmental crime 60–78; eco-global criminology 25–44; eco-justice, ecocide 45–59; environmental crime 7–24; researching environmental harm 79–98
conceptualizing environmental harm *30*
conflict timber 144
congregation of plastic waste 38, 56, 107, 158–159, 267
consciousness 60, 180, 268
conservation criminology 18–19, 63, 130, 140
conservation police 219
conservation-dependent species 153
considerations of harm **67**
consistent regulation 214
constraints in data collection **90**

constructionism 61
constructivist green criminology 19
contamination forensics 241–242
context bias 252
continuum of regulation **202**
contours of global capitalism 25–26, 31–35
contrarianism 102, 236
controlling trade 139
Convention on International Trade of Endangered Species 10, 35, 130–133, 138, *139*, 150, 221; appendices to *139*
Convention for Prevention of Maritime Pollution 35
conventional criminology *see* legal conceptions of harm
conventional street crime 77
conviction of crime 225
Corexit 74
corporate colonization of nature 34, 140–143
corporate crimes 77
corporate responsibility for environmental degradation 22
corruption 74, 221, 286–288, 291
cost-benefit analysis 259
Council of Europe 54
counter-terrorism 118–119
Cox, P. 14
creative architecture 277
crime, environmental 7–24, 29–31, 106–111, 276–295; and climate change 106–111, **110**; conclusion 23; definition of green criminology 8–9; and environmental harm 9–13; introduction 7–8; and justice 257–259; prevention of 276–295; studying environmental harm 13–17; systemic causes of environmental harm 17–22
criminal profiling 205–206
criminal responsibility 91
criminalization 276–280
criminogenic mechanisms 109
critically endangered species 153
cross-border transference 35, 107, 160
cross-pollination 148
cruelty 124–128
cultural domination 51
cyanide 68

'dangerous' breeds 118–119
data collection sources 88–92
'data dots' 242

data-deficient species 153
dealing holistically 53
dealing with illegal fishing 280–283, *281–283*
decriminalization 213
defining problem 291
definition of 'green criminology' 8–9
definition of transnational environmental crime 35–36
deforestation 12, 14, 82, 106, 113, 144–145, 239, 296–297
degradation of environment 12, 21–22, 54, 69–70, 106, 130, 154, 203–204, 233
demise of polar bears 40
denial 109, 113–114, 179, 243, 294
derogatory language 51
desensitization 118
desertification 37, 107, 154
detection of crime 225
determining seriousness of offences *262–264*
deterrence 274
Deville, A. 156
different types of space *73*
differing views of EMS *212*
dilemmas for crime prevention 291–294; *see also* issues for crime prevention
dimensions of environmental crime 60–78; categorizing environmental harm 67–70; conclusion 78; disasters and crime 76–77; eco-philosophy 65–67; introduction 60; social constructions of environmental harm 60–64; transference of harm across space–time 70–76
direct impact on environment 262
dirty energy 112
dirty industries 27, 54, 112, 115, 157, 173
disasters 28, 64, 74–77, 105, 109–110, 296
discourse 244–246
discrimination 16, 49, 123, 166
disease 69
displacement 105, 140, 292
disposal problems 34
disposal of toxic waste 9, 57, 107
dispossessed 16, 95, 172
disrespect 51
dissent 192
distributive justice 50–51, 270
DNA testing 88, 238–241, 282–283
Dodson, L. 93
dog fighting 125
dolphin fishing 35

domestic animals 120–121
dose–response relationship 244
downsizing 213
drinking water 32, 103, 106, 171, 187, 272, 296
drought 37, 68, 77, 102, 106–107, 144, 150
drug trafficking 39, 139–140, 228, 286
Duffy, R. 94
dumping rubbish 10, 15–16, 25, 30, 33, 158, 174, 180, 239, 272
duty of care 125
dynamics of toxic crimes 15

e-waste 17, 35, 156, 159–163, *160*, 229, 288
'Earth Community' 51
earth jurisprudence 56
earth rights 10–11, 56
earthquakes 76–77, 105, 109–110
eco-global criminology 18, 25–44, 81–82; conclusion 43; contours of global capitalism 31–35; horizon-scanning 36–43; introduction 25–26; as a perspective 26–31; transnational environmental crime 35–36
eco-justice 3, 45–59, 182–186, *182*; applying notions of justice 49–53; conceptions of harm 47–49; conclusion 58; ecocide 53–58; and green criminology 46–48; introduction 45; and non-human environmental victims 182–186
eco-philosophy 65–67, 277; anthropocentric perspective 66; biocentric perspective 66; ecocentric perspective 66–67
eco-terrorism 115, 126
eco-tourism 69, 73, 120, 126, 284
ecocentric perspective 66–67
ecocide 10–13, 15–16, 45–59, 112–114; *see also* eco-justice
ecological citizenship 30, 36, 47, 115, 189–190
ecological conceptions of harm 29–30
ecological justice 46–49, 182
ecology 28
economic criminals 127
economic gain 264
economic wild animals 120
effective policing 222–225
effective regulation 215
egg taking 127–129, 263
El Niño 77
elder knowledge 250–251, *250–251*

elephant poaching 9, 17, 82, 117, 130, 139, 283, 287
emissions trajectory 104
Empty Oceans, Empty Nets 250
EMS *see* management systems, environmental
endangered species 13–14, 126, 129–135, 139, 150, 153–154, 189, 284, 286
energy efficiency 105
enforced self-regulation 202
enforcement agencies **219**
enforcement of compliance 258
enforcement of regulation 205–210
engagement 51, 228–232; of NGOs 51, 228–232
Environment Agency 219, 257
Environment Enforcement Resolution 220
environmental courts 256–275; conclusion 274–275; crime and justice 257–259; introduction 256–257; problem-solving methods 267–274; specialist 261–267; value of environmental harm 259–261
environmental crime prevention 276–294
environmental forensic science 227, 237–242; automated video monitoring 241; contamination forensics 241–242; DNA testing 240–241; satellite surveillance 241
'environmental forensic studies' 242–244
Environmental Investigation Agency 91, 229
environmental issues 65–67
Environmental Protection Agency 180, 204, 207–210, 213–215, 218, 239, 257–260
environmental racism 15–16, 161, 167–168
environmental refugees 107
environmental victims 115, 175–193; conclusion 192; eco-justice 182–186; humans and environmental victimization 178–182; introduction 175; non-human environmental victims 182–186; victim mobilization 186–192; victimology 175–178
EPA *see* Environmental Protection Agency
ethnic minorities 49
EU *see* European Union
European Commission 161–162
European Union 217–218, 220, 223, 236, 257, 286–287

evidence 252–254; complications 253; limitations of investigation 253; resources 252–253; values/valuations 253–254
exotic pet market 37, 129–131, 134
expertise 227, 230, 238, 252, 261–262
exploitation of nature 46, 140–143
exploitation of resources 31, 57, 66, 106–107
exploratory compliance research *209*
exposure assessment 244
exposure to radioactivity 13
exposure to risk 248–249
extent of victimization 181
extinction 123, 129, 138–139, 153
extrinsic value of harm 96
Exxon Mobil 157

factory farming 14, 127–128, 291
factory ships 85
facts about e-waste ***160***
failed states 39
fairness 50–51, 80, 154, 270
famine 77
farmed food animals 122, 124–125
farming 66
Fattah, E. 176–177
feminization of nature 105, 179
feudalism 40
Field, R. 236–237
fire management 141, 237
fiscal crises 34–35, 76, 114, 204
Fish and Wildlife Service (US) 152
fishing with dynamite 68
fishing wars 107, 281
flex crops 146–150, 296
flora/fauna health 131, 263
fly tipping 30
focal considerations of harm 68
folk crime 82, 132
food riots 107
forensic studies 235–255; conclusion 254; environmental 242–244; environmental forensic science 238–242; evidence and investigation 252–254; introduction 235; politics of knowledge 247–251; science, knowledge, uncertainty 235–238; stake-holders and discourse 244–246
forest conservation 63
forest fires 77, 144
forestry 66

forms of harm 97
'fortress' society 2–3
fossil fuels 146
four propositions about justice *53*
fracking 112, 169, 171–173
fragmentation of habitat 134, 143
fraud 77, 105, 110, 221, 288
Freeland Foundation 229
freshwater quality 58
Fukushima Nuclear Power Plant 76, 191
functioning 51–53
future trends 2–3
futures horizon-scanning 41–42

galaxia fish 120, 152, 177
gene banks 151
general strain theory 17
genetically modified organisms 9, 15, 31–33, 70, 97, 105–107, 142, 146–150, 236, 296; *see also* flex crops
genocide 38–39, 57
geographical considerations of harm 68
geographical scale and harm **28**
geographical spaces 73
geography 28–29
Gibbs, C. 19
global commons *86*
global criminology 39
global data collection 82–89; data collection sources 88–89
Global Judges Programme 268
global resilience 296
global warming 28, 40, 54, 68, 101–114, 296–297; climate change and crime 106–111; resources and social conflict 104–106; *see also* climate change
globalization 32, 39, 71–73
globalizing spaces 73
GMOs *see* genetically modified organisms
'good society' 277, 294
Grabosky, P. 203, 210
grassland 145
Great Barrier Reef 40, 54, 104, 278
'green' environmental crime 14
'green' issues 70
Green Party 54
green zones 278
greenhouse gas emissions 69, 106, 112–115, 146, 154, 157, 169–173, 235, 296
Greenpeace 91, 222, 228–229, 231
guilt 283
Guiyu city 163

Gulf War 54
Gunningham, N. 203

habitat destruction 49
Hannigan, J. 61
Harding, R. 156
harm audits 97
harm, environmental 9–13, 60–78; illegality 10; serious harm 10–13; social construction of 60–64; *see also* crime, environmental
harm minimization 277
harm to animals 117–136; abuse and cruelty 124–128; animals and criminology 117–119; categorization of animals 119–123; wildlife crime/illegal trade 128–136
Harvey, D. 179
haves and have-nots 33
Hayman, G. 205–206
hazard identification 244
hazardous waste 30, 35, 159–165, *165*; *see also* toxic waste
heat waves 109–110
heavy metal pollution 90, 157
hoarding of food 109
hobby criminals 127
Hogan, M. 166
Holtom, R. 55
homicide 10, 56, 91, 189
horizon-scanning 36–43, 81–82, **83–84**, 228, 290–291
Hudson's Bay Company 140
human action as harm 1–3; future trends 2–3
human behaviour 108
human categorization of animals 119–123
human responsibility for environmental degradation 20–21
human rights 36, 47, 186, 288
human trafficking 39, 108–109, 228, 286
human victims of environmental degradation 178–182
hunting–gathering 102
Hurricane Katrina 9, 76–77, 102, 122

IEK *see* indigenous ecological knowledge
ignorance 205
ill health 263
illegal abalone market 14, 35, 85, 117, 130–132, *132*, 269, 273, 283
illegal action around cause 231

illegal environmental harms 13, 29–30
illegal fishing 10, 16, 25, 30, 35, 56, 85, 117, 154, 185, 222, 239–240, 280–283; dealing with 280–283, *281–283*
illegal trade in flora/fauna 10, 27, 30
illegal trade in wildlife 128–136, 229, 269, 283–286; and crime prevention 283–286
illegal transference of electronic waste 15, 17, 25, 35, 296–297; *see also* e-waste
illegality 10; *see also* prohibition
immediate impact on environment 262
impact assessment 252
impact of criminalization 181
impacts of climate change 42
imperative to expand 31–32
impetus for action 191
implementation 211
importance of biodiversity 138–140
inclusive regulation 214
Income Security Program 286
indigenous ecological knowledge 141, 237, 246
indigenous relationships with nature 20–21, 66, 72, 76, 95, 140–141, 172
individual analysis 108
INECE *see* International Network of Environmental Compliance and Enforcement
inequality 33
injustice 46–48, 105
innovation 211
insect blight 37
intelligence sharing 233
intentional destruction *see* ecocide
interfaces 8, *165*
intergenerational equity 41
International Consortium on Combatting Wildlife Crime 221
International Crime Against Peace 54
International Criminal Court 54
international criminology 39
International Environmental Court 56, 267, 274
International Fund for Animal Welfare 91
International Monetary Fund 213
International Monitoring, Control and Surveillance Network 228
International Network of Environmental Compliance and Enforcement 226–227, 233
International Organization for Standardization 211, 213

international security 105
International Standards Organization 204
International Tropical Timber Agreement 36
International Union for the Conservation of Nature 153
internet sources as data 91–92
internet trading in wildlife 129, 242–244, 285
interpersonal violence 117, 226
Interpol 36, 220–223, 227–229, 239, 286
interpretive focus groups 93
intervention and prevention 123, 195–295; environmental courts 256–275; environmental crime prevention 276–295; environmental forensic studies 235–255; environmental law enforcement 217–234; environmental regulation 197–216
intervention strategy 252
intrinsic value of harm 96
introduced wild animals 120
introduction of pests 153–154
Inuit 102
invasive introduction 143
investigation 252–254
ISO *see* International Organization for Standardization
ISP *see* Income Security Program
issue identification 244
issues with climate change *105*
issues for crime prevention 291–294; community crime prevention 293; defining the problem 291; politics of knowing 293–294; prevention, precaution 292; problems of displacement 292; questions of agency 293; tailoring responses 292
issues relating to animal abuse *126*
ivory 9, 14, 17, 35, 82, 117, 130, 242, 283

Japan 38, 64, 76
Joines, J. 163
justice conceptions of harm 29–30
justice, environmental 29–31, 46–48, 165–168, 182
justice horizon-scanning 41

Kamenetz, A. 190
kangaroos 54, 120
key issues in organized crime *288*

knowledge 235–238, 247–251; politics of knowing 247–251, 293–294
Kyoto Protocol 36

La Niña 77
laboratory testing 128, 134
lack of enforcement 205
land clearance 110, 138, 143–145, 150, 208, 239, 241, 260
land pollution 9, 30, 81, 156–159, 296
language of rights 136
languaging of environmental issues 47, 51, **245–246**
law enforcement 73, 77, 217–234; conclusion 233; introduction 217–218; networks/collaborative practices 225–228; NGOs in 228–232; official agencies 218–222; undertaking 222–225; valuing 232–233
learning lessons 53, 274
least concern species 153
Lee, M. 14
legal conceptions of harm 29–30
legal environmental harms 13, 29–30
legal timber coups 29, 46
legal–illegal divide 13, 29–31, 145, 279–280, 291
Levy, D. 212
licensing 264
limitations of investigation 253
limits of regulation 213–215
live export trade 122, 134
lobster poaching 14, 81, 130–131, 283
local data collection 82–89; data collection sources 88–89
localized issues 73
locally unwanted land uses 71
local–global continuum 72–73
locational considerations of harm 68–69
logging 10, 25, 30, 37, 67–69, 140, 144–145, 154, 189, 229, 240
looting 77, 108, 110
LULUs *see* locally unwanted land uses
Lynch, M. 7, 8, 18, 91, 167

McGarrell, E.F. 19
McGillivray, D. 268
McGurrin, D. 167
Mafia 37, 74, 289–290
malnutrition 125
malum in se 10–13, 232

malum prohibutum 10, 232; *see also* prohibition
man-made disasters 76–77, 104, 109–110
management systems, environmental 133–134, 210–213
Mandiberg, S. 253–254
Manual on Human Rights and the Environment 55
map of the world 85–89, *87*
mapping victim issues ***181–182***
marginalization 93–94, 187
market reduction approach to wildlife crime 285, **285**
masculinities criminals 127
mass industrial production 31–32, 122
massification 32
maximizing liberty 53
measuring environmental crime 96–97; measuring harm 97; scale 96; value 96
measuring harm 96-97
medical data exposing criminal harm 91
mega-mines 112, 173, 296–297
Melrose, S. 90
melting glaciers 96
mens rea 268
Mgbeoji, I. 141–142
migration of toxic substances 38
mining 66, 81, 138, 140, 144, 157, 168–172, 189
misappropriation of funds 77, 110
mitigation 264, 291
mobilization 60, 63, 69, 78, 282
models of environmental regulation 200–205
modus operandi analysis 290
monetarization of risk 71
money laundering 39, 144, 221, 286
money trails 287–288
monoculturalism 145, 147–149
monopolization 32
monsoon 73
Montreal Protocol on Substances that Deplete the Ozone Layer 10, 36
moral fissure 47
moral persuasion 281
morale 230
motivation for compliance 205
MRA *see* market reduction approach to wildlife crime
multilateral environmental agreements 35–36
murder 221, 286

National Environmental Security Task
    Forces 222
national security 105, 110, 115
native species 120
natural disasters 76–77, 102–105, 109–110
natural environment 73, 86
natural resources 9, 31–32, 296
'natural rights' 81
naturalistic generalization 90
nature of biodiversity 138–140
near threatened species 153
negligence 72
Neighbourhood Watch 293
neo-liberalism 31–32
NESTs *see* National Environmental
    Security Task Forces
networks 225–228
neurotoxins 179
neutralization 113
New Zealand 37
NGOs *see* non-governmental organizations
Niger Delta 55
NIMBYism 27, 71–72, 191, 292
non-compliance 204–208, 268
non-economic animals 121
non-governmental organizations 73, 91,
    103, 127, 188–189, 222–223, 228–232,
    230, 231–232; compared with official
    agencies *230*; and data collection 91;
    engagement in law enforcement
    228–232
non-human biota 55, 192
non-human environmental victims
    182–186
non-human oppression 183
non-intentional harm 40
non-intervention 230
non-renewable resources 296
'not in my backyard' syndrome *see*
    NIMBYism
notions of justice 50–53, **50**
Nurse, A. 127–129, 285

obsolescence 296
ocean gyres 107
offence patterns 264
official enforcement agencies 218–222, **219**
oil spills 55, 68, 70, 74, 77, 85, 190, 199,
    241–242, 277–278
old-growth forests 9, 38, 66, 291; *see also*
    clear felling
opportunities of regulation 213–215

organic pollutants 35
organized crime 14, 22, 37, 109, 164–165,
    228, 269, 286–291, ***288***
over-fishing 85, 123, 133, 199, 280, 283, 293
over-logging 199
over-use of land 37
overpopulation 21, 26, 154
ozone-depleting substances 10, 13, 35, 70,
    154, 199

paradoxical harms 105
parrot poaching 7, 9, 130, 135, 139,
    283–284, 287
participation in justice 51, 53, 69
pathological indoor environments 13
PBTs *see* persistent bio-accumulating and
    toxic compounds
peak oil 95
Pečar, J. 15–16
penalty infringement notices 268
People for the Ethical Treatment of
    Animals 125
people power 189; *see also* activism
perceived costs 211
perpetration of crime 10, 108–109, 286–291
persistent bio-accumulating and toxic
    compounds 159
personnel 211
perspectives within green criminology
    15–17, ***18–20***
pest/threat wild animals 120
pesticide exposure death 91, 236
pesticide regulation 13, 75
Pets Evacuation and Transportation Act
    2006 (US) 122
Piatelli, D. 93
PINs *see* penalty infringement notices
place-based activity analysis 108
planetary change 69
planetary sinks 107, 144
Plummer, K. 14
poaching *129*, 130–133, 218
polar bears 40, 64
political culture 31
political economic spaces 73
politics of knowing 247–251, 293–294
pollution 156–174; air, land, water
    156–159; conclusion 173–174;
    environmental justice and toxic sites
    165–168; hazardous/toxic waste
    159–165; introduction 156–174;
    and resource extraction 168–173

popularization 63
population responsibility for environmental degradation 21
potential limitations of investigation 253
powers of intervention 231
precautionary principle 41–42, 69, 80–82, 105, 292
premeditated harm 40
Preston, B. 183, 261
preventative measures 292
preventing environmental crime 276–295; conclusion 294; criminalization and prohibition 276–280; illegal fishing 280–283; illegal wildlife trade 283–286; introduction 276; issues for crime prevention 291–294; perpetrators and organized crime 286–291
prevention 195–295; *see also* intervention and prevention
prevention of wildlife crime *283–284*
primary crimes 14
principle of triangulation 88
Pring, C. 266
Pring, G. 266
pristine environments 72, 277
privatization 32
privileged information 269
problem-solving methods 267–274
problems of displacement 292
procedural justice 270
progressive theory 117–118
prohibition 276–280
Project LEAF 221–222
promotion of compliance 258
propaganda 248
proportionate regulation 214
prosecution 225, 227, 260, 267
prospective research 252
protected species 177
protecting biodiversity 150–154
protection of animals 133–136
protest 38; *see also* activism
public interest law 10, 55, 183–184
Putt, J. 224

quality-based limits 254
questions of agency 293

racism 16, 49, 123, 142, 179–180
radical green criminology 18
radicalism 212

radioactivity 13, 27, 30, 37, 77, 162, 218, 235, 248, 263
rape 77, 110, 189
rapid response agencies 224
rapid-onset disasters 77
realism 61
reasons for environmental regulation 198–200
receding coastlines 107
recognition 50–51
recycling 27, 33, 156, 160–161, 164, 173, 178, 296–297
REDD *see* Reducing Emissions from Deforestation and Forest Degradation
Reducing Emissions from Deforestation and Forest Degradation 146
reductions in biodiversity 143–146
reformism 212
regulation 197–216; approaches to compliance 205–210; conclusion 215–216; enforcement 205–210; environmental management systems 210–213; introduction 197; limits and opportunities of 213–215; models of 200–205; reasons for 198–200; self-regulation 210–213
regulatory pyramid 202–203, *202*, 205, 207, 213
regulatory toolbox *208*
relationship with regulatory authorities 263
release of chlorofluorocarbons 69, 199
renewable energy 57–58
reparation 115, 264
republican theory of justice 52
research subjects 92–95
researching environmental crime 79–98; conclusion 97–98; introduction 79–80; measuring environmental crime 96–97; subjects of research 92–95; undertaking research 80–92
resilience 76, 140, 150
resistance 85, 97–98, 192, 288
resource colonization 141–142
resource depletion 34
resource extraction 104–107, 168–173, 252–253
respiratory problems 69, 263
responsive regulation 199
restorative justice 183–184, 271
retrospective research 252
rhineroceros poaching 129, 283–284
Riccardi, M. 289

Rio Declaration 266
Rio Tinto 261
rising ocean levels 102, 106–109, 111, 183
risk 41
risk characterization 244
risk management 200, 245, 263
river 'rights' 184–185
Rivers, L. 19
Robinson, B. 208
role displacement 231
routinization of environmental concerns 62–63
Royal Commission on Genetic Modification (NZ) 147
Royal Parks Police 219
Royal Society for the Prevention of Cruelty to Animals 125–127, 218, 222, 229, 231
RSPCA *see* Royal Society for the Prevention of Cruelty to Animals
Ruggiero, V. 74

salvinia 151–152
sanctions 13, 35, 133, 256–260, 267–274
'Sandy' superstorm 104, 111, 296
satellite surveillance 88, 241, 284
Save the Tiger 123
scale of environmental harm 96
scarcity 32, 85, 103, 106, 109, 135
Schlosberg, D. 50
Schmalzbauer, L. 93
science 235–238
Science 103
secondary crimes 14
selective logging 67
self-generated knowledge 90
self-interest 3
self-regulation 172, 200, 202–207, 210–216
self-reliance 141
self-sustainment 135
sequestration 74, 145
serious harm 10–13
seriousness of harm 96
service animals 121
sewerage 158
sex trade 77
sexism 49, 123
Shell 55, 157
Shiva, V. 111
Sierra Club 189
Simon, D. 209

sites of national significance 10
sites of toxicity 165–168
situational approaches to deal with illegal fishing 282–283
situational crime prevention 17, 19, 278, **279**
Skinnider, E. 175, 181
Slovenia 15–16
slow-onset disasters 77
sludge surge 71, 162
smart regulation 199, 203, 212–213
smog 157
smuggling 57, 131, 153–154, 221, 228
Snider, L. 204, 213
snow leopards 284
social approaches to deal with illegal fishing 281–282
social conflict 2–3, 101–116, *107*; global warming 101–111; state–corporate crime 112–114; *see also* climate change
social construction of environmental harm 60–64, 230
social crime prevention 280
social media 242
sociocultural environment 73
'sock puppeting' 91
South, N. 14, 74
space debris 157
space–time transference of harm 70–76
specialist environmental courts 261–267
specieist criminology 19–20, 26, 47, 123, 130
species conservation 284
species decline 34
species justice 46–50, 182
species theft 126
stake-holder analysis 290
stake-holders 244–246
standard of proof 238
Standridge, P. 289
state of mind 263
'state of the world' indicators 57–58
state–corporate crime 112–114
steps to doing horizon-scanning **83–84**
stewardship 56, 272
strategic effectiveness 191
strategism 212
street crime 77, 293
street riots 109
stress offenders 127
Stretesky, P. 8, 18, 91, 166–167, 210
strict compliance 204

studying environmental harm 13–17; 'brown' types of environmental crime 14–15; 'green' types of environmental crime 14; perspectives within green criminology 15–17
subjects of research 92–96
subordination 50
substantive focus of eco-criminology 26–31; crime and justice 29–31; ecology 28; geography 28–29
substantive horizon-scanning 41
substantive justice 270
successful construction of environmental problem *63*
suffering of non-human animals 47, 124
suicide 56
super-exploitation of sharks 280
super-sized fishing trawlers 62
superstorms 104, 111, 296
supply and waste chain 211
supranational criminology 39
surface run-off 158
surrogate victims 55
survival status of species *153*
sustainability 12, 29–30, 62, 76, 130, 141, 204–205, 212, 284
Sutherland, W.J. 40
Suzuki, David 250
symbiotic green crimes 14
systemic causes of environmental harm 17–22; capitalism is responsible 22; corporations are responsible 22; human responsibility 20–21; population is responsible 21; technology is responsible 21
systemic crop failure 108

tactics of dissent 192
tailoring responses 292
tar sands 56, 112–113, 169
targeted regulation 214
Task Force on Organized Crime 220
Tasmania 250–251
tax evasion 221
technological responsibility for environmental degradation 21
technology-based limits 253
temperature change 40, 108
temporal considerations of harm 69–70
terminator technology 142
Texaco 157
theft 77, 81, 109, *129*

therapeutic justice 271
threats to biodiversity 137–155; bio-insecurity 140–143; conclusion 154; flex crops and GMOs 146–150; introduction 137–138; nature of biodiversity 138–140; protecting biodiversity 150–154; reductions in biodiversity 143–146
three approaches to eco-justice **49**
tiers of regulation **201**
tiger populations 117, 123, 139
tile-drained wetland 145
TNCs *see* transnational corporations
Tomkins, K. 224
Tomorrow's Children 251
torture 46, 49
tourism 69, 73, 177
toxic towns 165–168, 249–250, 296
toxic waste 14, 25, 156–174; and environmental justice 165–168; hazardous waste 159–165; pollution of air, land, water 156–159; resource extraction 168–173
trade in wildlife skins 284
traditional criminals 127
traditionalism 212
TRAFFIC 91
training 230
transaction analysis 290
transference of harm 27, 42, 70–76, 107
transformation of nature *34*
transgression 99–193; *see also* victimization
transnational activism 192
transnational corporations 22–23, 25, 34
transnational criminology 39
transnational environmental crime 25–44; definition of 35–36; *see also* eco-global criminology
transparent regulation 214
triangulation 88
trustworthiness 210
tsunamis 77, 102
types of activism **188**
types of data source **89**
types of transgression 48–50; ecological justice 48–49; environmental justice 48; species justice 48–49

ultraviolet radiation 105
UN *see* United Nations
UN Convention Against Corruption 288

UN Convention Against Transnational Organized Crime 288
UN Environment Programme 221
UN Framework Convention on Climate Change 36
UN Office on Drugs and Crime 221, 286
UNCAC *see* UN Convention Against Corruption
uncertainty 235–238
underground market *see* black marketeering
understanding compliance *206*
undertaking environmental research 80–89; global and local data collection 82–89
Union Carbide 186–191
United Nations 15, 54, 56–57, 143, 146, 178, 266–268
universal victimization 111
UNODC *see* UN Office on Drugs and Crime
unseasonal weather 102, 109
UNTOC *see* UN Convention Against Transnational Organized Crime
urban pollution 63; *see also* pollution

valuations 253
value of environmental harm 96, 259–261
valuing law enforcement 232–233
vegetation management *150*
victim mobilization 186–192
victimization 46, 99–193; abuse and harm to animals 117–136; climate change 101–116; environmental victims 175–193; pollution and toxic waste 156–174; threats to biodiversity 137–155
victimology, environmental 175–178
video monitoring 241
Vienna Convention for the Protection of the Ozone Layer 36

Vietnam War 54
vigilance 284, 293
violation of environmental laws 257–259; compliance 258
visibility 62–63
volcanic activity 105, 109–110
vulnerable species 153

Waikato River Enhancement Society 184–185
Waldman, L. 94, 180
Walters, R. 56
war-related degradation 12, 54
waste management 159–165
waste trafficking 57
water pollution 9, 30, 103, 156–159, 263, 296
WCO *see* World Customs Organization
welfare collapse 108
welfarism 124–125, 130
Wellsmith, M. 19
wetland 145
whale fishing 35, 64, 231
'white' issues 15, 70
White, R. 18, 20, 42
wider effects of harm 97
wilderness 66, 69, 71, 86, 277–278
wildlife crime 14, 120, 128–136; animal rights/protection 133–136
wildlife poaching 14, 129–133
wildlife smuggling 57
Williams, C. 22, 175–176
wind farms 289–290
win-win opportunity 212, 286
Woodroof, H.J. 40
World Bank 39, 213, 221
World Customs Organization 221
World Trade Organization 73, 213
World War Two 35, 162
wrongdoing 10
WTO *see* World Trade Organization

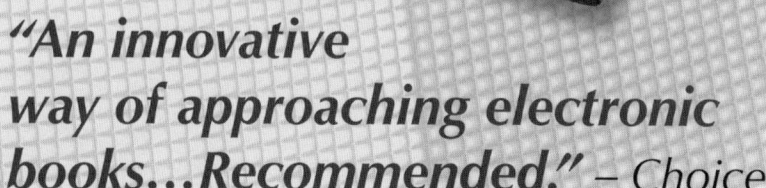